Oxford Bibliographical Society
Publications

THIRD SERIES VOLUME VI

PORTUGUESE WRITERS AND ENGLISH READERS

BOOKS BY PORTUGUESE WRITERS PRINTED BEFORE 1640 IN THE LIBRARIES OF OXFORD AND CAMBRIDGE

T. F. EARLE

THE OXFORD BIBLIOGRAPHICAL SOCIETY
OXFORD
2009

Published by the Oxford Bibliographical Society *care of* the
Bodleian Library, Oxford OX1 3BG

© 2009 Oxford Bibliographical Society

ISBN 0 901420 57 3

Inquiries about the Society and its publications should be
addressed to the Honorary Secretary at the
Bodleian Library

British Library Cataloguing in Publication Data
A catalogue record for this book is available
from the British Library

Typeset by Anne Joshua, Oxford
Printed in Great Britain by
Information Press, Eynsham, Oxford

TABLE OF CONTENTS

ACKNOWLEDGEMENTS

My first debt must be to the university and college librarians, at both Oxford and Cambridge, without whose devoted work this book would have been impossible. It would be invidious to mention names, but I have been particularly impressed by the friendliness and professionalism of some of the college librarians who attended to my enquiries while at the same time dealing with a multitude of other requests. It sometimes turned out that the most helpful college librarians were those who receive the least support from the governing bodies of the institutions where they work. I also have a very high regard for the staff of the Bodleian and of the Cambridge University Library.

Many colleagues have given me advice and encouragement during the years in which this book has been in preparation. In first place should come the editors appointed by the Oxford Bibliographical Society, Scott Mandelbrote and David Rundle, and the two anonymous readers who they asked to comment on a draft of the book. These four scholars made a great number of constructive suggestions and also saved me from a multitude of errors. I also owe a great deal to Clive Griffin, Paul Joyce, Ian Maclean, David McKitterick, Nigel Palmer, Julian Roberts and Ron Truman. Martha Repp's index of printers and places of publication was a model of accuracy and learning, and has been incorporated in the final version of the Index.

I am grateful to the Faculty of Medieval and Modern Languages at Oxford for having made me a number of research grants. My visits to Cambridge were enhanced by the splendid hospitality offered by Peterhouse.

ABBREVIATIONS

Abad	Abad, Julián Martín, *La imprenta en Alcalá de Henares*, 3 vols (Madrid: Arco, 1991).
Adams	Adams, H. M., *Catalogue of Books Printed on the Continent of Europe, 1501–1600, in Cambridge Libraries*, 2 vols (Cambridge: Cambridge University Press, 1967).
Allison	Allison, A. F., *English Translations from the Spanish and Portuguese to the Year 1700* (London: Dawsons, 1974).
Anselmo	Anselmo, António Joaquim, *Bibliografia das obras impressas em Portugal no século XVI* (Lisbon: Biblioteca Nacional, 1926; reprinted 1977).
ASC	All Souls College, Oxford.
Barbosa Machado	Barbosa Machado, Diogo, *Bibliotheca Lusitana*, 4 vols (Coimbra: Atlântida, 1965–67; 1st edition Lisbon: Antonio Isidoro da Fonseca, 1741–59).
BLA	Blackfriars, Oxford.
BLL	Balliol College, Oxford.
BNC	Brasenose College, Oxford.
BOD	Bodleian Library, Oxford.
Bod-inc.	Coates, Alan, et al. (eds), *A Catalogue of Books Printed in the Fifteenth Century now in the Bodleian Library*, 6 vols (Oxford: Oxford University Press, 2005).
Bush	Bush, Sargent, and Carl J. Rasmussen, *The Library of Emmanuel College Cambridge* (Cambridge: Cambridge University Press, 1986).
CCCC	Corpus Christi College, Cambridge.
CCCO	Corpus Christi College, Oxford.
CHC	Christ Church, Oxford.
CHR	Christ's College, Cambridge.
CLA	Clare College, Cambridge.
CUL	University Library, Cambridge.
EMM	Emmanuel College, Cambridge.
ENG	English Faculty Library, Oxford.
EXE	Exeter College, Oxford.
Faria (1977)	Faria, Francisco Leite de, *Estudos bibliográficos sobre Damião de Góis e a sua época* (Lisbon: Secretaria de Estado da Cultura, 1977).
Faria (1987)	Faria, Francisco Leite de, 'O maior sucesso editorial do século XVI: a *Imagem da Vida Cristã* de Frei Heitor Pinto', *Revista da Biblioteca Nacional*, Second Series, 2 (1987), 83–110.

Fidalgo	Fidalgo, Lorenzo Ruiz, *La imprenta en Salamanca*, 3 vols (Madrid: Arco, 1994–5).
FITZ	Fitzwilliam Museum, Cambridge.
Gaskell	Gaskell, Philip, *Trinity College Library: the First 150 Years* (Cambridge: Cambridge University Press, 1980).
G&C	Gonville and Caius College, Cambridge.
HEB	Oxford Centre for Hebrew and Jewish Studies Library.
HER	Hertford College, Oxford.
Hiscock	Hiscock, W. G., *A Christ Church Miscellany* (Oxford: privately printed, 1946).
HMAN	Harris Manchester College, Oxford.
HOA	History of Art Library, Oxford.
Inocêncio	[Innocencio, Francisco da Silva], *Diccionario bibliographico portuguez*, 22 vols (Lisbon: Imprensa Nacional 1858–1923).
JSC	Jesus College, Cambridge.
JSO	Jesus College, Oxford.
KEB	Keble College, Oxford.
Ker	Ker, Neil R., *Fragments of Medieval Manuscripts used as Pastedowns in Oxford Bindings* (Oxford: Oxford Bibliographical Society, 1954; reprinted with corrections and additions [edited by David Rundle and Scott Mandelbrote], 2004).
Kiessling (1988)	Kiessling, Nicolas K., *The Library of Robert Burton* (Oxford: Oxford Bibliographical Society, 1988).
Kiessling (2002)	Kiessling, Nicolas K., *The Library of Anthony Wood* (Oxford: Oxford Bibliographical Society, 2002).
KCC	King's College, Cambridge.
LIN	Lincoln College, Oxford.
Lumley	Jayne, Sears, and Francis R. Johnson, *The Lumley Library: The Catalogue of 1609* (London: British Museum, 1956).
Macray	Macray, William Dunn, *Annals of the Bodleian Library Oxford*, 2nd edition (Oxford: Clarendon Press, 1890; reprinted Oxford: Bodleian Library, 1984).
Macray, *Register*	Macray, William Dunn, *A Register of the Members of St. Mary Magdalen College, Oxford* 8 vols (London: Frowde, 1894–1915).
MGC	Magdalene College, Cambridge.
MGO	Magdalen College, Oxford.
McKitterick	McKitterick, David, *The Library of Sir Thomas Knyvett of Ashwellthorpe c.1539–1618* (Cambridge: Cambridge University Library, 1978).
MER	Merton College, Oxford.
MHS	Museum of the History of Science, Oxford.
Morrish	Morrish, P. S., *Bibliotheca Higgsiana: A Catalogue of the*

	Books of Dr Griffin Higgs (1589–1659) (Oxford: Oxford Bibliographical Society, 1990).
NEW	New College, Oxford.
ORI	Oriel College, Oxford.
Palau	Palau y Dulcet, Antonio, *Manual del librero hispano-americano*, 28 vols (Barcelona: Palau, 1948–77).
Pearson	Pearson, David, *Oxford Bookbinding, 1500–1640* (Oxford: Oxford Bibliographical Society, 2000).
PMC	Pembroke College, Cambridge.
PMO	Pembroke College, Oxford.
PET	Peterhouse, Cambridge.
PHI	Philosophy Faculty Library, Oxford.
QUC	Queens' College, Cambridge.
QUO	Queen's College, Oxford.
Rogers	Rogers, Nicholas, 'The Early History of Sidney Sussex College Library' in D.E.D. Beales and H.B. Nisbet (eds), *Sidney Sussex College Cambridge* (Woodbridge: Boydell & Brewer, 1996), pp. 75–88.
RSL	Radcliffe Science Library, Oxford.
SHE	St Edmund Hall, Oxford.
SID	Sidney Sussex College, Cambridge.
SJCC	St John's College, Cambridge.
SJCO	St John's College, Oxford.
STC	Pollard, A.W., and G. R. Redgrave, *A Short-Title Catalogue of Books Printed in England, Scotland, & Ireland, and of English Books Printed Abroad (1475–1640)*, 2nd edition, revised by W.A. Jackson and F.S. Ferguson, completed by Katharine F. Pantzer. 3 vols (London: The Bibliographical Society, 1976–91).
STCC	St Catharine's College, Cambridge.
TRH	Trinity Hall, Cambridge.
TRC	Trinity College, Cambridge.
TRO	Trinity College, Oxford.
UNI	University College, Oxford.
WAD	Wadham College, Oxford.
WEST	Westminster College, Cambridge.
Wheeler	Wheeler, G.W., 'Bodleian Press-Marks in Relation to Classification', *Bodleian Quarterly Record* , 1 (1916), 280–92 and 311–22.
Wijffels	Wijffels, Alain, *Late Sixteenth-Century Lists of Law Books at Merton College* (Cambridge: LP, 1992).
WOR	Worcester College, Oxford.

INTRODUCTION

FOREWORD

This book is about a historical fact few people know or even imagine possible. The fact is a bibliographical one: the presence in Oxford and Cambridge libraries of more than two thousand copies of books by Portuguese writers of the early modern period. Most historians of Elizabethan and Jacobean England think of the Portugal of those days as a country of navigators, colonizers and missionaries, men of action, not of ideas. There were many such in Portugal, but also many authors of scholarly books in demand in Oxford and Cambridge. Computerized cataloguing, coupled with a certain dogged determination in going round libraries in Oxford and Cambridge, reveals that the writings of Portuguese intellectuals, for the most part Catholics, were well known to the largely Protestant members of English universities in the early modern period.

It is possible to make claims about what was available in early modern Oxford and Cambridge because so many old libraries survive there. Oxford and Cambridge both have a plethora of libraries, not all of which belong to the central university. In Oxford today there are twenty college libraries whose collections date back to the sixteenth century – and in some cases even earlier – and in Cambridge sixteen. Their continued existence is something unique in Europe.[1] Undergraduates were not given access to libraries, not even to the libraries of the colleges to which all of them belonged, until the nineteenth century. However, the libraries formed the minds of their teachers who, then and now, had a close relationship with those they taught.

This was a time when the two universities and their constituent colleges had a monopoly on higher education in England. Anyone wishing to enter the Church, or the medical and legal professions, had to pass through them. So the reading habits of the teaching members of the universities are an important clue to the intellectual formation of the elite of the country as a whole. The thought that members of that elite not only had access to Portuguese books, but read and annotated them, and

---

[1] In recent centuries new colleges and other academic institutions have come into existence in both universities, and these have sometimes acquired old books. The Portuguese books are now divided among forty-eight libraries.

reflected about their contents, will be surprising to many people. Nevertheless, it is true, and it is the theme of the present study.

The college libraries have always been working libraries. They exist to meet the immediate needs of the intellectual community which they serve, not to contain the whole of knowledge. Scholars wanting special or unique material could always go to the university libraries, the Bodleian at Oxford, and – from the eighteenth century onwards, when it was placed on a secure footing – to the Cambridge University Library. These two institutions have the universal aims of great libraries, whether in the U.K. or elsewhere. They are also the places where individuals generally leave their collections, sometimes very large collections, like those of John Selden (in the Bodleian) or Bishop Moore (in the Cambridge University Library). These two book-lovers of the seventeenth century both probably wished to be remembered as men whose interests were all-embracing, for in the early modern period it was still thought possible for a single individual to have a grasp of the whole of knowledge, and libraries were formed to give effect to that belief.[2] However, the college libraries were, and are, not like that. Their holdings, uniquely, allow the researcher to see what early modern scholars as a group wanted to read – or at least, if not to read, what they thought they ought to have if they were to be taken seriously.

So the researcher in Oxford or Cambridge has access to libraries of very different kinds. In the central libraries of both universities you can find the rarities, including rare books by Portuguese authors of great historical importance. My own favourites are books published in Asia. Both the Bodleian and the Cambridge University Library have copies of the first edition, printed in Goa, of Garcia da Orta's treatise on the medicinal plants of the East (item **627**), and both these copies have annotations by contemporary or near-contemporary readers. Those in the Cambridge University Library are by Carolus Clusius (Charles de l'Escluse), the translator of Orta who made him into an international best-seller. Most exciting of all is the trilingual dictionary – of Japanese, Portuguese, and Latin – printed for the Japanese college of the Society of Jesus on the island of Amakusa, near Nagasaki (item **269**). Though strictly speaking anonymous, it is known to be the work of João Rodrigues (see the biographical note on this writer). This, the first dictionary of Japanese ever compiled, is one of the greatest triumphs of sixteenth-century

---

[2] For the universal quality of great libraries in the sixteenth and seventeenth centuries, see Fernando J. Bouza Álvarez, *Del escritorio a la biblioteca: la civilización escrita europea en la alta edad moderna (siglos XV–XVII)* (Madrid: Síntesis, 1992), pp. 123–6, and Jeremy Lawrance, '"Une bibliothèque fort complète pour un grand Seigneur": Gondomar's Manuscripts and the Renaissance Idea of the Library', *Bulletin of Spanish Studies,* 81 (2004), 1071–90 (1072–9). For the belief that individuals could have a grasp of all that was known see Mordechai Feingold, 'The Humanities', in Nicholas Tyacke (ed.), *The History of the University of Oxford: the Seventeenth Century* (Oxford: Clarendon Press, 1997), pp. 211–357 (216–17).

scholarship anywhere in the world and has the most electrifying effect on anyone who sees it. The Bodleian is very fortunate to have one of the few copies that exist, even if it only arrived in 1829.[3] Another very remarkable book by a Jesuit is item 447, Henrique Henriques's brief catechism and confessionary, composed by him in Tamil and printed in Cochin using a type-face which he had specially cut for this, the first printed book in the language. It has been in the Bodleian since the early days of the library.[4]

It has been a privilege to have had access to material of this kind, but the holdings of more ordinary books, shared between many libraries in both universities, have more significance, because they give an idea of the common intellectual culture of a whole epoch. And many of these books are by Portuguese writers. Most of them are in Latin. Their authors, like their readers, were university men. What they wrote mostly reflects the traditional faculty divisions to be found in nearly all European universities of the period: theology, medicine, and law, civil and canon. A fourth subject area, not quite so easy to define, might be called the contemporary history of Portugal. This includes substantial collections of books about quite disparate events which occurred in the widely scattered areas of the globe to which the Portuguese had ventured. One collection is of the writings of the Jesuit missionaries to India and the Far East, especially Japan, which explains the presence not just of the dictionary, but also of other works by Father Rodrigues, as well as those of his colleagues. The Japanese mission was by no means solely a Portuguese affair but it was one for which Portuguese writers provided much of the publicity. There is another important collection, of the polemics surrounding the extinction of the dynasty of Aviz at the battle of Alcácer-Quibir in North Africa, in 1578, and the subsequent occupation of the Portuguese throne by Philip II of Spain.

Very few of any of the books in any of the categories just described are in Portuguese, and still fewer are of what today would be called literature. Some of them were bought by modern collectors and librarians, but around two thirds can be shown to have arrived within a century or so of publication and were read by scholars interested in their intellectual content.

So this is a book mostly about multiple copies, the same book or the same writer found over and over again in all the old libraries of both universities. In the case of the most popular works that means forty copies or more. Some writers are represented by more than one hundred copies of their various publications.

Altogether there are 2,343 separate volumes in the short-title catalogue,

---

[3] There is also a modern facsimile edition (Tokyo: Toyo Bunko, 1953).

[4] Graham W. Shaw, 'A "Lost" Work of Henrique Henriques: the Tamil Confessionary of 1580', *Bodleian Library Record*, 11 (1982–85), 26–34.

1,426 in Oxford libraries (61%) and 917 in Cambridge ones (39%). The different numbers of books in the two universities is not a fact that has much significance, except in the case of the so-called Coimbra commentaries on Aristotle, which are discussed in Chapter Two. Even the presence of the commentaries in large numbers in Oxford, and their relative absence from Cambridge, is more a consequence of administrative action and syllabus design than of conflicting ideologies. Otherwise there are fewer Portuguese books in Cambridge because there were – and are – fewer college libraries in Cambridge, and because throughout the seventeenth century and until the arrival of Bishop Moore's library – usually called the royal library – in 1715, the Cambridge University Library was more neglected and more chaotic than the Bodleian.[5]

The short-title catalogue included at the heart of this volume is intended to show which books by Portuguese writers printed before 1640 entered university and college libraries, and where they are held. So far as possible the date of acquisition and the name of the donor are also included. The aim of the exercise is not just to compile a list, but to show that the Portuguese material was of real interest to early modern readers. It is possible to compile statistics in support of this claim, but to do so involves a number of problems.

The first is to define what is meant by 'early modern'. I have taken 1750 as the start of the later modern period, and throughout this book terms such as 'early provenance' should be taken as referring to the years before that date. Early modern collections cover the whole academic range of theology, medicine, law, and contemporary history. In the first half of the eighteenth century both universities were still receiving collections of this kind: the royal library is the largest, but at Christ Church the Wake and Orrery benefactions are also very extensive, and all of them include Portuguese material. The Peterborough Cathedral Library, which only came to Cambridge in 1970 is another large collection which dates from the late seventeenth and early eighteenth centuries. It was mostly the creation of university graduates, and the man 'mainly responsible for its enlargement and enrichment' was Bishop White Kennett (1660–1728), who had been first a student, then Fellow and Vice-Principal of St Edmund Hall, Oxford.[6]

What seems to be characteristic of modern library history, as opposed

---

[5] George I bought Moore's library after his death and shortly afterwards presented it to the university. Though the books only belonged to the king very briefly the collection is always referred to as the royal library. The arrival of the enormous gift forced the university to take its library seriously. See David McKitterick, *Cambridge University Library, A History: The Eighteenth and Nineteenth Centuries* (Cambridge: Cambridge University Press, 1986), p. 14.

[6] J. J. Hall (ed.), *Peterborough Cathedral Library: A Catalogue of Books Printed before 1800 and now in Cambridge University Library* (Cambridge: Cambridge University Library, 1986), pp. iv–v.

to early modern, is a decline in the belief that a single institution, still less a single individual, could amass a collection of books which included the universality of human knowledge. So after 1800 collectors specialized more, particularly in history, and there was also a much greater interest in writing in the vernacular as against the universal language, Latin.[7]

Somewhere on the borderline is the Crynes benefaction of 1745 to the Bodleian and a number of Oxford colleges. His books have the wide intellectual range characteristic of the early modern period (though there are no legal works by Portuguese writers) but Ian Philip thinks of him as a specialist, with a particular interest in sixteenth-century octavo editions.[8] Perhaps arbitrarily, I have included him among the early moderns.

The next – and very obvious – problem for the compiler of statistics is that of knowing when the books arrived in the libraries. Dating library acquisitions raises a multitude of questions which are discussed in Chapter Three. For the moment, the reader will have to take on trust the figures which have been arrived at using a variety of more or less dependable techniques. So – bearing in mind that what follows is necessarily provisional – we can say that that, out of the 2,343 volumes in the short-title catalogue, 1,481 (63%) arrived in Oxford and Cambridge before 1750. Of the rest 397 (17%) can be shown to be more recent acquisitions, and 465 (20%) are, for the moment, undateable.

Another interesting statistical question is to know the proportion of books by Portuguese authors among the totality of books in the libraries. It is not a question to which a complete answer can be given, but it can be answered with reference to the early history of the Bodleian, where the first catalogue, of 1605, has been republished with a scholarly introduction.[9] There are around 8700 entries in the catalogue (a figure which takes account of the fact that many titles are bound together), and of those eighty-one are by Portuguese writers. So in 1605 about one in every hundred works available to readers of the Bodleian was by a Portuguese writer – not a bad total for a country often assumed to have produced nothing at all.

Much of what follows will be bibliographical: a list of the books concerned, who acquired them and when, how they made the long journey from a study in Lisbon or Coimbra or Évora (or more far-flung places, like Goa in Portuguese India) to a library in Oxford or Cambridge. But this book is intended as a contribution to intellectual history also. If

---

[7] This point is treated in more detail in Chapter One.

[8] Ian Philip, *The Bodleian Library in the Seventeenth and Eighteenth Centuries* (Oxford: Clarendon Press, 1983), p. 84.

[9] [Thomas James], *The First Printed Catalogue of the Bodleian Library, 1605: a facsimile* (Oxford: Clarendon Press, 1986), Introduction, pp. xi–xiii.

nothing else, it helps to prove Jonathan Israel's assertion that 'during the
later Middle Ages and the early modern age down to around 1650,
western civilization was based on a largely shared core of faith, tradition,
and authority'.[10] So for at least a hundred years after the arrival of
Protestantism in England, Portugal and England shared and contributed
to an intellectual heritage, made the more accessible because it was
mediated through Latin, the universal language.

The idea that there was some intellectual community between scholars
in Portugal and in England in the sixteenth and seventeenth centuries
might seem reasonable enough, but it is disregarded and misunderstood
in both countries. In England, as already stated, modern historians –
there are some honourable exceptions, including Jonathan Israel himself
– seem to find it very difficult to conceive that Portugal has had an
intellectual tradition, still less that its products could be found in the
libraries of our ancient universities.

There is an exception to this rule, but it is not an exception which
necessarily leads to a clear vision of the realities of the reception of
Portuguese academic writing in England. Many people know how the
Bodleian Library at Oxford received its first collection of printed books
from Portugal. In 1596 the Earl of Essex, returning from the sack of Cadiz,
stopped to loot the library of Fernão de Mascarenhas, Bishop of Faro in
the Algarve, which he subsequently handed over to Sir Thomas Bodley,
the founder of the library which bears his name. The inclusion of
Mascarenhas's books does not greatly alter the total of Portuguese
works in the Bodleian, since only eight of his two hundred books are
by his fellow-countrymen. He was an intellectual with a European
outlook, like many of the writers and readers to be discussed in the
pages that follow.

The story of the loot has most recently been retold in an account of the
library's collections written by a group of distinguished members of its
staff.[11] The glamour of the tale has led them to the mistaken view that the
history of the Hispanic collections in the Bodleian in the early modern
period is one of derring-do and exotic purchasing, as seen in John Bill's
book-buying expedition to a hostile and dangerous Seville in 1604, or the
extremely rare Mexican codices and printed books in the Selden
collection, deposited in 1659.

Alas, the truth is much less exciting. Portuguese (and Spanish) books
normally arrived in Oxford through the well established commercial
channels of what came to be known in England as the Latin trade. This

---

[10] See his *Radical Enlightenment: Philosophy and the Making of Modernity 1650–1750* (Oxford: Oxford University Press, 2001), p. 3.

[11] Gregory Walker, Mary Clapinson and Lesley Forbes (eds), *The Bodleian Library: A Subject Guide to the Collections* (Oxford: Bodleian Library, 2004), pp. 110–11.

process – which is described in more detail in Chapter Four – had begun long before the raid on Bishop Mascarenhas's books, as the holdings of the college libraries demonstrate. The historians of the Bodleian's collections believe that for the rest of the seventeenth century after Selden's donation, and during virtually the whole of the following century, 'the Bodleian's Hispanic holdings remained in a state of suspended animation'.[12] That is simply not so. The short-title catalogue shows that hundreds of books by Portuguese authors (including those in the large benefactions of Thomas Barlow, Bishop of Lincoln, 1691, and Nathaniel Crynes, 1745) – not to speak of uncounted thousands of books by Spaniards – arrived in the period 1660–1750. Usually in Latin, and only occasionally glamorous (though they are sometimes) these are mainstream books on mainstream academic subjects. In the early modern period Portugal, and Spain, were part of the international Latin academic world which included England also, as a somewhat peripheral member.[13]

But in thinking otherwise Bodley's librarians are in excellent academic company. Let us start with one of the heroes of Oxford bibliography, the late Neil Ker, whose uncompromisingly titled *Fragments of Medieval Manuscripts used as Pastedowns in Oxford Bindings* is of great use in dating the arrival of books printed abroad in Oxford. Ker's book is a wonderful resource, and it much deserves its recent republication by the Oxford Bibliographical Society. Still, when it comes to Portugal, Ker, like many others, seems to have had a blind spot.

In what was probably a rare excursion into autobiography Ker says that it was the sight 'of an eleventh-century English manuscript of the sermons of Gaudentius inside the covers of Hector Pinto that made me think that a *Pastedowns in Oxford Bindings* would be worth compiling'.[14] Heitor Pinto was well-known in sixteenth-century Oxford as a theologian, and is well-known today in Portugal as the author of the vernacular *Imagem da vida cristã* [*Image of the Christian Life*]. That book, which is printed, in Latin translation, as an appendix to Volume IV of the complete works, attracted early modern readers in England too (see items **725–6**). Ker may not have known all that, but he could not have avoided knowing at least that Pinto was a Portuguese. This is because the title page of the 1584 Lyon edition of his *Opera Omnia*, to which he was referring, says plainly that the author of these Latin works was 'Lusitan[us]'. But Ker is silent about Pinto's

[12] Walker, Clapinson, Forbes (eds), *The Bodleian Library*, pp. 110–11.

[13] Bodley was very dismissive of learned printing in England at the start of the seventeenth century. See Julian Roberts, 'Importing Books for Oxford, 1500–1640', in James P. Carley and Colin G. C. Tite (eds), *Books and Collectors, 1200–1700: Essays presented to Andrew Watson* (London: The British Library, 1997), pp. 317–33 (318–19).

[14] See his *Records of All Souls College Library, 1437–1600* (Oxford: Oxford Bibliographical Society, 1971), pp. ix–x.

nationality, though not about that of the manuscript fragment, and he further muddies the waters, consciously or unconsciously, by spelling Pinto's Christian name incorrectly, thus hiding the characteristically Portuguese –ei- diphthong.[15] It could be said that it was not part of Ker's argument to discuss where Pinto came from, but in that case there was no need for him to mention that the manuscript fragment was English. He might also have asked himself whether it was purely by chance that he happened to light upon that particular book. I doubt whether it was. There are copies of the huge folio volumes of Pinto's collected works, with their fine bindings, in nine Oxford libraries and four Cambridge ones, where they are often a prominent object. All arrived there within a century of publication, and two have the characteristic bindings which Ker studied in his book. But perhaps he did not want to pursue these evident indications of the prestige of a Portuguese theologian.

Generally historians of Oxford University have very little to say about Portuguese intellectual achievements. The multi-volume history of the University completed in 2000 is a magnificent project. However, in it the Portuguese are rarely mentioned, and in the volume devoted to the seventeenth-century, which is the period when their influence was at its height, nothing is said about them at all.[16] In Britain academic indifference towards Portugal is probably a product of the nineteenth century, a period of imperial rivalry, racism, and a heightened consciousness of religious differences.[17] The indifference, at least, has survived into our own time, even in the work of a tolerant and well-informed historian like Diarmaid MacCulloch. His *Reformation: Europe's House Divided* has been rightly praised. All the same, it is a pity that in a book which stresses the political importance of theology in early modern Europe there is no mention of any Portuguese theologian, not even Jerónimo Osório (Hieronymus Osorius), the bishop of Silves in the Algarve and famous in English universities in the reign of Elizabeth as a Latin stylist and for his controversy with the Queen herself.[18]

MacCulloch has a chapter on the Portuguese as missionaries and colonialists, but in that he says nothing about the contributions of the

---

[15] Misspellings and misunderstandings of Portuguese names are very common in the catalogues of Oxford and Cambridge libraries. But Ker at least should have known the difference between Hector Pintus (Latin) and Heitor Pinto (Portuguese).

[16] T. H. Aston (ed.), *The History of the University of Oxford*, 8 vols (Oxford: Clarendon Press, 1984–2000).

[17] See P. J. Marshall, 'The Portuguese in Asia in British Historiography', *Portuguese Studies*, 20 (2004), 38–46.

[18] For an account of his impact in England by an English scholar see J. W. Binns, *Intellectual Culture in Elizabethan and Jacobean England: The Latin Writings of the Age* (Leeds: Cairns, 1990), pp. 272–8. However, the story is told in more detail by Bourdon and Guimarães Pinto (see note 20 below and Chapter One).

Portuguese to the scholarly understanding of the lands in the East which they were the first early modern Europeans to visit. He prefers instead to stress the violence and bigotry which frequently accompanied Portuguese attempts to catechize non-Christians.[19] Elizabethan and Jacobean scholars, however, knew that that there were individual Portuguese who had a keen intellectual interest in the non-European world and had written important books about different aspects of it. The works of Portuguese botanists, ethnographers, geographers and linguists fill the shelves of early modern libraries. Some of the writers concerned, Garcia da Orta and João Rodrigues, for example, have attracted the attention of modern specialists in Portuguese colonial history, perhaps most notably Charles Boxer.[20] But his warm appreciation of their work has received almost no attention among UK historians more generally.

It is surprising that in Portugal too there is very little appreciation of the intellectual achievements documented in this book. There twentieth-century historians, particularly those who have written for a wide public, have not tended to have much sympathy for the orthodox Tridentine and Jesuit tradition which for centuries dominated Portuguese theology. For example, J. S. da Silva Dias seems to condemn the universities of Évora and Coimbra simply because they were 'uma coluna inabalável de ideologia tridentina' [an unshakeable support of Tridentine ideology].[21] But the fact that a tradition may have become fossilized with the passing of the years does not mean that it was fossilized from the start. In the second half of the sixteenth century both the Council of Trent and the Society of Jesus were new, and the intellectual productions of men associated with them were exciting and stimulating. What they stimulated in Protestant England was not necessarily the same as the effect they had in Catholic Europe, but the English certainly wanted to know what the other side was thinking.

In my view, therefore, it is anachronistic to maintain, as Oliveira Marques does in his many times reprinted *História de Portugal,* that in the second half of the sixteenth century the Portuguese universities 'entraram em fase de estagnação' [entered a period of stagnation].[22] The bibliographical evidence is simply against such a view.

[19] Diarmaid MacCulloch, *Reformation: Europe's House Divided, 1490–1700* (London: Allen Lane, 2003), pp. 66–7.

[20] For bibliography, see the biographical notes included in the short title catalogue.

[21] J. S. da Silva Dias, *Camões no Portugal de quinhentos* (Lisbon: Biblioteca Breve, 1981), p. 35. For further discussion of this point, see also T. F. Earle, 'Portuguese Scholarship in Oxford in the Early Modern Period : The Case of Jerónimo Osório (Hieronymus Osorius)', *Bulletin of Spanish Studies,* 81 (2004), 1039–49 (1039–40).

[22] A. H. de Oliveira Marques, *História de Portugal,* 3 vols (Lisbon: Presença, 1997–98), II, p. 141. He makes partial exceptions for Pedro Nunes, Francisco Sanches, Pedro da Fonseca and the Coimbra commentators, but says nothing about theology, the discipline in which the Portuguese attained their greatest fame in the sixteenth and seventeenth centuries.

Francisco Leite de Faria has accumulated much of that evidence, in his various studies which show how many editions of books by early modern scholars in Portugal were published abroad. António Guimarães Pinto has followed a different line in his translations – most of them first translations – of the Latin works of Jerónimo Osório into Portuguese. He has also recently published an important study and edition, with translations, of the polemic between Osório and the English theologians.[23] Osório, whose books were owned by professors and by undergraduate students in England and who was – outside Portugal – by far the best-known Portuguese writer of the sixteenth century, has thus become accessible to modern readers.[24] But these and other specialist studies have not yet changed what is accepted opinion in Portugal about the backwardness of universities there.

Nor will it be easy to shake the rooted indifference of British scholars to intellectual trends in Portugal. Not even Charles Boxer, who in the twentieth century was the most distinguished British historian of Portugal, was able to do so, though he tried. He revealed a sympathetic understanding of the educational aims and achievements of the empire builders, especially of the Jesuits, in a chapter of his *The Portuguese Seaborne Empire*, which was intended for a wide public. Boxer was a historian of the highest quality whose work, and whose courage in maintaining what he believed to be the truth, deserve great admiration. His chapter on the Portuguese intellectual tradition reveals many of his best qualities, though his subtleties may escape some readers, and from time to time even he slips into the clichéd thinking that has made it so difficult for historians in the UK to understand their oldest ally.

Boxer gave his chapter a striking title, 'The "Kaffirs of Europe", the Renaissance, and the Enlightenment'. He immediately explains that it was a Portuguese, the famous seventeenth-century Jesuit António Vieira, who first blackened his fellow-countrymen's reputation with the phrase about Kaffirs, as a rebuke for their lack of intellectual curiosity, and that in later centuries other Portuguese, as well as foreigners, repeated the criticism.[25] Boxer therefore implies, but does not state clearly, that there has always been an intellectual elite in Portugal capable of self-criticism and aware of how their country might appear to outsiders. The printed works of some members of that elite form the subject-matter of the present book. Yet it would be very easy for a reader to come away with the idea

---

[23] António Guimarães Pinto, *Humanismo e controvérsia religiosa: lusitanos e anglicanos*, 3 vols (Lisbon: Imprensa Nacional-Casa da Moeda, 2006).

[24] This is a book about institutional library holdings as they exist today, not about private libraries which have mostly long since been dispersed. However, the evidence for the popularity of Osório is discussed briefly in the biographical notes attached to the short-title catalogue.

[25] C. R. Boxer, *The Portuguese Seaborne Empire, 1415–1825* (Manchester: Carcanet, 1991), p. 340. Boxer's book was originally published in 1969.

that all Portuguese were 'Kaffirs', nor does the racist slur do much for Anglo-Portuguese understanding.

Later in the chapter, perhaps because overmuch influenced by Portuguese historiography, Boxer makes a much more significant slip. In his account of Portuguese humanism he refers to King João III's well-known policy of sending young men to study abroad, especially to Paris, as a way of preparing them for a university career in Portugal. The king died in 1557, and the conventional view of Portuguese intellectual history sees in the 1550s the death of open-mindedness and of any hope of progress towards liberal reform. Boxer echoes the cliché by saying that 'no more Portuguese scholars were sent to study abroad with the idea that they would make suitable professors at Coimbra on their return' and then by claiming that between 1560 and 1715 Portugal was cut off from fresh inspiration and new ideas from outside.[26] That statement is quite untrue. Portuguese scholars travelled just as much after 1560 as before. After King João's time they tended to avoid France, troubled by the wars of religion, but many spent long periods in Catholic Spain and Italy before returning to their chairs, professorial or episcopal, in Portugal. The highly international character of the religious orders, to which so many of them belonged, encouraged foreign travel. And many went abroad by royal command. Andrade, Casal, Foreiro, dos Mártires and Soares all attended the final session of the Council of Trent (1561–3) at the request of King Sebastião, or rather, of the regent, Queen Catarina. The much published canonist Agostinho Barbosa spent most of the 1620s in Rome before returning to Portugal, and the casuist Beja Parestrelo was for many years a professor at Bologna. It was common for civil lawyers to spend all or part of their careers at Salamanca. Many further examples can be found here in the biographical notes on the authors in the short-title catalogue.

As already stated, Boxer was an admirer of Jesuit education, both at secondary and at university level. Of the latter he says that it was 'originally the best of its day and generation', that is, at the end of the sixteenth century, a time when printed books by Jesuits, Portuguese and others, flooded Oxford and Cambridge libraries. But he notes that it 'did not keep pace with the expansion of knowledge and the ferment of ideas in the seventeenth century', and he goes on to lament the Jesuits' preoccupation with grammar, dialectic, rhetoric and scholasticism.[27] Here Boxer gives not an incorrect impression, but rather a misleading one, as much by what he does not say as by what he does.

It is true that in the seventeenth century university education in Portugal did not keep pace with the expansion of knowledge and new

[26] *The Portuguese Seaborne Empire*, p. 349.
[27] *The Portuguese Seaborne Empire*, p. 346.

ways of thinking associated with men such as Galileo, Bacon, Descartes, Hobbes, or Locke. Even in the dynamic period up to 1640 Portuguese scholarship was sound, but only rarely innovative, a theme which will be taken up elsewhere in this book. But the implication that the Portuguese universities were, therefore, backward and cut off from the European mainstream is misleading, because exactly the same could be said of other universities, including Oxford and Cambridge. They too changed slowly. Students in the English universities continued to be expected to dispute in Latin throughout the seventeenth century, and Aristotelianism was still the dominant mode of philosophical thinking until after 1650. (There is further discussion of this point in Chapter Two). In his history of the mathematical sciences and the new philosophies at Oxford in the seventeenth century, Mordechai Feingold shows that the great innovators, Hobbes and Locke, were brought up on the old Aristotelian curriculum and appeared to have thriven on it, rather than otherwise. When they attacked it, it was with the advantage of hindsight and from the perspective of old age, in the late seventeenth or even early eighteenth century.[28]

However, in the period up to 1640, universities in England and in Portugal still had a great deal in common. And because the Portuguese universities enjoyed a religious stability lacking in England, they were able to keep up a continuous stream of publications which the English must have wanted – or they would not have bought those heavy tomes coming from Portugal. The many changes of religious allegiance which took place in the reigns of Henry VIII and his children required fellows of Oxford and Cambridge colleges to adapt, or to risk expulsion or worse. The Stuart monarchs also interfered in the governance of the universities, and teachers had to conform, outwardly at least, to a shifting scene in which first Calvinists and then Laudians were in the ascendant.[29] This was not a period when academic production can have been easy. In Portugal, though, untouched by the Reformation, university teachers were not required to change their religious beliefs every few years. That must have made it possible for them to reflect on intellectual problems in a calmer atmosphere, even if a rigorous censorship placed lengthy delays on the publication of even the most orthodox works. In the period 1578–1580 Portugal went through a violent change of regime, after the death of King Sebastião in battle in Africa and a Spanish invasion which placed Philip II on the throne of Portugal. But the change of monarch did not

---

[28] Mordechai Feingold, 'The Mathematical Sciences and New Philosophies', in Nicholas Tyacke (ed.), *The History of the University of Oxford: the Seventeenth Century* (Oxford: Clarendon Press, 1997), pp. 359–448 (359–60).

[29] For a good summary, see Nicholas Tyacke, 'Introduction', in Nicholas Tyacke (ed.), *The History of the University of Oxford: the Seventeenth Century* (Oxford: Clarendon Press, 1997) pp. 1–24 (6–8).

have religious consequences and academic production continued as healthily as before.

In writing this book I have tried to keep a sense of perspective. The Portuguese wrote many books and, in some cases at least, it can be shown that the English read them. But reading is an active process, and Oxford and Cambridge did not passively accept and reproduce what Coimbra or Lisbon had to offer. There were, for instance, English theologians bitterly hostile to post-Tridentine thinking who read Osório or Paiva de Andrade only with the intention of refuting them. Other English theologians had different agendas, but agendas of their own which were markedly different from those of the Portuguese. There are some examples in Chapter One.

It is important to keep in mind other perspectives. The rise of modern nationalism means that today even the most insular Englishman has some notion of a Portuguese identity which is more precise than simply 'Latin', or 'southern European', or 'Catholic'. It is for this reason that it is possible to feel a certain disappointment that so few modern English historians are able to recognize Portuguese intellectual achievement. But in the sixteenth and seventeenth centuries nationalism was still nascent, and English readers may not have been able to distinguish Portuguese from other Catholic foreigners, particularly Spaniards. This is despite the fact that most of the authors listed here felt a strong sense of national identity, and stated it on the title-pages of their books. Yet the proud proclamation that they were 'Lusitani' is undercut by many factors. Their books were usually written in Latin, they were often published outside Portugal, and there is nothing obviously Portuguese in the subject-matter, if it was theology, medicine, or law. In addition, after 1580 it would have seemed to Englishmen that Portugal no longer had a political existence separate from Spain. So in the early modern period there is a tension between the stirrings of nationalism and the existence in Western Europe of the common core of faith, authority and tradition that has already been referred to. Those tensions are further explored in Chapter Five.

This is a book about an almost entirely unknown bibliographical phenomenon. Because it is, I have thought it appropriate to provide summary information about the Portuguese writers and the English readers who produced and consumed the material discussed here. Every writer listed in the short-title catalogue, including the Jesuit writers, mostly missionaries, whose letters are included under the general heading 'Letters from Jesuits', is discussed briefly in the biographical notes attached to each entry. The English owners and donors of their books, for the most part equally unknown but much more numerous, get shorter shrift. Some of the more prominent among them are mentioned in the chapters that follow. The majority are only named in the short-title catalogue with the briefest of professional and biographical detail. If nothing is said about any of them that is because nothing is known.

This is a pioneering study, but other scholars have made my investigation possible, particularly the cataloguers of libraries. OLIS and Newton, the computerised union catalogues in use at Oxford and Cambridge respectively, are the latest development in a process of patient bibliographic effort that has continued for centuries. Much of the work contained in these catalogues is anonymous, making it impossible for the modern researcher to express gratitude, except in the most general terms. The compilers of more specialized lists are better known, especially the two cataloguers of foreign books, Paul Morgan at Oxford and H. M. Adams at Cambridge. To both I owe a great debt, though neither of them provides information about provenance, or about shelf-marks. The chronological boundaries of the present study are determined by those of Paul Morgan's. The sixteen volumes of his catalogue, never published and only available in the Bodleian in a print-out, include all foreign imprints in Oxford college libraries down to 1640. The Bodleian's holdings are excluded. Adams is more complete − he covers the Cambridge University Library as well as the colleges − but ends in 1600. For my purposes 1640 is the better end-date, because it allows the reader to see the highpoint and the beginning of the decline of the phenomenon of which this book is a record.

Portuguese writers were successfully publishing their books in the learned presses of Europe in serious numbers in the 1570s and 80s, and judging by the holdings of Oxford and Cambridge libraries, those numbers reached their peak in the early years of the seventeenth century. Today 125 editions of books by Portuguese writers issued between 1600 and 1610 can be found in the two universities, but in the 1630s that number had fallen by more than half, to fifty-three. It has to be remembered that the statistics refer only to the holdings of the English universities, and that they include all the books that can be found there today, including many which arrived centuries after publication. However, what happened with regard to the books by Portuguese writers does not seem very different from what was happening in the world of scholarly publishing in Europe generally at the time.

Ian Maclean has drawn attention to the economic causes of the collapse − or implosion, in his words − of the boom in scholarly books in the 1620s.[30] Since the publishers of Portuguese books tended to be the great European houses which are the subject of his study, it is natural that the results of the collapse are as visible in the case of Portuguese material as of

---

[30] Ian Maclean, 'The Market for Scholarly Books and Conception of Genre in Northern Europe, 1570−1630', in Georg Kauffmann (ed.), *Die Renaissance im Blick der Nationen Europas* (Wiesbaden: Harrassowitz, 1991), pp. 17−31 (18).

any other. Political events, particularly the dire consequences of the Thirty Years' War, also affected scholarly publishing. In the short-title catalogue there is no book published in Germany between 1634 and 1640. 1640 is also the date of the restoration of Portuguese independence from Spain, but that event, momentous though it was, does not seem to have affected Portuguese academic production, any more than the loss of independence in 1580. Oxford and Cambridge libraries continued to collect books written by Portuguese scholars after 1640.[31] But by 1640 the decline of Latin was becoming visible, and as vernacular languages were more frequently used for scholarly purposes, so the Portuguese contribution began to drop out of view.

However, by 1640 Portuguese academic books had been arriving in Oxford and Cambridge, in large numbers, for around eighty years. Even though by the middle of the seventeenth century those numbers were beginning to decline, more than enough had arrived to demonstrate this book's essential thesis, that the writings of Portuguese intellectuals were well known in English universities in the early modern period.

Morgan and Adams provided the starting-point for my investigation, and I have depended very heavily on OLIS and Newton too. But even these powerful tools have their limitations. Searching for writers by national origin, especially when it is concealed by Latin or other versions of Portuguese names, is something no computer can do. Only human intelligence and power of observation can do that, with all the limitations implied by the word human. Still, I hope to have introduced more order than existed before.

The forms of Portuguese names have given cataloguers great difficulties over the centuries, and those difficulties persist in the digital age. Variations in spelling mean that many writers have more than one entry in the computerized catalogues. In the short-title catalogue these anomalies have been tidied up, to the best of my ability, and modern spelling and accentuation are used. Writers are listed by the last element in the surname, the way which for many years has been normal in the Portuguese-speaking world (English-speaking librarians please note). The many and sometimes bizarrely varied alternative forms of names to be found in Oxford and Cambridge library catalogues are given in parenthesis at the head of each entry in the short-title catalogue.

Nevertheless, although the catalogue sometimes corrects OLIS and Newton, it is not intended to compete with them. A reader looking for more information about any of the books listed will naturally consult the computerized catalogues, or the printed bibliographies to which cross-references are provided. There very often he or she will find a much fuller

---

[31] A good example is the second editions of the works of the canonist Agostinho Barbosa, which appeared in the 1650s and 60s. There are several of them in Trinity Hall.

description than the one I have been able to give, though in the days before computerization and easy travel bibliographers provided only limited information about the location of books. Even today there are several college libraries whose antiquarian collections have not yet been computerized. There are also cases where what is on OLIS or Newton is very limited, most notoriously in the case of old books in the Bodleian, where the catalogue usually gives no more than author, title, place and date of publication, and a shelf-mark. Only a few libraries provide information about provenance, even in up-to-date computerized catalogues. So though one day, when every book in Oxford and Cambridge has a full computer record, including a record of the nationality of its author, this book will be obsolete, that day is some way off.

CHAPTER ONE

PORTUGUESE BOOKS IN OXFORD AND CAMBRIDGE LIBRARIES

Portuguese books can be found in libraries great and small, the Bodleian and the Cambridge University Library at one extreme, with collections that can be numbered in the hundreds, and the smaller college libraries at the other, with twenty books or fewer. Not all the books came as donations, but most of them did, either directly from the individuals who owned them, or from legacies intended for library purposes. Here too there is great variation. There are the donors of large collections, like Selden, Moore and Crynes, and the other fifteen benefactors who gave more than ten Portuguese books, and there are also around 260 smaller fry, men (nearly all) who presented their colleges with only one or two, very often as part of a larger gift.

Within all this statistical diversity there is, nevertheless, a remarkable homogeneity, especially in the early period. Up until the eighteenth century collectors, great and small, focussed on books in a single language, Latin, and in a relatively narrow range of subject areas. These correspond to the traditional faculty divisions of theology, law (civil and canon) and medicine. As explained in the Introduction, the special historical circumstances of Portugal, the country which had pioneered the exploration of Africa and Asia, led to the acquisition also by English libraries of many books about the lands hitherto unknown to Europeans. The old collectors concerned themselves, almost exclusively, with these four areas of interest, so that whether one goes into a small library or a large one which was formed in the early modern period, those are the books that one will find.

In the nineteenth century and afterwards collections and collectors are markedly different. Many more books in the vernacular appear on library shelves. This was the period when, in Oxford, the Taylorian began to acquire its holdings of Portuguese literature, almost unknown earlier unless it had been translated into Latin. The great prize, the first edition of the *Lusiads* of Camões (item **150**), came to the Bodleian after 1883. Collectors began to specialize, and not just in literature. The history of the medieval period and of the Discoveries, whose heroic period had ended before 1550, had not been of much interest to Elizabethan and Stuart readers who wanted to know about what was happening in their own

time. Victorian collectors changed all that. In Oxford Douce was a
collector of books about Portuguese history, and so were those who, at
Queen's and the Bodleian, spent the very generous bequest of Robert
Mason, who died in 1841.[1] The surprisingly large holdings of material in
Portuguese, also of literature and history, at All Souls probably came in
the nineteenth century. The builders of the British empire found
inspiration in their Portuguese predecessors, but also wanted to learn
from what they believed to have been their mistakes. Other kinds of
specialization were possible: H. W. Chandler's interest in Aristotelian
philosophy and Ingram Bywater's in neo-Latin literature and the classical
scholarship of the Renaissance. Their collections reflect the abundant
contributions of the Portuguese during the period under review.

   In Cambridge the arrival of the historian Lord Acton's library, of 60,000
volumes, in 1902 was the most important benefaction to the Cambridge
University Library since the royal library nearly two centuries previously.[2]
In some ways the Catholic Lord Acton's interests are a throw-back to the
earlier period, since he acquired Latin theology and law as well as history,
but his collection is, nevertheless, more specialized than those formed in
the seventeenth or eighteenth centuries. While Selden and Bishop Moore
included medical books by Portuguese doctors in their libraries, Acton
did not, for, unlike them, he was not trying to cover every subject taught
in the universities of his time. This survey of modern collecting would not
be complete without a mention of the eccentric H. A. Pottinger, who
would appear to have been little more than a thief, though one with
principles, since his magpie collection was all left in 1911 to his college,
Worcester.[3]

   However, there were local issues which even in the early modern period
might slant the collection of books one way or another. In the next chapter
one instance of seventeenth-century collection development will be
discussed – the acquisition by a large number of Oxford libraries of
the Coimbra commentators on Aristotle. The fact that relatively few of
these books can be found in Cambridge is an indication of the ways in
which the encyclopaedic urge was modified by the requirements of a
university curriculum. It seems likely, though, that it was an
administrative, and not an intellectual decision that led the universities
to acquire different guides to Aristotle. Keeping the exception constituted
by the Coimbra commentators in mind, then, it will be possible now to

   [1] He left £30,000 for the purchase of books. See Paul Morgan, *Oxford Libraries Outside the Bodleian: A Guide* (Oxford: Bodleian Library, 1980), p. 112.
   [2] David McKitterick, *Cambridge University Library, A History: The Eighteenth and Nineteenth Centuries* (Cambridge: Cambridge University Press, 1986), p. 14
   [3] 'Pottinger was a thorough-going, old-fashioned collector. His coats were made with poacher's pockets capable of accommodating a folio on each side'. See C. H. Wilkinson, 'Worcester College Library', *Transactions of the Oxford Bibliographical Society*, 1 (1927), 263–326 (265).

look at the broad sweep of the collections in early modern Oxford and Cambridge.

What the early modern universities really wanted to see in their libraries, more than accounts of exotic lands or even medical treatises, was theology. The extent and variety of Portuguese theology in Oxford libraries is surprising, especially as it is never mentioned by modern historians of the university and its intellectual life. In Cambridge, though, where the books are fewer, Basil Hall had certainly heard of some of them.[4] The Portuguese wrote so much, and in so many different branches of the subject, that they could continue to supply the market from the 1560s right through to 1640, even though during that period the religious temper of the universities changed very considerably.

The earliest Portuguese theological writings to arrive in any number are the controversial products of the Council of Trent. Portuguese bishops were present at the meetings of the Council, and also younger specialist theologians, who were sometimes commissioned to publicise the council's conclusions. Diogo Paiva de Andrade was such a theologian, an aggressive polemicist, one or other of whose two major works, *Orthodoxarum explicationum libri decem* and *Defensio Tridentinae fidei Catholicae* can be found, sometimes in more than one copy, in the Bodleian, the Cambridge University Library, nine Oxford colleges, and six Cambridge ones. There is a copy of the *Orthodoxarum explicationum* (item **49**) in the Cambridge University Library with the manuscript date of 1582 on the title page, and John Foxe, who died in 1587, also owned a book by Andrade.[5] There was a renewal of interest in Roman Catholic theology generally in the universities in the 1580s in which Portuguese theologians played their part.[6] Further, negative evidence about the dating of the coming of Portuguese polemical theology to England is its almost complete absence from the books left by Archbishop Matthew Parker to Corpus Cambridge in 1575. The exception is Osório's letter to Queen Elizabeth (item **668**).

The title 'Andradius contra Kemnicium', given to Andrade's work in the catalogue of Foxe's books, is an indication of its polemic nature. Martin Chemnitz was a German Lutheran theologian who was present at some of the meetings of the Council of Trent and whose books Andrade was ordered to attack. Andrade undoubtedly owed part of his success to his German publishers in Ingolstadt and Cologne, but he was also

---

[4] Basil Hall, 'Biblical Sholarship: Editions and Commentaries', in S. L. Greenslade (ed.), *The Cambridge History of the Bible, Volume III: the West from the Reformation to the Present Day* (Cambridge: Cambridge University Press, 1963), pp. 38–93 (92).

[5] Ralph Hanna, 'An Oxford Library Interlude: The Manuscripts of John Foxe the Martyrologist', *Bodleian Library Record*, 17 (2002), 314–26 (322).

[6] Gaskell, p. 10.

admired by his Protestant opponents. Even Chemnitz, who he had abused so thoroughly, praised him: 'Homo doctus sane et eloquens, cuius in Concilio Tridentino non minima fuit auctoritas' [a learned and eloquent man, of considerable authority in the Council of Trent], [7] and an anonymous reader wrote, in the copy of item 49 formerly kept in Peterborough Cathedral library but now in the Cambridge University Library: 'Andradius Payva a Doctor of Portugall is ye best learned man (in my opinion) of all ye Papistes'.

Portuguese writers supported each other in their international endeavours – a point to be explored further in a later chapter – and Andrade's *Defensio*, which was published posthumously, benefited from the preface written by another, and even more famous Catholic polemicist, Jerónimo Osório. Osório was one of the few Portuguese theologians whose work provoked detailed refutation in England. Since he had had the temerity to write an open letter to Queen Elizabeth herself, urging her to return to the faith of her ancestors, it could hardly have been otherwise. At the Queen's request Walter Haddon of Cambridge wrote a reply, which Osório countered with a work first published in Lisbon in 1567, and usually known in its numerous reprintings outside Portugal as *De religione*. However, the first, Portuguese edition (which has a slightly different title) reached Cambridge and in the University Library is a copy with extensive notes by Haddon himself (item **508**), though he died before completing his riposte. It was finished after his death by John Foxe, who also wrote a response to Osório's *De iustitia*.[8] In the same work Foxe took the opportunity of taking on Paiva de Andrade.[9] The responses show that Osório and Andrade were were not just received in Oxford but also read there before the end of the sixteenth century. So was the work of a third polemicist who had been at Trent, Gaspar do Casal, Bishop of Leiria and later of Coimbra. His *De quadripertita iustitia libri tres* (item **162**) had reached both Oxford and Cambridge by 1589. These three writers, who between them are responsible for well over 200 books in the college and university libraries, were of great interest to English theologians of the end of Elizabeth's reign. Osório especially offered a clear target for refutation,[10] while all three provided reliable and readable information

---

[7] Quoted by Léon Bourdon, 'Jerónimo Osório et Stanislas Hosius (1565–1578)', *Boletim da Biblioteca da Universidade de Coimbra*, 23 (1958), 1–105 (7n.)

[8] The most complete account of the controversy is to be found in Léon Bourdon, 'Jerónimo Osório et les humanistes anglais', in *L'Humanisme portugais et l'Europe* (Paris: Fondation Calouste Gulbenkian, 1984), pp. 263–333 (272–93). See also the texts published by Guimarães Pinto in *Humanismo e controvérsia religiosa: lusitanos e anglicanos*.

[9] Foxe's *De Christo gratis iustificante contra Osorianam iustitiam* was published in 1588. On pp. 35–77 there are frequent references to Andrade, and at p. 77 a detailed consideration of his *Orthodoxarum explicationum*, Book VI.

[10] Osório's intransigence in religious matters dismayed even his friends. See R. W. Truman, 'Jean Matal and his Relations with Antonio Agustín, Jerónimo Osório da Fonseca and Pedro Ximenes', in

about the new doctrines promulgated at Trent which their opponents needed to study so as to be able to formulate counter-arguments.

In the next century Portuguese theology, as represented in the English universities, took quite a different turn, one which seems to have suited the more eirenic reign of King James. The polemicists are replaced by encyclopaedists, learned canonists and others who were more concerned with scholarly accuracy than with confuting 'haereticam pravitatem'. Agostinho Barbosa, for instance, was the author of many compilations of papal bulls and decrees and especially of information about ecclesiastical privilege. He published mostly in Lyon in the 1620s and 1630s and his books arrived in Oxford not long afterwards. Magdalen has a large collection. From the short-title catalogue it might seem that Barbosa was an author more highly regarded in Oxford than in Cambridge, but that is not really the case. It is simply that Cambridge libraries tended to acquire his books in the later part of the seventeenth century, when second editions began to appear. Another writer rather similar to Barbosa was the Franciscan Manuel Rodrigues. A third, much in vogue in the early seventeenth century, was the Jesuit casuist Manuel Sá, whose tiny vest-pocket size *Aphorismi confessariorum* was printed and reprinted over and over again from 1599 onwards.

It is certainly tempting to see the Portuguese theologians of the seventeenth century as attractive to the 'avant-garde conformists' who, in MacCulloch's view, became more influential after 1600. These were men who wanted to emphasize the English Church's links with the universal catholic tradition while rejecting what they regarded as the excesses of Roman Catholicism.[11] King James himself encouraged the study of canon law, which had been abandoned in England earlier in the Reformation. For this writers like Barbosa and Rodrigues were important sources. Casuists like Manuel Sá, who discussed the resolution of cases of conscience, were bound to be useful even to Protestant clergy, especially as Protestants themselves were slow to produce literature of this kind, a regular cause for complaint in the seventeenth century.[12]

There is a risk, though, in assuming that the history of printing corresponds to the history of reception. There are sixty years between Paiva de Andrade's books and Agostinho Barbosa's, but in the 1620s they were offered for sale together. Henry Featherstone was a London bookseller who bought widely in Italy, where many Portuguese

M. H. Crawford (ed.), *Antonio Agustín Between Renaissance and Counter-Reform* (London: Warburg Institute, 1993), pp. 247–63 (253).

[11] Diarmaid MacCulloch, *Reformation: Europe's House Divided, 1490–1700* (London: Allen Lane, 2003), pp. 510–12.

[12] See Jeremy Taylor, *Ductor Dubitantium, or the Rule of Conscience in all her General Measures*, 2nd edition (London: Norton, 1671), Preface, p. i (first edition, 1660) and Thomas Barlow, *De Studio Theologiae or Directions for the Choice of Books in the Study of Divinity* (Oxford: Lichfield, 1700), p. 41.

theologians published. In his catalogue of 1628 both writers are listed, and the same phenomenon occurs in Robert Martin's catalogues of the same period.[13] A glance at the short-title catalogue will also show that the period elapsing between the publication of a book and its arrival in Oxford or Cambridge could vary quite unpredictably.

What seems to have happened is this. There was an undoubted shift in theological production in Portugal as the Council of Trent receded into the past. However, in distant England this may not have seemed obvious since the whole range of Portuguese scholarship was available more or less simultaneously. Its quality was such that it could inspire – or challenge – men in both universities who held a wide variety of religious opinion. Puritans, MacCulloch's 'avant-garde conformists' and their successors, the Anglicans of Charles II's reign, and crypto-Catholics all acquired the books, as a study of donors shows.

Thomas Barlow (1607–91) was an influential Oxford figure of the seventeenth century. A great reader and annotator, of Portuguese books among others, fellow of Queen's, Bodley's Librarian and finally Bishop of Lincoln, he left a large library to the Oxford institutions with which he had been associated. He was a staunch Puritan, disapproving of recent theological developments in the English church, and a royalist.[14] He read Barbosa, Rodrigues and Sá, but it seems likely that it was with the intention of extracting from their texts information injurious to the Catholic cause and not in any eirenic spirit. He once called Barbosa's *Remissiones* an 'Authentick Common-place-Book, and a Repository of all points of *Popery*',[15] and it was with that in mind that he annotated Rodrigues's account of the privileges of mendicant and non-mendicant Orders (item **774**), binding five pages of notes into his copy of the book. Some of the notes, which are carefully keyed to passages in the printed text, are simply intended to remind him of the topics discussed. However, he frequently draws attention to references to indulgences, always distasteful to Protestants, and underlines the statement that the Jesuit Order is mendicant. I suspect there is irony in the underlining, as the Jesuits were rumoured in Oxford to have an excessive fondness for trading.[16] When he came to the Jesuit writer Manuel Sá he made a careful, and legible note, clearly for the benefit of future readers, on Sá's statement that in certain circumstances kings may be put to death by their subjects. The idea was not an original one, but it must have

---

[13] See, for example, Henry Featherstone, *Catalogus librorum in diuersis locis Italiae emptorum, anno 1628* (London: John Legate, 1628) and Robert Martin, *Catalogus librorum, ex praecipiis Italiae emporiis selectorum* . . . (London: Thomas Harper, 1639).

[14] John Spurr, 'Barlow, Thomas (1608/9–1691)', *Oxford Dictionary of National Biography*, Oxford University Press, 2004 [http.www.oxforddnb.com/view/article/1439, accessed 21 Nov 2008].

[15] Barlow, *De studio theologiae*, p. 33.

[16] See the annotations, perhaps by Archbishop Wake, in item **464**.

seemed especially dangerous in a book which circulated very widely. The note explains that this passage of the *Aphorismi*, unlike many others, was never altered by any ecclesiastical censor. There is no explicit judgement, but it certainly seems likely that the royalist Barlow, who lived through the execution of Charles I, saw in this the depravity of Jesuits.

Sá was one of the writers who inspired Jeremy Taylor (1613–67), another royalist, Bishop of Down and Connor in Ireland, to correct what he conceived to be the errors of Roman Catholic teaching and produce his immense *Ductor Dubitantium*, about the resolution of cases of conscience. Sá heads the list of Catholic casuists whose work is held to be unreliable, but this time for quite a different reason. Taylor's objection is that he was insufficiently dogmatic, and in cases where the doctors of the Church disagreed allowed his readers to make up their own minds. Taylor complains that 'by this means they [Sá and others] entertain all interests, and comply with all perswasions, and send none away Unsatisfied'.[17]

However, it was possible for English writers to approach Portuguese theology in a more generous spirit. William Crashawe or Crashaw, whose many books were left to St John's, Cambridge in 1626, had no liking for Jesuits, those typical products of the Roman Church of his day, as he saw them. In *The Bespotted Jesuite* he accuses them of excessive devotion to the Virgin Mary, and part of the evidence for what he regarded as a serious error comes from the Portuguese Cistercian Cristóvão da Visitação, one of whose books he owned (item **901**).[18] But other writers fare rather better, especially if their work had been censored in the Indexes of Prohibited Books.

There are no copies of the earliest Portuguese Indexes in Oxford and Cambridge libraries. However, all the Indexes published in Portugal after the Council of Trent are to be found there (especially in Oxford), down to the comprehensive Lisbon edition of 1624. In addition there are several copies of the Index for Portuguese use edited by the distinguished Dominican Francisco Foreiro and published in Antwerp (items **449– 53**). The Indexes gave Protestants a wonderful weapon against their Catholic opponents. It made it very easy to say – and Crashawe said it – how the modern church of Rome had deviated from what he believed to be the true Catholic tradition. So the staunch Puritan could come to the defence of his Roman Catholic colleagues if their scholarly works had been 'razed out or perverted' by the new orthodoxy of the Council of Trent. At a time when the Church was particularly concerned to present a united front to the outside world theological works produced prior to the

---

[17] Taylor, *Ductor Dubitantium*, Preface, pp. ii and iv.
[18] *The Bespotted Jesuite* (London: Bartholomew Alsop, 1641), the Epistle, sig. Aa1v.

conclusion of the Council, even by writers of impeccable orthodoxy, were anxiously scrutinized for anything that might seem out of date. One such writer, among many, was Azambuja, who Crashawe knew by his Latin name, Oleaster, and whose commentary on the Pentateuch was in his library (item **67**). It had first been printed in the 1550s and soon fell foul of the new theology of the 1560s.

Crashawe only knew what was said about Oleaster in the Index. Had he been able to see the censors' own copy of item 67 he would have been delighted, because it was censored not just once, but several times, in 1575, 1613, 1640 and 1707. Even so, the censor thought it necessary to warn the reader that Oleaster is unsound on the question of the serpent in the Garden of Eden, to which he is said to have attributed 'quendam rationis ussum (*sic*) et facultatem naturalem sermonis' [some use of reason and the natural faculty of speech].[19]

Crashawe was pleased to defend Oleaster, and others like him. In the opinion of the English Puritan they were 'men of conscience, and not State-Papists' and 'knowne to be no babes in learning'. He could be eloquent on their behalf, though one must always suspect his motives: 'These Authors be Papists, so accounted, liued, and died, yet gave testimonies to many truths of our religion'.[20]

Later in the seventeenth century this was an attitude which became more common. Among the donors of books by the canonist Barbosa are three quite well-known Anglicans, Peter Gunning, Master of St John's, Cambridge, and Bishop of Ely, the diplomat and lawyer Sir Leoline Jenkins, Principal of Jesus, Oxford, and from the generation born after the Civil War, Archbishop William Wake.[21] All of these were traditionalists in the line of Archbishop Laud, concerned with ceremony and the Catholic roots of the Church of England, though disapproving of modern Popish errors. They did not annotate their copies of Barbosa, but it is reasonable to suppose that they read him because he provided the kind of information that they wanted, especially about such matters as ecclesiastical and episcopal privilege.

A major collector, colleague and contemporary of Barlow, but also rather different in religious outlook, was Richard Allestree. Professor of Divinity, whose library is preserved in the room in Christ Church which he intended for it, he was much less combatively anti-Catholic than

---

[19] The copy in question is in the Biblioteca Nacional de Portugal, with the shelfmark 3138v. The MS comment about the serpent is on p. 32.

[20] William Crashawe, *Romish Forgeries and Falsifications* (London: Matthew Lownes, 1606), the Epistle (sig. A4v) and the Preface (sig. C3v).

[21] For their biographies, see Kenneth W. Stevenson, 'Gunning, Peter (1614–1684)', Alan Marshall, 'Jenkins, Sir Leoline (1625–1685)' and Stephen Taylor, 'Wake, William (1657–1737), all in *Oxford Dictionary of National Biography*, Oxford University Press, Sep 2004; online edn. Jan 2008 [http://ezproxy.ouls.ox.ac.uk: 2117/view/articles/11748, 14732, 28409] accessed 22 Nov 2008.

Barlow. John Spurr contrasts the two men in this regard.[22] Allestree did not comment much on his reading, though a page of notes is included in his copy of Foreiro's edition of Isaiah (item **369**). Generally his choice of Portuguese books suggests an attitude of curiosity, rather than hostility. They include a number of liturgical works, published in Lisbon, and not otherwise represented in either Oxford or Cambridge (items **540–1 and 870–2**). This is not suprising in a churchman who was also seen as one of the heirs of Laud. Allestree also had three books about Ethiopia, indicating how Englishmen had to rely on the Portuguese for information about Christianity in that distant country. Ethiopia was especially significant because the first non-Jewish convert to Christianity came from there.[23]

At Cambridge, William Sancroft was appointed Master of Emmanuel in 1662, shortly after the restoration of Charles II, with the brief of bringing the notoriously Puritan college, which did not even have a properly consecrated chapel, into the Anglican fold. The royalist and traditionalist Sancroft, who had great success at Emmanuel, later became Archbishop of Canterbury. On his death in 1693 he left 6,000 books to his college, of which forty-one were by Portuguese writers. Sancroft had wide interests, but it is not surprising to find among his Portuguese books the Jesuit Cosme de Magalhães's work on ecclesiastical privilege (item **554**), as well as other works normally considered safe, like commentaries on the Bible.

Many people remained Roman Catholics, despite the Reformation. John Lumley, the first Baron Lumley (1533–1609) was a famous collector, the owner of the largest private library in Elizabethan England, and a committed Catholic, who married into the Arundel family.[24] Lumley did not have a university education, but in 1691, long after his death, part of his library came to Trinity, Cambridge. It includes books by Jesuit missionaries (items **464 and 493**) and by Osório (item **647**). Wadham possesses a collection undoubtedly formed by a Catholic, Sir William Godolphin (1634?–96), who converted while serving as ambassador in Spain. They were left to the college by a relative, Charles Godolphin, in 1720, and include a Spanish version of Heitor Pinto's very popular dialogues on religious and moral topics, the *Imagem da vida cristã* (item **728**).

In the universities the old religion was not easily extirpated from men's minds, and there were some who survived in important positions and yet

---

[22] John Spurr, 'Allestree, Richard (1621/2–1681) in *Oxford Dictionary of National Biography*, Oxford University Press, Sep 2004; online edn. Jan 2008 [http://ezproxy.ouls.ox.ac.uk: 2117/view/article/395] accessed 22 Nov 2008.
[23] Acts, ch. 8.
[24] Lumley, pp. 1–3.

seemed ambiguous in religious outlook. In Cambridge Andrew Perne, Master of Peterhouse, preached a sermon in 1564 in which he scandalised his hearers by insisting that the Church of Rome – for all its errors – was an essential part of Christian tradition.[25] He retained his Mastership – though he never became a bishop – and may have found consolation in Catholic thinking. At any rate, his donation of eight Portuguese books to his college, all but one of theology, was one of the largest received anywhere in Cambridge in the reign of Queen Elizabeth. In Oxford he was outstripped by William Paddy, who in 1602 gave fourteen books, mostly medical, to his college, St John's. In 1633 Paddy, now Sir William after a career as royal physician, gave more books to the college, among them works by Portuguese canonists (items **258, 386, 700**). Paddy, a colleague and ally of Laud, was a man of high church leanings.[26]

Dorothy Wadham, the true founder, in 1613, of the college which bears her name and that of her husband, was also suspected of Catholicism. She was a friend of Philip Bisse, Archdeacon of Taunton, who is not included in the *Oxford Dictionary of National Biography* but who owned what was one of the largest private libraries then in existence in Britain.[27] He gave twenty-five Portuguese books to Wadham, most of them of theology. Dorothy was extremely grateful – and one may speculate that this was in part because his were the kind of books that she wished her new foundation to own.[28]

I have suggested that the Portuguese theologians could meet different needs in the universities: material for refutation for the Puritans, information about the liturgy or ecclesiastical privilege for the Anglicans, spiritual consolation, perhaps, for those of uncertain allegiance. Fifty years ago Edward Wilson showed how some of the techniques of Spanish religious poetry of the Counter-Reformation period could quite easily be taken over into English.[29] Even earlier Peter Russell

---

[25] Patrick Collinson, 'Perne, Andrew (1519?–1589) in *Oxford Dictionary of National Biography*, Oxford University Press, Sep 2004; online edn. Jan 2008 [http://ezproxy.ouls.ox.ac.uk: 2117/view/article/21975] accessed 22 Nov 2008. See, in addition, Christopher Brooke, 'Learning and Doctrine', in Victor Morgan and Christopher Brooke, *A History of the University of Cambridge, 1546–1750* (Cambridge: Cambridge University Press, 2004), pp. 437–63 (451).

[26] H. R. Trevor-Roper, *Archbishop Laud 1573–1645* (London: Macmillan, 1940), p. 34. There is more information about Paddy's activities as a donor in Ralph Hanna, *A Descriptive Catalogue of the Western Medieval Manuscripts of St John's College Oxford* (Oxford: Oxford University Press, 2002), pp. xxii–v.

[27] Paul Morgan, *Oxford Libraries Outside the Bodleian: A Guide* (Oxford: Bodleian Library, 1980) , p. 152.

[28] At her behest the college acquired a portrait of him, holding a book. See Oliver Pointer, 'The Library', in C. S. L. Davies and Jane Garnett (eds), *Wadham College* (Oxford: Wadham College, 1994), pp. 92–9 (93).

[29] Edward M. Wilson, 'Spanish and English Religious Poetry of the Seventeenth Century', *Spanish and English Literature of the 16th and 17th Centuries* (Cambridge: Cambridge University Press, 1980), pp. 234–49 (244–9). Wilson's article was first published in 1958.

had pointed out that many English readers of Spanish put doctrinal differences aside in order to have access to scholarly information otherwise unavailable to them, or else to be able to read devotional material which was unexceptionable theologically.[30] This is likely to have been the case with the many editions of books of the Bible (Latin, Greek and Hebrew) produced by Catholic scholars throughout the period under review. It was to these that the Puritan Crashawe was referring when he said that there were papists who had given 'testimonies to many truths of our religion'.

Many Portuguese scholars had a particular skill in Hebrew, among them Azambuja, whom, as we have seen, Crashawe admired.[31] As early as 1567 Sir William Petre, the refounder of Exeter College, made a gift of new books published abroad, among them Heitor Pinto's commentary on Isaiah (Lyon, 1561, item 730). In this context it is interesting to note that the printer was a Protestant, Thibaud Payen.[32] Purchases of this type of material went on until 1640. Some of the editions achieved great fame. Francisco Foreiro, for instance, was the first commentator to approach Isaiah using the new techniques of textual criticism and philological investigation. He prints the Vulgate alongside the Hebrew text, but also a new, Latin translation of his own (items **368–9**). There are only fourteen copies of his edition in Oxford and Cambridge libraries, but several of them have extensive and legible annotation by philologically minded readers. Crashawe was one of those who owned a copy of the commentary. Foreiro continued to have such readers until the early eighteenth century, 150 years after his book was first published. The remarkable copy preserved in Worcester, with detailed notes, almost of print quality and in several languages, is a proof of this. The modern Biblical scholar Basil Hall has also noted that Foreiro's 'excellent commentary on Isaiah long remained . . . a standard work'.[33]

Another group of writers – priests for the most part, and who tended to be resident in Rome – are the Neo-Latin poets and orators whose work appears sporadically in the libraries, very often in compendia. Collectors, ancient and modern, have shown some interest in the writings of Bernardo Constantino, Tomé Correia, Aquiles Estaço and João Vaz da Mota, but their impact was minor compared to that of the theologians.

[30] P. E. Russell, 'English Seventeenth-Century Interpretations of Spanish Literature', *Atlante*, 1 (1950), 65–77 (69).

[31] See Manuel Augusto Rodrigues, 'Alguns aspectos da obra exegética de Fr. Jerónimo de Azambuja (Oleastro), O.P.', *Revista Portuguesa de História*, 17 (1977), 25–36 (25–6), and for an account of Portuguese Hebrew scholarship more generally, José Nunes Carreira, *Filologia e crítica de Isaías no comentário de Francisco Foreiro (1522?-1581)*, (Coimbra: privately printed, 1974).

[32] Clive Griffin, *Journey-men Printers, Heresy, and the Inquisition in Sixteenth-Century Spain* (Oxford: Oxford University Press, 2005), p. 98.

[33] Basil Hall, 'Biblical Scholarship: Editions and Commentaries', p. 92.

The next really important subject after theology was medicine. The works of Portuguese doctors, nearly all of them New Christians, or crypto-Jews, some of whom returned to their old faith when safely outside the reach of the Inquisition, can be found across Oxford and Cambridge libraries. Normally they wrote in Latin, though occasionally they would use a vernacular language. Hebrew, however, they avoided entirely, so their work was accessible to their Christian colleagues.[34] In this they were unlike the philosopher and theologian Isaac Abravanel who normally wrote only for the faithful (see items 1–17). The extraordinary paradox whereby so many of these men, many of them exiles from Portugal, nevertheless proclaimed their loyalty to the land where they had been born will be discussed in Chapter Five. Here the stress will be on their importance to the early modern university.

Doctors travelled with the soldiers, adminstrators and missionaries to Portuguese India and had the facilities to write and even publish books there. Garcia da Orta's botanical and medical treatise on the plants of India, the *Colóquio sobre os simples e drogas da Índia*, combined medical learning with information which was entirely new to European doctors and made an enormous impact in both English universities. Orta was, among other things, the first European doctor to describe the symptoms of cholera. It seems that Orta drafted his book in Latin, but was persuaded to publish in Portuguese, and in that language it first appeared 1563, attracting little publicity.[35] In the collection left by the eighteenth-century botanist William Sherard to the Bodleian is a copy of the first edition, with MS notes in Arabic script (item 627, now in the Plant Sciences library). Fortunately it came to the attention of a Flemish publicist, Carolus Clusius, while on a tour of the Iberian Peninsula with his pupil, a member of the Fugger banking family. Clusius abridged the book, translated it into Latin and published it through the Plantin press.[36] It became rapidly famous and there are twenty-two copies of Orta's work in Oxford and seventeen in Cambridge. Most of these are in Latin, but besides the two copies of the extremely rare Portuguese first edition, already mentioned, there are others in French and Italian. At least fourteen of the Oxford copies were acquired before the nineteenth century, and eleven of the Cambridge ones.

[34] Harry Friedenwald, *The Jews and Medicine*, 2 vols (Baltimore: Johns Hopkins, 1944), I, p. 167. However, Friedenwald admits that item 605, by Abraão Nehemias, may have been composed originally in Hebrew.

[35] See the dedications to Martim Afonso de Sousa and to the reader, which both mention the existence of a Latin version. Portuguese was used 'por ser mais geral' [because it is in general use], but that was only true of India.

[36] Item 628, p. 4. The Cambridge University Library owns Clusius's own copy of the Goa edition, signed and dated by him in January 1564.

Garcia da Orta's botanical work was continued by another doctor who served in Portuguese India, Cristóvão da Costa, as the title-page of item **242** makes clear. Costa is usually regarded as Portuguese, but he was more ambiguous about his nationality than Orta. On the title-pages of books he is always called an African, which probably means that he was born in Tangier, then a Portuguese possession and a city tolerant of Jews.[37] He also had family connections in Spain, and it was in Burgos, and in Spanish, that he published the book that made him famous. There are five copies of the first edition in Oxford (none in Cambridge), three with old provenance, which is an indication of the acceptability of Spanish in early modern England. But once again it was Clusius's Latin version, from which translations into French and Italian derive, that put his book into the libraries, with nine copies in Oxford and nine in Cambridge.

Orta's pioneering study is one of the most widely circulated of all the books in this survey. He, and Costa, showed how the Portuguese could be experts in the botany and *materia medica* of the tropics, but academic medicine in the early modern period dealt with many other subjects besides these and Portuguese doctors contributed to most of them. There are a number of editions and commentaries on works by Hippocrates (items **140, 168, 360–1, 534**), Galen (items **150, 358–9, 535, 742, 891–3**) and Dioscorides (items **128–32**). As well as such typically humanistic enterprises as these, there are also printed case-books. João Rodrigues de Castelo Branco, better known by his pseudonym Amatus Lusitanus, was the most famous author of these. He gradually accumulated seven 'centuries' of cures, in numerous editions. Oxford has thirteen of those appearing between 1554 and 1620, and Cambridge twelve. There were also books devoted to specific medical problems, like Rodrigo da Fonseca's disquisition on the stone (item **356**), or Rodrigo de Castro's very popular manual on the diseases of women (items **185–7**), of which there are eighteen copies divided roughly equally between the two universities. It is only anatomy and chemical, or alchemical, medicine that are lacking. Both these areas of medicine could be regarded as potentially dangerous to their practitioners, anatomy because it involved the dissection of human remains, chemistry and alchemy because of their association with magic. It may be for those reasons that Portuguese doctors tended to avoid them.

In the second half of the seventeenth century Oxford medicine had a period of glory, associated with William Harvey's discovery of the circulation of blood, but both before and afterwards English university medicine was relatively feeble compared with what was happening on the

---

[37] *Tratado das drogas e medicinas das Índias orientais*, translated and edited by Jaime Walter (Lisbon: Junta de Investigações do Ultramar, 1964), pp. vii–xii.

continent.[38] Famous English doctors, like Thomas Linacre or Harvey himself, studied in Italy, and the fact that several Portuguese doctors practised medicine there and taught in Italian universities would have greatly increased their prestige in Oxford and Cambridge. Rodrigo da Fonseca, for example, was a professor at Padua, considered the best medical school in Europe. Estêvão Rodrigues de Castro taught at the University of Pisa and was physician to the Medici family, an extremely prestigious position which had attracted the famous surgeon Vidus Vidius.[39] When one famous member of the family, Marie, moved to Paris to become Queen of France, Felipe Montalto was her physician there. Such appointments were a proof of the high standards achieved by Portuguese doctors.

Another sign of English doctors' appreciation of the work of their Portuguese colleagues was their habit of detailed annotation of medical works. Thomas Lorkin (?1528–91), Professor of Physick at Cambridge, was especially prolific. He left sixteen pages of notes in his copy of item 117 – a volume of Amatus Lusitanus's cases – and nine in item 125, another book by the same authority. Thomas Hopper of New College, who died in 1623, was also an enthusiastic annotator. It was also very common to write detailed marginal notes. Brian Twine did that in his copy of item 139, by Manuel Brudo, and there are marginalia in a number of William Sherard's copies of Latin editions of Garcia da Orta, as well as in his copy of the first, Portuguese edition.

A rather different and more famous reader of Portuguese medical works was Robert Burton. There are at least seventeen references in the *Anatomy of Melancholy* to Rodrigo de Castro and more than sixty to Montalto's study of mental illness (item **581**), though he does not seem to have owned a copy of either book. The stories contained in Amatus Lusitanus's case-books were also of great interest to him.[40]

Modern readers might reasonably expect Elizabethan and Jacobean scholars to have had a particular interest in the Portuguese discoveries. They did indeed acquire many books about what the Portuguese had achieved overseas, but they were not like modern collectors and historians. The historical context of the discoveries, and of the struggles with the Moslems and the Castilians which had led to the formation and

---

[38] Robert G. Frank, 'Medicine', in Nicholas Tyacke (ed.), *The History of the University of Oxford: the Seventeenth Century* (Oxford: Clarendon Press, 1997), 505–58 (506).

[39] V. Nutton, 'Humanist surgery', in Andrew Wear (ed.), *The Medical Renaissance of the Sixteenth Century* (Cambridge: Cambridge University Press, 1985), pp. 75–99 (87–8)

[40] For lists of the references to these three writers, see J. B. Bamborough, 'Biobibliography', in Robert Burton, *The Anatomy of Melancholy*, vol. VI, Commentary (Oxford: Clarendon Press, 2000), pp. 302, 329, 388. No books by Montalto nor Castro are listed in Nicolas K. Kiessling, *The Library of Robert Burton* (Oxford: Oxford Bibliographical Society, 1988), but, as Bamborough says, some of Burton's books may have been given away during his lifetime or dispersed after his death. See his Introduction to *The Anatomy of Melancholy*, I, p. xxii.

growth of the medieval kingdom of Portugal, was of no concern to them. Seeing the voyages as the culmination of a long historical process is a preoccupation of recent centuries. Nor were early modern people very interested in reading narratives of the famous voyages, of Bartolomeu Dias or Vasco da Gama, for instance. These had taken place in the fifteenth century and could almost be regarded as ancient, and therefore uninteresting history. It is in any case hardly surprising that the Protestant English did not want heroic stories about Catholics, who since 1580 had been the subjects of their principal enemy, the King of Spain. But they did want to know something about the events which had occurred, and were still occurring in their own time, and about the exotic lands which the navigators had brought to the attention of Europeans.

However, before going further there is another question which must be considered. It is impossible to assess the extent of knowledge about the Portuguese discoveries in English universities without taking into account the question of language. A good deal of what was available about the history of Portugal was in Portuguese, and that was not a language much studied in the English universities.

Modern languages were not unknown in early modern Oxford and Cambridge, but no evidence has emerged of a teacher of Portuguese. Only three of the books in the 1605 catalogue of the Bodleian Library are in the language. In Bodley's correspondence there is an almost comic letter in which he seems to boast to his first librarian, Dr Thomas James, that he could read the title-page of Garcia de Resende's *Crónica de D. João II*, even if James could not.[41] But there is no evidence that Bodley got any further than that. However, there were a few, at his university and at Cambridge, who thought that what the Portuguese had done overseas was important enough to make their language worth learning, and their books worth translating for the benefit of the English reader. Among them were Richard Hakluyt (Christ Church) and Samuel Purchas (St John's, Cambridge), who both included material from Portuguese sources in their compilations of travel literature.

A third geographer, Richard Willes (New College), the predecessor of Hakluyt and Purchas, states frankly that his translations of short texts by Galeote Pereira and Luís Fróis were made, respectively, from Italian and Latin.[42] His more famous successors also translated books by Portuguese writers in Latin, Spanish and Italian, but both – most unusually – show signs of being able to manage Portuguese too. Hakluyt translated the work of Lopes Vaz and of the anonymous Fidalgo de Elvas, and edited an

[41] See Letter 120, of 1605, in G. W. Wheeler (ed.), *Letters of Sir Thomas Bodley to Thomas James* (Oxford: Clarendon Press, 1926), pp. 127–8.
[42] Richard Willes, *The History of Travayle in the West and East Indies* (London: Richard Jugg, 1577), fols. 237r and 253v.

unknown English merchant's version of António Galvão's *Tratado dos Descobrimentos*.[43] Purchas published an abridged version of Lopes Vaz, who Hakluyt had translated before him, and selections about China from Gaspar da Cruz and Mendes Pinto. He also translated the whole of Fernão Cardim's treatise on Brazil, the manuscript of which had been purloined from its author while he was a prisoner in London.

Both these writers must have worked some of the time directly from material in Portuguese. Yet there is evidence that Hakluyt at least did not always feel comfortable with the language. His version of Galvão contains a dedication to Sir Robert Cecil in which he mentions 'Fernando Lopez de Castagneda' (*sic*) and, on various occasions, the 'Cape of Buona Sperança'. These Italianisms indicate that he may have preferred to read Castanheda in the Italian translation of 1577, which had been made by a Spaniard, Alfonso de Ulloa. John Pory (Caius), who was an associate of Hakluyt, was another writer who consulted Portuguese authorities in the original, but whose work shows obvious signs of strain. Pory discusses several Portuguese writers in his version, with commentary, of Leo Africanus. He goes out his way to explain how he knows what the phrase *os picos fragosos* [the craggy peaks] means, but then seems to hesitate over *povoação*: 'or perhaps Pouaçaon which (as I conjecture) may be all one with Poblacion in Spanish, which signifieth a Colonie or towne.'[44] He got that right, but his frequent recourse to Ramusio's *Delle navigationi . . .* suggests that he too tended to approach Portuguese through another language whenever it was possible to do so.

The early modern geographers were linguistically more adventurous than most university people, but the fact that some of them could read texts in Portuguese, albeit probably imperfectly, does not mean that they had a profound interest in Portuguese history. For them, books by Portuguese writers, in whatever language, were valuable as sources of information about the new worlds which the discoverers had brought to the attention of Europeans. Their authors, then, function as middlemen, enablers, rather than as people who had said or done anything particularly original.

Hakluyt includes António Galvão, but the latter, who seems to promise so much about the Portuguese discoveries, in reality is not greatly concerned with them. His book, which contains a good deal of fantasy, is about all maritime discoveries since the beginning of the world, and he has as much to say about the voyages of the Spanish as of the

---

[43] Purchas also found a translation of all or part of Francisco Álvares account of his journey to Ethiopia among Hakluyt's papers, but says of it: 'I know not who translated this Booke'. Purchas compared the translation with Ramusio's abridged Italian version. See *Purchas his Pilgrimes*, II (London: William Stansby for Henrie Fetherstone, 1625), pp. 1026–7.

[44] Leo the Moor, *A Geographical Historie of Africa*, translated by John Pory (London: George Bishop, 1600), pp. 3, 36, 49.

Portuguese.[45] Hakluyt no doubt valued it for its completeness, but the information about the Spanish Main would have been relevant to English colonial ambitions. That was certainly why he translated the Fidalgo de Elvas's account of the Spaniard Fernando de Soto's expedition to Florida, as the subtitle added by Hakluyt, 'Virginia richly valued', makes clear. Lopes Vaz was another Portuguese writer who was interested in what was part of the Spanish empire, the West Indies. When Hakluyt turned to books by Portuguese writers in Italian or Latin, Duarte de Sande and Galeote Pereira, it was for information about China and Japan, not properly what the Portuguese had done there.

The same books, or books on similar topics, appear in *Purchas his Pilgrimes*. The interest in Spanish America is maintained with the publication of Pedro Fernandes de Queirós's account of his Pacific voyages under the Spanish flag. As already noted, Purchas includes selections about China from Gaspar da Cruz and Mendes Pinto. Pedro Cardim's treatise on Brazil certainly deals with the Portuguese colony, but from the perspective of ethnography and natural history, not of discovery and conquest.

So neither Hakluyt nor Purchas translate the narrative histories of Barros and Castanheda, though, as already stated, they knew their work and consulted it. This is all the more surprising since the first volume of Castanheda was available to them, not just in Italian but also in English, in a version probably based on the Spanish translation of 1554.[46] The book is a great rarity (only three copies between the two universities), compared to the thirty or more of both Hakluyt and Purchas. They probably guessed the interests of early modern readers correctly, for it was not until the nineteenth century that the chroniclers of Portugal began to be acquired in earnest. That was the century when the Bodleian obtained its two copies of the first edition of João de Barros's *Décadas da Ásia* and All Souls its *Crónica de Dom Manuel* by Damião de Góis. Before that Barros had not been widely available and then only in an Italian translation. Of the classic vernacular historians of the voyage to India and its aftermath Castanheda fared the best in the early period, because of the translations made into a variety of languages. But even so there are only fourteen copies of his work, mostly in Cambridge. At least six even of these were acquired after 1800.

The English geographers were staunchly patriotic and Protestant, but their implied view of the overseas activities of the Portuguese was very

---

[45] For a critical analysis, see António Galvão, *Tratado dos Descobrimentos*, edited by Luís de Albuquerque (Lisbon: Alfa, 1989), pp. 115–9.

[46] On the title-page of the English translation (item **167**) even Castanheda's Christian name is given its Spanish form 'Hernán', making it unlikely that the translator worked from the Portuguese original, though he claims to have done so.

similar to that of a southern European, Giovanni Battista Ramusio.
Though not as popular as Hakluyt and Purchas, his compilation of
voyages can be found in many libraries. He prints half a dozen chapters of
Barros, but in the main avoids narrative history. The most extensive works
by Portuguese writers included by Ramusio in his *Delle navigationi* . . . are
the ever-popular Francisco Álvares on Ethiopia and Duarte Barbosa's
commercial and ethnographic guide to the countries of the East. He also
includes some short accounts of voyages, the anonymous 'Navigatione da
Lisbona all'isola de san Thome', fols 114v–118v, the 'Navigatione del
Capitano Pedro Alvares', fols 121v–127v, and the 'Navigatione verso le
Indie Orientali scritta per Thome Lopez', fols 133–145.[47]

The problem was that the Portuguese might have one view of the
significance of their achievements in Africa and Asia, and foreigners
another, in which heroic endeavour did not figure much. The only way
of bridging the cultural and linguistic gap, in the sixteenth century, was
to produce a sound narrative history written in Latin. This was
appreciated at the highest level in Portugal, and Cardinal-Prince
Henrique himself commissioned Jerónimo Osório, the best-known
Portuguese Latinist of the day, to translate Damião de Góis's
chronicle and adapt it for an international audience. Osório accepted
the challenge, for he saw in what his fellow-countrymen had done in
Asia the hand of God: 'This is what I commend in the present book. I
advise all those who read it to think carefully how varied and how truly
admirable are our feats . . . the seas, coasts and countries that have been
explored, the wars fought with unconquerable bravery against powerful
kings, the terrors scorned and despised, so that they understand that
praise for so much achievement is not due to human endeavour. Rather
there is every reason to give it to God, who on innumerable occasions
has revealed His presence to our forces.'[48] Here is a piece of splendid
Osorian rhetoric, the kind of thing that sometimes irritated his English
readers, but kept them turning the pages. Osório was adept at
tempering patriotism with religion, but in a way that reinforces his
belief in the unique qualities of the Portuguese, as the last sentence of
the extract shows. However, Osório did his work unwillingly and never

---

[47] The folio numbers come from item **745**. Duarte Lopes's account of the kingdom of the Congo,
printed by Ramusio, might be thought of as a Portuguese book, but *Relatione del reame di Congo*, which
appeared as a separate volume in Rome in 1591, and in Dutch, English, French and Latin later,
should be regarded as being by the Italian Filippo Pigafetta. Pigafetta used much information
provided by Lopes, but writes always from his own perspective.

[48] Item **488**, pp. 4–5: 'Illud, quod est praesentis operis, hortor et admoneo omnes, qui hos libros
euoluerint, ut animis secum reputent, quam variae res et vehementer admirandae sint a nostris
hominibus . . . effectae: quae maria, quae litora, quae regiones exploratae, quae bella contra Reges
potentissimos inuicta virtute gesta, qui terrores neglecti et contempti: ut intellegant, non esse
tantarum rerum laudem hominibus, sed Deo, qui praesentiam suam nostris saepenumero
declarabat, summa ratione tribuendam.'

referred to it in his correspondence.[49] Yet he was brilliantly successful and long after his death in 1580 the History continued to be admired by writers such as Dryden and Pope.[50] There are thirty copies of the various editions in Oxford and Cambridge, twenty at least with old provenance.

But even this book was outperformed by others of a different kind about the Discoveries. Osório had written a narrative history with a strong emphasis on the deeds of the Portuguese, though he was not afraid to criticize behaviour of which he disapproved.[51] But it still remained the case that what the English really wanted was to learn about the natural history of the places where the Portuguese had been, and the customs and beliefs of their human inhabitants. That perhaps may explain why there are thirty-eight copies of Orta's botanical study in the two universities, and forty-three of what was the most widely distributed book of all, Damião de Góis's *Fides, religio, moresque Aethiopum* and its companion piece, *Deploratio Lappianae gentis*.[52]

Góis made it perfectly clear that contact between Europeans and the Ethiopian Orthodox Christians had been made possible by the Portuguese discovery of the sea route to India. However, most of his book is taken up with transcripts of the correspondence of the emperors of Ethiopia and successive kings of Portugal, and above all with the long statement of the Ethiopian ambassador to Lisbon, Zagazabo, about the religion and customs of his fellow countrymen. The *Fides*, then, is not a heroic narrative, nor even a traveller's tale – Góis had never been to Ethiopia – but rather a political, religious and ethnographical study, whose value was enhanced by the way that Góis's principal informant delivers his statement almost without interrruption or comment.[53]

However, books have never sold just because of the importance of their contents. The *Fides* had the advantage of being quite short, so that it could easily be included in collections. Góis, or his publisher, Rescius, put one together themselves (item **396**). The book can be found in other well-

---

[49] Osório said, of the writing of history, 'ab eo . . . studio vehementer abhorrebam'[I was greatly averse to that study]. See the dedication of item 653. See also António Guimarães Pinto, 'Damião de Góis e D. Jerónimo Osório: a *Crónica de D. Manuel* e *De rebus Emmanuelis gestis*', in *Actas do Congresso Internacional: Damião de Góis na Europa do Renascimento* (Braga: Faculdade de Filosofia, 2003), pp. 307–48 (308).

[50] Léon Bourdon, 'Jerónimo Osório et les humanistes anglais', in *L'Humanisme portugais et l'Europe*, (Paris: Fondation Calouste Gulbenkian, 1984), pp. 263–333 (301).

[51] For a discussion of this point see Guimarães Pinto, 'Damião de Góis e D. Jerónimo Osório', pp. 310–11.

[52] To reach that number it is necessary to count the editions (many of them compilations) listed in the short-title catalogue under Góis and then add to the total the nine copies of Andreas Schottus's *Hispaniae illustratae* (item 826), all of which contain the *Fides*.

[53] It is not widely known that in the first edition of the *Fides* there are some brief marginal notes, presumably by Góis, commenting on the theological implication of Zagazabo's remarks. See item **404**, sigs G iii v.–G iv r.

known compilations, by Johannes Boemus (items **406–10**) and Andreas Schottus (item **826**). Some of Góis's other short geographical and historical writings were also reprinted by publicists like Belus (the Englishman Robert Beale, item **412**) and Simon Schardius (item **417**). All of these compilations, some limited to Spanish and Portuguese authors, others claiming to include 'Mores, leges et ritus omnium gentium', can be found widely in Oxford and Cambridge libraries.

Even with that proviso, however, Góis's mix of Christianity and exotic lands was a potent one. Ethiopia had provided the first non-Jewish Christian convert, and the *Fides* could certainly be read as pointing towards the possibility of union between all Christians throughout the world. This was an exciting prospect for some Jacobean Protestants who thought that unity between Protestants and the Christians of the East would be a way of isolating the Roman church. Andrew Willet (1562–1621), for example, mentions him several times in his *Synopsis papismi* of 1592.[54] Góis would have been disappointed by the polemical use made of his work, had he known about it, because his view of Christian unity was much more inclusive.

Protestants were also interested in reading about the missionary activities of Catholics, principally because of the geographical and ethnographical information which their reports contained. From its inception in 1540 the Jesuit Order was concerned with missionary work. Portuguese Jesuits went to Africa, to India, and to the Far East, above all to Japan, where during what Boxer called 'the Christian Century' they achieved remarkable success in conversion, without having either the military or the political superiority normally associated with Christian missionizing. Not all the missionaries were Portuguese: some of the most prominent, like St Francis Xavier, the founder of the mission, or Alessandro Valignano, the far-sighted Visitor to Japan of the 1580s and 90s, were Spanish and Italian respectively. The prestige of these individuals obscured the many Portuguese who surrounded them, as, paradoxically, did the characteristically Jesuit concern for the maximum publicity for their activities. Achieving effective publicity in Europe meant translation into widely known languages – Latin especially, but also Italian – of information coming from missionaries in the East. The published collections of letters from missions which fills library shelves in Oxford and Cambridge contains much material which had originally been written by Portuguese in their own language or in Spanish. However, the process of translation tended to hide the nationality of the original writer – even their names were Italianized or Latinized to the point of being unrecognizable. Jesuits in

[54] See Anthony Milton, *Catholic and Reformed: The Roman and Protestant Churches in English Protestant Thought* (Cambridge: Cambridge University Press, 1995), pp. 378–80.

the East, though not their colleagues who remained in Europe, were also usually silent about their nationality, perhaps in the interest of maintaining a united front against foreigners who were on the lookout for any sign of weakness or lack of unity. In these various ways the role of the Portuguese in bringing to Europe information about the East was obscured.

So the extraordinary appetite of readers in Oxford and Cambridge for knowledge about distant parts of the world was, to a very large degree, satisfied by Portuguese writers, even though the recipients of the information may not have realized it. In Oxford there are sixty-four collections of letters published before 1640 to which Portuguese Jesuits were contributors, and in Cambridge thirty-nine. In both universities at least half are of old provenance. Yet only one of these compilations is in Portuguese or has a Portuguese imprint (item **459**).[55] Altogether there are around eighty-nine authors of letters who were Portuguese – their names (including the confusing forms of them invented by translators), with brief biographical details, are listed in Appendix 1. In the matter of the Japanese mission – as in so many other areas of intellectual endeavour – the Portuguese were the agents, often disregarded, by whose efforts information was transmitted to distant England.

One such area, Aristotelian philosophy, was so fundamental to the thinking of the early modern universities that it requires a chapter to itself.

---

[55] It was in the Bodleian by 1605. The library is fortunate to have this compilation, because Bourdon considers it to have been one of the most important. See his *La Compagnie de Jésus et le Japon, 1547–1570* (Paris: Fondation Calouste Gulbenkian, 1993), p. 25.

CHAPTER TWO

FROM COIMBRA TO OXFORD: COMMENTARIES ON ARISTOTLE

The reception in Oxford of the commentaries on Aristotle composed in Coimbra at the turn of the sixteenth century is one of the most compelling proofs of the penetration of Portuguese intellectual culture into the heart of English academic life. The Coimbra commentators – or 'Conimbricenses', as they were normally called – issued five volumes of commentaries between 1592 and 1606, which were immediately reprinted in a multitude of editions. They began life as lecture notes delivered in the universities of Évora and Coimbra. Not all the lecturers were Portuguese, and the Spaniard Luis de Molina was disappointed that, when the notes of lectures which he claimed to have delivered were written up, he was not asked to contribute. No author's name appears in the printed texts, but they are known to have been Manuel de Góis (1543–97), Baltazar Álvares (1560–1630), Cosme de Magalhães (1551–1624), and Sebastião do Couto (1567–1639). Góis, the principal author, was especially dissatisfied with the requirement of anonymity.[1]

Altogether the commentators completed five volumes, numbered and given here in order of first publication: 1. *De Physica*, 2. *De Coelo* (usually printed with *Metereologica* and *Parva Naturalia*), 3. *De Generatione et Corruptione*, 4. *De Anima*, and 5. *In Universam Dialecticam*. The short work on the *Ethics* sometimes constitutes a separate volume.

There are today in Oxford more than one hundred copies of these books, mostly in the form of complete sets (though not always formed from editions issued by the same publisher), and spread between the Bodleian and thirteen college libraries.[2] If we add the twenty-five copies of the individual volumes of the commentary on Aristotle's *Metaphysics* by Pedro da Fonseca, a contemporary of the Conimbricenses and for a while their leader, though not formally part of the group, we reach an even more impressive total.

Many generations of Oxford undergraduates in the seventeenth century studied logic, dialectic and the natural sciences with tutors

---

[1] For a summary of the history of the project, and of the controversies surrounding it, see Pinharanda Gomes, *Os Conimbricenses* (Lisbon: Biblioteca Breve, 1992), pp. 35–63.

[2] And one modern Hall (Blackfriars Hall). There is more detailed information in the list provided at the end of this chapter.

who had access to the copies of the Coimbra commentaries kept in their colleges. (The same is not true of Cambridge, but that is an issue to be explored later).The bibliographical evidence is overwhelming, and should change opinion, especially in Portugal, about the books and their Jesuit authors. For some, including scholars of great erudition, like José Sebastião da Silva Dias, the commentaries are almost a symbol of Portuguese intellectual backwardness and resistance to change. But, throughout Europe, changes in intellectual habits were slow to come about, and Aristotle continued to be a key author in university programmes of study for fifty years after the Coimbra commentators had published their last book. Portuguese thought may have stagnated, as Silva Dias thinks, because no alternative to the neo-scholasticism of the commentaries took root there.[3] But that is not something for which the authors of the commentaries themselves can be held responsible.

Undoubtedly one of the reasons why the Coimbra commentaries survived for so long, in the Protestant as well as the Catholic world, was their generally high quality. That was, perhaps, guaranteed by the encouragement and patronage of successive generals of the Society of Jesus, and by their inclusion in the 'Ratio Studiorum', the programme of studies followed in all Jesuit educational institutions. In Oxford John Case (1539–1600), who was prominent in the Aristotelian revival at the end of the sixteenth century and a prolific author, was an admirer.[4] A number of tutors of the seventeenth century refer to them in their instructions to students. It is true that they do not give the commentaries any special emphasis, but there is no doubt that they were thought to be reliable authorities.[5] In the universities of Europe, Catholic and Protestant, they were widely used. [6] In modern times the Aristotelian scholar Charles Schmitt has gone further, and has claimed that 'Few other editions of classical texts from the sixteenth century can match them in the thoroughness and precision of the apparatus for understanding a specific Greek work, which they provided for the student or more advanced scholar.'[7]

Historians of Oxford and Cambridge, like Mordechai Feingold and

[3] See his 'O Cânone Filosófico Conimbricense (1562–1606)', *Cultura-História e Filosofia*, 4 (1985), 257–370 (288–9).

[4] J. W. Binns, *Intellectual Culture in Elizabethan and Jacobean England: The Latin Writings of the Age* (Leeds: Cairns, 1990), pp. 372 and 377.

[5] For some examples, see Mordechai Feingold, 'The Mathematical Sciences and New Philosophies', pp. 402–3.

[6] Pinharanda Gomes quotes a number of statements of approval, including from Leibniz, in *Os Conimbricenses*, pp. 115–20.

[7] See his *Aristotle and the Renaissance* (Cambridge, Mass.: Harvard University Press, 1983), pp. 39–40.

John Gascoigne, have found a number of reasons why Aristotelianism, whether mediated by Portuguese scholarship or not, persisted there until late in the seventeenth century. In universities where philosophical liberty prevailed it was possible to be selective, and the 'new philosophy', associated with Galileo, Copernicus and Descartes, could be used in conjunction with at least some of Aristotle.[8] In 1651 Isaac Barrow, who later became Master of Trinity, Cambridge, perhaps spoke for many when he said that the Scholastics built 'rather elaborate structures on flimsy foundations', but that they taught 'how to debate concisely and correctly, how to prosecute an inquiry judiciously, how to experiment warily'.[9] In other words, Aristotle provided a philosophical vocabulary and a training in argumentation. And, as with the case of the theology of which the Protestants universities disapproved, if you wanted to refute an opinion you had to understand it.[10]

Aristotelianism also represented continuity and stability and so appealed to the official mind. Feingold believes that the reason why, as late as the 1670s, the vice-chancellors of both Oxford and Cambridge compelled students to defend Aristotelianism in their disputations was to prevent public disorder between proponents of various systems of thought.[11] And it may be because of the actions of officialdom that the Coimbra commentators are so much better represented in Oxford than in Cambridge.

There are, as already noted, many sets of the commentaries in Oxford libraries, but very few in Cambridge. A set in the University Library has been there since before 1715, and Archbishop Sancroft left another to Emmanuel in 1693.[12] There is an incomplete set in St John's, but otherwise almost nothing. Fonseca's commentary on the *Metaphysics* is also very sparsely represented, though Helen Gulston, widow of Theodore Gulston of Merton, Oxford, gave a copy to Peterhouse in 1635. Aristotelianism was as important in Cambridge as in Oxford and the solution to the absence of the Portuguese commentators from Cambridge libaries is unlikely to lie in philosophical disagreement. Schmitt has also pointed out that there were many ways of teaching Aristotelianism, and while Oxford clearly preferred the commentaries, Cambridge may have made more use of compendia, like Johannes Magirus's *Physiologia peripatetica*, 1597, which was the textbook used by

---

[8] Mordechai Feingold, 'The Mathematical Sciences and New Philosophies', pp. 392–4.

[9] Quoted by John Gascoigne, 'Isaac Barlow's Academic Milieu: Interregnum and Restoration Cambridge', in *Science, Politics and Universities in Europe, 1600–1800* (Aldershot: Ashgate, 1998), pp. 249–90 (263).

[10] Feingold, 'The Mathematical Sciences and New Philosophies', pp. 402–3.

[11] Feingold, 'The Mathematical Sciences and New Philosophies', p. 390.

[12] The set in the Cambridge University Library is formed by items **198, 207, 216, 225, 229.** Emmanuel's are almost the same: **198, 207, 216, 225, 230.**

Newton.[13] The key to the mystery may be the Laudian statutes, which were much more prescriptive than those in force at Cambridge.[14]

Laud's statutes, promulgated in 1636 amid some controversy, nevertheless remained in force until the nineteenth century.[15] Though they do not mention the Coimbra commentators by name, a list of Aristotelian texts on natural philosophy is prescribed which corresponds exactly to what they had only quite recently published. Here the original Latin brings out the parallels much better than Ward's English translation. Both the statutes and the Coimbra commentators omit Aristotle's biological writings. The Sedleian lecturer is to read: 'Aristotelis Physica, aut libros de Coelo et Mundo, aut de Meteoris, aut eiusdem parva Naturalia, aut libros de Anima, necnon libros de Generatione et Corruptione'. Similarly, the lecturer in Metaphysics is to expound Aristotle's text and 'quaestiones Metaphysicas, quae apud scriptores antiquos et modernos agitantur', again an invitation to use a widely available modern book about these very matters.[16]

At the end of this chapter there is a list of the Oxford libraries which have the Coimbra commentaries arranged, so far as that is possible, to show how and when they were acquired. It is clear that compliance with Laud was not the only motive, since the Bodleian, All Souls and Wadham had acquired copies of the commentaries before the statutes were promulgated. However, the date of Charles May's gift to St John's, Laud's own college – 1634 – is suggestive, because it is the date of first printing of the statutes, and seven other college libraries obtained a complete or part set before the end of the seventeenth century (two sets, belonging to Corpus and Pembroke, were acquired in the nineteenth century). It certainly took some colleges quite a while to acquire their copies – forty years in the case of Magdalen. By the 1670s Aristotelianism was no longer the force it had been, but the statutes did not change, and it may be that the commentaries were circulating in the college before being deposited in the library.

Complete or partial sets are held in the following Oxford libraries:

[13] Charles B. Schmitt, *Aristotle and the Renaissance*, p. 52.

[14] I am grateful to Scott Mandelbrote for this suggestion. According to Christopher Brooke, the Cambridge statutes of 1570 'were deliberately drawn up' to avoid straitjacketing students. See 'Learning and Doctrine', in Victor Morgan and Christopher Brooke, *A History of the University of Cambridge, 1546–1750* (Cambridge: Cambridge University Press, 2004), pp. 437–63 (437).

[15] For the controversy, see Kenneth Fincham, 'Early Stuart Polity', in Nicholas Tyacke (ed.), *The History of the University of Oxford: the Seventeenth Century* (Oxford: Clarendon Press, 1997), pp. 179–210 (201–2). The statutes were first printed in 1634 and then emended by Laud acting on his own authority. The emendations do not, however, affect the list of books to be read. See the emended copies in the Bodleian, shelved at N.1.12. Jur. Seld., Arch. A C.4 , Caps.10.9 (1) etc.

[16] [The metaphysical questions which are discussed by ancient and modern writers]. See John Griffiths (ed.), *Statutes of the University of Oxford Codified in the Year 1636 Under the Authority of Archbishop Laud* (Oxford: Clarendon Press, 1888), pp. 36–7

Bodleian: A set in which vols 1–4 are in the 1605 catalogue and vol. 5, first published in 1606, is in the 1620 catalogue. All are shelved at AA 115–8 Art. (items **193, 202, 211, 219, 228**). They were issued by a variety of German printers. The library has another set, shelved at 4° E 12–17 Med., which it acquired probably in the early nineteenth century (items **196, 204, 213, 221, 227**). All were printed at Lyon by Cardon, except 204, issued by the bookseller Pillehotte who, like Cardon, had close links with the Jesuits. The existence of the closely matched set suggests a collector more interested in Lyon printing than in the intellectual content of the volumes.

All Souls: Vols 1,3,5 (items **195, 203, 228**) presented by Morgan Winne in 1610; vols 2,4 (items **212, 220**) have an Oxford binding with Ker centrepiece 6, in use after 1600.[17] By 1665 all five volumes were catalogued together.[18]

Balliol: The benefactors' register shows that the library had a complete set by 1656, given by Thomas Careles, John Harris and Henry Savage, all fellows of the college.[19] The books seem to have disappeared, because there is no sign of them in the library catalogues of 1673, 1701 and 1721. The library re-acquired vols 2 and 5 (items **214, 229**) when it took over the library of New Inn Hall, extinguished in the late nineteenth century.

Blackfriars Hall: Incomplete set, with vols 3 (item **194**) and 4 (item **222**). The Hall is a modern institution, refounded in Oxford in 1929.

Christ Church: The 1665 catalogue records vols 1–5 but it is not a wholly reliable guide because it does not give date or place of publication. However, the books are probably to be identified with those shelved today at Hyp.L.49–53, which are bound as a set and stamped W W on the cover (items **195, 205, 212, 222, 229**). As is usually the case with sets formed in the early modern period there seems to have been no concern to collect books printed by the same firm in the same city, though all these are from Germany.

Corpus: A set acquired in the nineteenth century (items **198, 206, 215, 223**). Vol. 5 is missing.

Jesus: An incomplete set. Vols 2, 3 and 4 were given by Principal Mansell in 1649 (items **198, 211, 220**). Mansell also owned a copy of vol. 1, now disappeared.[20]

Magdalen: All five vols are shelved together at D.3.4–7. Vol. 3 (item **195**)

[17] Ker, p. 216.
[18] They are listed in Catalogus librorum in Bibliotheca Chichleiana which came into use in that year. See Sir Edmund Craster, *The History of All Souls College Library*, edited by E. F. Jacob (London: Faber, 1971), p. 63.
[19] Catalogus librorum et benefactorum bibliothecae collegii de Baliolo, Oxon., pp. 38–40.
[20] See Jesus College LI.3, including 'Dr Mansell's books which are not allready in Jesus College Library'.

has an Oxford binding, roll no. xvii, in use up to 1631,[21] suggesting that it arrived before vols 1,2,4,5 which were given by Robert Pierce, who took his BCL in 1675/76 (items **204, 212, 222, 230**).

Merton: A complete set, stated to be from the library of F. H. Bradley (1846–1921). They are items **198, 201, 210, 225, 229**, from a variety of French and German printers, shelved at 120 f.7–11. However, the books are not among those known to have been presented by Bradley to his college and they all have marks of chaining. It is therefore very possible that they were in the college long before his time. Merton is one of the colleges that does not have a benefactors' register.[22]

New: A complete set, with identical binding and marks of chaining (items **198, 205, 212, 222, 229**). All five volumes are listed together in the catalogue of 1686. At New College shelf-marks are many and varied, but they all show that the books have always been kept together.[23]

Oriel: All five vols are in the library. Some were the gift of Henry Chamberlain, a student of the college. The seventeenth-century catalogues only list vols 1, 3, 5, but vols 3 and 2, and 1 and 4 are bound together. The cataloguers may have missed the second item in each case.

Pembroke: A complete set, donated by the Aristotelian H. W. Chandler in 1889 (items **195, 202, 211, 219, 226**). Chandler was able to acquire a copy of the first, Portuguese edition of item 226, otherwise unknown in Oxford except for the copy in the Bodleian, which came in 1961.

St Edmund Hall: An incomplete set, with vols 1, 2, 4 only (items **205, 211, 225**). Inscriptions, bookplates and a blind-stamped centrepiece binding suggest the books came to the library at least by the early eighteenth century.

St John's: A complete set was given by Charles May in 1634 (items **194, 205, 211, 222, 229**). He matriculated that year, aged 15. The bindings are similar and all have chain marks.

Wadham: Vols 1,2,3,4 were given by Edward Brounker (or Brunkard) in 1614 (items **195, 205, 212, 222**). In 1632 William Payton gave the *Commentarii in universam logicam Aristotelis,* a pirated work (item **232**) whose first publication in 1604 prompted the hasty completion of vol. 5.[24]

Worcester: An incomplete set. Vols 1, 3, 4 came from Gloucester Hall, the immediate predecessor of Worcester, which existed from 1560–1714

---

[21] Pearson, p. 69.

[22] N. R. Ker, 'Oxford College Libraries in the Sixteenth Century', *Bodleian Library Record*, 6 (1957), 459–515 (462).

[23] They are N.3.1–5, O.14.7–11, Auct.Y.33.5–9.

[24] For a discussion of the pirated edition, see Gomes, *Os Conimbricenses*, pp. 61–2.

(items **198, 208, 223**); vol. 2 (item **212**) with Ker centrepiece xi, in use before 1620.[25]

There are fifteen libraries listed here. One (Blackfriars Hall) acquired its books in the twentieth century, and there are three nineteenth-century sets, including one in the Bodleian, though the Bodleian acquired another early in its history. However, there is evidence, more or less conclusive depending on circumstances, that all the others have had their sets, complete or partial, probably since the seventeenth century – even if Balliol lost its one, deliberately or accidentally. The story of Pedro da Fonseca's commentary on the *Metaphysics* is simpler, but not dissimilar. At first it made little impression and the early Italian and French editions are poorly represented. But then in 1599 the Frankfurt publishers Schonwetter and Zetzner issued the first two volumes of the commentary together. They were acquired by the Bodleian and eight college libraries, All Souls, Christ Church, Magdalen, New College, Queen's, St John's, Wadham, and Worcester. Five years later, the same printers brought out volume 3, and that can be found in the same libraries (except for New College and Worcester). Finally, long after Fonseca's death, volume 4 appeared, in 1612. It is incomplete and inferior to the others and there are few copies in Oxford. The evidence presented in the short-title catalogue shows how these books have probably been in the Bodleian and the colleges since the seventeenth century, the exception once again being Pembroke, where the indefatigible Professor Chandler obtained the copies now in the library.

This account of the holdings in Oxford libraries of the Portuguese commentators on Aristotle has introduced the reader to some of the techniques used to determine the provenance and the date of acquistion of books. A more systematic discussion follows in the next chapter. Readers with experience of the libraries which are the subject of this book will hardly need the guide offered there. However, it is included partly with the hope of encouraging more scholars to explore the magnificent, but little used collections of early modern printed books to be found in Oxford and Cambridge.

[25] See Ker, p. 217.

CHAPTER THREE

THE OLD LIBRARIES OF OXFORD
AND CAMBRIDGE

Few places are as redolent of the past as the old libraries of Oxford and Cambridge. They often smell, quite strongly, of it – that is, if old leather, damp and dust constitute the authentic aroma of antiquity. In them it is easy to understand how the interest of books is more than the reproducible printed page, and how every copy of every book has its own history. This is especially true of the old college libraries, because they are very easy to use. The reader who has the run of one can collect a lot of information in a very short time, something that does not happen when books are stored underground in modern shelving systems only accessible via a catalogue. So the Bodleian and the many colleges in both universities which have kept their old libraries are much to be congratulated, even though they are expensive to maintain and almost impossible to supervise adequately.

The reader who can take a number of books from the shelves and consult them quickly can very soon begin to have an idea of the history of the library, whether the books were donated or purchased, and when. This is such an important aspect of the present study that the techniques used to establish provenance and date of accession need to be examined in some detail. If the aim is to assess the impact of Portuguese intellectual culture on the early modern universities of England it is necessary to know when books entered the libraries. This is the ideal to be aimed at, not necessarily a goal that can be achieved. In the case of any single book the evidence can be complete, scanty or totally non-existent.

The most satisfactory moments come when one takes from the shelf a book where all the evidence – inscription, shelf-mark, and binding – is consistent and points to a single donor and a single date. If, in addition, there is a correlation between an inscription and a benefactors' register, or between a shelf-mark, cancelled or current, and a catalogue, old or new, then you have a number of reasons for being certain of holding in your hands a volume which has been in the library concerned since the sixteenth or seventeenth century. Such moments are not rare, but there are many cases where you have to be satisfied with less than perfection.

Inscriptions, recording the date of a gift or bequest and the name of the donor, are quite common, hardly surprisingly in a period when most libraries relied on donations to increase their bookstock. Students and fellows gave books most often on leaving the college, or on death. Usually a librarian would make the entry in the books, on the fly-leaf or on the title-page; occasionally ownership is confirmed by the signature of the donor as well, as is the case with item 67, given by Bishop Lancelot Andrewes to Pembroke, Cambridge.

In Oxford inscriptions recording a donation were usually made by hand. They are common in the colleges, but much less frequent in the Bodleian. In Cambridge written inscriptions can be found, but there printed bookplates were also quite frequently used, in the colleges as well as in the Cambridge University Library. Bookplates bring a note of uncertainty, because anyone can stick a bookplate into a book at any time, including into a book that was published long before the bookplate was printed. That is true of inscriptions as well, but then handwriting and the form of language remain as additional clues as to the date of the donation. In Cambridge bookplates form a part of the evidence for identifying books belonging to a number of important collections which arrived at the turn of the eighteenth century: the Newton-Puckering collection at Trinity (1691), Archbishop Sancroft's at Emmanuel (1693) and Bishop Moore's at the Cambridge University Library (1715), the so-called Royal Library. In each of these cases additional evidence is usually available to confirm the identification.

Sir Henry Newton, who changed his name to Puckering to secure an inheritance, acquired many books from the collection of Lord Lumley, which was formed in the reign of Elizabeth and of which the catalogue of 1609 survives. Usually books with the Puckering-Newton bookplate also have Lumley's signature, or that of his wife, Jane (see item 305), and in addition can be identified in the catalogue.[1] Here bookplates are supported by two other kinds of evidence. In the cases of Archbishop Sancroft's donation and of the royal library bookplates are supported by catalogue entries and also by shelf-marks shared between the catalogues and the books themselves.[2]

Some might think the study of shelf-marks the last refuge of a mind rotted with pedantry. Yet they are one of the ways in which humanity has mapped its literary inheritance, and close attention to them can produce conclusive information about the history of the reception of books. In Oxford and Cambridge it is possible to make a broad distinction between

[1] The catalogue has been published by Sears Jayne and Francis R. Johnson, *The Lumley Library: The Catalogue of 1609* (London: British Museum, 1956).

[2] In Emmanuel there is an eighteenth-century manuscript class catalogue (LIB.1.2) which enables checks to be made. Books by Portuguese authors in the Sancroft collection are normally in classes S.2 to S.16. Some books in class S.17.8 are also his. Books in the royal library have characteristic shelf-marks with the form of a letter followed by two numbers. The letters ABDMRY are not found in shelf-marks in the Portuguese books. There is also a contemporary catalogue (ULIB 7/3/36).

the methods of the large, university libraries and of the smaller college ones. University librarians rarely have the time or the resources to reclassify material, so that shelf-marks, once given, tend to stick. The small collections of the colleges, on the other hand, subject to constant reshelving and re-housing, constantly acquire new shelf-marks. I have before me a book presented to a modern college in the 1940s which already has three cancelled shelf-marks. Clearly the usefulness of these marks varies greatly between libraries.

The Bodleian has rarely altered shelf-marks. It is also a library with a long tradition of reliable cataloguing, so much so that the catalogue of 1674 was widely used by other libraries, including some in Cambridge, like Trinity, to record their own holdings. Shelf-marks were included even in the first catalogue of 1605, and quite a number of these continue in use today.[3] If a book has an uncancelled 1605 shelf-mark (showing that the shelf-mark has not been recycled from one book to another) you can be sure that it has been in the library since then. The Bodleian has also been blessed with a number of shelf-mark historians, who have been able to find order in what to an outsider can seem complete chaos.[4] Wheeler shows how, especially in the nineteenth and twentieth centuries, the library's struggles with the immense amount of material it was expected to acquire and catalogue produced a series of datable shelf-marks. In earlier centuries the evidence is not so easy to interpret. The most unreliable shelf-marks are the oldest, those of the type '8°' or '4°', followed by letter, number and classification into one of the four classes of theology, law (Jur.), medicine and arts, because although they were not in general use after the first century of the library's existence, isolated examples can be found up until the early nineteenth century.[5] Such shelf-marks can only be used for dating when they are combined with other evidence, inscriptions (rare in the Bodleian), catalogue entries and binding (to be discussed shortly).

In the Cambridge University Library, too, shelf-marks are usually informative. The characteristic shelf-marks of the royal library have already been mentioned. Books already in the library were distinguished from the newcomers by the addition of a star to their shelf-mark, so you can easily separate the books that were deposited in 1715 from those acquired earlier – though there are aberrant marks Aa*

---

[3] Examples are items **46, 163, 185** and there are many others.

[4] G. W. Wheeler, 'Bodleian Press-Marks in Relation to Classification', *Bodleian Quarterly Record*, 1 (1916), 280–92 and 311–22. Another useful guide to the shelf-marks of the Bodleian and of other libraries is B. C. Bloomfield (ed.), *A Directory of Rare Book and Special Collections in the United Kingdom and the Republic of Ireland* (London: Library Association, 1997), pp. 496–516.

[5] Item **880** is a good example of a misleading shelf-mark. The classification Med. of a book which has nothing to do with medicine is an indication that it was a late accession, confirmed by an inscription.

and Dd* which are associated with the royal library. But the Cambridge University Library is smaller than the Bodleian, and librarians have had time and energy for reclassification. Shelf-marks like Syn. and Lib., normally used for acquisitions in relatively recent times, also turn up in books belonging to Bishop Moore's collection. This can be confirmed by the bookplate and by cancelled shelf-marks characteristic of the Royal Library (there is an example at **826**).

In Oxford the great benefactions of the seventeenth century, John Selden's and that of Thomas Barlow, Bishop of Lincoln, also have their own shelf-marks, Seld. and Linc. respectively. However, one of the consequences of the universal interests of the great collectors of the early modern period is that many of their books duplicated copies already in the institutional libraries to which they left their collections. In the early modern period there was a tendency to discard the copy acquired first and replace it with one from a prestigious donor. Of the fifty-six books by Portuguese writers presented to the Bodleian by Selden at least eight replaced works already in the library, as one can tell from the catalogues issued before the Selden benefaction was made.[6] Thomas Barlow was an Oxford man, and it is, therefore, not surprising that a large proportion – half – of the books in his personal library matched those already in the Bodleian.[7] In the Cambridge University Library about ten percent of the Portuguese books in the Royal Library are known to be duplicates.[8] Here is another factor which it is necessary to take into account when trying to date the arrival of books from shelf-marks.

College library shelf-marks are much less helpful. Sometimes special collections have their own marks, like Sancroft's at Emmanuel, or Allestree's at Christ Church, where the books have remained in the same room since they were bequeathed in 1681. Usually, however, college library shelf-marks are helpful only when they can be matched with entries in old catalogues, as at Balliol and Brasenose. At Clare the shelf-marks recorded in the catalogue of 1677–78 are matched by shelf-marks on the fore-edge of the books. That is also a reminder that books were usually shelved with their fore-edge outwards at that period, and that any book with a mark on the fore-edge is probably an early acquisition (unless it belonged previously to a library outside Oxford or Cambridge). Fore-edge studies reached a high point of sophistication in the work of Philip Gaskell, formerly librarian of Trinity, Cambridge, who was able to show

---

[6] They are items **181, 396, 492, 604, 749, 764, 809, 866**.

[7] Twelve out of the twenty-four Portuguese books with the 'Linc.' shelf-mark are duplicates: **35, 276, 284, 341, 359, 411, 583, 683, 700, 809, 841, 895**. Gwen Hampshire also notes that some books marked 'Linc.' may have been in the library before the benefaction was made in 1691. See her *The Bodleian Library Account Book, 1613–1646* (Oxford: Oxford Bibliographical Society, 1983), p. 155.

[8] They are items **110, 188, 354, 359, 368, 412, 628, 635, 856, 866**, ten out of a total of ninety-two items.

when a book arrived in his library by the position of the shelf-mark on the fore-edge, and by its size.[9]

Some colleges present special difficulties. One is New College, where the library has moved several times, creating a plethora of shelf-marks which are difficult to interpret. Among them are very unusual ones, like 'Auctar Wagon III-I', which suggest that the books may at some time have been housed in carts. Fortunately most of the college's Portuguese holdings can be dated by inscriptions and binding, as well as by the excellent catalogue of 1686. Libraries created by institutions which no longer exist are also problematic. Magdalen Hall, extinguished in the late nineteenth century, like a number of the medieval halls, is an example. Its interesting collection of ten books by Portuguese writers was transferred to Hertford College, which came into existence in its modern form in 1874–75. Magdalen Hall's catalogue of 1661 was the first to be printed of any college or hall, though by then the Bodleian had the catalogues of 1605 and 1620. None of the books now in Hertford with a Magdalen Hall stamp are listed in the catalogue, suggesting that they were acquired later.[10] With the exception of one medical book, presented in 1692, all of them are geographical or historical works, some in the vernacular (items **113–15, 135, 166**). Such interests suggest the hand of a nineteenth-century collector. The most difficult library of all to understand is one of the largest and most important, All Souls, and that too owes much to nineteenth-century scholarship.

All Souls has a collection of books in Latin by Portuguese writers which is broadly similar to that of other college libraries. The date of acquisition of these books can normally be determined using the techniques discussed here, though the shelf-marks are very unhelpful, and do not even allow allow you to distinguish between books that were in the college before the construction of the Codrington Library in the mid-eighteenth century and those that came later. However, the library also has the largest and most interesting collection of books in the Portuguese language of any Oxford or Cambridge college. It includes a unique copy of a work in that language by a major writer, Damião de Góis, which is otherwise unknown (item **403**). Yet when these books arrived in Oxford is not at all certain.

A tradition in the college – it is no more than that – associates the Portuguese books with Peter Fry Hony, a fellow who died in 1876. Several times he received the thanks of his colleagues for 'handsome presents' of books, but the Governing Body, preoccupied with its rents and leases, did

---

[9] Gaskell, pp. 97 and 103.
[10] Henry Wilkinson, *Catalogus Librorum in Bibliotheca Aulae Magdalenae* (Oxford: H. Hall, 1661). The catalogue shows that Magdalen Hall once possessed four of the five volumes of the Coimbra commentaries on Aristotle, but these did not survive the transfer to Hertford.

not specify what they were. His signature appears on a sale catalogue of the late 1820s in which there are several Portuguese books now in the library. Others are listed on the interleaved pages.[11] All Souls may have benefited from another important sale, in this case held in Paris in 1821, of the possessions of the British ambassador.[12] Baron Stuart de Rothesay (1779–1845) was minister in Lisbon, 1810–14, and also, while in Paris, negotiated the treaty by which Brazil became independent of Portugal. Six works by Portuguese writers printed before 1640 which are in the sale catalogue can be found today at All Souls. They may not be the same copies, but the coincidence is striking.[13] A Governing Body minute of 1827 mentions the fact that Hony had bought books for the library during extensive travels abroad, and perhaps the Stuart books came to the college through his agency. But where the great rarity, Góis's translation of Ecclesiastes, came from, and when, remains a mystery.

A book printed before 1640 which arrives in an Oxford library in the nineteenth century is likely to have had several owners. In these cases the binding is not likely to offer much evidence as to the date of acquisition. But when there are reasons for thinking that a book has been in Oxford or Cambridge since the early modern period then the binding becomes very important. In the sixteenth and seventeenth centuries new books were supplied unbound, and binding was the responsibility of the first owner. If the binding, and other distinguishing physical features of a book, are also of the sixteenth and seventeenth centuries then you have another element which can assist with dating. At the same time it is important to remember that second-hand books are not only found in nineteenth-century libraries. The library copy of a book presented by a donor is by that very fact second-hand, and donors of the early modern period did not always buy new.[14] So the evidence of binding always has to be treated with caution.

Oxford bindings of the Elizabethan and Stuart period were most famously studied by Neil Ker. His work, first published in the 1950s, has been developed and refined by David Pearson.[15] Ker described the development of various forms of decoration on Oxford books from the 1510s to the 1610s, especially roll-binding, where a strip or strips of

---

[11] *A Catalogue of a choice and valuable collection of books in all classes of Spanish Literature . . . to be sold by John Bohn* (shelfmark MZ.7.ST). No place or date, but the latest book listed is of 1826. For the Governing Body minutes see 'Acta in Capitulis Custodis et Collegii Omnium Animarum Fidelium Defunctorum de Oxon. (1801–51)' LR.5.a.4 Ms. 401 (d) October 27 1827.

[12] Charles Stuart de Rothesay, *Catalogue des livres de la bibliothèque du chevalier Stuart* (Paris: imprimé à l'hôtel de sa maj. Britannique, 1821). I am grateful to Angela Delaforce for this suggestion.

[13] They are items **50, 396, 653, 755, 866, 880**.

[14] Burton often bought second-hand, for instance. See Kiessling (1988), p. xxviii.

[15] Pearson. Corrections of detail were also made in the reprint by the Oxford Bibliographical Society of Ker's book in 2004. However, his conclusions remain unaltered.

decorative work is stamped into the cover, and ornamental centrepieces. A particular decorative motif can be associated with an individual binder, and sometimes even to a period in that binder's career. Ker is led to claim that: 'Nearly all Oxford bindings are datable within a decade or two; many can be dated within a few years; some are exactly dated.'[16] Even so, in making that claim Ker must have had in mind other forms of evidence – account-books, inscriptions – besides the bindings themselves, and with that proviso what he says can be applied to the Portuguese books.

Ker was primarily interested in the fragments of medieval manuscripts used as pastedowns, that is, as reinforcement of the binding, and the lists of books that he gives all have this feature. Some of the books by Portuguese authors have bindings with pastedowns (e.g., items **46, 67**), but many do not. Nevertheless, the characteristic stamped bindings remain as an indication of date of acquisition, as Ker himself says.[17] In the short-title catalogue the reader will find reference to books described by Ker, with their identifying number, and to blind-stamped centrepieces and other ornaments, also as numbered by him. I have normally recorded Pearson's modifications of the dates originally proposed by Ker.

Cambridge awaits its Ker and its Pearson, but the same kind of binding exists there. There are roll-bindings and centrepieces on at least ten books by Portuguese authors, and the date of acquisition of most of them is known.[18] That makes it possible to give at least an approximate date to the bindings. A few have medieval pastedowns (items **250, 609, 617, 661**). In the early seventeenth century stamped bindings went out of fashion in both universities and plain calf, sometimes decorated with fillets, was used instead.[19] The plain style does not provide much evidence for dating, except in broad terms, but it can sometimes be useful to know that a binding was made in the seventeenth century, and not later, and when that information is relevant it appears in the short-title catalogue.

The evidence of binding can sometimes be used in another, more speculative way. In early modern libraries books are very often bound together. This is normal in the case of short works – orations, pamphlets – but happens quite often with more substantial books. If a collection of short pieces printed within a few years of each other is bound in a single volume in a contemporary binding that is at least *prima facie* evidence for the date of acquisition. It is certainly not conclusive proof, but I have used information of this kind in the short-title catalogue as part of the evidence about a publication by a Portuguese author. Sometimes books can be seen as having been bound together in order to give the reader contrasting

---

[16] Ker, p. 203.
[17] Ker, p. 188.
[18] They are items **67, 96, 162, 250, 494, 609, 617, 643, 661, 775**.
[19] Ker, p. 214. Gaskell dates the change at Trinity to about 1604, p. 96.

views, Jesuit and virulently anti-Catholic, of the same material, as in the
Cambridge University Library's copy of item **550**.

Binding is not the only physical aspect of a book which can provide
evidence about the date of acquisition. Especially at Oxford, chain marks
are important too. The Bodleian chained folio and quarto books, and
other libraries went further. At Balliol there is a note in the *Catalogus
librorum et benefactorum bibliothecae* that all the books left by Thomas
Wendie in 1677 were to be chained, except very small ones (**120, 160,
240**) and those in limp bindings 'minoris formae aut mollis'.[20] However,
after around 1700 chains began to be removed, leaving behind usually
rusty marks which are an indication of early acquisition – though the
possibility that they might have once belonged to a chained library not in
Oxford cannot be excluded. New College is an example of a library where
the evidence of chaining is compelling, because all the books by
Portuguese authors, except for two, show the marks. The consistency
suggests that in the seventeenth century chaining was college policy.

Cambridge chained fewer books and stopped doing so maybe a century
before Oxford. The large library at Emmanuel, for example, which was
founded in 1584, was never chained.[21] However, what chain marks are to
Oxford, the paper tab is to Cambridge. Paper tabs are a branch of fore-
edge studies, mentioned earlier. When books were shelved with the spine
facing inwards a tab with the shelf-mark was sometimes fixed to the
leading edge of the cover. The tabs themselves have usually long since
disappeared, but they too, like chains, leave a characteristic mark behind.
They ceased to be used at Trinity early in the eighteenth century when
books began to be shelved in the modern way. Queens' and St John's also
made use of tabs in the seventeenth century.[22]

Here, then, are some of the ways in which the old libraries can reveal
something of their own histories. The evidence under review, which
includes everything except the printed text itself, varies greatly in quality
and scope from volume to volume. In this chapter its value as a means of
determining date of acquisition and provenance has been discussed.
However, the books, nearly all printed outside England, had a history
before they ever came into the hands of their English owners, and that is
the subject of the next chapter. To uncover that history, a different kind of
evidence has to be used. Some of it is extraneous to the books themselves
– commercial agreements, writers' correspondence, for example, though
letters, even quite private ones, are sometimes included among the

---

[20] For the Bodleian see Wheeler, 'Bodleian Press-Marks', p. 286. The Balliol catalogue is neither
paginated nor foliated.
[21] Bush, p. 5. However, Jesus, Oxford, was still chaining as late as 1765, C. J. Fordyce and T. M.
Knox, 'The Library of Jesus College, Oxford', *Oxford Bibliographical Society Proceedings & Papers*, 5
(1937), 53–115 (55)
[22] Gaskell, pp. 97 and 103.

preliminary matter of printed volumes. But the preliminary matter is often very revealing: title-pages, licences, prefaces, dedications and liminary poems can contain much information about how books crossed the political and ideological divides of early modern Europe.

CHAPTER FOUR

LINES OF COMMUNICATION

How did all these books reach early modern Oxford and Cambridge? The answer is obvious: through the international commercial networks that had developed in the sixteenth and seventeenth centuries to serve the book trade. Those networks did not normally include Portugal, and the authors who made an impact internationally did not publish there, or at any rate did not publish much there. Instead, they contrived to have their work printed in one of the great European centres of the trade – most usually Venice, Cologne, Lyon and Antwerp – from where books were exported to England, either directly or via the twice yearly Frankfurt book fairs.

The strong patriotic sense of most of the authors in this survey means that documentary evidence for the failings of Portuguese publishing is scanty, though some exists. In his private correspondence with the Polish cardinal Stanislaw Hozjusz (Hosius) Osório complains that the Portuguese printers of the first edition of *De Regis Institutione* (item **661**) were inexperienced and greedy. Guimarães Pinto believes that the abject letter by the printer, apologising for the many errors in that edition, was written by Osório himself.[1] Some of Osório's problems were caused by the fact that he lived in the Algarve, far from the centres of printing, such as they were, of Lisbon, Évora and Coimbra. The humanist André de Resende complains of the slowness and incompetence of Luís Rodrigues in a letter of 1547.[2] Only two of the nineteen copies of works by Resende in Oxford and Cambridge were published in Portugal.

Further evidence of the technical failings of Portuguese printers comes from Francisco Álvares, who told King João III in 1540 that he had had to import both men and materials from France before he could produce his account of his travels in Ethiopia, and that the standard of printing there and in Italy and Germany was higher than at home.[3] More than sixty years later a royal *alvará*, included in item **843** and dated 1601, explains

---

[1] For Osório's correspondence, see *Cartas,* translated and edited by A. Guimarães Pinto (Silves: Câmara Municipal de Silves, 1995) p. 78 (letter of 21 May 1572) and also p. 69 (letter of 30 January 1571). See also Pinto, 'Damião de Góis e D. Jerónimo Osório: a *Crónica de D. Manuel* e *De rebus Emmanuelis gestis*', p. 312.

[2] Venâncio Deslandes, *Documentos para a história da tipografia portuguesa nos séculos XVI e XVII* (Lisbon: Imprensa Nacional, 1888; facsimile Lisbon: Imprensa Nacional, 1988), p. 50.

[3] See the letter to the King in item **23**.

how Luís de Sotomaior also had to import materials for his edition of the Song of Solomon, probably to print the elaborate title page.

Sotomaior was a Dominican, and a historian of his Order, Luís de Cacegas, reported that this prestigious book, which had the support of the Pope, Clement VIII, never recovered its costs in Portugal, though the foreign editions sold well overseas.[4] Here Cacegas touches on the problem of distribution, which was probably the main reason why so many Portuguese writers preferred to publish abroad, though the evidence for this contention is mostly circumstantial. Portuguese books, especially if they were in Latin, did not have a large market at home. In a period long before the existence of international copyright agreements, Portuguese printers also found the foreign market difficult to penetrate.

There are very few Portuguese imprints listed in the catalogues of the Frankfurt book fair, for instance. It was via the fair that a great number of foreign books reached England.[5] Catalogues survive for the period 1565–1600, and during those years about 120 books by Portuguese authors were offered for sale. However, of these only eight were Portuguese imprints, and some of them arrived at the fair many years after they had been printed.[6] When, in the seventeenth century, English booksellers went to Italy to buy books for resale in London they found a situation that was not very different. In 1628 Henry Featherstone brought back twenty-six books by Portuguese authors, of which two had been printed in Portugal, and in 1639 Robert Martin had three Portuguese imprints out of twenty-seven.[7]

[4] Luís Cacegas, *Primeira parte da História de S. Domingos,* edited by Luís de Sousa, 2 vols (Lisbon: Panorama, 1866), I, p. 435. It took Sotomaior, and his college (S. Tomás) in Coimbra, a long time to repay the loan they had needed to raise to have the book published. See M. Lopes de Almeida, *Livros, livreiros, impressores em documentos da Universidade, 1587–1835* (Coimbra: Arquivo de Bibliografia Portuguesa, 1966), pp. 21–9, especially the document of 19.7.1608, which shows that several years after publication only a third had been repaid.

[5] See, for the fairs, R. J. W. Evans, *The Wechel Presses: Humanism and Calvinism in Central Europe, 1572–1627* (Oxford: Past & Present, 1975); Ian Maclean, 'André Wechel at Frankfurt, 1572–1581', *Gutenberg-Jahrbuch,* 63 (1988), 146–76; id. 'The Market for Scholarly Books and Conception of Genre in Northern Europe, 1570–1630', in Georg Kauffmann (ed.), *Die Renaissance im Blick der Nationen Europas* (Wiesbaden: Harrassowitz, 1991), pp. 17–31; id., 'Mediations of Zabarella in Northern Germany, 1586–1623', in Gregorio Piaia (ed.), *La presenza dell'aristotelismo padovano nella filosofia della prima modernità,* (Rome-Padua: Antenore, 2002), pp. 173–98. See for the English trade: Gwen Hampshire (ed.), *The Bodleian Library Account Book, 1613–1646;* Julian Roberts, 'Importing books for Oxford, 1500–1640', in Carley and Tite (eds), *Books and Collectors, 1200–1700: Essays presented to Andrew Watson* (London: The British Library, 1997), pp. 317–33; id., 'The Latin Trade', in John Barnard and D. F. McKenzie (ed.), *The Cambridge History of the Book in Britain, Volume 4 (1557–1695)* (Cambridge: Cambridge University Press, 2002) pp. 141–73; Jason Scott-Warren, 'News, Sociability and Bookbuying in Early Modern England: the Letters of Sir Thomas Cornwallis', *The Library,* 7th series, 1 (2000), 381–402.

[6] For the catalogues, see Bernhard Fabian (ed.), *Die Messkataloge des sechzehnten Jahrhunderts,* 5 vols (Hildesheim and New York: Georg Olms, 1972–2001). Item **839**, for example, printed in Coimbra in 1574, was advertised in the 1579 catalogue. Another book, Francisco de Cristo, *Praelectionum* (not in Oxford or Cambridge), was printed in Coimbra in 1564 but only advertised in 1582.

[7] Henry Featherstone, *Catalogus librorum in diuersis locis Italiae emptorum, anno 1628* (London: John Legate, 1628). Robert Martin, *Catalogus librorum, ex praecipuis Italiae emporiis selectorum . . .* (London: Thomas Harper, 1639).

Even the most prolific Portuguese printers sold very few books abroad. This might seem a paradoxical statement, since the firm of Craesbeeck, responsible for thirty-two books in Oxford and Cambridge, is one of the most productive of all – only comparable to Cardon of Lyon. But all but eight of the thirty-two books are in Portuguese, a language for which there was virtually no market outside Portugal in the early modern period, and most of the books published by Craesbeeck in the vernacular to be found in Oxford and Cambridge libraries can be shown to be recent acquisitions. Pieter Craesbeeck, the founder of the firm, was a Fleming, trained by Plantin, but once he had arrived in Lisbon, around 1592, he seemed to lose contact with the international trade.[8] His books in Latin are represented in the English universities by only one copy each, with two exceptions, the Index of prohibited books (item **453**) and a book by Beja Parestrelo (item **700**). As Crashawe's comments show, the Index was deeply fascinating to English scholars, partly as proof of the obscurantism of papists, partly because it showed exactly what they were thinking.[9] The presence in Oxford and Cambridge of four copies of item **700** is, however, probably a matter of chance. One or two other Portuguese imprints, not by Craesbeeck, also did surprisingly well: Pedro Nunes's mathematical works (item **609**), with eight copies, and António Luís's medical treatises (items **547–9**), seven copies. But these are very much exceptions. Also exceptional, but easily explicable, are the eight copies (six of them in Cambridge) of Osório's *In Gualterum Haddonum,* published by Francisco Correia in Lisbon in 1567 (item **674**). Haddon was a Cambridge man and readers there would have been anxious to get their copy of Osório's attack on him.

So Portuguese writers had to find other ways of ensuring that they would enter the international publishing circuit. There were considerable problems involved, some of them not those that a modern reader might expect. One was the possibility that a carefully composed manuscript of Tridentine theology, sent by ship to Northern Europe for printing – to Antwerp, for instance – might fall into the hands of ill-disposed, and learned Protestant pirates, who would issue it with emendations that would render it ideologically impure. Bishop Osório, for instance, was convinced that this would happen to his friend Diogo Paiva de Andrade's *Defensio Tridentinae fidei.* In the preface to the Christian reader he explains that, because the ship carrying the manuscript had been lost to pirates, the book had been issued in Lisbon (item **44**). This cannot have been a happy solution as far as Osório was concerned, given his low opinion of

[8] João José Alves Dias, *Craesbeeck: uma dinastia de impressores em Portugal* (Lisbon: Associação Portuguesa de Livreiros Alfarrabistas, 1996), p. ix.
[9] For Crashawe's views, see Chapter One, pp. xxxiii–iv. Barlow also revelled in the opportunities which the Indexes gave him. See his *De Studio Theologiae,* p. 40.

the standards of printing in his own country. In the end all was well, because when the book was published in Germany in 1580, simultaneously in Cologne and Ingolstadt (items **45–6**), it was a tremendous success. The German printers included the Portuguese licences, so they must have had access to the Lisbon edition, not some possibly adulterated manuscript. Only three copies of the Lisbon edition reached the English universities, but seventeen of the two German ones. Proof that Osório was not just being paranoid is provided by Cosme de Magalhães, the Jesuit author of a commentary on the book of Joshua (item **552**), as well as many other works. He expresses his gratitude to the Archbishop of Lisbon, Dom Miguel de Castro, who had allowed him to use the imperial postal service when sending the manuscript to Lyon, thus avoiding the potential hazards of maritime transport.

Those hazards included the possibility of damage by contact with sea water. Frei Jerónimo de Azambuja was the Dominican whose pre-Tridentine commentary on the Pentateuch could only be issued subsequently after severe emendation. However, when his work was delivered to Paris for a posthumous re-edition it was found to be 'corrosum' after its voyage, and its restoration gave the French editor considerable problems. [10]

Nevertheless, and despite these and other problems, Portuguese writers were often brilliantly successful in publishing in foreign countries, but it was at a cost which they did not appreciate. They were not usually in a position to know what effect their work had on foreign readers, and indeed a number of the most widely distributed Portuguese books were published posthumously. If they had known they would have been disappointed, because readers abroad very often failed to appreciate that the book they had before them was written by a Portuguese – though the fact of being Portuguese was an important aspect of the writers' self-image and was very frequently proclaimed on title pages and in prefaces. This paradoxical consequence of international success will be explored further in the next chapter.

The first writer in this survey to publish regularly outside Portugal was Jerónimo Osório. As a student in his twenties he had the opportunity to spend the years 1539–42 in Bologna, where he acquired a group of international friends who were to be very useful to him in later years. In 1542 Osório returned to Portugal and published, in Lisbon, the dialogues *De Nobilitate Civili* and *De Nobilitate Christiana* (item **651**: two copies in Oxford, of which the first did not arrive until 1659), and, seven years later, *De Gloria* (no copies in either Oxford or Cambridge). Two of the friends, Jean Matal and Antonio Agustín, however, remained in Rome. They

[10] See the Parisian Dominican Raymond de Hezeque's dedication of item **68** to Prince Henry of Lorraine.

had figured in the dialogues as interlocutors, expessed their admiration
for them on a number of occasions, and brought about their republication
in Florence in 1552 (item **636**: two copies of the complete work in Oxford,
two in Cambridge of *De Gloria* and four of *De Nobilitate*).[11]
Shortly afterwards Osório acquired another foreign admirer in the
Englishman Roger Ascham, best known as the author of *The Scholemaster*
(1570). Between 1553 and 1555 he sent what is essentially the same Latin
letter in praise of Osório's writing to four acquaintances, Sir William
Paget, Sir William Petre, Cuthbert Tunstall, and Cardinal Reginald Pole.
Those to Tunstall and Pole can be found, in manuscript, bound into the
copies of the Florentine edition of *De Nobilitate* kept at St John's
Cambridge, Ascham's college. In the early 1550s Ascham was in
Germany and the Low Countries, and it was probably there that he
acquired the recently republished dialogues. It was the edition produced
outside Portugal, as nearly always, that reached the English universities
first, and in greater numbers.[12]

Towards the end of his life Osório returned to Italy, where he published
items **681–2** (represented in the short-title catalogue only by later
editions). Otherwise he remained in Portugal, most of the time as bishop
of Silves in the Algarve, from where he cultivated his international contacts,
among them Roger Ascham.[13] He complained frequently of the
inadequacy of Portuguese printers, though his fears of piracy show that
he was aware, too, of the risks of publishing abroad. A way of spreading the
risks – and of achieving the maximum publicity – was by simultaneous
publication of books in different centres, a technique much favoured later
by Jesuit writers. So Osório's *De Regis Institutione* came out in the same
year, 1571–72, in Lisbon and in Cologne (items **661–2**). Cologne was
chosen because his French friend, Matal, had established a close
relationship with the influential printing firm of Birckmann, which was
based there.[14] The Portuguese and the German editions of 1571–72 both
found their way to Oxford and Cambridge in reasonable numbers, but the

[11] In the letter to Agustín published in the 1574 edition of Osório's *De rebus Emmanuelis gestis*,
quoted by Léon Bourdon, 'Jerónimo Osório et les humanistes anglais', pp. 326–7, Matal claims
that the two friends were only responsible for the republication of *De Gloria*. But since the other
dialogues were republished at the same time and by the same press this statement is unlikely to be
correct.

[12] It is surprising that Bourdon should think that Pole knew the dialogues in the Portuguese
edition. In 1553 Ascham described the book in terms which suggest that he had not seen it until that
year. Translations of three of the letters can be found in *Letters of Roger Ascham*, translated by Maurice
Hatch and Alvin Vos (New York: Lang, 1989). The letter to Tunstall has apparently never been
printed or translated. For further discussion see p. lxxxiii below.

[13] See his letter of 1567 in which he informs Ascham that he has completed his polemic against
Walter Haddon, in A. Guimarães Pinto (ed.), *Cartas*, pp. 51–2.

[14] For more details of Matal's activities as an agent, see Thomas F. Earle, 'Portuguese Scholarship
in Oxford', p. 1044. The Birckmanns imported books to England. See Julian Roberts, 'Importing
Books for Oxford', p. 323.

power of German publishing is evident in the way that Birckmann was able to issue and sell three subsequent editions (items **663–5**). In all, there are 15 copies of the German editions of the book in the libraries, as compared to five of the first and only Portuguese one.

Osório was a writer who set trends, but who also went further than anyone else. He did not just publish in Italy and Germany, but in England also, and was one of the very few Portuguese writers whose work appeared in London, in Latin and in the vernacular (items **642–3** and **652**).[15] His success abroad is all the more remarkable, given his isolated position in the southernmost province of Portugal. Most other Portuguese theologians had more access than he had to institutional support, or indeed the support which members of groups engaged in a common purpose can give each other.

One of the many regrets of Osório's life was that he was not allowed to attend the meetings of the Council of Trent in 1562–63, for fear that he would never return, according to his nephew and biographer.[16] Those Portuguese theologians who did go enjoyed a field-day where publishing was concerned, and several large and influential works came out almost simultaneously in 1563 and 1564, all through the Venetian printer Giordano Zileti. There is evidence of planning, as well as of mutual support, in this sudden arrival of Portuguese theology on the international market.

Gaspar do Casal, bishop successively of Funchal (though he never went there), Leiria, and Coimbra was at Trent between 1561 and 1563.[17] However, that gave him time to issue three long books which he must have brought with him from Portugal in a more or less finished state with the intention of finding a publisher in Italy. There he indeed found a publisher and an agent, in the jurist and polymath Girolamo Maggi, who among other things worked for Zileti as editor, copy-editor and proof-reader. Casal relied heavily on his judgement.[18] Maggi helped one of Casal's colleagues, who proved to be a more successful writer, Diogo Paiva de Andrade.[19]

---

[15] Others who also achieved this feat were José Teixeira, the political exile who lived for some time in London, and Bartolomeu Filipe.

[16] See *Vida de Jerónimo Osório, Português*, translated by A. Guimarães Pinto, in Osório, *Cartas*, p. 159

[17] For details of his career, see José de Castro, *Portugal no Concílio de Trento*, 6 vols (Lisbon: União Gráfica, 1944–1946), IV, pp. 39–40

[18] 'Hieronymus Magius meus, cuius ego plurimi iudicium facio' [My friend Girolamo Maggi, whose judgement I value very highly], in Casal's prologue to the Christian reader in item **160**. For a discussion of the importance of Zileti as a publisher of Portuguese material see D. Jerónimo Osório, *Tratado da Justiça*, translated and edited by A. Guimarães Pinto (Lisbon: Imprensa Nacional-Casa da Moeda, 1999), p. 28.

[19] See Maggi's letter to Andrade, included in the preliminaries to *De Quadripertita Iustitia* (item **161**). In the letter Maggi explains how he had proof-read Casal's text.

Casal used his participation at Trent as a way of advertising his books.[20] Andrade had greater institutional support in that he was a theologian whom the delegates to the Council had entrusted with the important task of explaining and justifying the conclusions reached by the Council.[21] It was perhaps this mark of approval, together with Andrade's statement that his intention in writing *Orthodoxarum explicationum libri decem* was to restore the whole of Germany to the Catholic faith, that brought him to the attention of the publisher Maternus Cholinus in Cologne. Andrade was thus launched, in the same year, north and south of the Alps and his international reputation was made. His posthumous *Defensio Tridentinae fidei Catholicae* had an even greater success. Other theologians who used their time at Trent to publish through Zileti were Francisco Foreiro, whose well regarded edition of Isaiah was discussed in Chapter One, and Bishop João Soares.

The physical presence of authors outside Portugal was usually essential if they were to launch themselves in the world of international publishing. Damião de Góis's Latin works, nearly all published during his twenty years or so in the Low Countries and in Italy, are the most obvious instance of this. Many of the most successful theologians also spent a large part of their careers abroad. The canonist Agostinho Barbosa, who was responsible for more than forty copies of books in Oxford and Cambridge (and many more if editions printed after 1640 are taken into account) spent the 1620s in Rome. Other writers on religious and philosophical topics who worked for long periods in Italy were Pedro da Fonseca, Nicolau Godinho, and Beja Parestrelo. The humanists Tomé Correia and Aquiles Estaço lived and died in Italy. As we shall see shortly, many Portuguese Jewish doctors also found refuge there.

Spain was the next most favoured country for the aspiring author. Manuel Sá, one of the most widely read religious writers of the early seventeenth century, divided his time between Jesuit colleges in Spain and Italy, where he died. Two of the most prominent Portuguese Franciscan writers were Felipe Diez and Manuel Rodrigues. Both were members of the Spanish Province of St James, and their books normally appeared first in Salamanca or Alcalá before going on to achieve wider distribution in France or Italy. A period in Salamanca seemed essential too for Portuguese civil lawyers if they wanted their books to enter the international market.

No civil lawyer achieved the fame of some of their colleagues in canon law, theology, or medicine. But their books reached the English universities, and Salamanca, with its presses closely linked to the

---

[20] See the title-pages of **161** and **163**.

[21] See the 'Epistola nuncupatoria' to King Sebastião, where he explains that the book was commissioned by Fernão Martins Mascarenhas, the King's representative at the Council.

European commercial network, was usually the entry point. Aires Pinhel is probably the most important of them, with fifteen copies of his books distributed between Oxford and Cambridge. When he arrived in Salamanca in 1559 he was already the author of two legal treatises which had been printed in Coimbra. One of the these (item **712**) reached both English universities, the other did not.[22] Nine years later he published the same treatises in Salamanca through Juan Baptista de Terranova, who was from an Italian family closely linked to the Juntas, or Giuntas, Florentines whose empire stretched to Lyon as well as to many cities in Italy and Spain. It was only five years after this that another Salamanca printer, Mathias Gast, issued Pinhel's books again. So short an interval between successive editions of the same books in the same city by different printers is unusual. It may well have been the consequence of co-operation rather than of sharp practice because Gast, too, had close links with the Giuntas.[23] Gast came from Antwerp, and it was presumably through his contacts that in 1573 Pinhel achieved the glory of simultaneous publication in two German cities, Cologne and Frankfurt, each taking one of his treatises (items **715** and **719**), and in Salamanca.[24] It was possible to bypass Spain, and one of Caldas Pereira de Castro's manuscripts was sent direct to Palthenius in Frankfurt.[25] He specialized in legal publications and had wide international interests.[26] However, this was an unusual case.

Although a very large proportion of the writers in this survey published their works in France, especially, if they were theologians, in Lyon, surprisingly few spent long periods in the country. In the early part of the sixteenth century it had been normal for Portuguese to study in France, encouraged by the system of scholarships set up by King João III.[27] However, only a few of these benefited from the publishing boom which, from the 1560s onwards, brought so many Portuguese books to Oxford and Cambridge. Among the exceptions are Jerónimo de Azambuja

[22] The treatise *De rescindenda venditione* was printed in Coimbra in 1558.

[23] See Luisa Cuesta Gutiérrez, *La imprenta en Salamanca: avance al estudio de la tipografía salmantina (1480–1944)* (Salamanca: Excma. Diputación Provincial de Salamanca, 1960), pp. 30–4, and Lorenzo Ruiz Fidalgo, *La imprenta en Salamanca*, 3 vols (Madrid: Arco, 1994–5), I, pp. 79–82 and 95–6.

[24] For the importance of Salamanca in the careers of other academic lawyers, see, in the biographical notes, Manuel Mendes de Castro, Manuel da Costa, the 'Doctor Subtilis', and Manuel Soares da Ribeira.

[25] The efforts of Castro's widow and son to get his works into print is documented, in part, by M. Lopes de Almeida. See his *Livros, livreiros, impressores em documentos da Universidade, 1587–1835* (Coimbra: Arquivo de Bibliografia Portuguesa, 1966), p. 27, and the companion volume, *Livros, livreiros, impressores em documentos da Universidade, 1600–1649* (Coimbra: Arquivo de Bibliografia Portuguesa, 1964), pp. 13–15, 19.

[26] See Palthenius's preface to the reader in item **179**. For his career, see R. J. W. Evans, *The Wechel Presses*, pp. 3–4.

[27] The classic study is Luís de Matos, *Les Portugais à l'université de Paris entre 1500 et 1550* (Coimbra: Por ordem da universidade, 1950).

(Oleander) and Francisco Foreiro, who also spent several years in Italy. António de Gouveia was another 'bolseiro d'el-rei' but one who, most unusually, never returned to Portugal. Francisco Sanches also rejected his Portuguese heritage, though for different reasons, and spent nearly the whole of his long career in Toulouse. But for most of the second half of the sixteenth century the wars of religion discouraged Portuguese from protracted visits to France. Only at the end of the century did the situation change, when political turmoil at home, following the extinction of the dynasty of Aviz and the invasion of Philip II, forced some loyalists into exile in France and also in England. These included José Teixeira, António de Sena, and the pretender to the Portuguese throne, António, the Prior of Crato.

Being physically present in a foreign publishing centre, whether for a long or a short period, was important for writers wanting an international reputation. Institutional backing was also very useful, and a great many of the theologians represented in Oxford and Cambridge were members of religious orders, which can be shown in several cases to have given practical support to their members' literary endeavours. It is true that Osório, in many ways the most successful of all Portuguese writers of the period, was not a monk or a friar, but he was exceptional.

Religious orders would often assist the publication of complete works, those massive compilations which could confirm an individual's reputation, but which were difficult and expensive to compile and publish. The Trinitarian Baltasar Pais is a good example. The two volumes of his *Opera Sacrae Scripturae* were published in Paris in 1631, when Pais was sixty. It was a massive undertaking in which eight different printers collaborated. The editor was a Trinitarian, Claude Ralle, who dedicated it to the General of the Order, Louis Petit. The work has the air of being a high-profile undertaking intended to enhance the prestige of the order. In that the Trinitarians were probably successful. Oxford and Cambridge have four copies each of the large and expensive volumes.

The six volumes of the Franciscan Filipe Diez's *Quadruplicium concionum*, sermons for every Sunday and feast day in the year, and the result of thirty years' preaching, were printed in Salamanca in 1585.[28] Here is another major publication of which a religious order could be proud. Several Franciscans contributed to the preliminaries, and on the title page is the Franciscan device showing the stigmata and the legend 'Signasti Domine servum tuum Franciscum signis redemptionis nostrae'. Despite its length the work was reprinted several times, in Venice and elsewhere. There are nine copies in English university libraries, all but two in Oxford.

---

[28] Diez's comment about the thirty years comes in the address to the reader of item **272**.

It was the Jesuit order which was the most successful in promoting its sons' literary work abroad. They brought off, more frequently than anyone else, the feat of simultaneous publication in different countries, most spectacularly with the Coimbra commentaries on Aristotle. Editions of each of the five volumes of commentaries appeared in the same year, or in consecutive years, in Lisbon and Lyon, or Lyon and Cologne (or sometimes Mainz), and all of them found their way to Oxford. In Horace Cardon, of Lyon, they had what amounted to an official printer, capable of dealing with the monstrous tomes that regularly arrived from Portugal.[29] Such was the order's effectiveness in placing Portuguese publications that some seventeenth-century Jesuits were able to break what was otherwise the firmly established rule that in order to publish abroad you had to go there, if only briefly. Neither Sebastião Barradas nor Cosme de Magalhães travelled much. In his dedication of item 550, to Aquaviva, Magalhães regrets never having met him because he had so little experience of foreign travel. Yet the numerous editions of his and Barradas's works in Oxford and Cambridge were all published outside Portugal.[30] Barradas was particularly successful, and there are 29 copies of his *Commentaria in concordiam et historiam Euangelicam* in the university and college libraries.

The Portuguese medical doctors whose works crowd the shelves of Oxford and Cambridge libraries did not have the kind of institutional support which the Jesuits and other religious enjoyed. All of them – there are around twenty names in the catalogue – had some connection by birth to the Jewish world. Some were observant Jews, some converted, seemingly wholeheartedly, to Christianity, some wavered between the two religions, but the lives of all of them must have been to some degree precarious. They had more reason than most to publish outside Portugal, and most of them did so, even those who maintained to their dying day their affection for the country where they had been born.

So it was that a number of these doctors, including some of the best known, found themselves obliged to leave. Their reasons for doing so are unclear. Persecution on religious or racial grounds is an obvious hypothesis, but they may have been looking for an outlet for their books.[31] Amatus Lusitanus, Estêvão Rodrigues de Castro and Rodrigo

---

[29] For Cardon's business relationship with Claudio Aquaviva, the General of the Order, see Henri-Jean Martin, 'Renouvellements et concurrences', in Henri-Jean Martin and Roger Chartier (eds), *Histoire de l'édition française*, I (Paris: Promodis, 1982), pp. 379–403 (401).

[30] The point refers only to Magalhães as sole author. The first editions of the Coimbra commentaries, in which he collaborated, were all issued in Portugal.

[31] See Estêvão Rodrigues de Castro, *Obras poéticas em português, castelhano, latim, italiano*, edited by Giacinto Manuppella (Coimbra: Acta universitatis conimbricensis, 1967), p. 61. Castro was 49 when he left Portugal in 1608, for reasons for which Manuppella could find no explanation.

de Castro all published extensively while abroad, but produced nothing while they were living in Portugal – or if they did, no trace of their efforts reached the English universities. The most prominent doctor who remained was probably Tomás Rodrigues da Veiga, whose family was in receipt of a bull from Sixtus V absolving its members from taxation as New Christians and requiring the king of Portugal to accept them as noblemen.[32] Yet Oxford only has one copy of his commentary on Galen printed in Coimbra (item **892**), while the ten copies of other books by him, distributed between the two universities, were all published abroad. The only exception – perhaps no more than a fluke – are the three medical works of António Luís already mentioned, published in a single volume in 1540 by Luís Rodrigues of Lisbon (items **547–9**). These survive in Oxford and Cambridge in seven copies, all probably of old provenance. Rodrigues did not achieve that degree of penetration into the English market again.

Jewish and New Christian doctors depended heavily on family networks and often refer to them in the preliminaries of their writings. The preface of Manuel Brudo's *De ratione victus* (item **141**), for instance, purports to be a dialogue between him and his father, in which he lets slip, perhaps as an advertisement, that his father had not only been a practising doctor in Portugal but had also spent forty years in the study of Greek and Arabic medical works. In the Gessner brothers' edition of the same book (item **140**) Konrad Gessner included an 'epistola nuncupatoria' which refers to Brudo's grandfather as well as his father – besides revealing that he had practised in England. Rodrigo da Fonseca is the most widely represented of all the Portuguese doctors, with 41 copies of editions of his various works spread between Oxford and Cambridge. In the dedication of item **360**, printed in 1586 and one of the earliest of his books to have reached England, he pays tribute to his uncle António, also a doctor, and expresses the love of the 'universa Fonsecarum familia' [the entire Fonseca family] towards his protector, Cardinal Ferdinando de' Medici.

These pieties suggest, though do not prove, that there was some element of mutual support between the members of these medical families, not perhaps all that different from the mutual support offered between the members of the wider family of the religious orders. In the case of Tomás Rodrigues de Veiga, the New Christian under papal protection whose case was mentioned above, it is possible to go a little further. One of his brothers was Simão Rodrigues, a wealthy merchant who lived in Antwerp. It cannot be a coincidence that two volumes of his commentary on Galen were published there by the prestigious firm of

---

[32] See the biographical notes attached to entries in the short-title catalogue.

Plantin (item **893**), and that the edition was energetically pushed, with seven copies in Oxford and Cambridge.[33]

So ambitious writers in Portugal, whether Christians or not, were largely united in thinking that the best way to bring their work to the attention of the learned world was to publish abroad. It was a policy that brought them fame but, as already hinted, had unforeseen disadvantages. In the next and final chapter those disadvantages will be examined, as part of an attempt to sum up the positive and negative aspects of the intellectual endeavours of the Portuguese in the early modern period.

---

[33] See J. Gentil da Silva, *Stratégie des affaires à Lisbonne entre 1595 et 1607: Lettres marchandes des Rodrigues d'Évora et Veiga* (Paris: S.E.V.P.E.N., 1956), pp. 3–5. Another brother was André Rodrigues de Évora, compiler of a well-known common-place book. See the biographical notes attached to their entries in the short-title catalogue. All three brothers were born in Évora.

CHAPTER FIVE

NATIONALISM AND INTERNATIONALISM

Portuguese scholars wrote mostly in Latin, the international language. If they were theologians, or canon lawyers, or doctors of medicine their books treated subjects of universal, not local interest. They very often lived abroad. And they did their best to ensure that their work came out in one of the major European publishing centres, not just in Lisbon or Coimbra. Yet for all this, or even because of it, they remained staunchly patriotic, concerned that their international readership should appreciate that they were not just professors, priests, or physicians to royalty, but also, and above all, that they were Portuguese. In those long and informative title-pages that were the norm in the early modern period some form of the word *Lusitanus* nearly always appears, in the midst of the list of degrees or other qualities by which the learned author would recommend himself to his public.

Bishop Gaspar Casal, for example, has a great deal to say about his work and about himself on the title-page of his *De quadripertita iustitia*. He claims to have considered the opinions of every Catholic theologian who had written about justification and to have refuted the erroneous views of heretics, some of whom are named. Then the bishop turns to his own achievements: a member of the Royal Council, making clear that he means the Royal Council of Portugal (*Lusitaniae . . . regis*), a former president of the board of censors, a delegate to the Council of Trent – and a Portuguese, if that was not obvious already. The word follows immediately after the author's name, in the ablative case, *Gaspare Casalio Lusitano.* The immensely productive canonist Agostinho Barbosa, who worked for many years in Rome, is also concerned that his national origin should not be forgotten. After stressing the importance of his *Remissiones doctorum* to confessors and to those practising in the ecclesiastical courts, he comes to his own qualities, and also gets in his Portugueseness twice: once because his distinguished patron is the grand inquisitor *in regno Portugalliae,* and also because he himself, once again in the ablative, is *Vimaranesi presbytero Lusitano.* The learned reader who recognized in the place-name the city of Guimarães, in northern Portugal, would get the geographical information about Barbosa three times.

Statements of this kind appear over and over again, in the work literally of hundreds of writers, whose patriotism very often extended beyond the title-page. Dedications and prefaces draw attention to the importance of the universities of Coimbra and Évora as places of learning, or recall with satisfaction the purity of the faith of the Portuguese, untouched by Protestant heresy.[1]

As already mentioned, patriotic effusions are not confined to Christian writers. Many doctors, New Christians, sometimes even practising Jews, who lived in exile still wanted to tell their readers where they had been born. One of the most famous of these, João Rodrigues de Castelo Branco, is better known by the pseudonym Amatus Lusitanus which he used for most of his long and distinguished career as a medical author. His career took him steadily eastwards, from Portugal to the Low Countries and then through Italy to the Ottoman Empire. He died in Thessalonica, where he dated his books according to the Jewish system and seemed to have returned entirely to the faith of his ancestors. But he never forgot that he was Portuguese. In a book written in Rome in 1551, but published in Lyon (item **132**) he includes a dedication to the town council (Senatus Rhacusinus) of Ragusa, or Dubrovnik, on the east coast of the Adriatic. To flatter the councillors, who he hoped would become his employers, he told them how many years before, while he was still living in Lisbon, the size of ships from Ragusa which had called at the port there had been admired. The implication of the story is that Lisbon represents the gold standard as far as ship-building is concerned. Other much published doctors who lived abroad but invariably recall their Portuguese origins on the title-pages of their books are Rodrigo de Castro, Estêvão Rodrigues de Castro and Rodrigo da Fonseca.

Inevitably, there are exceptions. Well over half the doctors who practised abroad were proud to be Portuguese, but a substantial minority was not. This includes some of the best known writers and scholars included in this survey: Judah Abravanel, better known as Leo Hebraeus, and Francisco Sanches, author of the tract about philosophical scepticism, *Quod nihil scitur*. None of the editions of the *Dialoghi di Amore* reveal much about its author, and certainly not that he was born in Portugal. Sanches seems positively to have rejected his home country. There is no statement of his nationality on the title-pages of his books, and in his biography of his teacher (included in item **817**) Sanches's pupil Delassus uses a quotation from Juvenal (X, 48–50) to make the point that great men sometimes first see the light in countries populated by fools.

Fear of religious persecution was probably why some of the exiles chose

---

[1] For the praise of the Portuguese universities, see the dedications, to King Sebastião and to Philip II, of the Roman editions of Pedro da Fonseca's commentary on Aristotle's *Metaphysics* (items **337** and **339**). Paiva Andrade praises the faith of the Portuguese in the Epistola Nuncupatoria (also to Sebastião) of his *Orthodoxarum explicationum* (items **48–9**).

to set their Portuguese experiences behind them, particularly Leo Hebraeus who was very likely to have been a practising Jew, like his father Isaac Abravanel, the author of many rabbinical commentaries on the Bible. The case of the New Christian Sanches, however, is less easy to understand, since he lived as a Catholic during his many years in Toulouse, and two of his sons became priests. However, in Portugal even the most devout New Christians seldom felt secure.[2] And career development may also have influenced his choice of country of residence, as pointed out in the previous chapter.

Another and quite different group of writers who did not always reveal their nationality to their readership were the Jesuits. The highly centralized order wished to present a united front to the outside world, and especially in the Japanese mission information about the national origin of Jesuit writers was systematically suppressed. The title-pages of books by Luís Fróis, Nicolau Pimenta and João Rodrigues never reveal where these celebrated writers came from. The reality of the Japanese mission was a great deal of squabbling between different national groups, especially Portuguese, Spaniards and Italians.[3] However, when their reports reached Europe all appeared, on title-pages at least, to be united in their membership of the Society of Jesus.

Readers in the English universities received many volumes of reports of missionary triumph and disaster, especially in the Far East, but also in Ethiopia and Brazil. These books were nearly always translations, into Latin or Italian, and very rarely in Portuguese or Spanish, the languages in which they were originally written.[4] The translations, which frequently extended to the authors' names, had the effect of concealing national origins, and the contribution of Portuguese Jesuits to the missions has, as a consequence, not always been fully appreciated.[5]

Back in Europe the Fathers were less coy about admitting their nationality, though there are plenty of exceptions. Manuel Álvares, composer of the Latin grammar which was in use in Jesuit schools for centuries, never said where he came from. Others, like Sebastião Barradas, Cosme de Magalhães and Francisco Mendoça – all well-known figures – name the city where they were born, but not the country. Since in two of these cases the city in question was Lisbon

---

[2] Francisco Sanches, *That Nothing is Known (Quod Nihil Scitur)*, edited and translated by Elaine Limbrick and Douglas F. S. Thompson (Cambridge: Cambridge University Press, 1988), pp. 6–7. For the persecution of New Christians in Portugal, see Francisco Bethencourt, *L'Inquisition à l'époque moderne* (Paris: Fayard, 1995), pp. 375–6.

[3] See M. Antoni J. Üçerler, 'Alessandro Valignano: Man, Missionary and Writer', in Daniel Carey (ed.), *Asian Travel in the Renaissance* (Oxford: Blackwell, 2004), pp. 12–41 (14–21).

[4] An exception is the two-volume compilation printed in Évora in 1598 (item **459**). The Bodleian has had its copy since the foundation of the library, but there are no others in either university.

[5] Clive Willis (ed.), *China and Macau* (Aldershot: Ashgate, 2002), p. xxv.

perhaps there was no need to say more. The Coimbra commentators are also associated on the title-pages of their books with the city and university of Coimbra, but not with Portugal. But again there was perhaps no need to state the obvious. Two of the most widely read of all Jesuit writers, Pedro da Fonseca and Manuel Sá, were Jesuits and no more during their lifetimes and 'Lusitani' only in editions of their books published after their deaths. But others, including Estêvão Fagundes and Brás Viegas, make no bones about saying that they were Portuguese.

However, the evasions and silences of some Jewish and Jesuit writers does not seriously alter the point that the readers of the vast majority of the books included in the catalogue could have learnt about the national origin of their authors from the title-page. Whether they did so is another matter. The reaction of English theologians to the works of their Portuguese colleagues is one indication of how intellectual communication in early modern Europe was not a process with an easily predictable outcome. Another is the apparent failure of many Englishmen – and of Frenchmen and Italians also – to appreciate that the books they were reading were by Portuguese writers, despite the very evident national pride of most of them.

Nationalism as an ideology is a product of the French Revolution, but most historians agree that nations have long pre-dated nationalism.[6] Hugh Seton-Watson included Portugal among the 'old, continuous' nations of Western Europe, because, in his words, like England and France it was 'a community of people, whose members are bound together by a sense of solidarity, a common culture, a national consciousness'.[7] Later writers on the medieval and early modern periods have added elements to that definition. For Adrian Phillips, whose main focus is English nationalism, what he calls an 'ethnicity' can only develop into a nation if there exists a written vernacular, used for literary purposes, a territorial core 'sufficient in size of population and local economy to be able to avoid economic strangulation' and 'a religion or historical tradition markedly different from that of the majority in the state of which it [the ethnicity] has been part'.[8]

If these criteria are used to measure the Portuguese experience the results are mixed. Portugal certainly possessed a flourishing vernacular literature from the twelfth century onwards. This would have promoted a national consciousness at home, but it was difficult to export, for the reasons explained in Chapter One. There were further problematic

[6] Anthony J. Smith, *Nationalism* (Cambridge: Polity, 2001), pp. 92–9.
[7] Hugh Seton-Watson, *Nations and States: An Enquiry into the Origins of Nations and the Politics of Nationalism* (London: Methuen, 1977), pp. 1 and 7.
[8] Adrian Hastings, *The Construction of Nationhood: Ethnicity, Religion and Nationalism* (Cambridge: Cambridge University Press, 1997), pp. 30–1.

aspects of Portuguese as a vernacular language which will be discussed shortly. The economic situation of Portugal in the early modern period falls outside the scope of this study. However, there is no doubt that publishing in Portugal suffered from a number of difficulties which prevented books printed there from penetrating European markets, except fleetingly. And then there is Hastings's last criterion, about religion and historical tradition, which also made the emergence of a distinctive Portuguese identity problematic.

Hastings's own view of the development of a Portuguese national consciousness is extremely misleading. For him, it grew out of the Crusades and was characterized 'by a particularly militant type of Catholicism, aggressive, nationalist, anti-Islamic'.[9] It is true that the Portuguese were always intensely proud of their Catholicism and of their loyalty to the Roman pope. But Hastings does not take into account the fact that the conquest of the Algarve from the Moslems was complete by the middle of the thirteenth century, and that consequently for the next 150 years or so emergent Portuguese nationalism defined itself by reference to its Christian neighbours to the east and north.

Portugal's Castilian neighbour, with which it enjoyed a frequently violent relationship, was a Catholic monarchy, like Portugal itself. Castile was the enemy, but also a country very similar in fundamental ways to Portugal. And although by the end of the fifteenth century Castile had absorbed the other medieval Iberian kingdoms of Aragon, Navarre and Granada, to the Portuguese it was not necessarily to be thought of as the dominant power in the Peninsula. King Manuel dreamt of becoming the ruler of a united Spain, and in 1498 his infant son (who died shortly afterwards) was recognized as the future monarch of Portugal and Castile.

The notion that there was a greater Hispania, a political unit larger than any of the medieval kingdoms, was probably an inheritance from ancient times. To the Romans Spain consisted of two provinces, later three, of which Lusitania was one. Any 'Lusitanus' might therefore be subsumed under the wider designation of 'Hispanus', and the ambiguity did not disappear with the rise of the vernacular languages. It could easily be a matter of pride.

When Camões, the national poet of Portugal, writing probably in the 1550s, wanted to place his country in its geographical context, he used the traditional image of Europe as a human figure, of which 'a nobre Espanha' [noble Spain] was 'the head'. Two stanzas later he comes to Portugal, which is 'quasi cume da cabeça / da Europa toda' [as it were the highest point of the head of all Europe].[10] The dream of single Iberia ruled from Lisbon famously backfired, and after 1580 the crowns of Portugal

---

[9] Hastings, *Construction of Nationhood*, p. 190.
[10] Camões, *Os Lusíadas*, III, 17 and 20. The poem was published in 1572.

and Spain were united, but under Philip II. After that not all Portuguese themselves would have been completely clear about their national status, and there was plenty of opportunity for confusion in the minds of foreigners. The countries, and their empires, were, in theory at least, governed separately, but there was always a risk that abroad Lusitania might be considered to be no more than a province.

There was another source of uncertainty about Portuguese national identity, and that arose from the linguistic choices made by Portuguese writers themselves, some of them at least. It was one thing to write in Latin, quite another to write in Spanish, though in both cases the motive was the same, to reach an international audience. Writing in Spanish – which became frequent after the loss of independence, but was not unknown before – can hardly have failed to confuse foreigners, to make them see the Portuguese, at the most, as another kind of Spaniards. The jurist Pedro Barbosa Homem calls himself 'Iurisconsulto Portugues' on the title-page of item 448 and apologises to the reader for using Spanish: 'Y pues no puede dudarse, que siendo nuestro Romance en las naciones estrangeras entendido, y hablado de muy pocos: por el contrario el Castellano es de casi todos' [There can be no doubt that, while our language is little understood or spoken abroad, almost everyone knows Castilian].

But although such a procedure would have been understood at home, abroad it would inevitably undermine the distinctness of the Portuguese in the wider Iberian world.

It is perhaps just as well that Barbosa Homem's book is a very rare one, but the same argument is used by other writers, the theologian Sebastião Gomes de Figueiredo and the poetess Bernarda Ferreira de Lacerda.[11] A much better-known writer, the mathematician Pedro Nunes, uses it too in his *Libro de Algebra* (item 625). In that book he describes himself on the title-page as 'Cosmographo Mayor del Rey de Portugal', and even addresses his patron, Cardinal-Prince Henry, in Portuguese. But the text of the treatise, which was published in 1566, is entirely in Spanish. Nunes may well have wished that the fruits of Portuguese scholarship should be as widely known as possible, but it was, inevitably, at a cost. Not using the Portuguese language removes one of the key elements of Portuguese nationhood.

A further doubt must have risen in the mind of foreign readers as to the status, perhaps even the existence of Portuguese as a language, and that would have derived from the reluctance of some writers (not all) to give it even a name. Barbosa Homem contrasts 'nuestro Romance [our vernacular]' with 'el Castellano', and Nunes says 'a lingoa Castelhana

---

[11] Item 321, address to the reader and item 503, prologue.

he mais commum em toda Espanha que a nosa' [The Castilian tongue is more common throughout Spain than our own], complicating matters further by the use of 'Espanha' to mean the whole of the Iberian peninsula. The short 'Demonstratio' by Nunes included in many editions of John of Holywood's *Sphaera emendata* was translated into Latin by his French friend Élie Vinet, who added a note that the text had originally been composed in 'Hispano Portugallico'. A reader in England might well have wondered what language that was.

Gaspar Barreiros, the humanist and nephew of the great vernacular historian João de Barros, damaged the status of Portuguese as a language independent of other languages in a different way. In his *Censura* (item **106**), he refers to his *Chorographia*, a learned account of a journey from Badajoz to Milan, which he had published in Portuguese in Coimbra in 1561 (no copy in either Oxford or Cambridge). He was proud that several Italians had read the travel book, despite the unfamiliar language, and he explains how they were able to do that: 'Alii, eo quod fuissent aliquod tempus in Hispania commorati, alii, adiuvante Hispanorum interpretatione' [Some because they had lived for some time in Hispania, others with the help of Hispanic interpreters].[12] Barreiros had revealed that the books which make up the *Chorographia* were 'Lusitane scriptos' [written in Portuguese], but by claiming that speakers loosely described as 'Hispani', who might come from anywhere in the Iberian peninsula, could interpret the text for Italians, he could be understood as suggesting that Portuguese and Spanish are the same language.

So the Portuguese writers represented in Oxford and Cambridge libraries sent mixed messages about themselves. Nearly all were proud to be Portuguese, and ensured that one of the first things their readers would learn about them was their nationality. Yet in all sorts of ways the clear nationalistic message was undermined. The next stage is to see how early modern readers – not all of them English – reacted to the sometimes confusing signals coming from Portugal.

Reaction can be gauged from marginal and printed comments on the work of Portuguese writers. Something can be learnt, too, from the preliminaries of books printed outside Portugal, which often contain revealing statements by non-Portuguese: printers, censors and authors of liminary poems and other publicity material. Some had no doubts about national origins, like our friend the anonymous reader from Peterborough who, around 1700, wrote those glowing words about the learning of Paiva de Andrade in his copy of item **49**. Vasco Figueiro is 'a Gentleman of Portingale', according to the title-page of item **324**. The translator of item **865** tells his readers that the author of the book is 'brother Ioseph Texere

---

[12] Item **106**, p. 13.

a Portuguese, one knowne to the greatest and meanest in Europe, as also here very well'. Part of the title of the translation of Walter Haddon's response to Osório's letter to Queen Elizabeth reads: 'A sight of the Portugall pearle, that is, the aunswere of d. Haddon . . . against the epistle of Hieronimus Osorius . . .'[13], and Francis Bacon, though critical of Osório's wordiness, knew well enough that he was 'the Portugal bishop'.[14]

Translators are necessarily aware of linguistic and national differences, but general readers may not be. Yet it is hard to imagine that Roger Ascham, for instance, did not know that Osório was Portuguese. It was he who introduced Osório's work to English readers of Latin, as was explained in Chapter Four, by sending his patrons and friends an enthusiastic appreciation of *De Gloria*, to him an apologia for firm Catholic rule, untainted by the immorality of Machiavelli. But Ascham's letter varies slightly from correspondent to correspondent, and as it does so uncertainty begins to grow about Osório's nationality.

In 1553 he wrote to William Paget that Portugal (Lusitania) had as much to be proud of in Osório alone as Italy in Bembo and Sadoleto, France in Christophe de Longueil and Joachim Périon, or Germany in Erasmus and Johannes Sturm. One Portuguese, therefore, was worth two Italians, Frenchmen etc.: 'Nec video iam cur plus aut Italia in Bembo et Sadoleto, aut Gallia in Longolio et Perionio, aut Germania in Erasmo et Joanne Sturmio, quam Lusitania nunc in uno Osorio gloriari possit'. But in 1555 there is a subtle change of emphasis in the letter to Cardinal Pole. Italy, France, and Germany are now represented by one writer each, and Lusitania has become Hispania: 'Immo tam praestans artifex est ut nec Italia in Sadoleto, nec Gallia in Longolio, nec Germania in Joanne Sturmio quam nunc Hispania in Osorio gloriari possit'.[15] Why the change? Perhaps because Lusitania did not sit well with Italia and Germania, terms which had geographical and cultural significance, but which did not designate political units. So Osório's national identity was sacrificed to stylistic elegance and to the wider republic of letters.

Robert Burton was a devoted reader of Portuguese material, especially the medical literature. But on one of the rare occasions when he says something about one of the authors of the books he quoted so frequently, the information he gives about nationality is incorrect. One of his favourite Portuguese books was item **353**, Rodrigo da Fonseca's *Consultationes medicae* of 1620–22. It has a typically informative title-page in which Fonseca says, amongst other things, that he was 'Olysipponensis' and that he held a chair of medicine at the University of Padua. Burton

---

[13] Walter Haddon, *A Sight of the Portugall Pearle*, translated by Abraham Hartwell (London: William Seres, 1565).

[14] Cited by Bourdon, 'Jerónimo Osório et les humanistes anglais', p. 297n.

[15] Quoted by Bourdon, 'Jerónimo Osório et les humanistes anglais', pp. 303–6.

picked up the information about the chair from the title-page, and knew from other sources that Castro was dead. However, he still called him a Spaniard.[16]

Here is an instance of a very learned English reader who did not trouble to distinguish the Iberian peoples from each other. Italian and French readers were not necessarily any better. Girolamo Maggi, the middleman so useful to Portuguese delegates at Trent with literary ambitions, must have got to know his clients quite well. But the eulogy of Hispania which he directs to Paiva de Andrade in item **161** does not distinguish that country from Lusitania, and this at a date well before the union of the Crowns.

Horace Cardon, the printer of Lyon responsible for so many Portuguese books, seems to confuse Lusitania and Hispania in the prefatory material to his edition of the Conimbricenses' *De Anima* (item **218**). He tells his readers that the commentaries 'iam pridem apud Lusitanos editi sint' [have already been published in Portugal] – which was quite true, as they had appeared in 1598 – but then, in the dedication to Nicolas Regnauld, lord of Vaudemar, explains how he has made a special journey to obtain MSS and printed works 'quae non nisi in ipsomet Hispaniae regno edita fuerant' [which had only appeared in the kingdom of Spain]. By this time,1600, Portugal and Spain were united, so technically Cardon is not being incorrect in seeming to equate them, but the effect of his words is to reduce the sense of a separate Portuguese identity.

Another reason why early modern readers may not have concerned themselves overmuch with Portugal as a national unit is, as already pointed out, that few of the books discussed here express a strong sense of difference from Catholic and European norms. Frequently they were written in response to commissions coming from outside Portugal, from the Jesuit General, for instance, or the Council of Trent. Consequently, the orthodoxy found so often in them could be paralleled elsewhere in southern Europe. And even the unique achievements of the Portuguese – the Discoveries – were downplayed by publicists like Hakluyt and Purchas, as appears in Chapter One. One of the few writers regarded today as having made an impact on the development of European thought, Francisco Sanches, seems to have rejected his national inheritance, as we have seen. And the theologians, valuable though their contribution was, seldom provoked controversy. Only Jerónimo Osório, and to a lesser extent Diogo Paiva de Andrade, drew a response from their English readers.[17]

---

[16] Robert Burton, *The Anatomy of Melancholy*, edited by Thomas C. Faulkner et al., 6 vols (Oxford: Clarendon Press, 1992–2000), II, pp. 230 and 403. Burton added the comment about Rodrigo de Castro in the edition of *The Anatomy of Melancholy* of 1628, six years after Fonseca's death.

[17] See Chapter One, n. 9.

And yet the bibliographical facts remain, the hundreds of books, the multiple copies spread across the old libraries of Oxford and Cambridge. The English universities remained, for much longer than most people believe, part of the international Catholic and Latin world. In this area, at least, the confidence about a national consciousness in England, expressed by writers like Hastings, needs to be modified.[18] Scholars in Oxford and Cambridge were slow to develop specifically English modes of thinking, and in the troubled sixteenth and seventeenth centuries, when scholarly creativity was difficult, they relied very heavily on what foreign writers had to tell them.

The Authorized Version of the Bible is often thought of as a formative influence on the development of English as a literary language. But behind it lies the work of innumerable commentators, many of them Portuguese. Anglicans learnt about the theology of the Counter-Reformation and about ecclesiastical law from the Portuguese controversialists and canonists. The doctors read and annotated not just writers like Orta, with their reports of new and exotic plant species, but also the practising physicans who worked in Germany and Italy – and who happened to be Portuguese. Generations of Oxford students, at least, learned to reason with the Coimbra commentators. Portugal has contributed more than its fair share – and certainly far more than anyone realises – to the intellectual life of the English universities.

The question then immediately arises of how much further it may be possible to go. There is no reason why in the Protestant world in the early modern period the English universities should have been unique in allowing themselves to be penetrated by Portuguese thinking. And indeed from the short-title catalogue it is easy to draw up a list of major writers whose works can be searched for elsewhere in Northern Europe. If Oxford and Cambridge are the model the theologians will always be in first place. Osório, Paiva de Andrade, and Casal among the controversialists, Barbosa and Rodrigues among the canonists, the commentators Azambuja (Oleander), Barradas, Foreiro, Mendoça, Sá – these are the writers who are likely to show up in catalogues. But it is highly probable that some of the doctors will be there also – Amatus Lusitanus, the two Castros, Rodrigo da Fonseca, Garcia da Orta – the historians – Osório (again) and Góis – and Pedro da Fonseca and the Coimbra commentators.

Here is a list which is manageable and yet which gives an idea of the breadth and depth of Portuguese intellectual life in the sixteenth and seventeenth centuries. The on-line catalogues reveal the presence of some or all of these writers in the Northern Protestant world: in the British

---

[18] 'England presents the prototype of both a nation and a nation-state in the fullest sense', Hastings, *Construction of Nationhood*, p. 4. This cannot be taken to apply to the universities.

Library and in Lambeth Palace (the London residence of the Archbishops of Canterbury), even in private houses like Lanhydrock in Cornwall,[19] in the National Library of Scotland in Edinburgh and in the library of St Andrews university (whose copy of *De Gloria* was presented by the sixteenth-century humanist George Buchanan, who had visited Coimbra), and on the other side of the North Sea in Utrecht and Leiden.

But in these libraries, too, the same problems exist that can be found in the English universities. The British Library's catalogue is unusually complete, but the other on-line catalogues are quite frank in admitting that they do not provide a record of all the antiquarian material in the library concerned. And all of them are patchy when it comes to the vital questions of provenance and the dating of the acquisition of books.

So the present study has to be seen for what it is, a pioneering excursion into a bibliographical world whose precise extent and significance for the moment can only be guessed at. It may be that wavering England was more open to Portuguese intellectual influence than Calvinist countries like Scotland or the Netherlands, but that is something that can only be ascertained by further studies at the same level of detail as the one attempted here.

---

[19] The first Lord Robartes, who owned the property in the seventeenth century, collected a magnificent library with many books published on the continent, including books by Portuguese authors.

SHORT-TITLE CATALOGUE

The short-title catalogue lists every copy of every edition of every work by a Portuguese author printed before 1640 and findable today in the university and college libraries of Oxford and Cambridge. Work is taken to mean a piece of writing with a separate title-page, but works without a title-page of their own which form part of compilations are listed, if they are mentioned on the title-page. The only exception are the compilations of letters from Jesuit missionaries, which are listed if they contain material by Portuguese writers, regardless of whether the writer in question is mentioned on the title-page.

It must be stressed that not all the information which a bibliographer might want is to be found here. Individual copies are located, by library and by shelf-mark, and whatever I have been able to discover about provenance and date of acquistion is stated, as briefly as possible. In the case of libraries which have several catalogues, compiled at different periods, reference is normally made only to the first occasion when a book is recorded. Brief details about owners of books are included where they are available. That is all. For further information about the books the reader should consult OLIS, Newton and the bibliographies to which cross-reference is made.

Some bibliographers – Adams in particular – multiply entries by regarding every change of date on a title-page, and every change of printer as evidence of a new edition. However, long and complex publications sometimes took early modern printers more than a year to finish, and they would alter the date as the edition progressed. They also quite frequently collaborated, each member of the consortium putting his name on the title-page of the copies for which he was responsible. For these reasons, and for the sake of clarity, I have tried wherever possible to reduce the number of entries.

The short notes which follow the name of each author listed in the catalogue are not intended as a full account of their lives. Rather they should be seen as complementary to the catalogue, and to the statements made in the Introduction. I have included details of writers' foreign experience, particularly if it is relevant to the printing of their works in publishing centres outside Portugal. I have also recorded whether or not they made a statement of nationality on the title-pages. Information about the number of copies of their books in early modern Oxford and Cambridge is included where it is not immediately obvious, and wherever an explanation for the presence or absence of their work is possible I have given one. Each article is followed by a brief bibliography.

Books in Oxford libraries are listed before Cambridge ones. References to the Bodlean Library and Cambridge University Library are placed before references to the college libraries, which follow in alphabetical order.

Abarbanel/Abravanel, Isaac (1437–1508)

Abravanel, who was born in Lisbon, was King Afonso V's treasurer. However, he was suspected of having taken part in the conspiracy led by the Duke of Bragança against Afonso's successor, João II, and forced to flee Portugal in 1483. He never returned and, like many other Portuguese Jews, spent his last years in Italy. Abravanel is the only author of books in Hebrew in this catalogue. In **17** there is a refutation of his views by the Christian writer Constantin L'Empereur.

Encyclopaedia Judaica, II, cols 109–11; Benzion Netanyahu, *Don Isaac Abravanel: Statesman and Philosopher.*

1 'Ateret zekenim : 'od lamad da 'at 'et ha-'am mah hem soro' ha-yesodot, Sabbioneta, 1557.
CUL S817.d.55.7.

2 Maayene ha-yeshuah, Ferrara, Shemuel Tsarefati, 1551. 4°
BOD (3 copies) Opp. Add. 4° IV.496 Previously 4° T11 Seld., and with 11 on the leading edge, so part of the Selden bequest deposited in 1659; Opp. 4° 235 Acquired in 1829; Opp. Add. 4° III.71.

3 Markhevet ha-mishnah perush le-mishnah torat 'el, Sabbioneta, Tobias Foa, 1551.
CUL S817.b.56.6.

4 Mashmi'a yeshu'ah, [Salonica], 1526.
CUL S817.b.52.4.

5 Pirke 'Avot : 'im perush . . . Mosheh bar Mayymon ve-'im perush Don Yitshak 'Abravan'el ve-kara' be-shem . . . Nahalat 'Avot, Be-Venetsiyah, Be-vet M.A. Yushtiniyano, 305, 1545.
CUL S817.b.54.11.

6 Pirke 'Avot, Venice, Giorgio di Cavalli, 1566–67. Fol.
BOD (3 copies) DD 23 Art. Seld. From the Selden bequest of 1659; Fol BS 146(1) With 146 on the leading edge. The shelf-mark indicates that the book was deposited between 1650–68. 17th-century calf binding with fillets, stamped HF. Chain mark; Opp. Fol. 333(4) Acquired in 1829.
CUL S816.b.56.1 SJCC Tt.2.23(1) From the bequest of David Dolben, Bishop of Bangor, 1635.

7 Perush ha-Torah, Venetsyah, Zuan Bragadin, 5339 [1579]. 4°

CUL 5816.b.57.5 **CLA** C.5.14 The book had a Portuguese owner **SJCC** Tt.4.26 (Adams A53).

8 Perush ha-Torah, Venice, Giovanni di Gara, 1579. Fol.
CHR P.12.20 (Adams A54).

9 R'osh 'amanah : bo shoreshe ve-r'ashe ha-'emunot, Cremona, 1557.
CUL S817.d.58.3.

10 Sefer Mif'alot 'Elohim, Venesiyah, Z. Digarah, 352, 1592.
CUL S817.d.59.19.

11 Haggadah, :Hagadah : im perush ha-hakham ha-shalem Don Yitshak Abravanel ha-noda bi-Yuda ve-Yisrael shemo Zevah Pesah, Riva di Trento, Yaakov Markariyah, 1560–61. Fol.
BOD Opp. Fol 219 (2) Acquired in 1829.
SJCC Tt.2.23 (2) bought with the bequest of David Dolben, Bishop of Bangor, 1635.

12 Seder Hagadah shel Pesah : be-lashon ha-kadosh u-pitronu be-lashon 'Ashkenazim . . . ve-'eleh mosif 'al ha-ri'shonim Perush Seli 'esh ve-hu' kitsur Zevah Pesah / meha-Rav Yitshak 'Abravan'el zatsal, Venetsyah : Nidpas . . . ke-mar Mosheh . . . ke-mar Gershon Frinatsu, be-vet Yiyovani Kaliyoni ha-madpis, 389, 1629.
CUL S817.a.62.1.

13 [Seder Hagadah shel Pesah : 'im perush Zevah Pesah le-ha'r Yitshak bar Yehudah 'Abravan'el . . .]. [Riva di Trento, 1561].
Notes: Title supplied in MS.
CUL Item no. 2 in volume S816.b.56.1.

14 Zevah Pesah : hu' perush be-hagado' ha-pesah, Venice, 1557.
CUL S817.d.58.3.

15 Sefer Zevah Pesah, Bistrovits, Kalonimus ben Mordekhai Yafeh, 1592. 4°
BOD Opp. 4° 1398(2) Acquired in 1829.

16 [Yehoshua'-Melakhim], [Pesaro], [1511?].
CUL S816.b.51.1.

17 Comment. in Esaiae prophetiam 30 cum additamento eorum quae r. Simeon e veterum dictis collegit, Lugduni-Batavorum, ex officina Bonaventurae & Abrahami Elzevirii, 1631. 8°
BOD (2 copies) 8° B 64(2) Art.; 8° A 12 Th. Seld. From the Selden bequest of 1659 **EXE** PE 22 With the signatures of Dr Williams and Henry Hastings. It may have belonged to another library, as it is marked 'duplicate' **LIN** L.11.16 College bookplate of 1703 and chain mark. Signature of Thomas Marshall, Rector 1672–85 **QUO** UU. G. 163.
CUL (2 copies) 6816.d.46 With the bookplate of the Royal Library, deposited in 1715; 6816.e.2 Binding repaired **CLA** C.8.26. **MGC** D.8.82 **QUC** M.16.16 In the catalogue compiled in the 1680s **SJCC** (2 copies) Uu.10.20; Pp.13.15 **TRC** F.1.45.

18 Liber de capite fidei, in quo continentur radices & capita vel principia religionis, Amstelodami, apud Guiliel. & Iohannem Blaeu, 1638, 4°
BOD 4° A 19 Th. Seld. From the Selden bequest of 1659 ASC S.R. 68.a.26. Chain mark BNC Lath.N.1.14, formerly L.14.14. In the 17th-century catalogue with shelf-mark L.14.15 CHC (2 copies) WF.7.20 (3–4); Allestree K.4.19 From the Allestree bequest of 1681 JSO A.4.8(1) MGO m.13.14(1–2) Marks of chaining on top edge SJCO F.4.31(2) Title on leading edge WAD M 40.25.
CUL (3 copies) Bury.42.11 Given to the grammar school at Bury St Edmunds in 1681. The school's library is now held on deposit in Cambridge; 6816.d.1 With the bookplate of the Royal Library, deposited in 1715; 6816.d.28 CCCC M.8.35 (1–2) QUC K.9.30 SJCC Tt.8.20 Given by Thomas Morton in 1628, while he was bishop of Lichfield TRC F.1.113.

Abravanel, Judah (see Leão Hebreu)

Aegidius, Benedictus (see Bento Gil)

Agostinho, Nicolau
Chaplain to and biographer of Teotónio de Bragança (1530–1602), Archbishop of Évora from 1578 to his death.

19 Relaçam summaria da uida do illustrissimo et reuerendissimo senhor dom Theotonio de Bragãça, quarto arcebispo de Euora, Euora, na officina de Francisco Simões, 1614. 4°
BOD Vet. G2 e.17 Acquired 1981.

20 Aliquot opuscula Graeca ex variis autoribus discerpta, Conimbricae, 1583, ex officina Antonii a Mariz, 1583. 8°
BOD 290 k.2 Acquired from Ebenezer Palmer after 1819 (Anselmo 882).

Almada, Manuel de (c.1510–1580) (Emanuel Dalmada)
Inquisitor and non-resident Bishop of Angra, in the Azores, he accompanied Princess Maria of Portugal on her journey to Brussels in 1565 to meet her husband, Alexander Farnese, whom she had just married by proxy. In the following year, he published in Antwerp, in great haste, his attack **(21)** on Walter Haddon's reply to Osório's letter to Queen Elizabeth **(668–70)**. His nationality and that of Osório are clearly stated on the title-page. Haddon was a Kingsman and it is not surprising that there are more copies of the book in Cambridge, all with early provenance, than in Oxford. In some of them there is a detachable satirical engraving showing Haddon (and other reformers) in the shape of dogs.
Léon Bourdon, 'Jerónimo Osório et les humanistes anglais', pp. 285–8; António Guimarães Pinto, *Humanismo e controvérsia religiosa*, I, pp. 118–37 and 147–50.

21 Epistola . . . aduersus Epistolam Gualteri Haddoni . . . contra . . . Hieronymi Osorij . . . epistolam, Antuerpiae, ex offina Gulielmi Silvij, 1566. 4°
BOD GG 41 Th., formerly D 1.4 Th. In the 1605 catalogue and listed under the old

shelf-mark in the 1620 catalogue **CCCO** LG.5.7(3) **CHC** f.1.13 Bequeathed by Robert Burton in 1640 (Kiessling (1988) 423). **CUL** (2 copies) E*.10.47 (D) Acquired before 1715; G.10.36 part of the Royal Library, deposited in 1715 **PET** I.9.32 Bequeathed by Andrew Perne, Master, in 1589 **SJCC** Oo.8.31 From the Crashawe collection, deposited in 1626 **TRC** E.9.4 Bequeathed by James Duport, vice-master, in 1679 (Adams D4).

Almeida, Manuel de (1581–1646)

A Jesuit missionary, most of whose life was spent in Asia. Other Jesuit writers, Pedro Pais and Baltasar Teles, were also involved in the compilation of **22**.

Inocêncio, V, p. 349; Fortunato de Almeida, *História da Igreja em Portugal*, II, p. 267.

22 Histoire de ce qui s'est passé es royaumes d'Ethiopie, en l'anné 1626, . . . : Et de la Chine, en l'année 1625, iusques en Feburier de 1626, *tr. from Italian*, Paris, chez Sebastien Cramoisy, 1629. 12°

BOD Vet. E2 f.159 Acquired after 1937.

Álvares, Francisco (–1540) (Francisco Alvarez)

He took part in the embassy of Dom Rodrigo de Lima to Ethiopia (1520–26), as chaplain to the expedition. To print **23**, the first edition (Lisbon, 1540), it was necessary to import both craftsmen and materials from Paris, as he explains in his prologue to the king. The 'estampas caratules de letras' to which he refers may be the ornamented capitals placed at the start of each chapter. Ethiopia was a topic of abiding fascination to early modern people. The original edition of Álvares's book, and the French and German translations, made little impact before the nineteenth century, but earlier it achieved wide circulation in Italian, Spanish and above all in English. (See **737** and the discussion in Chapter One.) The Spanish translation printed in Toledo (**29**) is attributed to Miguel de Selues but follows closely the work of Padilla (**27**). It has different preliminaries and in addition a table of contents.

Francisco Alves, *Verdadeira informação das terras do Preste João das Índias,* ed. Neves Águas (Mem Martins: Europa-América, 1989).

23 Ho Preste Joam das Indias. Verdadera informaçam das terras do Preste Joam, [Lisbon], em casa de Luis Rodriguez, 1540. Fol.

BOD (2 copies) Antiq. d.P. 1540.1 Spanish marginalia; Antiq. d.P.1540.2 Both copies were acquired between 1883 and 1936 **TAY** Arch. Fol. P. 1540 Acquired in 1936.

TRC X.13.17 Bequeathed by John Laughton in 1712. He was college, and later University, librarian (Adams A850; Anselmo 1015).

24 [Ho Preste Joam das Indias] Historiale description de l'Ethiopie, *tr. into French by Jean Bellère from the Italian version of Giovanni Battista Ramusio*, Anvers, chez Iehan Bellere, 1558. 8°

BOD Douce A 392 Part of the Douce bequest of 1834 **QUO** Sel. c. 6 Bequeathed by A. H. Sayce, who died in 1933.

CUL Kkk.685 Acquired in 1806 (Adams A847).

25 [Ho Preste Joam das Indias] Die Reiß zu deß Christlichen Koenigs in hohen Ethiopien . . . *in* General Chronicen, Franckfurt am Mayn, durch Johannem Schmidt in verlegung Sigmund Feyerabends, 1576. Fol., 3 parts in 1 vol.
    TAY U.S.R.3.A Acquired in 1879.

26 [Ho Preste Joam das Indias] Sehr herzliche schöne warhafftige Beschreibung . . . von den Landen des mechtigen Königs inn Ethiopien, den wir Priester Johan nennen . . . Eissleben, Joachim Heller, 1573. Fol.
    TRC Grylls 31.263 Bequeathed by William Grylls in 1863 (Adams A852).

27 [Ho Preste Joam das Indias] Historia de las cosas de Etiopia, *tr.* Fray Thomas de Padilla, en Anvers, en casa de Iuan Steelsio, [in colophon] en casa de Iuan Latio, 1557. 8°
    BOD 8° A 39 Art. Seld. From the Selden bequest of 1659 ASC SR.106.b.18. The same shelf-mark is used for All Souls' copy of **29 CHC** Allestree P.8.25 MS. notes. From the Allestree bequest of 1681.
    CUL N*.6.63 (G) In the library before 1715 (Adams A848).

28 [Ho Preste Joam das Indias] Historia de las cosas de Etiopia, Saragoça, en casa de Agostin Millan, 1561. Fol.
    CLA W.6.2 With the college bookplate of 1701. In the catalogue of 1677−78 with the shelf-mark C.36 (Adams A849).

29 [Ho Preste Joam das Indias] Historia de las cosas de Etiopia, *tr.* Miguel de Selues, Toledo, en casa de Pedro Rodriguez, 1588. 8°
    ASC SR.106.b.18 The same shelf-mark is used for All Souls' copy of **27**.
    There is another translation in Ramusio (**743**−8) and in **737**, *Purchas his Pilgrims* (1625), pt 2, bk 7, ch 5, pp. 1026−1121.

Álvares, Manuel de (1526–83) (Emmanuel Alvarez/Alvarus)

His Latin grammar was one of the most widely read books ever written by a Portuguese, and went through hundreds of editions (usually in an abridged form) between the sixteenth and the nineteenth centuries. The grammar was commissioned by Francisco de Borja, the Jesuit general, and is one of the greatest successes of Jesuit publishing. However, its fame was greatest in the Catholic world, and in early modern Oxford and Cambridge it was not widely used, though **35**, the Cologne edition of 1596, made some impact. The publishers, Birckmann, were represented in London and imported books directly from Germany. Generally, English students learnt their Latin from the grammars of Priscian and Thomas Linacre.

    Like a number of other Jesuit writers, especially missionaries, Álvares makes no statement of his nationality on the title-page. However, he is known to have been born in Madeira. The first official edition of the complete grammar was published in Lisbon in 1572. There is no copy in Oxford or Cambridge. The first abridged version appeared in Venice in 1570. It is represented here by a later edition (30).

Francisco Rodrigues, *História da Companhia de Jesus na Assistência de Portugal*, II.2, pp. 50–1; J. M. Fletcher, 'The Faculty of Arts', in McConica (ed.), *The History of the University of Oxford*, III, pp. 157–99 (172); Julian Roberts, 'Importing Books for Oxford, 1500–1640', p. 323.

30 De constructione octo partium orationis liber, Dilingae, excudebat Sebaldus Bayer, 1572. 8°
WOR TC.19.28 Bequeathed by H. A. Pottinger, 1911.

31 De institutione grammatica libri tres, Venetiis, apud Iacobem Vitalem, 1575. 4°
BOD Vet. F1 e. 192 Acquired in 1976.

32 De institutione grammatica libri tres, Lugduni, apud Alexandrum Marsiliem Lucensem, 1580. 8°
SJCC Hh.1.68(3) With the college bookplate of 1710 (Adams A858).

33 De institutione grammatica libri tres, Mediolani, apud haeredes Francisci et Simonis Tini, 1595. 8°
BOD Byw. J 4.10 Bequeathed in 1914 by Ingram Bywater.

34 De institutione grammatica libri tres, Romae, apud Gulielmum Facciotum,1595. 8°
CUL Aa*.6.59 Part of the royal collection deposited in 1715 (Adams A859).

35 De institutione grammatica libri tres, Coloniae Agrippinae, in Officina Birckmannica, sumptibus Arnoldi Mylii, 1596. 4°
BOD (2 copies) 4° A 56 Art. Seld. From the Selden bequest of 1659; D 4.1 Linc. (Barlow bequest of 1691). A copy is recorded in the 1605 catalogue, but it is no longer identifiable. It may have been replaced by one of those listed above **BNC** Lath. B.8.6 Printed bookplate recording the gift of Henry Mason, prebendary of St Paul's and formerly a student of the college, who died in 1647. In the 17th-century catalogue with the shelf-mark L.12.6. Chain mark **CCCO** OO.3.13 Bequeathed by Richard Samways, fellow, who died in 1669.
CUL (3 copies) O*.4.31 (D) Acquired before 1715; Aa*.5.50; Aa*.10.29 both part of the Royal Library, deposited in 1715 **CLA** R.7.6 With the college bookplate dated 1701, a medieval pastedown and a former shelf-mark D 19? on leading edge. In the catalogue of 1677–78 with the shelf-mark D.20 **PMC** 11.5.4 With the college bookplate of 1700. Erased signature, perhaps that of Henry Molle (?1597–1658), of King's (Adams A860).

36 De institutione grammatica libri tres, *with additions by* Antonii Vellesii (António Velésio), Eborae, excudebat Emmanuel de Lyra typographus, 1599. 4°
BOD Marl. D 46 Annotations in ink and pencil. From the collection of William White, Master of Magdalen College School, who graduated from Wadham in 1625. Deposited in the Bodleian in 1985 (Anselmo 776).

37 De institutione grammatica libri tres, Romae, apud Bartholomaeum Zannettum, 1613. 16°

BOD Vet. F2 g.8 Acquired since 1937.

38 De institutione grammatica libri tres, Romae, apud Franciscum Caballum, 1637.
CUL M*.12.62 (G) Acquired before 1715.

39 De institutione grammatica, libri tres, *with additions by* Antonii Vellesii Ameensis, Vlissipone, apud Paulum Craesbeek, 1638. 8°
ASC g.12.28.

40 Grammatica siue institutionum linguae latinae liber primus [-secundus], Antuerpiae, apud Ioach. Trognaesium, 1609. 8°
BOD Marl. L 40 From the collection of William White, Master of Magdalen College School, who graduated from Wadham in 1625. Deposited in the Bodleian in 1985.

41 Grammatica sive institutionum linguae latinae, Antuerpiae, (Liber 1) Jacobus Meursius, (Liber 2) Martinus Nutius, 1680 (Liber 1), 1636 (Liber 2). 8°
WAD E 37.14 Bequeathed by Alexander Thistlethwaite, who had been a student of the college, in 1771.

Andrade, António de (Andrada)

42 Prosigue el descubrimiento del gran Catayo, o Reynos del gran Thibet, Segovia, Diego Flamenco, 1628. 8°
BOD Arch. Seld. A subt. 11 From the Selden bequest of 1659. One of a collection of pamphlets. For letters by this author included in compilations see Appendix 1.

Andrade, Diogo Paiva de (1528–75) (Payva Dandrada)

An Augustinian whose career as a writer gained enormously from his period at Trent, where he arrived in 1561. He earned the admiration of Pius IV for his ability as a theologian and was commissioned to write a refutation (**48–9**) of the writings of the German Lutheran Martin Chemnitz, who was an observer at the early meetings of the council. Though not a Jesuit himself, he took up their cause against Chemnitz on the grounds that in Portugal the Jesuits were a national institution, responsible for the education of the King (see Praefatio, fol. 4). His book was printed in the same year in Venice and Cologne and was apparently widely read in Germany (see the licence issued by Frei Bartolomeu Ferreira in **44**). All this must have prepared the ground for the great success of his second book in Oxford and Cambridge (**44–6**). Of this there are at least twenty copies, of which all but one arrived in the early modern period. Nearly all were printed in Germany, and a mere three are of the Lisbon edition. John Foxe probably owned a copy. Jerónimo Osório contributed an address to the Christian reader of the book, which must have increased sales, since by that time Osório was well

known in England. (Further discussion in Chapter One). Andrade is invariably described as 'Lusitano' on the title-page of his books.
José da Costa, *Portugal no Concílio de Trento*, IV, pp. 146–7; Manuel Augusto Rodrigues, 'Algumas notas sobre a vida e a obra de Diogo de Paiva de Andrade'.

43 Concio habita ad patres in concilio Tridentino congregatos, Brixiae, apud Ioannem Baptistam Bozolae, (BOD 4° C36(3) Th: Venetiis, apud Iordanum Ziletum), 1562. 4°

BOD (5 copies) 4° C36 (3) Th. This copy is listed in the 1620 catalogue; 4° A 28(24) Th.; 4° A 84(23) Th. BS. The shelf-mark suggests that it was acquired after 1650, Wheeler, p. 288; Antiq. e.I. 8(21) Formerly 4° S 159 and entered the Bodleian between 1826 and 1850; Vet. F1 e. 215(15) From the library of Lincoln's Inn and entered the Bodleian after 1937 **CCCO** LE.14.32(6) Imperfect but complete copy which continues at end of the volume in item no. 56. Chain mark.

CUL C.11.55 (10) Probably a recent acquisition, signed J. F. Van de Velde (Adams A1020).

44 Defensio Tridentinae fidei catholicae et integerrimae quinque libris compraehensa, Olysippone, per Antonium Riberium, 1578. 4°

WAD i13.22 Given by Dr Philip Bisse, July 1613. Slight annotation in liber V.

G&C F.33.34 Bequeathed by William Branthwaite, Master, in 1619. He was one of the revisers of the Bible. MS. note at end keyed to marginal notes to Book 3, fols 190–207, 'De libris canonicis'. Further notes to Book 4, about the Vulgate, on fols 247–51. Note in Hebrew fol. 260v. Binding with blind-stamped centrepiece made around 1600, but not the same as **48**. MS. pastedown. In earlier times **44** and **48** were shelved consecutively **PET** L.1.41 Cambridge centrepiece binding, with MS. binding strips at front board. Bequeathed by Andrew Perne, Master, in 1589 (Adams A1022; Anselmo 937).

45 Defensio Tridentinae fidei Catholicae et integerrimae quinque libris comprehensa, Coloniae, apud Maternum Cholinum, 1580. 8°

BOD Antiq. f.G. 1580.2 Given by All Souls College in 1928. The book is listed in the college's catalogue of 1665–89 **CCCO** E.7A.6 Bequeathed by Richard Cobb, Bachelor of Theology and fellow, who died in 1597. Chain mark **CHC** (2 copies) Hyp.N.5 The shelf-mark also appears on the leading edge, suggesting that it was acquired in the 17th century; Th.D.3 Bought with money given by Otho Nicolson in 1613. Nicolson was a benefactor with no obvious connection to the college (Hiscock, pp. 6–7).

CUL F*.14.5 (F) Acquired before 1715, marginal marks **SID** N.7.38 In the catalogue of 1674. With the title on the top edge, a practice which continued until the 1640s (Rogers, p. 78), and also on the fore-edge (Adams A1025).

46 Defensio Tridentinae fidei Catholicae et integerrimae quinque libris comprehensa, Ingolstadij, apud Dauidem Sartorium, 1580. 8°

BOD (2 copies) 8° A 5 Th. Belonged to Gilbert Hawthorne of Corpus who matriculated in 1588. In the 1605 catalogue with the current shelf-mark; 8° G 16 Linc. From the Barlow bequest of 1691 **MGO** Q.03.24 Bequeathed by Arthur Throckmorton, who gave many foreign books to the library, in 1626. Chain marks **JSO** F. 10. 19 With the signature of Robert Bryan **NEW** BT3.145.5 Oxford binding, Ker no. 1106, using roll xii, which was in use 1575–1621 (Pearson, p. 67). Probably to be identified with the copy given by Arthur Lake in 1617 on leaving to become bishop of Bath and Wells. In the catalogue of 1686 **UNI** K.38.8 Perhaps a sixteenth-century binding. Evidence of chaining.

CUL (2 copies) Acton. d.6.30 Lord Acton's library was presented in 1902; 7.39.55 Bequeathed by John Hackett, Bishop of Lichfield (1592–1670) **EMM** S3.5.37 Bequeathed by Archbishop William Sancroft in 1693 **MGC** D.7.5 With blind-stamped binding and printed waste as paste-down, suggesting that the book was acquired around 1600 **SJCC** Uu.15.26 From the Crashawe collection, deposited in 1624, and in the catalogue compiled around 1640 (Adams A1024).

47 De Societatis Iesv origine libellvs, Lovanii, apud Rutgerum Velpium, 1566. 8°

BOD 8° G 66a Th. MS. notes and underlining. It came from the library of the Augustinian monastery in Ingolstadt, which suggests that it was not an early acquisition **CHC** WD.8.5 From the Wake bequest of 1737, with annotations by someone hostile to Jesuits. This copy and the Bodleian one are bound with **464**.

CUL Acton e.6.13 Lord Acton's library was presented in 1902 (Adams A1021 and I110).

48 Orthodoxarum explicationum libri decem, Venetiis, ex officina Iordani Zileti, 1564. 4°

BOD Antiq. e.I. 1564.2, acquired between 1883 and 1936 **CHC** Hyp.G.44 Bought with mony given by Otho Nicolson in 1613. Nicolson was a benefactor with no obvious connection to the college (Hiscock, pp. 6–7). **QUO** UU. k. 230 Marginal notes.

G&C F.34.29 Bequeathed by William Branthwaite, Master, in 1619. He was one of the revisers of the Bible. For the binding see **44**. MS. pastedown **TRC** E.8.54 (Adams A1027).

49 Orthodoxarum explicationum libri decem, Coloniae, apud Maternum Cholinum, 1564. 8°

BOD 8° A 4 Th. In the 1605 catalogue with the current shelf-mark. The gift of Gilbert Hawthorne of Corpus, who matriculated in 1588 **MGO** Q.5.20 Bequeathed by Arthur Throckmorton, who gave many foreign books to the library, in 1626. Chain marks.

CUL (3 copies) F*.15.26 (F), with motto and date 1582 on title page; Peterborough F.2.46 With a note on the flyleaf 'Andradius Payva a Doctor of Portugall is ye best learned man (in my opinion) of all ye Papistes'. (For Peterborough Cathedral Library, see the Introduction, p. xiv); Hhh.26, probably acquired in the 19th century **SJCC** Uu.15.24 From the Crashawe collection, deposited in 1626, and in the 1640s catalogue; some MS. notes (Adams A1026).

Andrade or Andrada, Diogo de Paiva (the younger) (1576–1660)
Son of Francisco de Andrade and nephew of Diogo Paiva de Andrade. None of his Latin poems or plays, or his moralistic writing in Portuguese reached early modern Oxford or Cambridge. In **50**, which is a historical work, he is critical of Bernardo de Brito's *Monarquia Lusitana* (**135**).

Biblos: *Enciclopédia Verbo das Literaturas de Língua Portuguesa*, I, cols 261–2.

50 Exame d'antiguidades, Lisboa, Iorse (*sic*) Rodriguez, 1616. 4°

ASC III.7.13 Some 17th-century notes in Portuguese and underlining, which indicate that it is unlikely to be an early acquisition. Perhaps bought at the Stuart sale in 1821. **CUL** Ee.6.64. Rebound in 1964.

Andrade (or Andrada), Francisco de (1540?–1614)
Poet and historian. No complete original work in Portuguese by him reached early modern Oxford or Cambridge. However, he placed six chapters of his own about the history of the Turks, compiled from various sources, at the start of his translation of Marinus Barletius's chronicle of the fifteenth-century Albanian hero Scanderbeg. See the preface to King Sebastião of **51**. The book is one of the very few in Portuguese to have been in the Bodleian since 1605. It is bound with John Pory's translation of Leo the Moor's *A Geographical Historie of Africa* (London: George Bishop, 1600). Pory made use of Portuguese material and had some knowledge of the language (see Chapter One, p. xlii).
Biblos: Enciclopédia Verbo das Literaturas de Língua Portuguesa, I, cols 273–4.

51 Chronica do valeroso principe & invencivel Capitão Iorge Castrioto . . . escrita em Latim por Marino Barlecio Scutarino, *translated into Portuguese by Andrade*, Lisboa, em casa de Marcos Borges, 1567. Fol.
BOD CC 4(2) Art., formerly P.4.9. Art, chain marks. It is listed in the 1620 catalogue with the shelf-mark P.4.9 and in the 1605 catalogue with a different shelf-mark (Anselmo 367).

Anjos, Luís dos (1591–1625)
An Augustinian. The only copy of his work in either Oxford or Cambridge is in the Bodleian and was acquired recently. Devotional works of this kind in the vernacular were of little interest to readers in the early modern period.
Inocêncio, V, 209–10.

52 Iardim de Portugal, em que se da noticia de alguas sanctas, & outras molheres illustres em virtude, Coimbra, em casa de Nicolao Coutinho, 1626. 4°
BOD Vet. G2 e. 18 Acquired in 1981.

António, Prior do Crato (1531–95)
Dom António, illegitimate son of Prince Luís, was a pretender to the Portuguese throne after the death of King Sebastião in 1578. Forced into exile after Philip II had become king, he spent several periods in the 1580s in England, where Elizabeth I gave him some support. There are doubts as to whether he wrote **54** (Peixoto, pp. 52–4), but it did well, in Latin and various vernaculars. Other writers associated with his cause were of interest in the early modern period (see António de Sena and José Teixeira).
Dicionário de história de Portugal, I, pp. 157–9; Jorge Peixoto, *Relações de Plantin com Portugal.*

53 Excellent et libre discours du droict de la succession royale au royaume de Portugal, *tr. from Latin by Iean Micard, with letters by and to Dom António, Prior do Crato*, Paris, chez Iean Micard, 1606–7. 12°

BOD 8° B 63(2) Art.
SID L.7.19 In the anonymous section of the catalogue of 1674, under 'Portugallia'. With the title on the top edge, a practice which continued until the 1640s (Rogers, p. 78) TRC W.12.87 Probably acquired after 1800. At one point it belonged to an Italian, Giacinto Castelvetri, resident in London.

54 Explanatio veri . . . juris, quo serenissimus Lusitaniae rex Antonius . . . primus nititur, ad bellum Philippo regi Castellae pro regni recuperatione inferendum, Lugduni Batavorum, in typographia Christopheri Plantini, 1585. 4°

BOD (3 copies) 4° K 2(8) Jur. Robert Burton bequest of 1640 (Kiessling (1988) 40); 4° B 18(2) Art BS; 4° D 5(10) Jur. Seld. From the Selden bequest of 1659 SJCC HB4/4.a.6.14(2).
CUL (2 copies) Dd*.3.10 (E); Dd*.3.32 (E) both with the bookplate of the Royal Library which was deposited in 1715 TRC P.7.148[1] With a large 33 on the fore-edge and evidence of a paper tab, indicating that it was in the library in the 1660s (Gaskell, pp. 97, 103). Bound with a number of other short works, none later than 1637. See **57** (Adams A1243).

55 [Explanatio veri . . . juris] Iustificatie van den doorluchtighen . . ., Dordrecht, Peeter Verhagen, 1585. 4°

CUL Gg.15.65(9), in a volume of Dutch pamphlets from the 16th and 17th centuries (Adams A1245).

56 [Explanatio veri . . . juris] The explanation of the true and lawfull right . . ., Leyden [i.e. London], Christopher Plantyn, [i.e. Thomas Purfoot?],1585. 4°

BOD 55 d.156 (STC 689.3) SJCO P.scam.1.lower shelf. 9(7).
EMM S14.2.42 (3) Bequeathed by Archbishop William Sancroft, 1693. SJCC Hh.3.25(5).

57 [Explanatio veri . . . juris] Iustification du serenissime don Antonio roi de Portugal premier de ce nom, touchant la guerre qu'il faict à Philippe roi de Castille, ses subiectz & adherens, pour estre remis en son roiaume. Auec vne histoire, summaire de tout ce qui s'est passé à ceste mesme occasion, iusques en l'an M.D.LXXXIII inclusiuement. A Leyde, en l'imprimerie de Christophle Plantin., 1585. 4°

MER 75.G.3(2). Part of the bequest of Griffin Higgs (1589–1659) fellow (Morrish 12).
TRC W.15.137[3] Marginal marks and notes in French. It was probably in the library in the 1660s, as there is a large 32 on the fore-edge and vestiges of a paper tab (Gaskell, pp. 97, 103). Bound with other short works, all of the 16th century. See **54** (Adams A1244).

Apresentação, Egídio de (1539–1626) (Aegidius de Praesentatione)
An Augustinian and professor at Coimbra. It is likely that seven of the nine copies of **58–9** are of early provenance, which is unusual for books

published in Portugal but not elsewhere. There may be a connection to the the work of another Coimbra Augustinian and writer on scholastic theology, Manuel de Lacerda, also published by Gomes de Loureiro (**504**).
Barbosa Machado, I, 747–9.

58 De immaculata beatae Virginis conceptione ab omni originali peccato immuni libri quatuor, Conimbricae, apud Didacum Gomez de Loureyro, 1617. Fol.
BOD E 5.14 Th. Bound with **59**, vol. 3 **QUO** 62. B. 6. 17th-century binding and chain marks.
CUL E*.10.3(C) Acquired before 1715.

59 Disputationes de animae, et corporis beatitudine. Ad priores quinque quaestiones primae secundae D.Thomae, & ad quaestionum 12. primae partis, Conimbricae, ex officina Didaci Gomez Loureyo, 1609–15. 3 vol. Fol.
BOD E 5.12–14 Th. **CHC** O.C.2.14, 3 vols in 1. Part of the Orrery bequest of 1732 **JSO** F.5.11–13 In the 1649 catalogue. Presented by Lady Maria Cockayne, widow of Sir William Cockayne, Lord Mayor of London, between 1626 and 1630 **QUO** 54. B. 22–24 17th-century binding.
CUL G*.10.4 (C) Acquired before 1715 **SJCC** O.5.5 Given by Thomas Morton (1564– 1659), bishop successively of Chester, Lichfield and Durham.

Augustinian order

60 Ordinario dos canonicos regulares da ordem do . . . padre S. Augustinho, Lisboa, per Ioam Fernandez, 1579. 4°
CUL F157.d.12.1 Acquired in 1957 (Adams L994; Anselmo 547).

61 Ordinario dos religiosos eremitas de nosso p. s. Agostinho da prouincia de Portugal, Lisboa, impresso por Pedro Crasbecke, 1605. 4°
BOD Vet. G2 e.16 Acquired after 1937.

Aveiro, Pantaleão de (1520?–)

A Franciscan, who made his journey to the Holy Land in 1561. Early modern libraries acquired very few accounts of journeys in Portuguese, and Frei Pantaleão's book probably did not reach either Oxford or Cambridge until the late nineteenth century.
Luís Graça, *A visão do oriente*, pp. 19–22.

62 Itinerario de terra sancta, e suas particularidades, Lisboa, em casa de Simão Lopez, 1593. 4°
TAY Finch.H.69 The title page is torn. Part of the Martin bequest of 1895.
TRC U.19.20 probably a recent acquisition (Anselmo 798).

Aviz, Order of

63 Regra da cavalaria e ordem militar de S. Bento de Avis, Lisboa, por Yorge Roiz, 1631. Fol.
BOD Vet. G2 d.7 Acquired after 1937 **TAY** Vet. Port. I C.8, acquired in 1936.

Azambuja, Frei Jerónimo de (Hieronymus ab Oleandro) (–1563)
A Dominican, he matriculated at Louvain in 1536. He was present at the Council of Trent, 1545–9, but the rest of his career was spent in Portugal. He was particularly active in the Inquisition. Cambridge University Library has two copies of part of his commentary on the Pentateuch in the first, Portuguese editions (**64–5**), but the complete work only arrived in force in early modern Oxford as well as Cambridge after it had been reprinted in Antwerp and Lyon. His commentary on Isaiah was first published in Paris long after his death, at the instigation of the Portuguese provincial, Pedro Calvo. The French editor Hezecque, also a Dominican, complains in his letter to the reader that the manuscript had been damaged by sea-water on its journey from Portugal. In **66** and **68** Azambuja is described as 'Lusitanus', and in **67** as inquisitor in Lisbon. For the commentary on Isaiah Azambuja prepared his own translation, which he compares with the Vulgate. Of the twenty-five copies of books by him in Oxford and Cambridge twenty-two were acquired in the early modern period. He was a figure of interest, and even some sympathy to Protestant theologians because his books, written before the new orthodoxy of the Counter-Reformation had become established, were subjected to a strict censorship (see Chapter One, pp. xxxiii-iv).
Luís de Matos, *Portugais à Paris,* p. 88; José de Castro, *Portugal no Concílio de Trento,* II, pp. 80–90.

64 Commentaria in Leviticum, Olisipone, apud Ioannem Blavium, 1557. Fol.
CUL F*.4.36 (C) Acquired before 1715. Bound with **65** and **730** (Adams O153; Anselmo 321).

65 Commentaria in librum Deuteronimi, Olysipone, ex officina Ioannis Blavii, 1558. Fol.
CUL (2 copies) F*.4.36 (C) Acquired before 1715. Bound with **64** and **730**; Qq.2.6 (B) Bound with **66** (Adams O154; Anselmo 323).

66 Commentaria in Mosi Pentateuchum, Antuerpiae, in aedibus Viduae & Haeredum Ioannis Stelsij, 1568–69. Fol.
CCCO GG.4.16 Entered Corpus 6 July 1612, chain mark **CHC** Allestree B.2.3 From the Allestree bequest of 1681 **NEW** BT3.118.8 Oxford binding, Ker centrepiece xvii, in use 1600–25 (Pearson, p. 80). Evidence of chaining. In the catalogue of 1686.
CUL Qq.2.6 (B), formerly E.3.19. Evidence of a paper tab, suggesting that it was acquired in the 17th century. Bound with **65 G&C** F.15.14. Bequeathed by William

Branthwaite, Master, in 1619. He was one of the revisers of the Bible. 17th-century
Cambridge binding with fillets (Adams O148–9).

67 Commentaria in Pentateuchum Mosi, 2a editio, Lugduni, apud
Petrum Landry, 1586. Fol.
    BOD M 4.1 Th. Deposited in 1596. In the 1605 catalogue. Part of the Mascarenhas
collection (see Foreword, p. xvi) **QUO** 78.D.4 Oxford binding. Ker no. 1360, in use 1565–
1620 (Pearson, p. 75) **WAD** J 1.25 Given by Dr Philip Bisse, 1613.
    CUL E*.3.19 (B) Edition dated 1588. Bequeathed by John Hacket, Bishop of
Lichfield (1592–1670), with a note at the end indicating that it was in England by
1630 **EMM** 301.3.2 (with date of publication 1588) Bequeathed by Dr John Richardson,
in 1626. He was one of the translators of the Bible **PMC** 3.9.38 Given by Lancelot
Andrewes, bishop of Winchester, in 1589 and with his signature. The binding has a
blind-stamped centrepiece **SJCC** Pp.1.20 Part of the Crashawe collection, deposited in
1626 **SID** O.2.15 **TRC** D.4.53 Binding with gilt armorial centrepiece stamped E S,
bequeathed by Sir Edward Stanhope, who had been a fellow from 1564 to 1572, in 1608
(Adams O150–2).

68 In Isaiam prophetam commentarii, Lutetiae Parisiorum, sumptibus
Sebastiani Cramoisy, 1622. Fol.
    BOD L 7.9(2) Th. In the 1635 appendix to the 1620 catalogue **BNC** Lath. G.1.6,
formerly R.4.6. In the 17th-century catalogue with the old shelf-mark R.4.6. Chain mark.
Oxford binding, Ker rolls xvii and xxi, associated with the bookbinder Roger Barnes, who
died in 1630, Ker, p. 213, Pearson, p. 127 **MGO** d.11.3 Chain marks, indicating that it was
acquired in the 17th century **ORI** A.e.19 Chain mark, indicating that it was acquired in
the 17th century. In both the 17th-century catalogues **QUO** 76.c.17 Bought with money
left by Robert Mason in 1841.
    CUL F*.3.6 (B) Acquired before 1715 **SJCC** Pp.5.18, bought with money given by John
Carey, Earl of Dover (1608–77) **TRC** D.17.29 Binding with gilt armorial centrepiece
stamped M S. The crest is that of the Stanhope family, so this book was given by Sir
Michael. He left money to the college for the purchase of books in 1625 (Gaskell,
p. 128 n.1), but he clearly gave books also, perhaps influenced by his brother's interests
(see **67**).

Baptista, João (o Feio) (16th century)
A Franciscan friar, of whom otherwise nothing is known.

69 Calendairo romano perpetuo, [Lisbon], impresso por Antonio
Ribeiro, 1588. 8°
    BOD 8° O 30 Th. In the 1674 catalogue. One previous Portuguese owner, perhaps
Diogo Frances (Anselmo 978).

Barbosa, Agostinho (1590–1649)
An extremely productive canonist, whose works were eagerly sought
after in Oxford and in Cambridge. Of the thirty copies of books by him
in the Bodleian and Oxford college libraries twenty-five were acquired
in the seventeenth or early eighteenth centuries. In Cambridge there
appear to be only thirteen, but the figure is misleading, as Trinity Hall
alone has eleven books by him, mostly in editions printed after 1640

(and so not included in this catalogue). The licences printed in **79** (Rome, 1631; Lyon, 1632; Venice, 1635) show that there was often great competition to publish his work. The years that he spent in Rome were particularly important for his intellectual development. He published **82** in Lisbon in 1618, suggesting that he had not yet left for Italy, but he must have done so not long afterwards, as in the dedication of **73** to Urban VIII, composed in 1626, he speaks of himself as having been in Rome for more than five years 'iam altero abhinc lustro'. In the same document he explains how for him Rome was a place for study, especially of law, and the praise of Rome was a theme he returned to more than once (in **77**, Ad lectorem, and **87**, dedication to Olivares). According to the secretary of Agustín Spínola, Archbishop of Santiago, writing in 1635 **(81)**, the Iberian Peninsula seemed like a prison to Barbosa, but he was certainly in Spain in the 1630s and in Lisbon at least for a while around 1634, from where he signed the dedication of **70**, to Dom Miguel de Castro, Bishop of Viseu. On the title-pages of his books he is invariably described by some form of the word 'Lusitanus', and he certainly needed to maintain some contact with Portugal, for he was able to live abroad thanks to being treasurer of the cathedral of Guimarães, a position made available to him by Paul V a month after his arrival in Rome (see the Ad lectorem of **77**). At his death he was bishop of Unguento, in Otranto.

Fortunato de Almeida, *História da Igreja em Portugal,* II, p. 576.

70 Collectanea bullarii, Lugduni, sumptibus Laurentii Durand, 1637. 4°
MGO G.08.10, Chain marks. In the benefactors' register as having been acquired in 1639.

71 Collectanea doctorum, qui suis in operibus Concilii Tridentini loca referentes, illorum materiam incidenter tractarunt, Lugduni, sumptibus Laurentii Durand, 1634. 4°
BOD 4° P 41 Jur. In the 1674 catalogue **MGO** h.07.11 Chain marks. In the benefactors' register as having been acquired in 1639 **QUO** II.d.678.

72 Collectanea doctorum tam veterum quam recentiorum, in ius pontificium vniuersum . . . in quo duo priores decretalium libri continentur, Lugduni, sumptibus Laurentii Durand, 1636–37. 5 vols. Fol.
BOD T 11.3–7 Jur. In MS. additions to 1620 catalogue **MGO** F.5.3–7 All with chain marks. In benefactors' register as having been acquired in 1639 **NEW** BTI.90.3–7. In the catalogue of 1686.
QUC H.1.5-, formerly 8.1.5, H.a.16. Same binding and pastedowns as **74**, and with the author's name on the fore-edge. In the catalogue of the 1680s with the shelf-mark H.1.5 **TRH** M*.4.12 and 14 (vols 1,4,5 in 2). With the college bookplate of 1700.

73 Collectanea doctorum tam veterum, quam recentiorum, qui super rubricas, textus, & glossas pontificii, & caesarei iuris vniuersi . . . scripserunt, Romae, ex typographia Reuerendae Camerae Apostolicae, 1626. 2 vols. Fol.

BOD A 5.7,8 Jur. In the 1635 appendix to the 1620 catalogue **ASC** bb.1.14–15 Chain mark. Bought with money left by John Jessop, who was elected as a fellow in 1572.

74 Collectanea ex doctoribus tum priscis, tum neotericis in codicem Justiniani, Ludguni, sumptibus Gabrielis Boissat, & sociorum, 1637–8. 2 vols. Fol.

BOD T 11.8,9 Jur. MS. addition to the 1620 catalogue **MGO** F.5.8–9 Chain marks. The final vol. has signature of Thomas / John Head and drawings.

QUC H.4.23-. 17th-century Cambridge binding with fillets and with a pastedown with text in English. The author's name and an abridged title appear on the fore-edge. In the catalogue of the 1680s with the shelf-mark H.4.29.

75 De canonicis et dignitatibus, aliisque inferioribus beneficiariis cathedralium, & collegiatarum ecclesiarum, Lugduni, sumptibus Laurentii Durand, 1634. 4°

BOD 4° H 7 Jur. In the 1674 catalogue **JSO** A.8.5 Gall From the bequest of Sir Leoline Jenkins, lawyer and diplomat, 1685 **MGO** k.05.12 Chain mark. In the benefactors' register as having been acquired in 1639.

TRC N.7.41 With the bookplate of John Colbatch, Anglican chaplain in Portugal from 1693–1700, who died in 1748.

76 Iuris ecclesiastici vniuersi libri tres, Lugduni, sumptibus Laurentii Durand, 1634. Fol.

ASC aa.7.8 Chain mark Listed in the catalogue of 1665–89 **MGO** F.05.11. In the benefactors' register as having been acquired in 1639. Chain mark **SJCO** U.3.2 Given by John Harflett on graduating B.A. in 1622.

77 Pastoralis solicitudinis, siue de officio et potestate episcopi, tripartita descriptio, Parisiis, apud Michaelem Somnium, 1625. Fol.

BOD B 4.2 Jur. In the 1635 appendix to the 1620 catalogue.

CUL G*.1.15(B) Acquired before 1715 **SJCO** K.4.12 Bought with money given by John Carey, Earl of Dover, in 1677 **TRH** M*.4.15. With the college bookplate of 1700.

78 Pastoralis solicitudinis, siue de officio et potestate episcopi, tripartita descriptio . . ., Lugduni, sumptibus Laurentii Durand, 1628. Fol.

NEW BTI.90.2 In the catalogue of 1686 **QUO** 34.B.19 With the signature of Joannes Morphy sacerdos.

79 Pastoralis solicitudinis, siue, de officio et potestate parochi, tripartita descriptio, Venetiis, ex typographiia Iaconi Sarzinae, 1635. 4°

BOD 4° H 8 Jur. In the 1674 catalogue **CHC** OH.4.21 Binding stamped Edward Gwynn, with initials on back cover. He matriculated in 1671, aged 18, and took his BA in 1675–76.

80 Pastoralis solicitudinis, siue, de officio, et potestate parochi tripartita descriptio, 3a editio, Lugduni, sumptibus Laurentii Durand et Laurentii Arnaud, M.DC.XL.X [really 1640]. Fol.
BOD Vet. E2 c.11 (2) Acquired after 1937.
CUL H.2.42 With the bookplate of the Royal Library, deposited in 1715.

81 Praxis exigendi pensiones contra calumniantes, & differentes illas soluere, Lvgdvni, sumptibus Laurentii Durand, 1636. 4°
BOD 4° P 40 Jur. In the catalogue of 1674 **MGO** h.09.13 Chain mark. In the benefactors' register as having been acquired in 1639.
TRH K*.3.8. With the college bookplate of 1700.

82 Remissiones doctorum, qui varia loca Concilii Tridentini incidenter tractarunt, Ulyssipone, ex officina Petri Craesbeeck, 1618. 8°
BOD 4° B 21 Th. Seld. From the Selden bequest of 1659. In the 1674 catalogue.

83 Remissiones doctorum, qui varia loca Concilii Tridentini incidenter tractarunt, Lugduni, sumptibus Horatii Cardon, 1619. 8°
BOD 8° B 22 Jur. Seld. From the Selden bequest of 1659. In the 1674 catalogue.

84 Sacrosancti Concilii Tridentini canones et decreta . . . cum . . . remissionibus Augustini Barbosae, Coloniae, sumptibus Antonii Hierati, 1620.
SJCC S.9.32 Bequeathed by Peter Gunning, Master, in 1684.

85 Sacrosancti Concilium Tridentinum, additis . . . remissionibus Augustini Barbosae, Lugduni, sumptibus Iacobi Cardon, 1631.
CUL H.4.21 With the bookplate of the Royal Library, deposited in 1715.

86 Tractatus de canonicis, et dignitatibus, aliisque inferioribus beneficiariis cathedralium, & collegiatarum ecclesiarum, 3a editio, Lugduni, sumptibus Laurentii Durand, et Laurentii Arnaud, 1640. Fol.
BOD Vet. E2 c.11 (1) The binding is stamped Edward Gwynn, of Christ Church, who matriculated in 1671, aged 18, and took his BA in 1675–76. The book, at one time in Ely Cathedral Library, was acquired by the Bodleian in 1975.
CUL H.2.42 With the bookplate of the Royal Library, deposited in 1715.

87 Variae tractationes iuris in quibus continentur quinque tractatus legales, Lugduni, sumptibus Laurentii Durand, 1631. Fol.
CHC WS.2.4 Included in the catalogue of the Wake bequest, which entered the library in 1737 **MGO** F.05.10 Chain marks. In the benefactors' register as having been acquired in 1639.
CCCC SP.199. In the Parker register, p. 95, but received after Archbishop Matthew Parker's death in 1575 **SJCC** Ll.13.14 (1) **Squire Law Library** E.9.8

Barbosa, Aires (1470?—1540), editor

He is said to have introduced the study of Greek to the Iberian Peninsula. He studied in Salamanca and later, under Poliziano, in Florence. From 1495–1523 he taught at Salamanca before returning to Portugal as tutor

to the royal princes. The only book by him to have arrived in either Oxford or Cambridge in the early modern period is this edition of Arator's Latin poem on the Acts of the Apostles. His nationality is stated on the title-page.
Dicionário de história de Portugal, I, pp. 297–8 (article by Luís de Matos).

88 Aratoris cardinalis Historia apostolica, cum comentariis Arii Barbosae, Salmanticae, in aedibus Ioannis de Porris, 1516. Fol.
BOD A 14.4 Th. Formerly A 6.6 Th. In the 1605 catalogue with the old shelf-mark (Fidalgo 112).

Barbosa, Duarte (–1546/47)

Customs official in the port of Cananor in south India, and author of a pioneering account of the geography, ethnography and commerce of Asia, remarkable for its freedom from Eurocentric prejudice. It was complete in manuscript in 1516, though additions were made later. It was first published by Ramusio, in Italian, and it was through Ramusio that the book became known to early modern Oxford and Cambridge (**743–8**). Ramusio's version is based on the Portuguese original and on a Spanish translation.
O Livro de Duarte Barbosa, I, p. 36.
Duarte Barbosa, [O Livro de Duarte Barbosa] Libro di Ododardo Barbosa Portoghese.

Barbosa, Pedro (–1606)

A lawyer, who was a professor in Coimbra, a judge in Lisbon and a member of the royal council, under Kings Sebastião and Henrique. Towards the end of his life, under the Dual Monarchy, he served in Madrid, and his *Tractatus absolutissimi* are dedicated to Philip II. All his published work dates from this period. Some of his books were published posthumously, by his son, Miguel de Vasoncelos y Brito, and by his nephew, Pedro Barbosa de Luna. In his dedication of **91** to Dom Alonso Hurtado de Mendoça, Archbishop of Braga, Miguel hints that his father was murdered. The title-pages of his books state that he was Portuguese.
Grande Enciclopédia Portuguesa e Brasileira, IV, p. 198.

89 Commentarii ad interpretationem tituli, ff. de iudiciis, Francofurti, e Collegio Musarum novenarum Paltheniano, 1615. Fol.
BOD B 7.11 Jur. Chain mark.

90 Commentariorum ad interpretationem tituli ff. soluto matrimonio, quemadmodum dos petatur, Madrid, apud Ludovicum Sanchez, 1595. Fol.
BOD MM 16,17 Jur. 2nd series In the 1605 catalogue **SJCO** U.3.32 Given by Sir William Paddy in 1633.

91 Memorial de la preferencia que haze el reyno de Portugal, y su conseio, al de Aragon, y de las dos Sicilias, Lisboa, Geraldo de Vinha, 1627. 4°
CUL Hisp. 7.62.4 Acquired in 1912.

92 Tractatus absolutissimi . . . Commentando in tit. ff. soluto matrimon. quemadmod. dos pet. incidentibus, Francofurti, e Collegio Musarum Paltheniano, 1606. 2 vols in 1. Fol.
BOD B 4.1 Jur. Chain mark.

93 Tractatus absolutissimi . . . Commentando in tit. ff. soluto matrimon. . . ., Francofurti, sumptibus haeredum D. Zachariae Palthenii, typis Hartmanni Palthenii, 1625. Fol.
JSO F.5.12 Gall. Part of the bequest of Sir Leoline Jenkins, lawyer and diplomat, 1685.

Barbuda, Luís Coelho (16th–17th centuries)
A historian, of whom little is known.

94 Empresas militares de Lusitanos, Lisboa, por Pedro Craesbeeck, 1624. 8°
BOD 243 f.31 Acquired from another library after 1864.

Barradas, Sebastião (1542–1615)
A Jesuit, whose career seems to have been spent entirely in the universities of Évora and Coimbra. He did not need to study or work abroad to be immensely successful in the English universities, perhaps the most successful of all Portuguese writers if we measure success by the speed with which his work arrived. The Mainz edition of his *Commentaria in concordiam et historiam evangelicam* (**96**) appeared over a period of fourteen years between 1601 and 1615, and six Oxford libraries acquired one or more volumes during the course of publication. Copies reached Cambridge a little later. The eagerness of the Bodleian was such that before 1605 it obtained a manuscript (MS Bodl. 112) of parts of the book not yet printed. Altogether there are forty-five copies of the multi-volume *Commentaria* and of other works by Barradas in Oxford and Cambridge, of which thirty-six are of early provenance. All the title-pages describe him as 'Olisiponensis'.
Barbosa Machado, III, pp. 680–1; Falconer Madan and H. H. E. Craster, *Summary Catalogue of Western MSS in the Bodleian Library* II, Part 1, 1965.

95 Opera omnia, Moguntiae, sumptibus Hermanni Mylii Birckmanni, 1627. Fol.
JSO C.6.9–10 QUO 60.F.10 Two vols in one. Given by Thomas Wethereld, fellow, in 1636 UNI G.12.5 Tomus 5 only, Itinerarium filiorum Israel WOR TT.1.7–8. With the printed sale note of a London bookseller, C. J. Stewart, indicating that the book was probably acquired in the 19th century.

96 Commentaria in concordiam et historiam Euangelicam, Moguntiae, sumptibus Arnoldi Mylii, [in some copies] Hermanni Mylii, excudebat Balthasar Lippius, 1601–15. 4 vols. Fol.

BOD B 17.14–17 Th. In the 1605 catalogue, where vol. 2 is described as 'nondum excus. MS'. The MS. (MS. Bodl. 112) was given by Josiah White, fellow of New College ASC SR 8° d Bought in 1615, from the gift of William Raleigh, Warden CCCO LC.17.c.1–2 Vols 1 and 2 only, bequeathed by President John Reynolds, who died on 21 May 1607. Chain mark. Corpus's set is made up with **98 CHC** NC.3.2 One vol. only, dated in the colophon 1610 **MER** 83.HH.4–5 Ker Rolls xvii and xxi. They were used by Roger Barnes from the early 17th century until his death in 1631 (Pearson, p. 69). Chain mark. **NEW** BT3.113.9–10 4 vols in 2 Probably to be identified with the copy given by Arthur Lake in 1617, on leaving to become bishop of Bath and Wells. In the catalogue of 1686 **PMO** U5c Vols 3–4 only **SJCO** F.2.20 Acquired in 1613 with money left by Henry Price (1562–1600), fellow. St John's set is made up with **97 WAD** J.2.11–14 Given by Philip Bisse in 1613 (v. 1–4, v. 4 dated 1612).

CUL (2 copies) Z.14.1-, Z.14.5-, both with the bookplate of the Royal Library, deposited in 1715 **JSC** B.1.19 2 vols in 1. College bookplate of 1700 and in the catalogue of 1705 **KCC** A.28.24 **PMC** 7.3.14 (vols 1–2); 6.3.26–7 (vols 3–4) All given by Mark Frank, fellow, in 1662. Medieval pastedown and blind-stamped centrepiece of around 1600 **SID** O.3.18–21 (4 vols). In the catalogue of 1674. With the title on the top edge, a practice which continued until the 1640s, and on the fore-edge (Rogers, p. 78) **SJCC** P.4.1 (vols 1–2) Part of the Crashawe collection, deposited in 1626.

97 Commentariorvm in concordiam & historiam quatuor Euangelistarum, tomus tertius, Lvgdvni, sumptibus Horatij Cardon, 1608. Fol.

SJCO F.2.21–2 St John's set is made up with **96**.

98 Commentariorvm in concordiam & historiam Euangelicam, tomus primus [-quartus et ultimus], Lvgdvni, sumptibus Horatij Cardon, 1610–12. 4 vols. Fol.

CCCO LC.17.c.3 Vol. 4 only, which entered the library on 8 August 1612. Corpus's set is made up with **96 MGO** c.12.03–06 Chain marks and Oxford roll binding, roll no. XXVI, in use 1610–20. Stamped RW, i.e., the binder Robert Way (Pearson, p. 72). Acquired with money left by Nathaniel Vertue, fellow, who died in 1609.

CLA A1.2.7–10 With the 1701 college bookplate. In the catalogue of 1677–78 with the shelf-mark Aa. 13. The same shelf-mark appears on the fore-edge.

99 Commentaria in concordiam et historiam evangelicam, Antverpiae, apud Petrum, & Ioannem Belleros, et Socios, 1617. 4 vols. Fol.

CUL (2 copies) Z.14.7, Z.14.9, both with the bookplate of the Royal Library, deposited in 1715. In the catalogue of the library, with the shelf-mark C.1.35 **EMM** 303.2.49–50 (4 vols in 2), formerly G.1.1–2. With 17th-century Cambridge binding and evidence of a paper tab. Listed in the 18th-century catalogue, under G.1.1–2. This is a part of the catalogue including nothing printed after 1712, and it is reasonable to assume that the book was in the college before that date **QUC** L.2.2, formerly 9.5.2, N.b.1.17th-century Cambridge binding, with fillets and parchment pastedown. Author's name and abridged title on fore-edge. College bookplate of 1700. In the catalogue of the 1680s with the shelf-mark L.2.2.

100 Commentaria in concordiam et historiam evangelicam, Moguntiae, sumptibus Hermanni Mylii Birckmanni, excudebat Balthasar Lippius, 1618. Fol.

LIN K 2.23–4 4 vols in 2. With the college bookplate of 1703 and chain marks, indicating that it was acquired in the 17th century.
TRC C.16.4–5, 4 vols in 2. Bought with money left by Thomas Whalley, Fellow, in 1637. Binding stamped T W. Fore-edge numbers in black and red.

101 Commentaria in concordiam et historiam evangelicam, Antverpiae, apud Petrum, & Ioannem Belleros, et Socios, 1621–22. 4 vols. Fol.

HMAN F1621/3 Vol. 3 only. The title-page is missing. With the bookplate of Exeter Library, i.e. of Exeter Academy, extinguished in the late 18th century. It may have belonged earlier to an academy in Taunton (1670–1759). Harris Manchester College came to Oxford in 1889. Repaired 17th-century binding ORI B.c.20–22 Four vols in three. Bequeathed by John Tolson, 'nuper praepositi', in 1644. In both the 17th-century catalogues.
MGC B.11.8, formerly H.1.13, 2 vols in 1. 17th-century Cambridge binding with fillets.

102 Commentariorum in concordiam et historiam evangelicam tomus primus [-quartus], Lugduni, sumptibus Iacobi Cardon & Petri Cavellat, 1621–36. Fol.

UNI K.18.3–4, given by William Smith, fellow, in 1685.

103 Itinerarium filiorum Israel ex Aegypto in terram repromissionis, Lugduni, sumptibus Iacobi Cardon et Petri Cavellat, 1620. Fol.

BOD 5 DELTA 65 Entered the library between 1824 and 1861.

104 Itinerarium filiorum Israel ex Aegypto in terra repromissionis, Antuerpiae, apud Hieronymum Verdussium, [in some copies] apud Petrum & Ioannem Belleros, 1621. Fol.

BOD B 1.14(1) Th. In the 1635 appendix to the 1620 catalogue ASC S.R. 80.b.9 Oxford binding. Ker rolls xvii and xxi, used by Roger Barnes from the early 17th century to his death in 1631 (Pearson, p. 69). Chain mark and college note . . . 'empt. p. colleg.' JSO A.6.14 In the catalogue of 1649.
CUL F*.3.18 (B) Acquired before 1715 CHR B.8.18, formerly D.5.9 (so shelved close to 781, which was acquired in the early 17th century). With two college bookplates. 17th-century Cambridge binding with fillets EMM (2 copies) S8.3.40 Bequeathed by Archbishop William Sancroft in 1693; 309.1.29 JSC B.1.18 In the catalogue of 1705 QUC L.3.6, formerly 9.2.6, N.l.7 17th-century Cambridge binding with fillets. Paper pastedown. With the author's name on fore-edge and the college bookplate of 1700. In the catalogue of the 1680s with the shelf-mark L.3.6 SID R.2.6 In the catalogue of 1674. With the title on the top edge, a practice which continued until the 1640s (Rogers, p. 78) TRC D.4.59

Barreira, Isidoro de (–1634/48)

A member of the Order of Christ, represented here by a devotional work in Portuguese which was not of interest to the early modern universities.
Barbosa Machado, II, 916; Inocêncio, III, 234–5.

105 Historia da vida, e martyrio da gloriosa virgem santa Eria, Lisboa, por Antonio Aluarez, 1618. 8°
BOD Vet. G2 e.20 Acquired from Livraria de J. G. Mazziotti Salema Garção, after 1937.

Barreiros, Gaspar de (–1574) (Caspar Varrerius or Varrer)
The nephew of the historian João de Barros, he attended the university of Salamanca. In later life he spent two periods in Rome, from 1546–9 and 1561–4. Barbosa Machado claims that he got to know Bembo and Sadoleto while there. There are no early editions of his *Chorographia* (the account of his journey to Rome) in Oxford or Cambridge, no doubt because it was published in Portuguese. In the dedication of **107**, dated 1563, to the Venetian cardinal Antonio Amulio, he shows himself to be a staunch defender of Latin against the vernacular languages, even Italian, but he was proud nevertheless of his *Chorographia,* which despite the unfamiliar language was read in Italy (see **106**, p. 13). Some of the ambiguities of Barreiros's position are explored further in Chapter Five, p. lxxxii. Early modern readers in England were interested in his *De Orphyra regione,* because it is a commentary on various passages from the Old Testament, and in the *Censura,* because the Babylonian historian Berosus was an important source for the history of Biblical Israel. Editions of *De Orphyra regione* normally state on the title-page that the author was Portuguese, but the information is missing from the *Censura,* perhaps because **106**, the first edition, is deficient in other respects, including in having no printer's name.
Gaspar Barreiros, *Chorographia;* Barbosa Machado, II, pp. 333–6; Américo da Costa Ramalho, 'Um humanista em viagem: Gaspar Barreiros (1546)', pp. 81–93.

106 Censura in quendam auctorem, qui sub falsa inscriptione Berosi Chaldaei circunfertur, Romae, [no printer], 1565. 4°
BOD (3 copies) 4° V 17(1) Th. In the 1620 catalogue with the current shelf-mark; 4° D 17(5) Art. Seld. From the Selden bequest of 1659. In the 1674 catalogue; Byw. T 9,8 Bequeathed in 1914 by Ingram Bywater
CUL Dd*.3.50 (E) With the bookplate of the Royal Library, deposited in 1715 (Adams B252 and V280).

107 Censura in quendam auctorem, qui sub falsa inscriptione Berosi Chaldaei circumfertur, [Heidelberg], H. Commelinus, 1598–99. 8°
BOD (3 copies) Crynes 621 Part of the Crynes legacy of 1745; Douce H 70 From the Douce legacy of 1834; Byw. K 5 12 MS. notes. Bequeathed in 1914 by Ingram Bywater
ASC With the signature of J. Thirlestane 1614 BLL 0660 h 14 WOR G.14.14 Bequeathed by H. A. Pottinger in 1911.
TRC (2 copies) Y.3.90 (2) It belonged to the antiquarian Beaupré Bell (1704–41) in 1726. Marginal notes; Z.8.21 (4) Given by Thomas Parne (1694–1753) while he was a student at Trinity, so before 1720, when he became a fellow (Adams V279).

108 De Ophira regione in sacris litteris disputatio, Antuerpiae, sumptibus viduae et haeredum Io. Belleri, 1600. 8°

BOD 8° C 12 Th. Seld. From the Selden bequest of 1659. In the 1674 catalogue. The book previously belonged to John Causton, of Corpus Christi, Cambridge, who incorporated at Oxford in 1597.

TRC I.4.108 In the college's copy of the interleaved Bodleian catalogue of the 18th century. With annotations in English and Latin and an MS. index. The book also had at one time a French owner.

109 Commentarius De Orphyra regione, in sacris litteris Lib. III Regum & II Paralipomenon, Roterodami, apud Ioannem Leonardi Berevvout, 1616. 8°

BOD (2 copies) 8° M 4(3) Th. Seld. From the Selden bequest of 1659. In the 1674 catalogue; 203 g.105 British Museum duplicate, acquired after 1864. CHC Arch. Inf. C.6.1 17th-century binding **MER** 67.C.2 17th-century parchment binding.

CUL F*.6.35 (F) Acquired before 1715.

110 De Ophyra regione & ad eam navigatione commentarius, Hardervici Gelrorum, excudebat Nicolaus a Wieringen gymnasij typographus, 1637. 8°

BOD (2 copies) 8° P 3 Art. Seld. From the Selden bequest of 1659. In the 1674 catalogue; 8° P 224(2) Th. **SJCO** K.scam.1.upper shelf. 27 Part of the Crynes collection, deposited in 1745.

CUL (3 copies) O*.15.37 (F) Acquired before 1715; O.12.20 from the Royal Library, deposited in 1715, and in its MS. catalogue; Peterborough F.3.6 Belonged to Edward Judkin, who had studied at Pembroke College, and John Vokes, who had studied at St John's. (For Peterborough Cathedral Library, see the Introduction, p. xiv). **EMM** 329.7.115, formerly Q.5.62 and listed in the 18th-century catalogue under the old shelfmark. No book in this part of the catalogue was printed after 1712, and it is reasonable to assume that the book entered the library before then **MGC** G.17.34, formerly M.5.57 **SJCC** D.11.27 Given by Thomas Baker, fellow (1656–1740) **TRC** W.12.138 Acquired after 1800.

Barros, João de (1496–1570)

The best-known historian of the Portuguese in Asia. Oxford has an impressive collection of early editions of his work but, with one exception, these were not acquired before the eighteenth century. The exception is **115**, the Italian translation of *Décadas* I and II made by a Spaniard, Alfonso de Ulloa, which can also be found in Cambridge. Yet even of this there are only three complete copies known to be of early provenance. Some chapters of the translation, however, were available to sixteenth- and seventeenth-century readers because they were reprinted by Ramusio (see **743–8**). Barros had to wait until the nineteenth century before there was widespread interest in all of his work.

111 Asia, [Decades 1–2], Lisboa, Germão Galharde,1552–53. Fol.

BOD (2 copies) Arch. SIGMA 71,72 Purchased in 1828; 243 h.18 2 vols in one. Acquired after 1864 **QUO** Sel.c.184–5 Mason bequest of 1841 (Anselmo 648).

112 Terceira decada da Asia, Lisboa, por Ioam de Barreira, 1563. Fol.
BOD (2 copies) HH 74 Art. Acquired after 1710. Lacks the title page and index. Some cropped marginalia in Portuguese; 243 h.19 Acquired after 1864. On the title page there is the MS. statement 'esta visto segun el expurgato.del año de 1640', showing that the book was still in the Iberian Peninsula at that time (Anselmo 176).

113 Quarta decada da Asia, *ed. by* Ioaõ Baptista Lavanha, Madrid, na Impressaõ Real, [in colofon] por Anibal Falorsi, 1615. Fol.
BOD (3 copies) HH 75 Art. Acquired after 1710. Maps; Arch. SIGMA 74 Maps. Acquired between 1826 and 1850; 243 h.20 Acquired after 1864 **HER** oh.j.02(3) From Magdalen Hall (extinguished 1874–75), bound as a set with **114**. **QUO** 27.D.11 Bequeathed by Robert Mason in 1841.

114 Decada primeira [-terceira] da Asia, Lisboa, impressa per Iorge Rodriguez, aa custa de Antonio Gonçaluez mercador de liuros, 1628. 3 vols. Fol.
BOD (set is complete, but Decade 3 has a different shelf-mark) HH 72,73 Art. Decades 1–2 have a similar binding, Decade 2 with some marginalia in Portuguese; Arch. SIGMA 73 Decade 3 only, parchment binding, acquired between 1826 and 1850, presumably later than Decades 1–2 **HER** oh.j.02(1) (contains Decades 1–2), oh.j.02(2), from Magdalen Hall (extinguished 1874–75). Bound as a set with **113 QUO** 27.D.12–14 Bought with money left by Robert Mason in 1841.

115 [Asia] L'Asia del S. Giovanni di Barros, *Italian tr. of Decades 1–2 by* Alfonso de Ulloa, Venetia, appresso Vincenzo Valgrisio, 1561–2. 4°
BOD (2 copies) 4° B 14 Art. In the 1605 catalogue where the book is listed as having been printed in 1601. However, the shelf-mark is unchanged. Some notes and under-lining; Locke 9.83b Formerly owned by John Locke, the philosopher (1632–1704) given to the Library by Paul Mellon in 1978 **HER** oh.i.45(1–2) from Magdalen Hall (extinguished 1874–75).
CUL T*.4.53 (D) Acquired before 1715 **TRC** W.22.1. Repaired binding. With 4 previous shelf-marks and in the interleaved Bodleian catalogue used by the college in the 18th century, but not attested before that date (Adams B254–5).

Bartolomeu, monk of Alcobaça (16th century) (Bartholomeo de Alcobaça)
As he explains in his Prologo, Bartolomeu was a monk of the Cistercian abbey of Alcobaça. While a student at Coimbra he compiled this liturgical work, basing his work on French texts. Vernacular writing of this kind was not acquired in early modern times.

116 Liuro ordinario do officio diuino segundo a ordem de Cister, Coimbra, impresso por Ioam Alvares & Ioam da Barreira, 1550. 8°
BOD Vet. G1 f. 11. Acquired in 1950 (Anselmo 274).

Bermudes, João (16th century)
For around twenty years after 1535 Bermudes was in Ethiopia, part of the time as self-styled patriarch, but his period there was the source of some

controversy. Early modern Oxford and Cambridge only knew of his career through the translation printed by Purchas (**737**).

Grande Enciclopédia Portuguesa e Brasileira, IV, p. 570; R. S. Whiteway (ed.), *The Portuguese Expedition to Abyssinia in 1541–1543 . . . with . . .the short account of Bermudez.*
[Esta he hua breve relação da embaixada q*ue* o Patriarcha Dom João Bermudez trouxe do Emperador da Ethiopia] A briefe Relation of the Embassage, *translated from Portuguese* in Samuel Purchas, Purchas his Pilgrimes, vol. II, pp. 1149–74.

Branco, João Rodrigues de Castelo (Amatus Lusitanus) (1511–68)
The *Encyclopaedia Judaica* describes him as 'one of the greatest Jewish figures in medical literature in the first half of the sixteenth century', but he retained his Portuguese identity throughout his career, despite being forced to leave Portugal in 1533. After a period in Antwerp he practised for many years in Italy, before moving to Ragusa (Dubrovnik) and finally Thessalonica, in the Ottoman empire. All his books, including **128**, published before he adopted the pseudonym Amatus Lusitanus, state his national origin on the title-page. See Chapters One and Five for further discussion, pp. xl, lxxvii.

Amatus Lusitanus was much read by early modern doctors, and nearly all of the thirty-eight copies of his various works listed in the catalogue were acquired before 1750. There are annotated copies of **117, 118, 119, 120, 122, 123, 124, 125,** and **132**.

Encyclopaedia Judaica, II, cols 795–8.

117 Curationum medicinalium, centuriae duae, Parisiis, apud Egidium Gourbin, [in colofon] excudebat Benedictus Prevotius, 1554. 16°
SJCO H.scam.1.lower shelf. 23 Given by William Paddy in 1602.
CUL P*.14.46 (G) (the printer was Franciscus Bartholomeus) Bequeathed by Thomas Lorkin, Professor of Physick, in 1591, with 16 pp. of MS. notes (Adams A912).

118 Curationum medicinalium centuriae II priores, Lugduni, apud Gulielmum Rouillium, 1567. 8°
CUL Kkk.69 It was given by Gonville and Caius college library in 1911. At Gonville and Caius it had the shelf-mark E.m.25. with 12 on fore-edge. It was probably acquired by the college at the same time as **121–2**. Underlining and marginalia. The binding is different from that of the CUL's copy of **122**, which was also given by Gonville and Caius **G&C** K.2.8. Formerly E.h.25. With I and 17 on fore-edge but no sign of a tab. With a blind-stamped centrepiece binding of around 1600 and an MS. pastedown (Adams A913).

119 Curationum medicinalium . . . centuriae duae, quinta videlicet ac sexta, Venetiis, ex officina Valgrisiana, 1560. 8°
BOD 8° A 14(1) Med. In the 1620 catalogue, with the current shelf-mark **NEW** BT3.243.18 Contains notes in the same hand as **123**. Given by Thomas Hopper, medical practioner, in 1623. In the catalogue of 1686.
CUL (2 copies) N*.16.9 (F) Bequeathed by Thomas Lorkin, Professor of Physick, in 1591. Marginalia; K.17.77(2) Bound with **124**, which has the bookplate of the Royal Library, deposited in 1715 (Adams A917).

120 Curationum medicinalium, centuriae duae, quinta et sexta [-septima], *with* colloquium eruditissimum . . . de curandis capitis vulneribus, Lugduni apud Gulielmum Rouillium, 1564–7. 4 vols 12°

HMAN X1567/1 [1–2] With the signature of John Bank, 1583, and Latin marginalia. 16th-century binding with blind-stamped centrepiece, not identical to any listed by Ker NEW BT3.241.3 Vol.4 In the catalogue of 1686 QUO H.S.b.46 1–3 Vols 1–3. Bequeathed by Theophilus Metcalfe, M.D., in 1757, with MS. notes in his hand SJCO G.scam.1.upper shelf. 15 Vols 3–4. Given by William Paddy, 1602.

121 Curationum medicinalium, centuriae duae, quinta et sexta [-septima], *with* colloquium eruditissimum . . . de curandis capitis vulneribus, Lugduni apud Gulielmum Rouillium, 1576.12°

G&C K.2.10 Formerly E.h.27 Trace of a tab on the fore-edge. Perhaps the book listed in the catalogue completed in 1646 as having been printed in 1567 (Adams A918).

122 Curationum medicinalium, centuriae duae, tertia et quarta, Lugduni, apud Gulielmum Rouillium, 1565. 8°

CUL Kkk.70 From the library of Gonville and Caius College, given in 1911. With a blind-stamped centrepiece binding and an MS. pastedown. However, the binding is different from that of **118**, which was also given by Gonville and Caius. While in the college the book had the shelf-mark E.m.26, like **118** and **121**. There is a note suggesting that it was bought in 1572 from S. May of Cambridge for 18d. G&C K.2.9. Formerly E.h.26 With a tab on fore-edge and marginalia (Adams A913–14).

123 Curationum medicinalium centuriae quatuor, *with* Commentatio de introitu medici ad aegrotantem, de[que] crisi & diebus decretorijs, Basileae, Froben, 1556. Fol.

BOD P 3.8(1) Jur. In the 1620 catalogue with the current shelf-mark MER 46.F.3(2) Gift of Robert Barnes (1514–1604), fellow, but not among those which he gave in 1594. Chain mark NEW BT3.251.4 Given by Thomas Hopper, medical practioner, 1623. With detailed and legible Latin marginalia, in the same hand as **119**. In the catalogue of 1686.

CUL K.14.15 Part of the Royal Library, deposited in 1715, and in its MS. catalogue (Adams A915).

124 Curationum medicinalium centuriae quatuor, *with* Commentatio de introitu medici ad aegrotantem, de[que] crisi & diebus decretorijs,Venetiis, apud Balthesarum Constantium, 1557. 8°

CUL K.17.77 With the Royal Library bookplate of 1715, and in its MS. catalogue. Marginalia. Bound with **119** (Adams A916).

125 Curationum medicinalium . . . centuria septima, Venetiis, apud Vincentium Valgrisium, 1566. 8°

BOD 8° A 20(1) Med In the 1605 catalogue, included with De morbo gallico scriptores. The current shelf-mark appears in the 1620 catalogue.

CUL N*.16.10 (F) Bequeathed by Thomas Lorkin, Professor of Physick, in 1591, with 9 pp. of MS. notes (Adams A919).

126 Curationum medicinalium . . . centuria septima, Lugduni, apud Gulielmum Rouillium, 1570. 16°

G&C K.2.12 Signature of John Argent, President of the Royal College of Physicians, 1625–34. Fore-edge tab. Blind-stamped centrepiece binding of around 1600 (Adams A920).

127 Curationum medicinalium centuriae septem, *with* Commentatio de introitu ad aegrotantem, simulque de crisi et diebus decretoriis, Burdigalae, ex typographia Gilberti Vernoy, 1620. 4°
BNC Lath J.4.1 In the catalogue probably of the 17th century with the shelf-mark F.12.15, which is still visible in the book today QUO NN.s.661.
CUL K.14.47 With the bookplate of the Royal Library, deposited in 1715, but signed Joseph Fenton. In the catalogue of the Royal Library with the present shelf-mark. 17th-century Cambridge binding with fillets.

128 Index Dioscoridis, Antuerpiae, excudebat vidua Martini Caesaris, 1536. Fol.
SJCO Z.4.35(2) Given by William Paddy, 1602. Fol.
CUL (2 copies) K.4.2 with the bookplate of the Royal Library, deposited in 1715; K.3.35(5) Part of a volume with the bookplate of the Royal Library, deposited in 1715 (Adams A923).

129 In Dioscoridis Anazarbei De medica materia libris quinque enarrationes eruditissimae, Venetiis, apud Gualterum Scotum, 1553. 4°
CUL K.4.48 From the Royal Library, deposited in 1715, and in its MS. catalogue (Adams A921).

130 In Dioscoridis Anazarbei De medica materia libris quinque enarrationes eruditissimae, Argentorati, Wendelinus Rihelius, 1554. 4°
MER 46.E.15 Decorated with Ker rolls xii and xviii, which were used by the binder Dominic Pinart between 1575 and 1605 (Pearson, p. 67). Left by Roger Gifford, D. Med., fellow, in 1597.
CUL CCC.47.20 Given by John Martyn (1699–1768), Professor of Botany, in 1729/30.

131 In Dioscoridis Anazarbei De medica materia libris quinque enarrationes eruditissimae, Venetijs, ex officina Iordani Zilleti, 1557. 4°
QUO NN.s.660 Given by Sir John Floyer, D. Med. (1649–1734). It also belonged to Anthony Hewett (1603–84).

132 In Dioscoridis Anazarbei De medica materia libros quinque . . . enarrationes eruditissimae, Lugduni, apud viduam Balthazaris Arnoleti, 1558 (in some copies apud Theobaldum Paganum, apud Gulielmum Rovillium, or apud Matthiam Bonhomme). 8°
BOD 8° P 49 Med. MGO R.09.09 With the shelf-mark on the leading edge. Belonged to N. Carrus, MS. annotations SJCO HB4/4.d.1.10 Given by William Paddy, 1602. Shows price.
CUL P*.6.21 (F) Bequeathed by Henry Lucas, benefactor and founder of the Lucasian professorship of mathematics, in 1663. He owned the book by 1654. TRC S.23.17 It belonged to Thomas Lorkin, Professor of Physick, who died in 1591 (Adams A922).

Brandão, António
See Brito, Bernardo de

Brandão, Luís Pereira (between 1530 and 1535–)
Author of an epic poem, in Portuguese, about the death of King Sebastião at the battle of Alcácer-Quibir. Though the date of acquisition of **133** is not known, it is unlikely to be early. See also Jerónimo Corte-Real.
Biblios: Enciclopédia Verbo das Literaturas de Língua Portuguesa, I, cols 759–61.

133 Elegiada, Lisboa, Manoel de Lyra, 1588. 8°
CUL XII.20.62 The title page is missing (Adams P652; Anselmo 748).

Brito, Bernardo de (1569–1617)
The founder of the Cistercian school of historians based in the monastery of Alcobaça. Because he wrote exclusively in Portuguese his writings made no impact on early modern Oxford. The old editions now in All Souls were probably bought by Peter Frye Hony, a fellow of the college, after 1826. See Chapter Three, pp. lix–lx, for further discussion of Hony's work as a collector.

134 Geographia antiga de Lusytania, Alcobaça, por Antonio Aluarez impressor de liuros, 1597. Fol.
ASC SR.89.d.1/1 Bound with Monarchia Lusitana, vol 1.

135 Monarchia Lusytana, Alcobaça, [in colophon: per Alexandre de Siqveira, & Antonio Alvarez impressores de livros], 1597. Fol.
(4) **BOD** Vet. G1 d.13 Acquired after 1937 **ASC** SR.89.d.1/1 **HER** iii.04.01(01) From Magdalen Hall (extinguished 1874–75) **TAY** Arch.Fol.P.1597. Acquired from the Martin collection, 1895. A copy which has been heavily restored, with many pages supplied in MS.

136 Primeyra parte da Chronica de Cister, Lisboa, por Pedro Crasbeek, 1602. Fol.
ASC SR 67.c.1.

137 Segunda parte da Monarchia Lusitana, Lisboa, por Pedro Crasbeeck, 1609. Fol.
ASC SR. 89. d. 1/2.

138 Terceira parte da Monarchia Lusitana, Lisboa, por Pedro Craesbeeck, 1632. Fol.
ASC SR. 89. d. 1/3.

Brudo, Manuel (c.1500–c.1585)
A New Christian doctor, who practised in England before settling in Italy. Like many New Christians he was also known by another name, Manuel Rodrigues. All three editions of his well-known work about diet (**139–41**) state on the title-page that he was a Portuguese. Ten of the twelve copies now in Oxford and Cambridge are of early provenance. Brudo first published in Venice, but even then was in negotiation with the Zurich firm of Gessner, as the letter from Konrad Gessner included in the first

edition proves. Gessner published the second edition of 1555, having spent a good deal of time, as he claims, in purging Brudo's Latin of Grecisms and improving his punctuation. Part of Gessner's sales pitch for Brudo is the fact that he came of a family of Portuguese doctors and that he had practised 'magna cum laude' in Portugal, England and Italy. See his 'Epistola nuncupatoria'. There is further discussion of the importance of family networks to Jewish doctors in Chapter Four, p. lxxiv.

Friedenwald, II, pp. 465–6; António Manuel Lopes Andrade, 'Os senhores do desterro de Portugal . . .', p. 68.

139 Liber de ratione victus in singulis febribus, Venetijs, [in colophon, apud haeredes Petri Rauani & socios], 1544. 8°

BOD Vet. F1 f. 5 The shelf-mark would indicate acquisition after 1937, but the book is in the 1605 catalogue with the title De victu febricitantium, apparently in 4 copies **CCCO** N.13.2 Part of the bequest of Brian Twyne, fellow, of 1644. MS. notes. **MER** 73.F.11 Bequeathed by Helen Gulston, widow of Theodore Gulston, M.D. and fellow, in 1635.
CUL Kkk.66 From the library of Gonville and Caius College, deposited in 1911. Like **118** and **122**, it was probably acquired by the college in the early modern period **G&C** K.22.27 Formerly Hh.3.b With 34 on fore-edge. In the MS. catalogue completed in 1646 with the old shelf-mark **WEST** Westminster College moved from London to Cambridge in 1899 (Adams B2904).

140 De ratione victus in febribus secundum Hippocratem, in genere et singillatim libri III, *in* Enchiridion rei medicae triplicis, Tiguri, per Andream Gessnerum F. & Iacobum Gessnerum fratres, 1555. 8°

BOD 8° E 6 Med. Ker Centrepiece xvi, in use between c.1580 and c. 1620 (Pearson, p. 78) **SJCO** G.scam.1.upper shelf. 2 Given by William Paddy, 1602.
CUL N*.14.38 (F) Bequeathed by Thomas Lorkin, Professor of Physick, in 1591.

141 De ratione victus in singulis febribus . . . libri III, Venetiis, per Ioannem Rubeum, 1558–59. 8°

BOD (2 copies) Crynes 859(2) Crynes bequest of 1745; Antiq. f.I. 1559.5 Bought in 1918 **NEW** BT3.242.8 Signed Thomas Hopper, medical practioner, who gave books in 1623, and with marginal notes in his hand. Brudo is mentioned in the catalogue of 1686, in association with Amatus Lusitanus, but without a shelf-mark.

Cabedo, Jorge de (1549–1604)

A jurist, who served for some time on the council of Portugal in Madrid. His work is poorly represented in the English universities, but **143**, despite being concerned with the laws of Portugal, went through several editions in Germany and the Low Countries.

Grande Enciclopédia Portuguesa e Brasileira, V, p. 262; Barbosa Machado, II, pp. 794–5.

142 De patronatibus ecclesiarum regiae coronae regni Lusitaniae, Olysipone, 1602. 4°

CUL H.6.62 From the Royal Library deposited in 1715, and in its MS. catalogue.

143 Practicarum observationum sive decisionum supremi senatus regni Lusitaniae pars prima [-secunda], *with, in Portuguese,* Aresta Senatus, Antuerpiae, apud Ioannem Keerbergium, 1620. Fol.
BOD W 1.4 Th. Seld. From the Selden bequest of 1659, and with his Greek motto. In the 1674 catalogue. Chain mark.

Calvo, Pedro (1551–)
A Dominican and the Provincial of his Order, author of a number of works in Portuguese not represented in either Oxford or Cambridge. On the title-page of **144,** a collection of Latin homilies, he is described as having been born in Oporto, thus making public his Portuguese identity.

144 Homiliarum totius anni tomus I, Ulissipone, apud Vincentium Alvarez, 1615. 4°
BOD D 1.13 Th. In the 1635 appendix to the 1620 catalogue. Chain mark **QUO** 60.C.26 Apparently acquired in 1964.

Camões, Luís de (?1525–1580) (Camoens)
Although the author of *Os Lusíadas* and the best-known name in Portuguese literature his work made almost no impact in the early modern universities. Even Fanshawe's English translation of the epic, which was printed in 1655 and so falls outside the scope of this survey, is sparsely represented in the libraries. The Bodleian's copy of **145,** the first edition of the Portuguese text, was acquired between 1883 and 1936. The only copy of a book by Camões printed before 1640 known to have reached either Oxford or Cambridge in the early modern period is **148,** a translation into Spanish left to Wadham by the Catholic William Godolphin.

145 Os Lusiadas, Lisboa, Antonio Gõçalvez, 1572. 4°
BOD Antiq. e.P. 1572.1 With the signature of C. R. Fox, 1825 but acquired between 1883 and 1936 (Anselmo 697/8).

146 Os Lusiadas, Lisboa, por Pedro Crasbeeck, 1609. 4°
ASC nn.12.3 MS. notes.

147 Os Lusiadas . . . commentados pelo licenciado Manuel Correa, Lisboa, por Pedro Craesbeeck, 1613. 8°
TAY Arch.8°.P.1613 Part of the Martin collection, acquired in 1895. The titlepage is missing.

148 [Os Lusiadas] La Lusiada, *tr. into Spanish by* Luys Gomes de Tapia, Salamanca, Ioan Perier, 1580. 8°
WAD G 18.16 Given by Charles Godolphin in 1720, and with the signature of D. Guilmo., i.e. Sir William, Godolphin (?1634–96), who was an exile in Spain (Fidalgo 1014).

149 Rimas . . . segunda parte, *with* Da creação, & composição do Homem, Lisboa, na officina de Pedro Crasbeeck a custa de Domingos Fernandez mercador de livros, 1616 [Da creação . . . , 1615]. 8°
TAY Arch. 8°.P.1616 Acquired 1937. This is an incomplete copy.

Campos, Francisco v. Diez, Felipe

Cardim, Fernão (1548/49–1625)

Jesuit missionary, ethnographer and natural historian of Brazil, who was captured by English privateers in 1601 and held prisoner in England until 1603. During that time his manuscripts were stolen. They found their way into the possession of Samuel Purchas who published an English translation, attributed incorrectly to Manuel Tristão. Cardim's original Portuguese text was not published until the nineteenth century.

Fernão Cardim, *Tratados da Terra e Gente do Brasil*, edited by Ana Maria de Azevedo, pp. 12–13, 18–25.
A Treatise of Brasil, *tr. from Portuguese and included in* **737**, Samuel Purchas, *Purchas his Pilgrimes*, vol. IV pp. 1289–1325.

Cardoso, Fernão Rodrigo (–1608)

A doctor, who was professor of medicine at Coimbra until he became *Prothomedicus* [chief physican] in Lisbon in 1585. But the dedication of **150** to the Venetian nobleman Francisco Bollizza, of Kotor in Montenegro, in which Cardoso makes no mention of his previous career, perhaps indicates an intention, never realized, of moving to the east coast of the Adriatic, a safe haven for Portuguese Jewish doctors. There is a marked difference, too, between the title-pages of **150** and **151**. The latter was published in Lisbon and has a detailed account of his Portuguese career.
Barbosa Machado, II, pp. 52–3.

150 Methodus medendi, Venetiis, apud Vincentium Somaschum, 1618. 4°
BOD 4° T 5 Med. In the 1635 appendix to the 1620 catalogue.

151 Tractatus de sex rebus non naturalibus, Olyssipone, ex officina Georgii Rodriguez, 1602. 4°
BOD 4° M 12 Med. In the 1620 catalogue with the current shelf-mark.

152 Tractatus de sex rebus non naturalibus, Francofurti ad Moenum, Iacobi de Zetter, 1620.
EMM 324.8.46, previously E.5.59, G.6.15 With 17th-century Cambridge binding and evidence of a paper tab. Listed in the 18th-century catalogue under E.5.59.

Cardoso, Jerónimo (–1569) (Hieronymus Cardosus)

A humanist, who earned his place in Portuguese literary history by being the first scholar to publish a Portuguese and Latin dictionary (Lisbon,

1563; no copy in either Oxford or Cambridge). Cardoso's dictionary is the only work about the Portuguese language to appear in the short-title catalogue, but the presence of a mere six copies – even if four of them are certainly of old provenance – shows that there was little interest in the early modern period in learning a vernacular tongue spoken in a distant part of Europe.

Biblos: Enciclopédia Verbo das Literaturas de Língua Portuguesa, I, cols 989–90 (article by Sebastião Tavares de Pinho).

153 De uario amore aegloga quae Silenis inscribitur, de[que] uini inuentione, [no place, date or printer]. 4°
BOD 4° R 11(3) Th. Seld. From the Selden bequest of 1659. In the 1674 catalogue. Bound with **651, 758**.

154 Dictionarium Latinolusitanicum et vice versa Lusitanicolatinum . . . Conimbricae, excussit Ioannes Barrerius, 1588. 8°
MGC F.6.20, formerly A.6.5.

155 Dictionarium Latino Lusitanicum et vice versa, Olyssipone, excussit Alexander de Syqueira typographus, expensis Simonis Lopezii bibliopolae, 1592. 4°
BOD 4° C 44 Art. Seld. From the Selden bequest of 1659. In the 1674 catalogue (Anselmo 1058).

156 Dictionarium Latino Lusitanicum, et vice versa, Olyssipone, excussit Antonius Aluares Typographus, 1601. 4°
BOD 4° C 43 Art. In the 1620 catalogue with the current shelf-mark ASC nn.2.10.

157 Dictionarium Latino Lusitanicum, et vice versa, Olyssipone, ex officina Petri Craesbeeck, 1619.
EMM S.15.1.37 Bequeathed by Archbishop William Sancroft in 1693.

158 Dictionarium Latino Lusitanicum, et vice versa, Olyssipone, ex officina Petri Craesbeeck, 1630.
CUL M*.10.17 (D) Acquired before 1715. With signature of M. Castell on the titlepage and scribbles, some in Spanish, on the endpapers.

Casal, Frei Gaspar do (1510–84) (Gasparo Casalius)

An Augustinian, he was successively bishop of Funchal, Leiria and Coimbra. He was present at the Council of Trent in 1561, and while in Italy published three books (**160–3**), all in 1563, through the Venetian firm of Zileti. There is further discussion in Chapter One, p. xxx. In the prefatory letters included in **160** and **162** Casal explains that these combative anti-Protestant works were intended to be accessible to non-specialists. Oxford and Cambridge libraries were eager to have them, and there are sixteen copies, spread between the two universities, almost all acquired before 1715. The three copies of **159** and **164** also arrived in the

early modern period. On the title-page of all his books he is identified by some form of the word 'Lusitanus'.
José de Castro, *Portugal no Concílio de Trento*, IV, pp. 39–44.

159 Axiomata Christiana ex divinis scriptis . . ., Conimbricae, apud Ioannem Barrerium et Ioannem Alvarem, 1550. 4°
CUL F.3.119. With the bookplate of the Royal Library, deposited in 1715 (Adams G265; Anselmo 267).

160 De coena et calice Domini . . . libri tres, Venetiis, ex officina Iordani Zileti [in colophon: Ioan. Gryphius excudebat], 1563. 4°
BOD 4° A 46 Th. In the 1674 catalogue.
CUL F*.11.25 (D) Acquired before 1715 SJCC Uu.14.4 Given by Thomas Morton, 1564–1659, bishop successively of Chester, Lichfield and Durham (Adams C814).

161 De iustificatione humani generis libri tres, 2a editio *of* **162**, Venetiis, apud Baretium Baretium et socios, 1599. Fol.
BOD C 6.6 Th. In the 1605 catalogue. In the 1620 catalogue with a different title but with the shelf-mark which is still in use today. Chain mark and 6 on the fore-edge, which are also indications of old provenance JSO G.8.8. Bequeathed by Edward Herbert, Baron Cherbury (1583–1648), diplomat and writer on religion.
CUL E*.9.20 (C) Acquired before 1715. The title-page is missing. Some marginal notes to Book 1. TRC E.10.30 With a repaired blind-stamped centrepiece binding and a small 19 and 18 and a large 2 on the fore-edge. The small numbers date from around 1605 (Gaskell, p. 97), but it was in the library by 1600 (Gaskell, p. 163, Adams C815 or 817).

162 De quadripertita justitia libri tres, Venetiis, ex officina Iordani Zileti, 1563. Fol.
BOD G 7.10 Th. In the 1674 catalogue. With a chain mark and 10 on the fore-edge CCCO L.C. 13 G.12 In the 1589 catalogue transcribed by Liddell, pp. 403–16. The book perhaps belonged to Thomas Greaves, a fellow of Corpus, still living in 1637 EXE 9I 1563.3 Gift of Thomas Masters who left the college in 1661 MGO 1.18.3 Chain mark WAD I 32.24 Given by Philip Bisse in 1613.
CUL E*.8.34 (C) Acquired before 1715. The book at one time belonged to the Academic Library of Würzburg G&C M.6.1 Bequeathed by William Branthwaite, Master, in 1619. He was one of the revisers of the Bible. 17th-century Cambridge binding with fillets SJCC O.2.11 Given by Thomas Morton in 1628, while he was bishop of Lichfield PET O.8.7 Bequeathed by Andrew Perne, Master, in 1589 (Adams C816).

163 De sacrificio missae & sacrosanctae eucharistiae celebratione . . . libri tres, Venetiis, ex officina Iordani Zileti, 1563. 4°
BOD 4° C 10 Th. In the 1605 catalogue with the current shelf-mark.

164 De sacrificio missae, et sacrosanctae eucharistiae celebratione . . . libri tres, Antuerpia, apud Ioannem Withagium, 1573. 8°
QUO UU.e.55 The third of three works bound together, Ker no.1476. The binding is decorated with centrepiece iii, in use from the late 1580s to 1620 (Pearson, pp. 75–6). It was often used on small books.
CUL H*.14.6 In the library before 1715 (Adams C818).

Castanheda, Fernão Lopes de (−1559)

A historian of Portuguese India, whose first-hand knowledge of the country makes his work particularly valuable. The first volume of his history appeared in Portuguese in 1551, but early modern Oxford and Cambridge read him in translation. The English translator claims to have followed the Portuguese original, but gives the Spanish version of the historian's name (Hernan Lopes de Castaneda) on the title-page, suggesting that he may have used the Spanish translation of 1554. Further discussion in Chapter One, p. xliii. The French version, bound with a work by Osório, is listed at **658−60**.

Biblos: Enciclopédia Verbo das Literaturas de Língua Portuguesa, I, cols 1035−7.

165 [História do descobrimento e conquista da Índia pelos portugueses] Historia del descubrimiento y conquista de la India . . ., Anvers, en casa de Martin Nucio, 1554. 8°

CUL Syn. 8.55.7 Acquired from Thorpe, perhaps in 1906 **CLA** W.8.5 With the signature of Sir Bernard Hampton, the 1701 college bookplate and the shelf-mark C3 on the fore-edge. In the catalogue of 1677/78 with the shelf-mark C.16 **EMM** S.12.5.9 Bequeathed by Archbishop William Sancroft in 1693 **TRH** L*.8.22, formerly L.10.39. With the signature of Sir Bernard Hampton and the college bookplate of 1700 (Adams L1467).

166 [História do descobrimento e conquista da Índia pelos portugueses] Historia dell' Indie Orientali, scoperte, & conquistate da' Portoghesi, *tr. into Italian by* Alfonso Vlloa. Parte prima [-seconda], in Venetia, appresso Giordano Ziletti, 1577. 2 vols 4°

BOD (2 copies) 4° L 8,9 Art; Vet. F1 e. 33,34. Entered the library after 1937 **HER** ggg.03.04, from Magdalen Hall (extinguished 1874−75).

167 [História do descobrimento e conquista da Índia pelos portugueses] The First Booke of the Historie of the Discoverie and Conquest of the East Indies . . . *tr. by* N[icholas] L[ichefield], London, Thomas East, 1582. 4°

BOD Vet. A1 e. 27. Entered the library after 1937 (STC 16806).

CUL (2 copies) T.10.58 With the bookplate of the Royal Library, deposited in 1715 (STC 16806); Peterborough A.4.35 Given to Peterborough Cathedral Library by White Kennett (1660−1728; see the Introduction, p. xiv).

Castro, Estêvão Rodrigues de (1559−1638)

A Jewish doctor, who left Portugal in 1608, eventually settling in Pisa and Florence where he was in the service of the Medici. He is identified on the title-page of all his books by some form of the word 'Lusitanus', and his literary work, of which there is a modern edition, is in Portuguese as well as in a number of other languages. In some library catalogues, including OLIS and Newton, he is confused with another doctor, Rodrigo de Castro. Of the fourteen copies of books by him now in Oxford and

Cambridge at least twelve arrived before 1750. There are annotations in **170** and **173**.

Obras poéticas, ed. Manuppella, pp. 51–74.

168 Commentarius in Hippocratis Coi libellum de alimento, Florentiae, in typographia Sermartelliana, 1635. Fol.

BOD R 1.5(1) Med. In the 1674 catalogue **CHC** O.p.2.16 From the Orrery bequest of 1732. Chain mark.

169 De meteoris microcosmi libri quatuor, Florentiae, apud Iunctas, 1621. Fol.

BOD R 1.11 Med. In the 1635 appendix to the 1620 catalogue, with the shelf-mark unchanged **UNI** Given by G. Hudson, perhaps George Hudson (?1679–1749) who was a fellow of Queen's. It is now in **MHS** at G/RODxos.

SJCC L1.4.25 Bequeathed by John Collins, fellow and Professor of Physick, in 1634.

170 De meteoris microcosmi libri quatuor, 2a ed., Venetiis, apud Euangelistam Deuchinum, 1624. Fol.

CHC Op.2.17 From the Orrery bequest of 1732. Chain mark **MER** 52.I.23 Chain mark. 17th-century binding. Marginal annotations throughout.

171 Il curioso, nel quale in dialogo si discorre del male di peste, Pisa, Francesco Tanagli, 1631.

CUL K.15.85 With the bookplate of the Royal Library, and in its MS. catalogue. Deposited in 1715.

172 Quae ex quibus, opusculum in quatuor libros divisum, Florentiae, apud Petrum Cecconcellium, 1627. 12°

BOD 8° O 1 Med. In the 1635 appendix to the 1620 catalogue, with the shelf-mark unchanged **BLL** 0845 a 06 Recorded for the first time in the 1871 catalogue.

SJCC Mm.15.14.

173 Tractatus de complexu morborum, Florentiae, apud Zenobium Pignonium, 1624. 8°

BOD 8° R 25 Med. In the 1635 appendix to the 1620 catalogue **BLL** 0845 a 09 Probably the copy left by Nicholas Crouch, fellow, in 1690. It contains an MS. index and a chain mark. In the 1709 catalogue, but without a shelf-mark.

CUL K.17.34 With the Royal Library bookplate. Deposited in 1715.

Castro, Francisco de Caldas Pereira e

A jurist not mentioned in the *Grande Enciclopédia Portuguesa e Brasileira* and referred to only in passing by Barbosa Machado, as the father of the epic poet Gabriel Pereira de Castro. However, there are fifteen copies of books by him in Oxford and Cambridge, nearly all of which arrived by the seventeenth century. Some, like **176** and **179–80** were published by the Frankfurt firm of Zacharias Palthenius. Palthenius specialized in legal publications, and he was also a member of the Wechel family who were noted for their cosmopolitanism and breadth of interest. In his preface to the reader Palthenius explains his difficulty in obtaining an MS. of **179**,

'Hispanico idiomate scripta', which he had translated. Further discussion in Chapter Four, p. lxxi.

R. J. W. Evans, *The Wechel Presses*; Ian Maclean, 'The Market for Scholarly Books and Conceptions of Genre in Northern Europe, 1570–1630', p. 24.

174 Analyticus commentarius, seu electio, ad celebratissimam l. si curatorem habens, C. de integrum restitutione minorum, Vlyssippone, excudebat Emmanuel de Lyra, typographus. Expensis . . . Simonis Lopez bibliopolae, 1583. Fol.

MER 46.C.6(2) Oxford binding using rolls xii and xviii, which were used together from 1575 to 1605 (Pearson, p. 67). In the Wijffels List C of legal books in the library around 1600. Chain mark.

TRC N.8.38 With a small 13 and 14 on the fore-edge, an indication of early provenance. Stamped with gilt crest and the letters E S, indicating that it was left by Sir Edward Stanhope, who had been a fellow from 1564 to 1572, in 1608. There is a signature, G. Nunez?, perhaps of a previous owner (Adams C179; Anselmo 733).

175 Analyticus commentarius, seu relectio ad celebratissimam l. Si curatorem habens, C. De in integrum restitutione minorum. Francofurti, ex officina typographica Nicolai Bassaei, 1585–6. Fol.

BOD C 9.3 Jur. Deposited in 1596. Part of the Mascarenhas collection. In the 1605 catalogue and, with the current shelf-mark, in the 1620 catalogue. (See Introduction, p. xvi.) Bound with **178**.

TRH P*.2.28, formerly L.2.4 With the college bookplate of 1700. Bound with **178** (Adams T881).

176 Analyticus commentarius, sive ad typum instrumenti emptionis & venditionis tractatus, Francofurti, sumptibus Haeredum Doctoris Zachariae Palthenii, typis Hartmanni Palthenii, 1619. Fol.

BOD F 4.8 Jur. (2) In the 1635 appendix to the 1620 catalogue.

177 Commentarius analyticus, de renouatione emphyteutica, Vlyssippone, excudebat Emmanuel de Lyra, 1585. Fol.

BOD Fol. BS 161 (2) Lacks titlepage. In the 1674 catalogue. Bound with **182 ASC** dd.7.12(2) 17th-century Oxford binding, chain mark (Anselmo 740).

178 Consilia seu responsa duo, Francofurti, ex officina Nicolai Bassaei, 1585. Fol.

BOD C 9.3 Jur. (2) Bound with **175 ASC** aa.infra 2.7(2) Oxford binding, perhaps of the 16th century; chain mark.

TRH P*.2.28, formerly L.2.4. With the college bookplate of 1700. Bound with **175**.

179 De universo iure emphyteutico, syntagma tripartitum, Francofurti, in D. Zachariae Palthenii . . . officina, 1612. Fol.

BOD C 10.3 Jur. In the 1620 catalogue with the current shelf-mark.

G&C H.6.8.

180 Explicatio vera l. Si curatorem habens, C. De in integrum restitutione minorum, *in* Tractatus de in integrum restitutionibus, Lugduni, apud Antonium de Harsy, 1586. Fol.

NEW BT1.75.3 Chain marks. Ker centrepiece xxxii, in use around 1605 (Pearson, p. 83). With an MS. pastedown which both Ker and Pearson seem to have missed. In the catalogue of 1686, under De Restitutionibus, and with the shelf-mark V.12.1 which is visible in the volume.

181 Receptarum sententiarum, seu quæstionum forensium et controuersiarum civilium, libri duo. *Followed by* Solemnis et analyticæ relectio tituli De inofficioso testamento *and* Consilium primum [-liii], Francofurti, in D. Zachariae Palthenii . . . Officina, 1612. Fol.
BOD O 1.16 Th. Seld. From the Selden bequest of 1659, but in the 1620 catalogue.

182 Singularis, et excellens tractatus et analyticus commentarius, et syntagma de nominatione emphyteutica, Ulyssippone, [Emmanuel de Lyra], 1585, Fol.
BOD Fol. BS 161 (1). Bound with **177**.

Castro, João de (1500–48)
Viceroy of India, whose *roteiros* or guides to navigation in the Indian Ocean are famous for their scientific approach. Purchas's publication (**737**) of one of them, from a MS. procured by Sir Walter Raleigh, seems to have been the first in any language.
Inocêncio, III, pp. 345–7; *Dicionário de História de Portugal,* I, pp. 529–30.
A Rutter . . . of the Voyage which the Portugals made from India to Zoez, *translated from Portuguese* in Samuel Purchas, Purchas his Pilgrimes, Vol. II, pp. 1122–48.

Castro, Manuel Mendes de (16th–17th centuries)
A jurist who studied in Salamanca, taught in Coimbra, and divided his career as an advocate between Madrid and Lisbon.
Barbosa Machado, III, pp. 309–10.

183 Repertorio das ordenações do reyno de Portugal novamente recopiladas, Lisboa, Pedro Craesbeeck, 1623. 4°
WAD G 24.25 Given by Charles Godolphin in 1720. Part of the collection of Sir William Godolphin (?1634–96).

184 Repetitio L. cum oportet VI de bon. quae lin. in potest. constitut. ex matron. & c. Augustae, Typis Praetorianiis, sumptibus Sebastiani Mylii, 1608. 8°
ASC ww.12.23(4) Signature of S. Wach.

Castro, Rodrigo de (1546/50–1627/28) (Rodericus a Castro)
A Marrano doctor who subsequently reconverted to Judaism. He left Portugal for Hamburg in 1594. In some library catalogues, including OLIS and Newton, he is confused with another doctor, Estêvão Rodrigues de Castro. His Portuguese origin is stated on the title-page of his books, with the exception of **189**, which is a brief pamphlet. There is a 'laus Lusitanorum' in **186**, p. 89, which shows his attachment to his native

land. Of the twenty-nine copies of books by him now in Oxford and Cambridge libraries at least twenty-three can be shown to have arrived before 1750, and there are in addition a number of copies (not listed here) which were printed after 1640. There are annotations in copies of **185** and **188**.

Encyclopaedia Judaica, V, cols 244–5.

185 De universa mulierum morborum medicina, Hamburgi, in officina Frobeniana, 1603. Fol.

    BOD S 1.9(3) Med. In the 1605 catalogue with the current shelf-mark **NEW** BT3. 232.7 Bound with other works, and with the signature of Thomas Hopper, medical practioner, on the first item. He gave books to the college in 1623. In the catalogue of 1686 **ORI** L.e.3 Given by John Sanders, or Saunders, a doctor, while he was provost, 1644–52/3. Chain mark. In both the 17th-century catalogues **WOR** I.8.6 Heavily and legibly annotated. Endpapers repaired.

    CLA T.2.10 With the 1701 bookplate and the motto Castrum et fortitudo mea Deus. In the catalogue of 1677–78 with the shelf-mark T 26, which also appears on the fore-edge of the book **G&C** K.20.28 This copy was printed in Cologne, without a printer's name. With the author's motto Castrum et fortitudo mea on the title-page.Underlining **JSC** G.2.13 typis Philippi de Ohr. Bequeathed by Lionel Gatford, D.D. and a former student of the college, in 1715. MS. notes to Book 3 **PMC** 10.8.29 With the college bookplate of 1700 and the motto Castrum et fortitudo mea Deus. The author's name and the title of the book appear on the fore-edge, indicating that it was probably acquired in the 17th century **SJCC** Mm.9.3 Bequeathed by John Collins, fellow and Professor of Physick, in 1634.

186 De universa muliebrium morborum medicina, altera ed., Hamburgi, Frobeniano, 1617. 4°

    WAD K 21.9 Given by John Goodridge (1580–1654), one of the founding fellows.

    TRC S.10.125 In the catalogue of the new library (1675–95) it has the number Q.Delta.5, and Q is an element in several of the cancelled shelf-marks in the book.

187 De universa muliebrium morborum medicina, 3a ed., Hamburgi, ex bibliopolio Frobeniano, 1628. 4°

    BLL 0825 e 10 Listed in the 1709 catalogue with the shelf-mark N.13.2 (and others) which are still visible in the volume. Probably to be identified with the gift of Nicholas Crouch, fellow, in 1690. Chain mark **CHC** O.M.4.2 From the Orrery bequest of 1732 **HER** SSS.2.14 From Magdalen Hall, to which it was given by Samuel Thurner, who was a doctor, in 1692. Chain mark **JSO** I.7.5 Gall. Bequeathed in 1724 by Griffith Davies MD and fellow **MGO** r.6.4 Chain mark.

    SJCC Mm.5.17 **KCC** F.8.10 Listed in the catalogue of 1738.

188 Medicus-politicus sive de officiis medico-politicis tractatus, quatuor distinctus libris, Hamburgi, ex bibliopolio Frobeniano, 1614. 4°

    ORI 2Ne7 Given by John Sanders, or Saunders, while he was provost, 1644–52/3. Chain mark. In both the 17th-century catalogues **TRO** M.5.29(2) Signed Francis Combe (1601–41), who was related to the founder of the college, Sir Thomas Pope. Listed in the chained catalogue. Some pencil annotations. Combe was also a benefactor of Sidney Sussex. See **324 WAD** K 21.10 Given by John Goodridge, one of the founding fellows, in 1651.

    CUL (2 copies) M*.11.12 (E) Acquired before 1715. Signed M. Wigmor; K.5.15

From the Royal Library, deposited in 1715, and in the MS. catalogue **SJCC** Hh.9.11 (1) **TRC** S.21.19 Among the medical books left by John Nidd in 1659. He owned the book by 1654.

189 Tractatus brevis de natura, et causis pestis, quae hoc anno M.D.XCVI Hamburgensem ciuitatem affligit, Hamburgi, excudebat Jacobus Lucius Junior, 1596. 4°

BOD (2 copies) 4° C 11(3) Med. In the 1620 catalogue with the current shelf-mark; Ashm. 1036 (8) From the collection of Elias Ashmole, 1617–92, founder of the Ashmolean Museum.

G&C K.32.33 (4) Bound with other medical and vetinerary works, the latest printed in 1631 (Adams C1014).

Cerqueira, Luís (1552–1614)

A Jesuit, and Bishop of Japan. In his preface to the priests of his diocese he states that this manual for the administration of the sacraments has been adapted to suit local conditions. There is no statement of his nationality in the book, but he was born in Alviro, in the diocese of Évora. De Backer & Sommervogel; *Gutenberg comes to Japan: The Jesuit Mission Press, 1590–1620.*

189.01 Manuale ad sacramenta ecclesiae ministranda, Nangasaquii, in collegio japonico societatis Iesu, 1605. 4°

BOD Arch. Be. 22 The book was at one time in Peking. With a shelf-mark similar to **269,** and likely to have entered the library at about the same time, 1827–9. This was a period when the Bodleian acquired a number of very rare books published by the Jesuit mission press in Japan, e.g. **765–6.**

Chagas, Gerardo das (–1610)

He was a Cistercian. His compilation about the privileges of the Benedictine order may have been printed in the monastery of Alcobaça, which a few years later was responsible for the production of the famous history of Bernardo de Brito. It is evident from the title-page that some commonly used characters, like c cedilla, were missing from the font available to the printers. It is one of the few books in Portuguese listed in the 1605 Bodley catalogue. Barbosa Machado, II, p. 377.

190 Defensam do dereito e justiza que tem a Ordem de Sam Bernardo do Reino de Portugal no padroado dos mosteiros da mesma Ordem, *no publisher or place,* 1594. Fol.

BOD B 15.20 (1) Th. Formerly B.17.15 Th. Chain mark. In the 1605 catalogue (Anselmo 1236).

Chaves, Tomás de (–1570) (editor)

A Dominican, who studied in Salamanca under the famous Spanish Dominican and canon lawyer Francisco de Vitoria. He edited **191** - a

book by Vitoria – and prepared it for publication. It is typical of Oxford to have, not the first Spanish edition of 1560, nor the Lisbon edition of 1564 (João da Barreira), but a later reprint published in the Low Countries (not listed by Palau).
Barbosa Machado, III, p. 742; Palau, XXVII, pp. 373–5.

191 Summa sacramentorum Ecclesiae, ex doctrina R.P.F. Francisci a Victoria, Antuerpiae, in aedibus Petri Belleri, 1580. 12°
BOD 8° V 14 Th. In the 1620 catalogue with the current shelf-mark.

Coelho, Jorge (?–1563)
Humanist and secretary to Cardinal-Prince Henrique (1512–80). Amongst the shorter pieces contained in **192**, which is one of the earliest books listed in the short-title catalogue, there are a number of Latin poems dedicated to the Portuguese royal family. The book was acquired in the twentieth century. Even in this Portuguese edition the author is described as 'Lusitani' on the title-page.
José Sebastião da Silva Dias, *A política cultural da época de D. João III*, pp. 241–52; Barbosa Machado, II, 802–4.

192 De patientia Christiana liber vnus. Item nonnulla alia quae in fine videbis, [Lisbon], apud Ludovicum Rothorigum, 1540. 4°
BOD Vet. G1 e.19 Entered the library after 1937 (Anselmo 1018).

Conimbricenses
The complete commentaries form sets which can be found in a number of libraries. For a discussion of the sets, and of other questions relating to these famous commentaries see Chapter Two. Altogether there are around 100 copies of thirty-nine editions of the various volumes in Oxford, but only twenty in Cambridge. Of these at least 70% were acquired before 1750. (Some are not authentic, like **232**, which is a pirated edition, and **235**, which is a compilation probably put together by the printer).
  The first editions of the commentaries on Aristotle produced in Coimbra were all printed in Portugal, but no copy of them reached Oxford before the nineteenth century. In the early modern period university and college libraries were supplied principally by Zetzner of Cologne and Cardon and Pillehotte of Lyon. Their editions, which appeared virtually simultaneously and often contain the same preliminary material, are an indication of how anxious the Jesuits were to see the commentaries in use throughout Catholic Europe.
Pinharanda Gomes, *Os Conimbricenses*; Francisco Rodrigues, *História da Companhia de Jesus na Assistência de Portugal*, II.2.116–19; Amândio A. Coxito, 'O curso conimbricense', *História do Pensamento Filosófico Português*, vol. 2, pp. 503–43.

193 Commentarii . . . in libros de generatione et corruptione Aristotelis. 2a ed., Moguntiae, in officina typographica Ioannis Albini, 1600. 4°
BOD AA 116 Art. In the 1605 catalogue with the shelf-mark C.8.6. Part of a set. Chain mark **WOR** RR.s.6 Lacks the title page.

194 Commentarii . . . in libros de generatione et corruptione Aristotelis, Moguntiae, Ioannis Albini, 1601.4°
BLA With the signature of Henry Hall. 17th-century binding with fillets **PMO** 2e.6 Bound with **199, 216, 225 SJCO** Delta.4.24(1) Given by Charles May 1634 who matriculated that year, aged 15. Bound with **211**.

195 Commentarii . . . in libros de generatione et corruptione Aristotelis, 2a ed., Moguntiae, in officina typographica Ioannis Albini, 1606. 4°
ASC I inf 1–6 Part of a set given by Morgan Winne, fellow, in 1610. Bound using Ker centrepiece xi(a), in use 1610–20 (Pearson, p. 78). Chain mark **CHC** Hyp.L.51 It is part of a set, and probably the item listed in the 1665 catalogue. Chain mark **MGO** D.3.4 Chain mark. Oxford binding roll xvii, which was in use until 1631, Pearson, p. 69 **PMO** 1F15 Bequeathed by H. W. Chandler, 1889. Bound with **202 WAD** (2 copies) K 12.21 Given by Edward Brounker, or Brunkard, one of the founding fellows, in 1614. Bound with **222**; O 30.9.

196 Commentarii . . . in libros de generatione et corruptione Aristotelis, 2a ed., Lugduni, sumptibus Horatii Cardon, 1606. 4°
BOD 4° E 17 Med. Signed Grott 1809. Part of a set probably acquired in the 19th century.

197 Commentarii . . . in duos libros de generatione et corruptione Aristotelis, Lugduni, sumptibus Horatii Cardon, 1613. 4°
ORI 2TG11 Chain mark. Bound with **214**. In both the 17th-century catalogues.

198 Commentarii . . . in libros de generatione et corruptione Aristotelis, 3a ed., Moguntiae, 1615, in officina typographica Ioannis Albini, 1615. 4°
BOD (2 copies) 2902 d.22 Acquired after 1864; Vet. D2 d. 9 Acquired in 1961 **CCCO** Fol.I.17 Owned by Samuel Parr in 1816, indicating that it entered the library after that date. Bound with **215 JSO** K.12.21(1) In the 1649 catalogue. Bound with **220 MER** 120.F.9 From the library of F. H. Bradley, 1846–1924, but probably in Merton before that date. Chain mark, signed Anne Thompson on endpaper **NEW** BT3.258.5 Part of a set, with identical binding and signs of chaining. Listed together in the catalogue of 1686 **WOR** E.10.8, from the library of Gloucester Hall (extinguished in 1714).
CUL P*.10.7 (D) Acquired before 1715, and with one previous owner whose name has been obliterated. Part of a set. **EMM** S.6.2.28 Bequeathed by Archbishop William Sancroft in 1693 **SJCC** Ff.10.7 Given by Thomas Bendish (?1607–?74), ambassador at Constantinople.

199 Commentarii . . . in libros de generatione et corruptione Aristotelis, 3a ed., Coloniae, sumptibus haeredum Lazari Zetzneri, 1633. 4°
PMO 2e.6 Bequeathed by H. W. Chandler, 1889. Bound with **194, 216, 225**.

200 Commentarii . . . in octo libros Physicorum Aristotelis, Conimbricae, typis et expensis Antonii a Mariz, 1592. 4°
BOD Vet. G1 d. 18 Acquired in 1961 (Anselmo 901).

201 Commentarii . . . in octo libros Physicorum Aristotelis, Lugduni, sumptibus Ioannis Baptistae Buysson, 1594. 4°
MER 120.F.8 (2 pts in 1) From the library of F. H. Bradley, 1846–1924, but probably in Merton before that date. Chain mark.

202 Commentariorum . . . in octo libros Physicorum Aristotelis . . . prima [-secunda] pars, Coloniae, sumptibus Lazeri Zetzneri, 1600. 4°
BOD AA 115 Art. In the 1605 catalogue. Part of a set **ORI** 2Qa18 From Sir David Ross's donation of 1971 **PMO** 1F15 Bequeathed by H. W. Chandler, 1889. Bound with **195**.

203 Commentariorum . . . in octo libros Physicorum Aristotelis . . . prima [-secunda] pars, Coloniae, sumptibus Lazari Zetzneri, 1602. 4°
ASC I infra 8 Part of a set given by Morgan Winne, fellow, in 1610. Bound using Ker centrepiece vi, in use 1605–20 (Pearson, p. 77). Chain mark **QUO** BB.f.162(1) Title page of Part I missing. Bound with **233**.

204 Commentarii . . . in octo libros Physicorum Aristotelis . . . prima [-secunda] pars, Lugduni, apud Ioannem Pillehotte, 1602. 4°
BOD 4° E 12 Med. Signed Grott 1809. Part of a set probably acquired in the 19th century **MGO** D.3.6 The gift of Robert Pierce, son of President Thomas Pierce and commensalis. Robert matriculated 1668–9, aged 12, BCL 1675–6. Bound with **212**. Chain mark. Part of a set.

205 Commentariorum . . . in octo libros Physicorum Aristotelis . . . prima [-secunda] pars, Coloniae, sumptibus Lazari Zetzneri, 1609. 4°
CHC (2 copies) Hyp.L.50. It is part of a set, and is probably referred to in the 1665 catalogue. Chain mark; Z.P.5.7 **NEW** BT3.258.3 Part of a set, all with identical binding and signs of chaining. All five vols are listed together in the catalogue of 1686 **SEH** 4° D1 With the signature of Nathaniel Dod, 14 April 1619. On the title-page a note stating that it is in the college library with the date 1749. Chain mark **SJCO** Delta.4.23(1) Given by Charles May in 1634. Bound with **222**. Part of a set with similar bindings and chain marks **WAD** K 12.22 Given by Edward Brounker, one of the founding fellows, in 1614. Bound with **212**.

206 Commentariorum . . . in octo libros Physicorum Aristotelis . . . prima [-secunda pars, Coloniae, sumptibus haeredum Lazari Zetzneri, 1616. 4°
CCCO Fol.I.16 A copy owned by Samuel Parr in 1816, indicating that it entered the library after that date. Bound with **223**.

207 Commentariorum . . . in octo libros Physicorum Aristotelis . . . prima [-secunda] pars, Coloniae, sumptibus haeredum Lazari Zetzneri, 1625. 4°
BOD Vet. D2 d. 6 Given by Mrs Hardie in 1963 **PMO** 2.e5 Bequeathed by H. W. Chandler 1889. Bound with **231 WAD** K 13.3 Given by Phineas Bury, 1635–78/9.
CUL P*.10.6 Part of a set, deposited in the library before 1715 **EMM** S.6.2.39 Bequeathed by Archbishop William Sancroft in 1693 **SJCC** Ff.10.5(1) Bound with **234**.

208 Commentariorum . . . in octo libros Physicorum Aristotelis . . . prima [-secunda] pars, Lugduni, sumptibus Iacobi Cardon & Petri Cavellat, 1625. 4°

ORI 2TG12 Given by Henry Chamberlaine, who entered Oriel 1633/4 and died 1666. Chain mark. Bound with 224. In both the 17th-century catalogues, with the date of publication as 1616 **WOR** E.10.6 From the library of Gloucester Hall (extinguished in 1714).

209 Commentarii . . . in quatuor libros de Coelo Aristotelis, *with* Parva Naturalia, In libros Meteororum, In libros Ethicorum, Olisipone, ex officina Simonis Lopesii, 1593. 4°

BOD Vet. G1 d.17 Acquired 1961 (Anselmo 794–7).

210 Commentarii . . . in quatuor libros de Coelo Aristotelis, *with* Parva Naturalia, In libros Meteororum, In libros Ethicorum, 2a ed., Lugduni, ex officina Iuntarum, 1594. 4°

MER 120.F.7(1) From the library of F. H. Bradley, 1846–1924, but probably in Merton before that date. Chain mark.

211 Commentarii . . . in quatuor libros de Coelo, Meteorologicos & Parua Naturalia Aristotelis *with* In libros Ethicorum, 4a ed., Coloniae, Lazari Zetzneri, 1599–1600. 4°

BOD AA 118(1) Art. Formerly C.8.7, in the 1605 catalogue with shelf-mark C.8.5, altered to C.8.7 in 1620 Chain marks. Bound with **219 JSO** K.15.5 From the library of Dr Mansell, deposited in 1649 **PMO** 1F14 Bequeathed by H. W. Chandler, 1889. Bound with **219 SEH** 4°D2 With blind-stamped Oxford binding of around 1600 and college bookplate of 1704. Chain mark **SJCO** Delta.4.24(2) Given by Charles May 1634 who matriculated that year, aged 15. Part of a set, with similar bindings and chain marks.

212 Commentarii . . . in quatuor libros de Coelo, Meteorologicos & Parua naturalia Aristotelis, 5a ed., *with* In libros Ethicorum, Coloniae, impensis Lazari Zetzneri, 1603. 4°

ASC i.infra 1.8 Oxford binding, Ker centrepiece vi, in use 1605–20 (Pearson p. 77), and chain marks **CHC** Hyp.L.53. It is part of set, and is probably the copy listed in the 1665 catalogue **MGO** D.3.6(2) The gift of Robert Pierce, son of President Thomas Pierce and commensalis. Robert matriculated 1668–9, aged 12, BCL 1675–6. Bound with **204**. Chain mark. Part of a set **NEW** BT3.258.7 Part of a set, with identical binding and signs of chaining. All five vols are listed together in the catalogue of 1686 **WAD** K 12.22 Given by Edward Brounker, one of the founding fellows, in 1614. Bound with **205 WOR** II.1.21 Oxford binding, Ker centrepiece xi or xi(a), in use from the early 1590s to 1620 (Pearson, pp. 77–8).

213 Commentarii . . . in quatuor libros de Coelo, Meteorologicos, Parua Naturalia & Ethica Aristotelis, Lugduni, sumptibus Horatii Cardon, 1608. 4°

BOD 4° E 13 Med. Signed Grott 1809. Part of a set probably acquired in the 19th century.

214 Commentarii . . . in quatuor libros de Coelo, Metereologicos, Parva Naturalia, & Ethica Aristotelis, Lugduni, sumptibus Ioannis Pillehotte, 1616. 4°

BLL 1555 d 09(1) The book came from New Inn Hall, which was a medieval hall extinguished in the 19th century. Signature of John Hippisly of King's College Cambridge, 1664. **EXE** AAL 43 CA Lacks title page. **ORI** 2TG11 Chain mark. Bound with **197**, which is in both the 17th-century catalogues.

MGC B.15.3 17th-century Cambridge binding with fillets.

215 Commentarii . . . in quatuor libros de Coelo, Meteorologicos & Parua Naturalia Aristotelis, 5a ed., Coloniae, sumptibus haeredum Lazari Zetzneri, 1618. Fol.

CCCO Fol.I.17, signed Samuel Parr 1816, which suggests the book entered the library after that date. Bound with **198**.

216 Commentarii . . . in quatuor libros de Coelo, Meteorologicos & Parva Naturalia Aristotelis, 5a ed., *with* In libros Ethicorum, Coloniae, sumptibus haeredum Lazari Zetzneri, 1631. 4°

PMO 2e.6 Bequeathed by H. W. Chandler, 1889. Bound with **194, 199, 225**.

CUL (2 copies) P*.10.5 (D) In the library before 1715. Bound with **225** and part of a set; Path.c.225 **EMM** S.6.2.38 Bequeathed by Archbishop William Sancroft in 1693 **SJCC** Ff.10.6 Given by Thomas Bendish (?1607—?74) ambassador at Constantinople.

217 Commentarii . . . in tres libros de anima Aristotelis, Conimbricae, typis & expensis Antonii a Mariz Universitatis Typographi, 1598. 4°

BOD Vet. G1 d.16 Acquired in 1961 (Anselmo 916).

218 Commentarii . . . in tres libros de anima Aristotelis, 2a ed., Lugduni, apud Horatium Cardonum, 1600. 4°

BOD (2 copies) Antiq. d.F. 1600.1 Acquired 1900; Byw. D 1.13 c.20 From the Bywater bequest of 1914.

219 Commentarii . . . in tres libros de anima Aristotelis, 3a ed., Coloniae, impensis Lazari Zetzneri, 1599–1600. 4°

BOD AA 118(2) Art. Bound with **211**. In the 1605 catalogue. Chain mark **PMO** 1F14, bound with **211**. Bequeathed by H. W. Chandler in 1889. **PHI** B.7.4. With Ker centrepiece xi or xia and ornament 63, in use between 1590 and 1620, but not necessarily in Oxford (Pearson, pp. 77–8, who notes that the design 'generated many variants both in Britain and abroad'). Bequeathed by Thomas Fowler, President of Corpus Christi College, in 1904.

220 Commentarii . . . in tres libros de anima Aristotelis, 4a ed., Coloniae, impensis Lazari Zetzneri, 1603. 4°

ASC i-inf.1–9 With the signature of Walter Pinfield or Tinfield. MS. index. Ker centrepiece vi, in use c. 1605–20 (Pearson, p. 77). **JSO** K.12.21(2) In the collection of Dr Mansell, deposited in 1649. Bound with **198**.

221 Commentarii . . . in tres libros de anima Aristotelis, 3a ed., Lugduni, apud Horatium Cardon, 1604. 4°

BOD (2 copies) 4° E 16 Med. Signed Grott 1809. Part of a set probably acquired in the 19th century; Antiq.d.F.1604.1 Acquired in 1909.

222 Commentarii . . . in tres libros de anima Aristotelis, 4a ed., Coloniae, impensis Lazari Zetzneri, 1609. 4°
BOD 4° C 13 Art. Seld. From the Selden bequest of 1659. In the 1674 catalogue **ASC** I inf 1–4 Part of a set given by Morgan Winne, fellow, in 1610 **BLA** Unbound copy. Formerly belonged to Hinckley Priory **CHC** Hyp.L.52 Bound with **233**. The vol. is part of a set, and is probably that listed in the catalogue of 1665. Chain mark **MGO** D.3.7, Chain mark. The gift of Robert Pierce, son of President Thomas Pierce and commensalis. Robert matriculated 1668–9, aged 12, BCL 1675–6. Part of a set **NEW** BT3.258.6 Part of a set. All five vols are listed together in the catalogue of 1686. Rebound **SJCO** Delta.4.23(2). Bound with **205**. Part of a set, with similar bindings and chain marks. **WAD** K 12.21 Gift of Edward Brounker, one of the founding fellows, in 1614. Bound with **195**.

223 Commentarii . . . in tres libros de anima Aristotelis, 4a ed., Coloniae, sumptibus haeredum Lazari Zetzneri, 1617. 4°
BOD Vet. D2 d. 15 part of the collection of Robert Finch of Balliol (1783–1830), formerly in the Taylor Institution **BNC** Lath. I.5.9, formerly K.5.10, among others. In the catalogue probably compiled in the 17th century with the shelf-mark K.5.11. Chain mark. **CCCO** Fol.I.16 A copy owned by Samuel Parr in 1816, indicating that it entered the library after that date. Bound with **206 WOR** E.10.9 From the library of Gloucester Hall (extinguished in 1714).

224 Commentarii . . . in tres libros de anima Aristotelis, 5a ed., Lugduni, sumptibus Iacobi Cardon & Petri Cavellat, 1627. 4°
ORI 2TG12 Given by Henry Chamberlaine, who entered Oriel 1633/4 and died 1666. Bound with **208**, which is in both the 17th-century catalogues.

225 Commentarii . . . in tres libros de anima Aristotelis, Coloniae, sumptibus Haeredum Lazari Zetzneri, 1629. 4°
MER 120 f.10 From the library of F. H. Bradley, 1846–1924, but probably in Merton before that date. MS. index **PMO** 2e.6 Bequeathed by H. W. Chandler in 1889. Bound with **194, 199, 216 SEH** 4°D3 College bookplate of 1704. 17th-century binding with fillets. Chain mark. On flyleaf: 'Liber Auli Sancti Edmundi in usum studiosorum inibi commorantium'.
CUL P*.10.5 (D). Acquired before 1715. Bound with **216** and part of a set **EMM** S.6.2.27 left by Archbishop William Sancroft in 1693 **SJCC** Ff.10.3.

226 Commentarii . . . in vniuersam dialecticam Aristotelis, Conimbricae, ex officina Didaci Gomes Loureyro, 1606. 2 vols 4°
BOD Vet. G2 d. 18 Acquired in 1961. Vol 2 has no title page **PMO** 1B7, 2 vols. in 1. Bequeathed by H. W. Chandler in 1889.

227 Commentarii . . . in vniuersam dialecticam Aristotelis . . . prima [-secunda] pars, Lugduni, sumptibus Horatii Cardon, 1607. 2 vols 4°
BOD 4° E 14,15 Med. Signed Grott 1809. Part of a set probably acquired in the 19th century ORI 2Qa16 Two vols in one. From Sir David Ross's donation of 1971.

228 Commentarii . . . in vniuersam dialecticam Aristotelis, Coloniae Agrippinae, apud Bernardum Gualtherium, 1607. 4°

BOD AA 117 Art., formerly Art C.8.6 In the 1620 catalogue with shelf-mark C.8.7. Chain mark **ASC** i-inf 1–7. Part of a set given by Morgan Winne, fellow, in 1610. Chain mark.
CUL Ven.4.60.1 With the signature of J. Venn, 1888. The book, which is a duplicate from Lund University library, was deposited in Cambridge in 1889.

229 Commentarii . . . in vniuersam dialecticam Aristotelis, Coloniae Agrippinae, apud Bernardum Gualterium, 1611. 4°
BLL From New Inn Hall, a medieval hall extinguished in the 19th century, with the signature of John Hippisly of King's College Cambridge 1664 **CHC** Hyp. L.49 Part of a set, and probably the one listed in the 1665 catalogue. All five vols are stamped W.W. The same stamp is found on the college's copy of **340–1**. Chain marks **MER** 120 f.11 From the library of F. H. Bradley, 1846–1924, but probably in Merton before that date. Chain mark **NEW** BT3.258.4 Part of a set, with identical binding and signs of chaining. All five volumes are listed together in the catalogue of 1686 **SJCO** Delta.4.22 Given by Charles May in 1634. Part of a set with similar bindings and chain marks.
CUL P*.10.8 (D) Acquired before 1715. Bound with **234**, and part of a set **MGC** F.5.26. Parchment binding.

230 Commentarii . . . in vniuersam dialecticam Aristotelis, prima [-secunda] pars, Lugduni, sumptibus Iacobi Cardon & Petri Cavellat, 1622. 4°
MGO D.3.5 Gift of Robert Pierce, son of president Thomas Pierce and commensalis. Robert matriculated 1668–9, aged 12, BCL 1675–6. Part of a set **ORI** 2T.G13 Signature of Henricus Camerarius, probably Henry Chamberlaine, who entered Oriel 1633/4 and died 1666. In both the 17th-century catalogues, under the title In Arist: Log.
EMM S.6.2.25 Bequeathed by Archbishop William Sancroft in 1693.

231 Commentarii . . . in vniuersam dialecticam Aristotelis, Coloniae, sumptibus haeredum Lazeri Zetzneri, 1630. 4°
PMO 2.e5 Bequeathed by H. W. Chandler in 1889. Bound with 207.

232 Commentarii . . . in uniuersam logicam Aristotelis, [Basel], Frobeniano, 1604. 2 vols 4°
BOD 4° C 32 Jur. In the 1620 catalogue **WAD** K 38.11 Two vols in one. Given by William Payton, one of the founding fellows, in 1632.

233 In libros Ethicorum Aristotelis ad Nichomachum aliquot . . . disputationes, 4a ed., Coloniae, impensis Lazari Zetzneri, 1603. 4°
CHC Hyp.L.52 Bound with **222**.**QUO** BB f.162 (2) Bound with **222**.

234 In libros Ethicorum Aristotelis ad Nichomachum aliquot . . . disputationes, 4a ed., Coloniae, impensis haeredum Lazari Zetzneri, 1621. 4°
BOD Wood 644(2) Bequeathed by Anthony Wood, antiquarian, in 1695. Bound with a variety of other works, including the English poems of Mrs Killigrew. (Kiessling (2002) 259).
CUL P*.10.8 (D) Bound with **229**, and in the library before 1715 **SJCC** Ff.10.5 (2) Bound with **207**. Given by Thomas Bendish (?1607–?74) ambassador at Constantinople.

235 Problemata quae in . . . physicis commentariis enodantur, Moguntiae, in officina typographica Ioannis Albi, 1601. 12°
BOD 8° C 18 Art.BS. In the 1674 catalogue.
MGC I.10.62 Parchment binding.

Constantino, Manuel (?–1614)

Born on the island of Madeira, about which he wrote a history, but from 1588 to his death lived in Rome, as a preacher and professor of philosophy. He is identified by some form of the word 'Lusitanus' on the title-page of all his poems and orations, except those dedicated to the Spanish Cardinal Bernardo de Sandoval.
Barbosa Machado, III, pp. 230–1.

235.01 Ad Bernardum Cardin. de Sandoval . . . Carmen, Romae, apud Nicolaum Mutium, 1599 4°
BOD Antiq. e.I. 1599/2 Acquired 1900.

235.02 Ad . . . Petrum Cardinalem Aldobrandinum . . . De discessu tanti Principis ex urbe Ferrariae in almam Vrbem, Romae, apud Aloysium Zannettum, 1599. 4°
BOD Antiq. e.I. 1599/2 Acquired 1900.

235.03 Ad . . . Petrum Cardinalem Aldobrandinum . . . Epistolarum liber unicus, Romae, apud Aloysium Zannettum, 1599 4°
BOD Antiq. e.I. 1599/2 Acquired 1900.

235.04 Ad . . . Petrum Cardinalem Aldobrandinum . . . in Iacobi Mazonii . . . funus, Romae, apud Aloysium Zannettum, 1599 4°
BOD Antiq. e.I. 1599/2 Acquired 1900.

235.05 Ad . . . Petrum Cardinalem Aldobrandinum pro Ferrariae victoria carmen, Romae, apud Aloysium Zannetum, 1599 4°
BOD Antiq. e.I. 1599/2 Acquired 1900.

235.06 Gratulatio pro summo pontificato . . . Pauli V, Romae, 1607. 4°
CUL Acton d.54.1 (24) Lord Acton's library was deposited in 1902.

235.07 Insulae Materiae historia, cui accesserunt orationes duae . . .& alia latina monumenta, Romae, ex typographia Nicolai Mutii, 1599. 4°
BOD Antiq. e.I. 1599/2 Acquired 1900.

235.08 Oratio in funere Philippi II, Romae, apud Aloysium Zannetum, 1599. 4°
BOD Antiq. e.I. 1599/2 Acquired 1900.

235.09 Oratio . . . in funere Seraphina a Portugallia, Johannis Brigantiae ducis filiae, Romae, ex typographia Stephani Paulini, 1604. 4°
CUL Acton d.54.1(16) Lord Acton's library was deposited in 1902.

235.10 Vehemens deprecatio ad . . . Virginem Mariam . . . pro salute . . .
Clementis VIII, Romae, apud Aloysium Zannettum, 1599 4°
BOD Antiq.e.I.1599/2 Acquired 1900.

236 Constituições do arcebispado de Lisboa
Lisboa, Belchior Rodrigues, 1588. 4°
BOD AA 117(1) Th. Seld. From the Selden bequest of 1659. Chain mark (Anselmo
997).

Correia, Tomé (1536–95) (Thomas Correa, Thome Correia)
A humanist and writer on literary theory. After studying in Coimbra he
taught briefly at Évora, but most of his professional life was spent in
Italy, particularly in Rome and Bologna, where he died. He never
mentions his nationality on the title-pages of his works, unlike Manuel
Constantino, Aquiles Estaço and João Vaz da Mota, who also worked in
Rome. However, his funeral oration on Martín de Azpilcueta was
delivered in the Portuguese church there (Santo Agostino dei Porto-
ghesi) and in the oration he refers to himself and to his congregation as
'Lusitani', sig. A2v. Information about the provenance of copies of his
work is scanty.
Biblos: Enciclopédia Verbo das Literaturas de Língua Portuguesa, I, cols 1304–6 (article by
Aníbal Pinto de Castro).

237 De elegia . . . libellus, *with* De epigrammate, Bononiae, apud
Alexandrum Benatium, 1590. 4°
BOD 4° 245 AS Bequeathed by Benjamin Heath, M.A. of University College, in 1766.

238 In librum de arte poetica Q. Horatij Flacci explanationes, Venetiis,
apud Franciscum de Franciscis Senensem, 1587. 16°
BOD Meerm. 985 Acquired in 1824.
CUL Dd*.5.42 (G) With the bookplate of the Royal Library, deposited in 1715.

239 Oratio habita ad Xystum V. Pont. Max., Romae, expensis Valerij
Pasini, 1585. 4°
BOD 4° W 24(1) Jur.

240 Oratio in funere sapientissimi viri Doctoris Navarri D. Martini ab
Azpilcueta, Romae, ex typographia Iacobi Tornerij, & Bernardini
Donangeli, 1586. 4°
BOD 4° W 24(2) Jur.; 4° E 16(17) Th. BS Acquired after 1668.

Corte-Real, Jerónimo (1530?–1588)
A prolific epic poet, some of whose work antedates that of Camões.
However, early modern Oxford and Cambridge had no interest in
vernacular literature in Portuguese. See, for another example, Luís
Pereira Brandão (**133**).
Hélio J. S. Alves, *Camões, Corte-Real e o sistema da epopeia quinhentista.*

241 Felicissima victoria concedida del cielo al señor don Iuan d'Austria en el golfo de Lepanto, [from colofon] Lisboa, por Antonio Ribero, 1578. 4°

BLL 0700 d 08 19th-century binding. In the 1871 catalogue (Anselmo 938).

Costa, Cristóvão da (?1515–?92) (Cristobal Acosta)
A doctor, probably a New Christian, always described in the preliminaries to his books as an African. His study of Indian plants and medicine is closely related to Orta's pioneering book of 1563 (**627**). He was probably born in Tangier, which had been a Portuguese possession since 1470. He seems to have been in the service of Dom Luís de Ataíde, viceroy of India from 1568–71. There he wrote the treatise which made him famous (**242**). It was first printed, in Spanish, in Burgos where he worked as a doctor from 1576–86. A later work, **248**, was published in Venice, but it is not clear from the rather vague preface 'de un amigo del autor' whether, like many Jewish doctors, he moved to Italy.

Altogether there are five copies of the first edition of *Tractado delas drogas* in Oxford, an indication of the effectiveness of Spanish publishing, as opposed to Portuguese, and of the acceptability of the Spanish language. The eighteenth-century botanist William Sherard owned a copy of the first edition and of the French and Italian translations. However, it was the Latin version by Clusius that made the most impact in early modern Oxford and Cambridge. There are marginalia in copies of **243** and **244**.

Cristóvão da Costa, *Tratado das drogas e medicinas das Índias orientais,* tr. and ed. by Jaime Walter; M. N. Pearson, 'Hindu Medical Practice in Sixteenth-Century Western India', pp. 107–10.

242 Tractado delas drogas, y medicinas de las Indias Orientales, Burgos, por Martin de Victoria, 1578. 4°

BOD (2 copies) 4° A 12 Med. In the 1605 catalogue with the current shelf-mark; 4° F 43 Med. **PLS** Sherard 3 From the collection of William Sherard, deposited in 1726 and 1728 **RSL** RR. w. 481 Acquired between 1749 and 1835 **WAD** G 20.23 Given by Charles Godolphin in 1720. Part of the collection of Sir William Godolphin (?1634–96).

243 [Tractado delas drogas, y medicinas de las Indias Orientales], Aromatum & medicamentorum in orientali India nascentium liber, *tr. by Carolus Clusius,* Antuerpiae, ex officina Christophori Plantini, 1582. 8°

CHC Ok.6.11(1) Signatures of Edward Windsor and Nicholas Wyat, perhaps the Nicholas Wyat who took his BCL degree at Christ Church 1568–9. It may have formed part of the Orrery collection, bequeathed in 1732. Bound with **630 NEW** BT3.226.13 Repaired Oxford binding, with Ker centrepiece iv, in use between c.1600 and 1620 (Pearson, p. 77) **SJCO** HB4/4.a.1.17(3) MS. marginal notes and underlinings.

EMM (2 copies) 333.3.13 It is likely that this copy was left by Archbishop William Sancroft in 1693; 331.4.118 (3) The third of three short botanical works associated with Clusius, all published by Plantin in the same year. The first is signed William Sheppard. There were a number of students with this name in Cambridge in the early 17th century, but none at Emmanuel. **MGC** H.17.16(3) Bound with item **630**. With MS. indices (Adams C2725).

244 [Tractado delas drogas, y medicinas de las Indias Orientales], Aromatum & medicamentorum in orientali India nascentium liber, *tr. by Carolus Clusius,* Antuerpiae, ex officina Plantiniana, apud viduam, & Ioannem Morteum, 1593. 8° (Bound with **631**).

BOD Douce O 101 Part of the Douce collection left in 1834 **PLS** Sherard 166. From the collection of William Sherard, deposited in 1726 and 1728. With marginalia and MS. notes on the flyleaf and endpages **RSL** RR. w. 453 Acquired after 1835. Bound with **631 SJCO** HB4/4.a.4.21(2) The gift of Dr Reynolds or Reanolds President of Corpus (1549–1607).

CUL (2 copies) P*.6.53 (F) Given by Henry Lucas, benefactor and founder of the Lucasian professorship of mathematics, in 1663. It had been in his possession since 1654; CCD.47.88 Given by John Martyn, Professor of Botany, (1699–1768) and with the signature of John Banister (1540–1610) **SJCC** Ll.11.14 In the catalogue compiled around 1640 (Adams O322).

245 [Tractado delas drogas, y medicinas de las Indias Orientales], Aromatum et medicamentorum in orientali India nascentium historia, *tr. by Carolus Clusius and included in his Exoticorum liber nonus,* 3a ed., Antuerpiae, ex officina Plantiniana Raphelengii, 1605. Fol. (Bound with **632**).

CHC G.2.4 **MGO** R.17.7 Given by John Goodyear, who was an important donor of medical books, in 1664 **RSL** RR. x. 308 (1) Acquired between 1749 and 1835 **SJCO** Y.2.12 From the Crynes bequest of 1745 **UNI** Given by Elias Wrench and now in **MHS** at P/ CLUos **WAD** J 26.7 Bequeathed by Richard Warner, who graduated B.A. in 1734. His library, particularly rich in works on natural history and botany, was left to the college in 1775. A copy now disappeared is listed in the Bodley catalogue of 1620.

CUL L.2.6 From the Royal Library, deposited in 1715 **CLA** L1.1.19 With the bookplate of 1701. In the catalogue of 1577–78 with the shelf-mark S.8 **EMM** 314.2.19 Probably among those left by Archbishop William Sancroft in 1693.

246 [Tractado delas drogas, y medicinas de las Indias Orientales] Traicté . . . des drogues & medicamens qui naissent aux Indes, *tr. from Latin by* Anthonie Colin, Lyon, aux despens de Iean Pillehotte, 1619. 8° (Bound with **634**).

BOD Douce CC 41 Part of the Douce collection left in 1834 **PLS** Sherard 59(2) From the collection of William Sherard, deposited in 1726 and 1728.

247 [Tractado delas drogas, y medicinas de las Indias Orientales] Trattato . . . della historia, natura, et virtu delle droghe medicinali . . ., Venetia, presso a Francesco Ziletti, 1585. 4°

PLS Sherard 387 From the collection of William Sherard, deposited in 1726 and 1728. **CUL** K.8.51 Repaired binding, but probably from the Royal Library, deposited in 1715 (Adams A121).

248 Tratado en loor de las mugeres, y dela Castidad, Onestidad, Constancia, Silencio, y Iusticia, . . . Venetia, presso Giacomo Cornetti, 1592. 4°

BOD 4° A 5 Art. In the 1605 catalogue and in the 1620 catalogue with the current shelf-mark.
CUL Hisp.7.59.1 From the library of Norman MacColl, presented in 1905 (Adams A120).

Costa, Manuel da (1541–1604) (Acosta, Emanuel)

Jesuit historian, who seems never to have left Europe. His history of the missions in the East, translated into Latin by Giovanni Pietro Maffei, achieved wide circulation because it was included in compilations. See **487** and **489–96**. There is some uncertainty as to the language Costa wrote. Barbosa Machado says it was Portuguese, but the title-page of **250** claims that Maffei translated from Spanish.
Barbosa Machado, III, pp. 236–7.

De rebus indicis ad annum usque a Deipara Virgine MDLXVIII commentarius, *in* Rerum a Societate Iesu in Oriente gestarum volumen, Coloniae, apud Geruinum Calenium & haeredes Iohannis Quentel, 1574. 8°
For copies of this edition see **487**.

249 Historia rerum a Societate Jesu in Oriente gestarum ad annum . . . 1568, Paris, apud Michaelem Sonnium, 1572. 8°
SJCO HB4/1.a.4.8 Given by William Paddy, 1602.

Historia rerum a societate Iesu in Oriente gestarum, ad annum usque Christi Domini M.D. LXVIII, Antuerpiae, in officina Martini Nutii, 1605. 8°
Included in Maffei Historiarum indicarum. See **489–96**.

250 Rerum a Societate Iesu in oriente gestarum ad annum vsque a Deipara Virgine M.D.LXVIII commentarius, *tr. from Spanish by Giovanni Pietro Maffei, together with a selection of letters,* Dilingae, apud Sebaldum Mayer, 1571, 8°
BOD (2 copies) Antiq. f.X. 28 (3) Acquired 1928; Vet. D1 f.10 Acquired after 1937
CHC f.10.37 Bequeathed by Robert Burton, 1640. Oxford binding of around turn of 17th-century (Kiessling (1988) 5) **WOR** XY. b.47 Bequeathed by H. A. Pottinger in 1911.
EMM 324.5.18, formerly P.5.77, which is the shelf-mark given to the book in the 18th-century catalogue. However, it may have been acquired earlier, since it has a blind-stamped centrepiece binding and medieval pastedowns, suggesting that it was bound between 1560–1620. Many books at Emmanuel are second-hand; this one perhaps belonged to a Catholic who was impressed by the missions and wrote 'miracula Xaverii' at Fol. 9r. It is possible that his signature has been removed (Adams A129).
The edition of 1574 (Cologne) is included in **487**.

Costa, Manuel da (1512–62) (Acosta, Emanuel)

Jurist and humanist poet. He studied in Salamanca from 1527–32 before becoming, in 1537, one of the first professors of civil law in the refounded university of Coimbra. In 1561 he retired from Coimbra and returned to Salamanca. Nothing that he published in Portugal, and none of his literary compositions, reached Oxford or Cambridge, but of the four legal works that are in the university and college libraries three at least arrived very early, around 1600 (**252–4**). All four state his nationality on the title-page.

Pedro Urbano González de la Calle, 'Contribución a la biografía de Manuel da Costa "Doctor Subtilis" '.

251 Omnia quae quidem extant in ius canonicum et ciuile opera, Lugduni, sumptibus Philippi Tinghi Florentini, 1576. Fol.

JSO D.1.9.Gall.

252 Omnia quae quidem extant in ius canonicum et ciuile opera, Lugduni, in officina Q. Philippi Tinghi apud Simphorianum Beraud, et Stephanum Michaelem, 1584. Fol.

BOD B 6.8 Jur. Formerly C 9.1.Jur. In the 1605 catalogue, and in the 1620 catalogue with the shelf-mark C.9.1. Chain mark.

TRH M*.3.5, formerly O.2.1 and with 18 on the fore-edge, suggesting that it was acquired in the 17th century. College bookplate of 1700 (Adams C2726).

253 Cap. Si pater, De testament. lib. sexto, et. [section]. Cùm in bello. l. Qui duos ff. De reb. dub. Commentaria, Salmanticae, in aedibus Vincentij à Portonarijs, 1569. Fol.

MER 60.G.9 In Wijffels List C as having entered the library around 1600.

254 In nonnullas leges et paragraphos commentarii, Lugduni, apud haeredes Iacobi Iuntae, 1564. Fol.

MER 64.E.9 Chain mark. In Wijffels List C as having entered the library around 1600.

Costa, Nuno da (16th–17th centuries) (Nuñez Acosta)

Like many doctors, he lived in Italy, perhaps in Venice, since **255** is dedicated to a Venetian senator. Nevertheless, on the title-page he is described as 'Lusitanus'.

255 De quadruplici hominis ortu, *with* Pro geniti hominis cura de arte medendi liber unus, Patauii, apud Laurentium Pasquatum, 1594. 4°

CUL N*.10.35 (E) Acquired before 1715. The foot of the title-page is missing EMM 331.4.87, formerly 17.3.21, the shelf-mark listed in the 18th-century catalogue. Lacks Pro geniti . . . Repaired binding (Adams C2727).

Couto, Diogo do (1542–1616)

Historian of Portuguese Asia, who continued the work of João de Barros. Today he is regarded as the greatest figure in Portuguese historiography

of the second half of the sixteenth century, whose work is especially valuable because he spent many years in India. There was little interest in vernacular narrative history written by Portuguese in the early modern period, and it was only in the nineteenth century that copies of books by him printed before 1640 reached Oxford or Cambridge.
George Davison Winius, *The Black Legend of Portuguese India.*

256 Decada quarta [-setima] da Asia, dos feitos que os portugueses fizeram na conquista e descobrimento das terras, & mares do Oriente, Lisboa, Pedro Crasbeeck, 1602–16. 4 vols Fol.
BOD 243 h.21–24 Acquired after 1864 QUO Sel.c.186–189 Bought with money left by Robert Mason, 1841. Decade 6 is imperfect.

Cristo, Francisco de (–1587) (Franciscus, a Christo)
An Augustinian, professor at Coimbra from 1563–81, and stated on title-pages to be a native of the city. It is unusual for a Portuguese theologian who apparently did not study abroad to be represented by two works of early provenance both published in Portugal.
Fortunato de Almeida, *História da Igreja em Portugal,* II, p. 436; Luís de Matos, *Portugais à Paris,* p. 82.

257 Commentariorum in tertium librum Sententiarum [of Petrus Lombardus] libri duo, Conimbricae, typis Antonii a Mariz, 1585–86. Fol.
BOD D 1.14(1) Th. In the 1605 catalogue. Chain marks (Anselmo 888).

258 Enarrationes in collectanea primi libri Magistri Sententiarum, Conimbricae, typis Antonii a Mariz, 1579. Fol.
SJCO O.4.14 Given by Sir William Paddy, 1634.
CUL I*.4.5 (c) Acquired before 1715 (Anselmo 874).

Cruz, Gaspar da (–1570)
A Dominican and, according to C. R. Boxer, the author of the first book about China to be printed in Europe. It was based on extensive first-hand experience. Of the two copies in Oxford (none in Cambridge) one is of seventeenth-century provenance.
C. R. Boxer, *South China in the Sixteenth Century,* pp. l–lv.

259 Tractado em que se co[n]tam muito por este[n]so as cousas da China co[m] suas particularidades e assi do reyno dormuz, Euora, em casa de Andre de Burgos, 1569–1570. 4°
BOD D 9.32 Linc. From the Barlow bequest of 1691 ASC SR.15.n.11 Stamp of Nicolas de Azara (Anselmo 399).
Partly translated in **737,** Samuel Purchas, *Purchas his Pilgrimes,* vol. III, pp. 166–98.

Cruz, Luís da (1542–1604) (Ludovicus Crucius)
Jesuit poet and dramatist who was a native of Lisbon, according to the title-pages of his books. It is an indication of early modern Oxford and

Cambridge's relative indifference to the literary work of Portuguese writers, even when in Latin, that there should only be six copies of books by him in university and college libraries, of which three are of early provenance. Cruz's school plays were performed in Jesuit colleges outside Portugal and he was widely admired as a Latinist. According to Nigel Griffin, 263 did him great honour, because it was 'the first published collection of Jesuit Latin compositions anywhere in Europe'. If he had been a theologian the story would have been very different.

Nigel Griffin, 'Italy, Portugal and the Early Years of the Society of Jesus', p. 144.

260 Interpretatio poetica latine in centum quinquaginta psalmos, Ingolstadii, excudebat Adam Sartorius, 1597. 12°

TRC A.12.68 Bequeathed by John Laughton in 1712. He was college, and later University librarian.

261 Interpretatio poetica latine in centum quinquaginta psalmos, Madriti, ex officina Ludovici Sanchez, 1600. 16°

BOD Ps. Lat. 1600 f.1 Bought 1882.

262 Liber Psalmorum cum poetica interpretatione Latine, Neapoli, apud Tarquinium Longum, 1604. 4°

BOD 4° M 19(2) Th. In the 1620 catalogue with the current shelf-mark **ASC** SR.67.a.11 19th-century binding.

263 Tragicae, comicaeque actiones, Lugduni, apud Horatium Cardon, 1605. 8°

BOD 8° C 74 Art. (2 copies) In the 1620 catalogue with the current shelf-mark; Broxb. 39.2 From the Broxbourne Library, donated in 1978.

Cunha, Rodrigo da (1577–1643)

Bishop of Portalegre and Oporto, and finally Archbishop of Lisbon, famous for his resistance to Castilian rule and his support of the restored Portuguese monarchy. Writers of historical works in Portuguese did not normally interest readers in the English universities in the early modern period, and nearly everything by Cunha was acquired in the nineteenth century or later. There are also copies of books by him in Oxford which were printed after 1640.

Dicionário da História de Portugal, I, 773–4.

264 Catalogo e historia dos bispos do Porto, Porto, por Ioaõ Rodriguez, 1623. 4°

BOD Vet. G2 d.12 Acquired after 1937. Marginal notes in Portuguese **QUO** 28.A.17 Bought with money left by Robert Mason, 1841.
CUL F162.b.12.3.

265 Primeira [e segunda] parte da Historia Ecclesiastica dos arcebispos de Braga, Braga, Manuel Cardozo, 1634–35. Fol.

CUL Acton b.17.63 Lord Acton's library was presented in 1902.

266 Pro . . . Papae Pauli V statutu nuper emisso in confessarios, apud Matthaeum Donatum Benavente, 1611. 4°
CUL Acton d.2.153 Lord Acton's library was presented in 1902.

267 Tractatus de confessariis solicitantibus, 3ª ed. Vallisoleti, 1632. 4°
CUL Acton d.2.152 Lord Acton's library was presented in 1902.

Dalmada, Manuel (see Manuel de Almada)

Delgado, João Pinto (after 1582–1654)
A New Christian, originally from a family based in the Algarve. He fled from Portugal to France and Flanders, but only found lasting sanctuary in Amsterdam. His poems, entirely in Spanish, were dedicated to Cardinal Richelieu, who gave covert support to the Jewish community of Rouen, where **268** was published.
João Pinto Delgado, *Poema de la reina Ester, Lamentaciones del profeta Jeremías, Historia de Rut y varias poesías*, ed. by I. S. Révah, p. xxxii.

268 Poema de la Reyna Ester, Lamentaciones del Propheta Ieremias, Historia de Rut, y varias poesias, Rouen, chez Dauid du Petit Val, 1627. 8°
ASC Gallery nn.12.19.

Dias, Manuel, see Almeida, Manuel de

269 Dictionarium Latino Lusitanicum, ac Iaponicum
Amacusa, in Collegio Iaponico Societatis Iesu, 1595. 4°
BOD Arch. B e.41 Bought 1829. Strictly speaking, the book is anonymous, but it is known to be the work of João Rodrigues (see below)

Diez, Felipe (–1601) (Filipe Dias, Philippe Diez)
A Franciscan, noted especially for his preaching. He was educated in Salamanca and spent the whole of his career in Spain. Even the form of his name usually used is Spanish – in Portuguese it would be Filipe Dias. It is no doubt for these reasons that there is no entry for him in the *Grande Enciclopédia Portuguesa e Brasileira* or in Fortunato e Almeida. However, his Portuguese nationality is proclaimed on the title-page of every one of his books, including those in Spanish, and Barbosa Machado confirms that he was born in Bragança. His collected sermons, which covered every Sunday in the year, were a publishing success only comparable to that achieved by the Spanish Dominican Luis de Granada, according to Fidalgo. In Protestant England his sermons were widely acquired, and taking the two universities together there are at least twenty-one copies of books by him with early provenance. Another Franciscan, Francisco Campos, compiled **270–2**, which form an index of his work. In the letter

to the reader included in **270** Campos explains how **273** is a pirated edition, which is an indication of Diez's popularity as a preacher.
Barbosa Machado, II, 70–2; Fidalgo, *La imprenta en Salamanca*, I, p. 113.

270 Compendium siue index moralium conceptuum, *edited by* Francisco Campos, Salmanticae, excudebat Ioannes Ferdinandus, 1588. 4°
BOD 4° V 56 Th. Chain mark (Fidalgo 1237).

271 Compendium, sive index moralium conceptuum, *edited by* Francisco Campos, Venetiis, Societatem Minimam, 1597. 4°
WAD i5.13 Given by Dr Philip Bisse, 1613.
CUL H*.6.17 (D) Acquired before 1715 (Adams C491).

272 Compendium siue index moralium conceptuum, *edited by* Francisco Campos, Venetiis, apud Societatem Minimam, 1603. 4°
BOD KK 34(2) Th., previously P 36 Th. Chain mark.
EMM 333.4.62 There is an old shelf-mark, 18.4.55, which is not found in the 18th-century catalogue, making the date of acquisition uncertain.

273 Concionium quadruplicium, Lugduni, Savinianus Pesnot, 1586. 6 vols 4°
WAD H 18.19–24 Given by Dr Philip Bisse, 1613.
CUL Peterborough D.10.3- (For Peterborough Cathedral Library, see the Introduction, p. xiv.)

274 Conciones quadruplices, Venetiis, apud Dominicum de Farris, 1589. 4 vols in 3, 4°
WOR XB.2.1–3 With pastedowns in German which suggests that the book was not bound in Oxford.
EMM 301.5.78 (3 vols in 2) Bequeathed by John Breton, Master, in 1675 (Adams D451).

275 Conciones quadruplices, Venetiis, apud Ioannem Florinam, 1591. 2 vols. 4°
WAD i13.24–5.

276 Conciones quadruplices, Venetiis, apud Damianum Zenarium, [in colophon, apud Dominicum de Farris], 1596. 4 vols in 3, 4°
BOD A 8.16–18 Linc. Part of the Barlow bequest of 1691, but also in the 1620 catalogue, indictaing that it is a replacement. Chain marks.

277 Conciones quadruplices, Venetiis, apud haeredes Io. Ant. Bertani, 1600. 4 vols 4°
CCCO G.5.13–14 (vols1–2) and G.6.1(vols 3–4) Similar bindings, though vol 3 has been repaired, chain marks. The set was left by President John Spenser in 1614.

278 Conciones quadruplices, Moguntiae, sumptibus Antonii Hierati 1614. 1 vol., 4°
PMO U6a 4 vols in 1.With the signature of Thomas Throckmorton and motto in his hand, Habeas fiduciam. Printed bookplate showing that it was left by John Hall, Bishop of Bristol and Master, 1710.

MGC B.6.6 With Lusitanus on fore-edge, indicating early acquisition **SID** X.4.4 and 6–7. In the catalogue of 1674. With the title on the top edge, a practice which continued until the 1640s (Rogers, p. 78), and on the fore-edge.

279 Marial de la sacratissima Virgen Nuestra Señora, Salamanca, por Juan Fernandez, 1596. 4°
BLL 0570 e 08 In the 1871 catalogue.
CUL E.4.24 From the Royal Library, deposited in 1715, and in its MS. catalogue (Adams D452; Fidalgo 1423A).

280 Quadruplicium concionum, Salamanca, excudebat Ioannes Ferdinandus, 1584–1585. 6 vols 4°
CHC Hyp. G. 104–9 All the vols are signed by Fray Francisco de Aguirre, suggesting that the college was not the first owner. Marginal notes (Fidalgo, 1128–9 and 1157–60).

281 Quinze tratados, Salamanca, en la imprenta de Artus Taberniel, 1602. 4°
BOD 4° D 11 Th. In the 1605 catalogue, with the current shelf-mark.

282 Summa praedicantium, Venetiis, apud Ioannem Florinam, 1591. 2 vols 4°
WAD I 13.24–25 Given by Dr Philip Bisse, 1613.

283 Summa praedicantium, Lugduni, apud Petrum Landry, 1596. 4°
CUL H*.4.20 (D) In the library before 1715 (Adams D453).

284 Summa praedicantium, Antuerpiae, ex officina Martini Nutij, 1600. 2 vols 4°
BOD B 26.13 Linc. From the Barlow bequest of 1691, but also in the 1605 catalogue
SJCO R.4.36 Given by Nicholas Linnebye, fellow, in 1605.
EMM 333.2.20 Entered the library between 1597 and 1621 (Bush p. 184; Adams D454).

285 Summa praedicantium, Antuerpiae, ex officina haeredum Martini Nutii, 1613. 2 vols 4°
PMO U6a With the signature of Thomas Throckmorton and motto in his hand, Habeas fiduciam. Printed bookplate showing that it was left by John Hall, Bishop of Bristol and Master, 1710.
CUL H*.10.44 In the library before 1715 **SID** X.4.5. In the catalogue of 1674.

286 Summa praedicantium, Venetiis, apud Sebastianum de Combis, 1614. 4°
SJCC Oo.8.46.

Encarnação, João da (16th–17th cent.) (Iohannes ab Incarnatione)
Little is known of this Franciscan friar and editor of Duns Scotus except that, according to the title-page of **287**, he came from Lisbon.
Barbosa Machado, II, 651.

287 R.p.f. Ioannis Duns Scoti . . . in librum primum Sententiarum . . . Petri Lombardi, Conimbricae, typis Didaci Gomez Loureyro, 1609. Fol.
BOD Vet. G2 d. 24 Acquired after 1937.

Estaço, Aquiles (1524–1581) (Achilles Statius)
This humanist, Achilles Statius in Latin, almost shared his name with the Greek novelist of the second century A.D., Achilles Tatius, a fact of which Estaço was aware (see the poem dedicated to Tatius in **302**, fols. 3v–5r). As a boy he was tutored by João de Barros, as he explains in the dedication of **300**. After studying in Coimbra he left for Louvain, Paris and finally, between 1555 and 1559, Rome from where, unusually for a Portuguese, he never returned. However, he remained in contact with Portugal. Most, though not all, title-pages state his nationality, and one of the compositions in **301** records a recent Portuguese naval victory over a fleet from Atjeh (Sumatra). Another is an oration delivered in the name of King Sebastião.

Early modern Oxford and Cambridge were not especially interested in the work of the Portuguese humanists, though in Oxford there are four copies with old provenance of Estaço's commentary on the Greek poet Aratus's *Phaenomena.* Yet even this is bound with other commentaries and may not have been the selling point. Modern collectors have acquired his books, especially Ingram Bywater, who bequeathed nine items by Estaço in 1914.

Biblos: Enciclopédia Verbo das Literaturas de Língua Portuguesa, II, cols 389–92 (article by Sebastião Tavares de Pinho); Luís de Matos, *Portugais à Paris,* pp. 101–2 and 113; Jozef Ijsewijn, 'Achilles Statius, a Portuguese Latin Poet in Late 16th-Century Rome'.

288 Ad aliorum commentationes, *on Cicero's Topica,* epidoma, Parisiis, apud Thomam Richardum, 1549. 4°
CHC AB.6.9(3) Marginal notes. Bound with **430**.

289 Appendiculae explanationum in libros tres M. Tullii Ciceronis, impensis Martini Nutii, Antwerp, 1553. 8°
CUL L.20.49 From the Royal Library, deposited in 1715, and in its MS. catalogue. Bound with **290, 292, 300** (Adams S1665).

290 Castigationes ac explanationes in Topica M. Tullii Ciceronis, Lovanii, excudebat Servatius Sassenus, impensis viduae Arnoldi Birckmanni, 1553. 8°
ASC g.11.7(4) Signed Richard Rykens and Theophilus Sijvkens.
CUL L.20.49 From the Royal Library, deposited in 1715. Bound with **289, 292, 300** (Adams S1666).

291 Catullus cum commentario, Venetiis, in aedibus Manutianis, 1566. 8°
BOD (2 copies) Auct. 2 R inf. 88 Acquired after 1825. Bound with **303**; Byw. L 5.18 Bequeathed in 1914 by Ingram Bywater. Bound with **293** ASC e.6.15 CHC O.h.6.17 Bound with **303**.
TRC N.1.109 Probably acquired after 1800.

292 Commentarii in librum Ciceronis de fato, Louanij, ex officina Seruatij Sasseni, 1551. 8°

BOD (3 copies) 8° S 17(2) Jur. Belonged to Richard Eedes, Student (Fellow) of Christ Church (1555–1604). Ker no.1455, centrepiece ii, in use 1580–97 (Pearson, p. 75); Byw. L 7.9 Bound with 300; Byw. T 2.8 From the Bywater bequest of 1914 **QUO** CC.a.13 It is item 6 in a composite volume, Ker no. 1948, centrepiece in use c. 1610–20 (Pearson, p. 82). **CUL** L.20.49 With the bookplate of the Royal Library, deposited in 1715. Bound with **289, 290, 300 CLA** G.8.26 (2) Bound with **300 TRC** Z.8.140 One work included in this volume has the signature of Richard Remington. There were a number of students with this name at Cambridge in the 17th century, but none at Trinity (Adams S1667).

293 C. Suetonij Tranquilli libri ij. de inlustribus grammaticis et claris rhetoribus cum A. Statij commentatione, Romae, 1565. 8°
BOD Byw. L 5.18 (2) Bequeathed in 1914 by Ingram Bywater. Bound with **291**.

294 De reditibus ecclesiasticis qui beneficiis et pensionibus continentur, commentarioli ii, Romæ, apud haeredes Antonii Bladii Impressores Camarales, 1581. 8°
BOD Diss. U 108 (ex Biblioth. Nürenbergiana).

295 Gregorij Baetici . . . de Trinitate, sive de fide, *edited by Estaço*, Romae, in aedibus Populi Romani, 1575. 4°
BOD Antiq. e.I.1575.4 Given by All Souls College, 1928.

296 In Arati Phaenomena, *with text by Estaço in Greek*, Florentiae, in officina Iuntarum, Bernardi filiorum, 1567. Fol.
BLL 0635 d 10 In the 1709 catalogue with the shelf-mark D.12.15 which is still visible. Chain mark **CCCO** I.78(1) Chain mark. From the bequest of Brian Twyne, fellow, of 1644 **MER** 111.C.3(1) Chain mark **SJCO** Delta.3.12 (3) Given by Archbishop William Laud in 1634.

297 Inlustrium virorum ut exstant in urbe expressi vultus, Romae, formis Antonij Lafrej, 1569. Fol.
BOD (3 copies) Vet. F1 d. 14 With older Bodleian shelf-marks, but not in the early catalogues; Vet. F1 d.65 With bookplates of John Sparrow (1906–92) and Arthur H. S. Yeames. Lawn C. 55(2) Bequeathed by Brian Lawn in 2001 **CHC** AF.4.9(2) 17th-century bookplate.

298 In Q. Horatij Flacci poëticam commentarij, Antuerpiae, apud Martinum Nutium,1553. 4°
BOD Byw. T 2.9 Bequeathed in 1914 by Ingram Bywater.
CUL F155.d.6.1 With the bookplate of M. D. Babington, of Trinity, who died in 1851 (Adams S1668).

299 M. T. Ciceronis De optimo genere oratorum liber . . . commentarii, Lutetiae, apud [Michaelem] Vascosanum, 1551. 4°
BOD Byw. L 7.8 Bequeathed in 1914 by Ingram Bywater.

300 M. T. Ciceronis De optimo genere oratorum liber . . . commentarii, excudebat Seruatius Sassenus, impensis viduae Arnoldi Birckmanni, Louanii, 1552. 8°
BOD Byw. L 7.9 Bound with **292**. Bequeathed in 1914 by Ingram Bywater.

CUL L.20.49 With the bookplate of the Royal Library, deposited in 1715 CLA G.8.26 (1) With the 1701 college bookplate. Bound with 292 (Adams C1723).

301 Oratio oboedientialis, *with* Monomachia navis Lusitanae *and* insignia regum Lusitaniae, Romae, apud Iosephum de Angelis, 1574. 4°
BOD (2 copies) G.Pamph. 1829 (17) Probably from the bequest of Charles Godwyn, fellow of Balliol, 1770; Byw. T 2.10 Bequeathed in 1914 by Ingram Bywater. CUL Syn.6.57.3 Oratio only, probably acquired in 1875. Marginal note (Adams S1669).

302 Syluae aliquot vna cum duobus hymnis Callimachi, Parisiis, apud Thomam Richardum, 1549. 4°
BOD Byw. T 2.7 Bequeathed in 1914 by Ingram Bywater CHC Oa.4.4(1) Bound with works by eight other Latin poets, the latest dated 1611.

303 Tibullus, cum commentario, Venetiis, in aedibus Manutianis, 1567. 8°
BOD (2 copies) Auct. 2 R inf. 88 Acquired after 1825. Bound with 291; Byw. T 7.19 Bequeathed in 1914 by Ingram Bywater CHC O.h.6.17 Bound with 291. TRC N.1.111 Acquired probably after 1800.

Estaço, Gaspar (–1626)

Canon of Guimarães, not related to Aquiles Estaço. Barbosa Machado says he studied in Rome. His only printed work, which is in Portuguese and about the antiquities of Portugal, arrived in Oxford in the nineteenth century, like so many other books about Portuguese history.
Barbosa Machado II, 349.

304 Varias antiguidades de Portugal *with* Trattado da linhagem dos Estaços, Lisboa, por Pedro Crasbeeck, 1625. 4°
QUO 27.A.23 Bought with money left by Robert Mason, 1841.

Évora, André Rodrigues de (– after 1578) (Andreas Eborensis)

Libraries in English-speaking countries have a tendency to confuse this author of a successful commonplace book with the better known humanist André de Resende, who was also born in Évora and is usually referred to on title-pages as Andreas Resendius Eborensis. The error, which is found in OLIS and Newton, is repeated by Ann Moss and by the collaborators in *Private Libraries in Renaissance England*. The presence or absence of the surname Resende indicates which Andreas Eborensis is meant.

André Rodrigues de Évora came from a family of New Christians but, like many others, is described as 'Lusitanus' on the title-pages of successive editions of his book. One of his brothers was the doctor Tomás Rodrigues da Veiga (see below). Another member of the same family was the wealthy merchant Simão Rodrigues de Évora, who lived in Antwerp. Perhaps because of their links to the international Jewish or

New Christian community the brothers' books were very successful abroad. The commonplace book went through several editions in France, Germany and Italy, of which Oxford and Cambridge have five, all published in France. Although there are only eight copies in all in libraries today (six with old provenance) the book was quite well known in Elizabethan Oxford, and four inventories of private libraries of the 1570s and 1580s list it.

André Rodrigues de Évora, *Sentenças para a ensinança e doutrina do Príncipe D. Sebastião*, ed. Luís de Matos, pp. 24–8; Barbosa Machado, I, 145; Ann Moss, *Printed Commonplace-Books and the Structuring of Renaissance Thought*, pp. 201–2; *Private Libraries in Renaissance England*, IV, see Austin (no Christian name), William Battbrantes, Philip Johnson; VI, see Robert Dowe; J. Gentil da Silva, *Stratégie des affaires à Lisbonne entre 1595 et 1607*, pp. 3–5.

305 Sententiae et exempla, Lugduni, apud Theobaldum Paganum, 1557. 2 vols 8°

SJCO HB4/1a.3.19–20 Given by William Paddy 1602.

EMM 329.7.6, formerly Q.4.28, and listed with that number in the 18th-century catalogue. No book printed after 1712 appears in this part of the catalogue, and it is reasonable to assume that the book entered the library before then. How much earlier is unknowable, because the title-page is missing. 2 vols in 1. Medieval pastedown. **TRC** III.13.95 Signed Jane Lumley (1537–78), and in the Lumley catalogue of 1609. It also has the Newton-Puckering bookplate. It was deposited in the college library in 1691. Vol 1 only (Adams A1050, Lumley 100).

306 Sententiae et exempla, Parisiis, apud Gulielmum Iulianum, 1569. 2 vols 8°

BOD 8° E 9,10 Th. In the 1605 catalogue with current shelf-mark **BLL** 0650 a 12 Vol. 1 only. In the 1871 catalogue.

307 Sententiae et exempla, 3a ed., Parisiis, apud Gulielmum Iulianum, 1583. 2 vols 8°

WAD H 15.1–2 Given by Philip Bisse, 1613.

308 Sententiae et exempla, 5a. ed., Parisiis, apud Nicolaum Niuellium, [*in some copies* apud Michaelem Gadouleau] 1590. 8°

CUL Acton d.47.448 Lord Acton's library was presented in 1902 **SID** E.7.54 With the title on the top-edge, a practice which continued until the 1640s (Rogers, p. 78), and in the catalogue of 1674 (Adams A1051–2).

Fagundes, Estêvão (1577–1645) (Fagundez, Stephanus)

A Jesuit and moral theologian, who spent most of his career in Portugal but studied for some time in Salamanca (see **309**, p. 20). All his books were published abroad, sometimes after considerable delay. The royal licence of **310**, for instance, is dated 1630, but the two large volumes did not appear until ten years later, after two changes of printer. Except for **309**, which is a pamphlet, all his books state his nationality on the title-page. All nine copies of them now in Oxford and Cambridge were acquired in the seventeeth century, not long after publication.

Barbosa Machado, I, 755–56.

309 Informatio pro opinione de esu ouorum, & lacticiniorum tempore Quadragesimae, [Salamanca], 1630. Fol.
BOD Arch Seld. A subt. 11. In a vol. with many Spanish pamphlets, some MS, from the Selden collection, deposited in 1659.

310 In quinque priora[-posteriora] praecepta Decalogi tomus primus [-secundus], Lugduni, sumptibus Laurentij Anisson et haeredum G. Boissat, 1640. 2 vols. Fol.
BOD F 4.14,15 Jur. In the 1674 catalogue. Chain mark MGO k.18.9–10. Forms vols 1–2 of a set with **311**, chain mark SJCO N.2.20 2 vols in 1, bought with money left by William Thomas in 1639.

311 Tractatus in quinque Ecclesiae praecepta, Lugduni, sumptibus Iacobi Cardoni et Petri Cauellat, 1626. Fol.
BOD C 14.15 Th. In the 1635 appendix to the 1620 catalogue MGO k.18.11 Chain mark. It is vol. 3 of a set with **310**, and so must have been acquired after 1640.
QUC I.11.19. 17th-century Cambridge binding with fillets. Author's name on foreedge. Bought with money given by John Davenant, Bishop of Salisbury, in 1626 (Benefactors' register, pp. 10–12). In the catalogue of the 1680s with the current shelfmark. College bookplate of 1700 SJCC Nn.2.17 Given by Thomas Morton in 1639, while he was bishop of Durham.

312 Tractatus in quinque Ecclesiae praecepta, 2a ed., Lugduni, sumptibus Iacobi Cardon, 1632. Fol.
SJCO N.2.21 Bought with money left by William Thomas in 1639. Chain mark.

Faria, Manuel Severim de (1583–1655)

Master of the choir of Évora cathedral. The book listed here, **313**, is a minor classic of Portuguese literature, which contains, among other things, some of the earliest biographies of literary figures (Camões and João de Barros) in the language. The only copy in Oxford was acquired in the nineteenth century because of the engraved portraits which it contains. There are none in Cambridge.
Biblos: Enciclopédia Verbo das Literaturas de Língua Portuguesa, II, cols. 476–7.

313 Discvrsos varios politicos, Evora, impressos por Manoel Carvalho, 1624. 4°
HOA XXII.Eb.45. Part of the collection of Frederick William Hope (1797–1862).

Ferreira, António (1528–1569)

Author of the tragedy *Castro* and one of the best known vernacular poets of the Renaissance. Early modern libraries did not usually acquire literature in Portuguese.
António Ferreira, *Poemas Lusitanos*, ed. by T. F. Earle.

314 Poemas Lusitanos, Lisboa, por Pedro Craesbeeck,1598. 8°

TAY ARCH.8°.P.1598. Acquired in the twentieth century (Anselmo 517).

Fialho, Francisco Fernandes (16th–17th cents) (Franciscus Fernandez Fialho)

A jurist of whom little is known. Barbosa Machado claims that **315** was written during the author's youth. It owes its presence in Oxford to having been part of the collection of Fernão Mascarenhas, bishop of Faro, whose library was presented to Bodley by the Earl of Essex.
Barbosa Machado, II, 143–4.

315 Titulorum omnium iuris ciuilis declaratio, Eborae, in aedibus Martini Burgensis calchographi regiae academiae, 1587. 4°
BOD 4° F 1 Jur. In the 1605 catalogue with the current shelf-mark. Deposited in 1596. Part of the Mascarenhas collection (see Introduction, p. xvi) (Anselmo 427).

Fidalgo de Elvas (16th century)

An anonymous Portuguese historian, known simply as the 'gentleman from Elvas', whose account of the discovery of Florida by Don Fernando de Soto was published in Évora in 1557 by André de Burgos (no copy in either Oxford or Cambridge). It was translated by Hakluyt and published in London in 1609 and 1611. For further information about Hakluyt's translations see Chapter One, pp. xli–iii.

316 [Relaçam verdadeira dos trabalhos que o governador Dom Fernando de Soto . . .] Virginia richly valued, By the description of the maine land of Florida . . ., *translated by Richard Hakluyt*, London, Felix Kingson for Matthew Lownes, 1609. 4°
BOD 4° F2 (2) Art. BS (STC 22938) **SJCO** HB4/3.a.2.17 (1).
CLA B¹.2.26(4) (STC 22938).

Figueiredo, Manuel de (1568–?1622)

He was appointed *cosmógrafo-mor* (Hydrographer to the king) in 1608, and composed an important work in the history of navigation, the first printed sailing-directions for the voyage to India (**317**). It was first published in 1608 and went through several editions in Portugal. Figueiredo, Nunes and Diogo Sá are the only Portuguese mathematicians represented in the early modern English universities. Because Nunes was available in Latin there are many more copies of his work than of the others.
Dicionário de História de Portugal, II, p. 237; C. R. Boxer, *The Tragic History of the Sea*, p. 13.

317 Hydrographia, exame de pilotos, Lisboa, impresso por Vicente Aluarez, 1614. 4°
BOD B 19.29(1) Linc. (Barlow bequest of 1691) **ASC** n.4.2.

Figueiredo, Sebastião Gomes de (- 1611)

A canon of Braga, he studied in Salamanca, where **321** (in Spanish) and **318** (in Latin) were published. The dedicatee of **318** is Agostinho de Castro, Archbishop of Braga, whose career had taken him to Italy and Germany. His patron's foreign experience, and the fact of having published in Salamanca (usually a better starting-point for an international career than Lisbon or Coimbra) may have brought him to the attention of Cardon in Lyon.

All five copies of Figueiredo's work, which he explains is of special interest to preachers (see preface to the reader of **321**), reached Oxford in the years immediately following publication. The three Cambridge copies arrived later, but within the early modern period. In all his works, Spanish as well as Latin, he is described as 'Lusitano'.

Barbosa Machado, III, p. 689.

318 Explicatio Psalmi quinquagesimi Miserere mei Deus, Salmanticae, apud Ioannem Ferdinandum, 1598. 4°

BOD II 46(2) Th. In the 1605 catalogue. Chain mark (Fidalgo 1464).

319 Explicatio Psalmi quinquagesimi, Miserere mei Deus, ed. postrema, Lugduni, Horatius Cardon, 1603 [in colofon 1601]. 8°

WAD H 30.12 Given by Philip Bisse, 1613.

EMM S.7.5.10 Bequeathed by Archbishop William Sancroft in 1693 TRC D.41.38 Bequeathed by John Laughton in 1712. He was college, and later University librarian. Latin MS. annotation.

320 Homiliarivm dominicale, a Dominica prima Aduentus, vsque ad Dominicam Trinitatis, Lvgdvni, svmptibvs Horatii Cardon, 1606. 8°

BOD 8° G 47 Th. In the 1620 catalogue, with the current shelf-mark **WAD** H 30.13, given by Philip Bisse, 1613.

EMM 323.5.104, formerly H.6.4 Bequeathed by John Breton, Master, in 1675.

321 Milicia christiana de los tres enemigos del alma, Salamanca, en casa de Juan Fernandez, 1596. 4°

BOD 4° G 12 Th. In the 1620 catalogue, with the current shelf-mark (Fidalgo, 1424).

Figueiró, Pedro de (–1592) (Petrus a Figueiro)

An Augustinian canon of Santa Cruz in Coimbra for nearly fifty years. He was so learned in Hebrew that he was given the nickname 'Hebraicus'. He had the backing of his order which, many years after his death, arranged for the publication of **322**, an enormous volume consisting solely of commentaries on the Old Testament. Though there are licences issued in Lisbon and Coimbra in 1611, the book may not have appeared in Portugal.

All six copies of books by Figueiró now in Oxford and Cambridge are of old provenance. His nationality is stated on the title-pages.

Barbosa Machado, III, pp. 579–80.

322 Operum . . . Tomi duo, [Lyon], sumptibus Horatii Cardon, 1615. Fol.
BOD G 2.1 Th. In the 1635 appendix to the 1620 catalogue. Chain mark **CHC** I.1.2.7 Chain mark. **SJCO** G.2.15 Given by William Harrison in 1615.

323 Commentarii in Lamentationes Hieremiae prophetae, et in Malachiam prophetam, Lugduni, ex officina Iuntarum, 1596. 8°
BOD 8° F 32 Th. In the 1605 catalogue, with the shelf-mark F.31.
EMM S7.4.47, also 334.5.14. With the Sancroft-Emmanuel bookplate and part of the bequest of 1693 **SJCC** Uu.11.4 From the Crashawe collection, deposited in 1626 (Adams F446).

Figueiro, Vasco
On the titlepage of **324** he is called 'a Gentleman of Portingale', and at the start of the text 'Segnior Vasco Figueiro'. The tract is a warning to the French about the threat posed to them by Philip II, and so forms part of the extensive literature associated with the loss of Portuguese independence in 1580. It is not clear what was the original language.

324 The Spaniards monarchie, and leaguers Olygarchie. Englished by H.O., London, Richard Field for John Harison, 1592. 4°
BOD Douce T 241 Part of the Douce bequest of 1834 (STC 10865).
G&C H.11.3(3) **SID** Bb.4.14 (2) Bequeathed by Francis Combe in 1641. Combe was also a benefactor of Trinty, Oxford (see **188**) **TRC** VI.8.82 (6) Bound with fourteen other tracts, the latest printed in 1622. Binding repaired, but with 3 on the fore-edge, which is an indication of acquisition in the 17th century (all three listed in STC 10865).

Filipe, Bartolomeu (1498 or later–?1590) (Bartolomé Felippe or Filippe)
A jurist who studied at Salamanca and Coimbra and the author of one of the few books of political economy in the short-title catalogue. (Another is Osório's *De Regis Institutione,* **661**–5). In the dedication, to Cardinal Archduke Alberto, of **326** Filipe explains how he published in Portugal only because he was unable to obtain a licence in Spain. The first, Coimbra edition, which is in Spanish, is absent from Cambridge and only reached Oxford in the twentieth century. The 'Turin edition' (**327**) is also in Spanish, though the dedication, by the printer to the author, is in Italian. The printer who, according to the British Library catalogue, was really John Wolfe, says that he only obtained a copy of the first edition 'per ispetial fauore' of a friend of the author, an indication of the poor distribution of Portuguese books abroad.

John Thorius, the English translator of **325**, thought that Filipe was a Spaniard (see the dedication to John Fortescue). On the other hand, the spurious 'Turin edition' is dedicated to 'Signore Bartolomio Felippe

Portughese'. It is not clear why the text was printed in London in Spanish with a false imprint and a dedication in Italian. However, **330** is a genuine Italian publication, issued in Venice. Filipe was Portuguese, as he reveals, not altogether umambiguously, in the dedication of **326**.
R. W. Truman, 'Dr Bartolomeu Filipe of Coimbra'.

325 [Tractado del conseio y delos consejeros delos principes] The Counseller. A Treatise of Counsels and Counsellers of Princes, *tr. by* John Thorius, London, printed by John Wolfe, 1589. 4°
  BOD 55 d 135, acquired between 1861 and 1883, probably in 1882 (STC 10753).
  CUL Peterborough G.3.10 For Peterborough Cathedral Library, see the Introduction, p. xiv. In 1650, before it came to Peterborough, the book belonged to P. de Cardonnel, a Christ Church man who also owned **678 EMM** S.5.3.41 left by Archbishop William Sancroft in 1693 **TRC** VI.1.154 Signed John Lumley and in the 1609 catalogue of his collection. With the Newton-Puckering bookplate, showing that it reached the library in 1691 (Lumley 996).

326 Tractado del conseio y delos consejeros delos principes, Coimbra, impresso en casa de Antonio de Mariz impressor dela vniuersidad, 1584. 4°
  BOD Vet. G1 e. 13 Acquired after 1937 **TAY** Finch.G.85 Bought in 1939 with money left by Robert Finch of Balliol (1783–1830) (Anselmo 885).

327 Tractado del conseio y de los conseieros de los principes, Turino, impresso en casa de Gio. Vincenzo del Pernetto [really London, J. Wolfe], 1589. 4°
  BOD 4° F 4 Art. (STC 10752.7).
  CUL Syn.7.58.84 With the bookplate of the Royal Library, indicating that it came to Cambridge in 1715. Listed in the catalogue of the Royal Library with the shelf-mark O.10.21. It was part of the collection of Sir Thomas Knyvett (?1539–1618), of Ashwellthorpe, Norfolk, which was acquired by Bishop Moore. Knyvett bought the book on 20 July 1589 and had read it by February 1590 (STC 10752.7; McKitterick 1388) **CLA** E1.2.15 With the signature of George Ruggle, fellow, who gave books in 1621, and the 1701 college bookplate. Parchment binding, waste material in English **TRH** H*.6.28 With an MS. index of Spanish words, keyed to the text, the college bookplate of 1700, an illegible former shelf-mark and 33 on the leading edge, suggesting that it may have been acquired in the 17th century (Adams F221).

329 Tractado del conseio y de los conseieros de los principes, Turino, impresso en casa de Gio. Vincenzo del Pernetto [really London, J. Wolfe], 2nd impression, 1598. 4°
  TRC S.3.114(1) (Adams F222).

330 [Tractado del conseio y delos conseieros delos principes] Trattato del conseglio, et de' conseglieri de' prencipi, *tr. by* Giulio Cesare Valentino Piouano di Carpeneto, Venetia, appresso la Compagnia Minima, 1599. 4°
  WAD f 17.12 Bequeathed by Alexander Thistlethwaite, a former student (1718–71).
  SID D.4.2 In the catalogue of 1674 (Adams F451).

Fonseca, António da (1517–after 1559)

A Dominican, and one of the group of scholars sent by King João III to study abroad. From 1535 he was in Paris, where he obtained a licence in theology (1542). The following year he became professor of theology at Coimbra. His edition (339), with notes, of the commentary on the Pentateuch of Cardinal Cajetan (also a Domincan), is the earliest of the many commentaries on Biblical texts by Portuguese scholars in Oxford. On the title-page Fonseca is described as Portuguese.
Luís de Matos, *Portugais à Paris*, pp. 86–87.

331 Commentarii illustres planeq[ue] insignes in Quinque Mosaicos libros Thomae de Vio Caietani, *with explanatory notes by Fonseca*, Parisiis, apud *variously* Guillelmum de Bossozel, Ioannem Boule, Ioannem Paruum, Ioannem Yuernel, 1539. Fol.

BOD C 9.3 Th. (Paruus) Chain mark, and with 3 on the leading edge, an indication of early provenance. In the 1605 catalogue **MER** 82.I.15 (Yuernel) **SJCO** F.2.24 (Paruus) Given around 1559 by Henry Cole, dean of St Paul's (1500–80). Marginal notes.
CUL E*.2.25 (B) (Paruus) Acquired before 1715 **G&C** F.15.8 Bequeathed by William Branthwaite, Master, in 1619. He was one of the revisers of the Bible. Much marginal annotation **PET** O.7.21 The book has been in the library since the 17th century **PMC** 6.4.14 (Boule).With the college bookplate of 1700. The binding has been repaired, obscuring previous shelf-marks **SJCC** Oo.4.3 (Paruus) Bought with money given by Bishop Thomas Morton between 1628 and 1639 **TRC** D.2.14 (Bossozel) Given by Thomas Nevile, Master, along with other books of divinity in 1611–12. 17th-century Cambridge binding stamped T N.

Fonseca, António da, M.D. (16th–17th centuries)

Fonseca is described on the title-page of his book as 'Ulisipponensis', and as 'Lusitanus' by a fellow-countryman, António Denis Manrique, who dedicated a liminary poem to this army doctor.

332 De epidemia febrili grassante in exercitu regis catholici in inferiori Palatinatu, anno 1620. & 21. tractatus, Mechlinae, apud Henricum Haye,1623. 4°

BOD 4° M 11(3) Med. With the shelf-mark on the fore-edge, indicating that it was acquired soon after publication.
SJCC Mm.12.20 Given by John Collins, fellow and Professor of Physick, in 1634.

Fonseca, Damião da (1573–?1640) (Damián de Fonseca)

A Domincan who spent all his professional life outside Portugal, in Spain, Italy and Poland.
Grande Enciclopédia Portuguesa e Brasileira, XI, p. 556.

333 Iusta expulsion de los Moriscos de España . . . Roma, Iacomo Mascardo, 1612. 8°
TRC W.12.76.

334 [Iusta expulsion de los Moriscos de España] Del giusto scacciamento de Moreschi da Spagna . . . *translated by* Cosimo Graci, Roma, Bartholomeo Zannetti, 1611. 4°
CUL 6000.c.30 Acquired in 1987.

335 Relacion de lo que passo en la expulsion de los Moriscos del reyno de Valencia . . . Roma, Iacomo Mascardo, 1612. 8°
ASC SR.88.F.7.

Fonseca, Gabriel da
Friedenwald says he was a Marrano. On the title-page of his book he is called 'Lusitani'.
Friedenwald, I, p. 225.

336 Medici Oeconomia, Romae, apud Andream Phaeum, 1623. 8°
BOD 8° E 21 Med. On the endpaper there is a note in Portuguese stating that the book was bound 27 April 1623, indicating that the Bodleian did not obtain its copy first hand.

Fonseca, Pedro da (1528–99)
A Jesuit and philosopher, whose commentary on Aristotle's *Metaphysics* was eagerly sought after in seventeenth-century Oxford, though not in Cambridge. For further discussion of this point see Chapter Two. Of the twenty-five copies now in the libraries more than twenty are of old provenance.

Fonseca taught at Coimbra and had close links to the 'Conimbri-censes', but was not strictly speaking part of the group. He was regarded by his contemporaries as being a more independent-minded thinker than his colleagues (Pinharanda Gomes, p. 60), and he also spent the period 1573–81 in Rome, where the first volume of his commentary was published (**337**). That has a dedication to King Sebastião which makes no secret of its author's nationality, but the fact is not stated on the title-page of the book. It was only after his death that Fonseca was regularly called a Portuguese (**339**, printed in 1589, is an exception). No edition of his *Institutionum Dialectarum* mentions his nationality. For further discussion of the Jesuit self-image see Chapter Five, pp. lxxviii–ix.
Pinharanda Gomes, *Os Conimbricenses*; Francisco Rodrigues, *História da Companhia de Jesus na Assistência de Portugal,* II.2. pp. 102–10.

337 Commentariorum . . . in libros Metaphysicorum Aristotelis . . . tomus primus, Romae, apud Franciscum Zanettum et Bartholomaeum Tosium, socios, 1577. 4°
BOD 4° F 66 Art. In the 1605 catalogue. From the Mascarenhas collection, deposited in 1596 (see Introduction, p. xvi). Bound with **339**.

338 Commentariorum . . . in libros metaphysicorum Aristotelis . . . Tomus primus, *with* Institutionum dialecticarum libri octo, Lugduni, ex officina Iuntarum, 1591–1593. 2 vols. 4°

MER 112.B.11–12 Chain mark. With the signature of F. H. Bradley, 1846–1924, but the book may have been in the library before his time. Bound with **348**. Some underlining.

339 Commentariorum . . . in libros Metaphysicorum Aristotelis . . . tomus secundus, Romae, ex officina Iacobi Tornerii, 1589. 4°

BOD 4° F 67 Art. In the 1605 catalogue. From the Mascarenhas collection, deposited in 1596 (see Introduction, p. xvi). Bound with **337**.

340 Commentariorum . . . in libros Metaphysicorum Aristotelis . . . tomus primus [-secundus], Francofurti, typis Ioannis Saurij, impensis Ioannis Theobaldi Schonvvetteri *and* impensis Lazari Zetzneri, 1599. 2 vols 4°

BOD 4° F 3 Art. Seld. From the Selden bequest of 1659. In the 1674 catalogue ASC i.infra 1.10–11 Gift of Crofts Potts, 1621. Potts became M.A. in 1620. Chain marks CHC Hyp. L.19–20 Both vols stamped W.W., like **341**. Chain marks MGO D.3.1 Chain mark. The gift of Francis White MA, 1614, and Ludimagister, 1614–17 NEW BT3.258.9 This rebound copy was published by Zetzner. In the catalogue of 1686 PMO 1.e.3 Bequeathed by H. W. Chandler, 1889 QUO BB.f.110–1 Given by Thomas Barlow, 1630 SJCO Delta.4.11–12 16th/17th-century calf binding. The title is on the leading edge WAD K 21.23/4 Given by John Goodridge (1580–1654), who was a founding fellow WOR E.10.7 Oxford binding, Ker no. 1527, with centrepiece v, in use from early/mid 1580s-1605, Pearson, p. 77. Given in 1634 by the same John Goodridge to Gloucester Hall (extinguished in 1714), where he had been 'commensalis', and where he took his M.A. in 1606.

PET K.4.2 Given by Helen Gulston, widow of Theodore Gulston, M.D. and fellow of Merton, probably in 1635. Same binding as **341** (Adams A1849).

341 Commentariorum . . . in libros Metaphysicorum Aristotelis . . . tomus tertius, Coloniae, impensis Lazari Zetzneri bibliopolae, 1604. 4°

BOD D 11.4 Linc. From the Barlow bequest of 1691, but a copy with a different shelf-mark is listed in the 1605 catalogue ASC i.infra 1.12 Old shelf-marks indicate that it has always been kept close to the 1599 ed., as the entry in the catalogue of 1665–89 'tom. 3 Fr. 1599' suggests. Early 17th-century Oxford binding, chain marks CHC Hyp. L. 21 The binding is stamped W.W., like **340** MGO D.3.2 Chain mark. The gift of Francis White, who gave item **340** PMO 1.e.4. Bequeathed by H. W. Chandler, 1889 QUO BB.f.112 Given by Thomas Barlow (1607–91), who left a second copy to the Bodleian SJCO Delta.4.13, bound with **343**. Chain mark WAD K 21.23/4 3 vols in 2 Given by John Goodridge, who also gave **340**.

PET K.4.3 Given by Helen Gulston, widow of Theodore Gulston, M.D. and fellow of Merton, probably in 1635. Same binding as **340** and bound together with **343**.

342 Commentariorum . . . in Metaphysicorum Aristotelis . . . decimum, vndecimum & duodecimum . . .tomus IV, Lugduni, sumptibus Horatii Cardon [Colophon: ex typographia Iacobi du Creux, dicti Molliard], 1612. 4°

BOD 4° M 44 Art. In the 1620 catalogue. Chain mark.

343 Commentariorum . . . in Metaphysicorum Aristotelis . . . decimum, undecimum, & duodecimum . . .tomus IV, Coloniae, sumptibus Lazari Zetzneri bibliopolae, 1613. 4°
SJCO Delta.4.13 Bound with **341**. Chain mark.
PET K.4.4 Bound with **341**.

344 Commentariorum . . . in libros metaphysicorum Aristotelis . . . tomi quatuor, Coloniae, sumptibus Lazari Zetzneri, 1615. 4 vols in 2. 4°
JSO K.14.20–21 Bequeathed by Edward Herbert, Baron Cherbury (1583–1648), diplomat and writer on religion, and in the catalogue of 1549 **ORI** 2Qa15 From Sir David Ross's donation of 1971.
CUL P*.10.2 (D) Acquired before 1715 TRC T.3.65- (4 vols in 2). Bequeathed by John Paris, who became a fellow in 1707.

345 Commentariorum . . . in libros Metaphysicorum Aristotelis tomi quatuor, Coloniae, sumptibus Lazari Zetzneri bibliopolae, 1615–29. 4 vols in 1. 4°
PMO 1.e.5 Bequeathed by H. W. Chandler, 1889.

346 Institutionum dialecticarum libri octo, Olyssippone, apud haeredes Ioannis Blavii, 1564. 4°
BOD 4° F 22 Art. In the 1620 catalogue with the current shelf-mark. Signature of Christopher Dugdale, possibly one of the two persons of this name (father and son) listed by Foster as having been at Oxford before 1620. Marginalia.
TRC T.23.51 Acquired probably after 1800 (Adams A319; Anselmo 358).

347 Institutionum dialecticarum libri octo, Conimbricae, apud Ioannem Barrerium, 1575. 4°
PHI A.7.6. Bequeathed by Thomas Fowler, President of Corpus Christi College, in 1904. It had previously belonged to Mark Pattison and Ingram Bywater.
CUL F157.d.12.2 Acquired from Librería Puvill, Barcelona, in the 20th century (Anselmo 221).

348 Institutionum dialecticarum libri octo, Lugduni, ex officina Iuntarum, 1591–1593. 2 vols 4°
MER 112.B.11–12 Chain mark. With the signature of F. H. Bradley, 1846–1924, but the book may have been in the library before his time. Bound with **338**. Some underlining.

349 Institutionum dialectarum libri octo, Ingolstadii, ex typographia Adami Sartorii, 1600. 8°
CUL Ven.8.60.1 With the signature of J. Venn, 1883. The book at one time belonged to a Russian library (Adams F701).

350 Institutionum dialecticarum libri octo, Lugduni, sumptibus Petri Rigaud, 1608. 8°
BOD 8° F 7 Art. Seld. From the Selden bequest of 1659. In the 1674 catalogue.

351 Institutionum dialecticarum libri octo, *with* Isagoge philosophica, Ingolstadii, ex typographeo Adami Sartorii, 1611. 8°

BOD Vet. D1 f.320 Acquired after 1937 from Balliol College library.

352 Institutionum dialecticarum libri octo, *with* Isagoge philosophica, Coloniae, apud Petrum Cholinum, 1616. 8°
PMO 12.b.20.

Fonseca, Rodrigo da (–1622) (Rodericus de Fonseca)

A doctor, proud of his Portuguese and specifically Lisbon origins, which he never ceased to proclaim on the title-pages of his books, but who worked for many years in Italy, in the universities of Pisa and Padua. The medical school at Padua was regarded as the best in Europe (Bylebyl, p. 335). Towards the end of his life he was negotiating with King Sigismund III of Poland for a place there (see the dedication of vol. 1 of **353**). Barbosa Machado says that he had a Christian burial in Rome, but modern writers regard him as Jewish. He was physician to Duke Ferdinand de Medici and claims that his cure for head wounds won the approval of the Spanish royal family, whose chief at the time was Philip II (see the title-page of **365**). He was also on good terms with the Archbishop of Pisa, to whom he dedicated **361** and praised extravagantly in **358** (see the dedication to Duke Ferdinand). All this suggests someone of complex religious allegiancies. For Burton's attitude to him see Chapter Five, pp. lxxxiii–iv.

Altogether there are forty-two copies of books by Fonseca in Oxford and Cambridge, of which at least thirty-six are of old provenance. There are marginal notes throughout **353**, perhaps by Ashmole, and endpaper notes to **355**.

Barbosa Machado III, pp. 647–8; *Encyclopaedia Judaica*, XI, col. 1194; Friedenwald, I, p. 63; Jerome J. Bylebyl, 'The School of Padua: humanistic medicine in the sixteenth century'.

353 Consultationes medicae, *with* De consultandi ratione *and* Consultatio de plica Polonica, Venetijs, apud Ioannem Guerilium, 1620–22. 2 vols. Fol.

BOD E 1.14(3) Med. In the 1635 appendix to the 1620 catalogue CHC O.k.2.13 From the Orrery bequest of 1732. There are marginal notes throughout, perhaps by Elias Ashmole (1617–92), founder of the Ashmolean Museum, whose name appears on the flyleaf MGO r.15.01–02, Chain mark. The copy may possibly have belonged once to another library. Vol. 2 was purchased by Johannis Abdy in Padua, perhaps in 1648. NEW BT3.237.15 Given by Thomas Hopper, medical practioner, 1623. In the catalogue of 1686.

354 Consultationum medicinalium tomus primus [-secundus], *with* De consultandi ratione *and* Consultatio de plica Polonica, Francofurti ad Moenum, typis Wechelianis, apud Danielem & Davidem Aubrios, & Clementem Schleichium, 1625. 2 vols. 8°

BOD Lister A 62 Given by Dr Martin Lister (?1639–1712), physician and zoologist

BLL 815 a.11 Vol. 2 only. In the 1709 catalogue **CCCO** N16.13–14 Bequeathed by William Creed, fellow, in 1711, chain mark **JSO** I.3.10 Gall. Bequeathed by Edward Herbert, Baron Cherbury (1583–1648), diplomat and writer on religion. **QUO** NN.s.1313 (1–2) From the library of Theophilus Metcalfe, M.D., 1690–1757, with a note on the endpaper **SJCO** HB4/4.a.1.22(1–2) With the signature of John Merrick (1671–1757), fellow, or of his son, also John, fellow 1721–1733 **WOR** HH.9.10–11.

CUL (2 copies) K.17.73 From the Royal Library, deposited in 1715, and in its MS. catalogue; Hh.19.21 Vol 1 only. Given by John Worthington, fellow of Peterhouse, between 1691 and his death in 1738.

355 Consultationum medicinalium tomus primus [-secundus] *with* De consultandi ratione *and* Consultatio de plica Polonica, Venetiis, apud Ioannem Guerilium, 1628. 2 vols in 1. Fol.

BOD Vet. F2 c. 4, Aquired, probably after 1835, by the Radcliffe Library, which was established using funds left by John Radcliffe (bap. 1650–1714). It entered the Bodleian after 1937 **QUO** NN.n.371 Given by Sir John Floyer, M.D., 1649–1734, with endpaper notes.

KCC F.3.2 In the 17th-century catalogue, which was begun in 1612 **TRC** S.11.12 Bought with money given by Sir Thomas Sclater, fellow, in 1676.

356 De calculorum remedijs, Romae, apud Io. Angelum Ruffinellum [colophon: apud Titum, & Paulum Dianum fratres],1586. 4°

CCCO NN.8.7(2) from the bequest of Brian Twyne, fellow, of 1644. Chain mark. Bound with **360** **QUO** NN.s.1310.

CUL K.9.6 From the Royal Library, deposited in 1715, and in its MS. catalogue **SJCC** Mm.4.8 (3) left by John Collins, fellow and Professor of Physick, in 1634 (Adams F702).

357 De hominis excrementis libellus, Pisis, apud Io. Baptistam Boschettum, & Ioannem Fontanum Socios, 1613. 4°

BOD 4° L 3(1) Med. In the 1674 catalogue **CCCO** LC.3.b.21 Signature of William Creed, fellow, 1686, and left to the college in 1711 **QUO** NN.s.1311 Bequeathed by Theophilus Metcalfe, M.D. in 1757.

SJCC Mm.5.38 (1) From the bequest of John Collins, fellow and Professor of Physick, of 1634.

358 De tuenda valetudine, et producenda vita liber, Florentiae, apud Bartholomaeum Sermartellium Iuniorem, 1602. 4°

BOD 4° S 26(3) Med. In the 1605 catalogue, bound with **360, 363**.

CUL (2 copies) K.15.21; T.14.16(2) Both from the Royal Library, deposited in 1715. Both copies are listed in the MS. catalogue.

359 De tuenda valetudine, et producenda vita liber, Francofurti, ex officina Paltheniana, 1603. 8°

BOD 8° I 76(1) Linc. Stated to be a duplicate of r.51 & g.79, indicating that there were copies in the library before the arrival of the Barlow bequest in 1691.

CUL (2 copies) N*.14.21(F) Acquired before 1715; K.18.63 From the Royal Library, deposited in 1715, and in its MS. catalogue.

360 In Hippocratis Legem commentarium, Romae, ex typographia Titi & Pauli de Dianis fratres, 1586. 4°

BOD 4° S 26(1) Med., formerly Med F.1.13. In the 1605 catalogue, with shelf-mark

F.1.14. Bound with **358, 363**. Chain mark **CCCO** NN.8.7(1) From the bequest of Brian Twyne, fellow, of 1644. Bound with **356**.

SJCC Mm.4.8 (2) Bequeathed by John Collins, fellow and Professor of Physick, in 1634 (Adams F703).

361 In Hipp.[ocratis] Prognostica commentarii, Patavii, apud Franciscum Bolzetam, 1597. 4°
NEW BT3.229.16 Chain mark. Probably to be identified with the book left by Thomas Hopper, medical practioner, in 1623. In the catalogue of 1686.

362 In primum, & secundum Aphorismorum librum commentaria, Florentiae, apud Bartholomaeum Sermartellium, 1591. 4°
CHC Op.3.21(2) From the Orrery bequest of 1732. Bound with other works, of which the latest is dated 1609. Chain mark.

363 In septem Aphorismorum Hippocratis libros commentaria, Venetiis, apud Franciscum de Franciscis Senensem, 1595. 4°
BOD 4° S 26(2) Med. In the 1674 catalogue. Bound with **358, 360**.
G&C K.4.37 (Adams F704).

364 Leonardi Iacchini . . . Methodus curandar. febrium, *edited by Fonseca,* Pisis, apud Jo. Fontanum 1615. 4°
BOD (2 copies) 4° M 15(2) Med. In the 1674 catalogue; Lister C 13. Given by Dr Martin Lister (?1639–1712), physician and zoologist.

365 Opusculum, quo adolescentes ad medicinam facile capessendam instruuntur, *with* consultationes aliquot, Florentiae, apud Michaelangelum Sermartellium, 1596. 4°
BOD Vet. F1 e.213 Acquired after 1937 **NEW** BT3.225.17(2) In the catalogue of 1686.

366 Tractatus de febrium, Venetiis, apud Ioannem Guerilium, 1621. 4°
BOD 4° C 3(2) Med. In the 1635 appendix to the 1620 catalogue **QUO** NN.s.1312 Modern rebinding.

Foreiro, Francisco (?1522–81) (Franciscus Forerius) see also Index librorum prohibitorum
A Dominican born in Lisbon, according to the title-pages of his books. He studied in Paris from before 1534 to 1537/8, and was at Trent and later Rome between 1561 and 1566. He made use of his time in Italy to issue his edition and commentary on Isaiah (**368**) through the firm of Zileti who published several Portuguese theologians. Carreira (p. 218) claims that he was the first to apply the new techniques of textual criticism to a book of the Old Testament. Although there are only seven copies in Oxford, and another seven in Cambridge (all with old provenance) this was a commentary that was read. There are marginal notes in four copies, including some perhaps by Allestree (**369**). Most remarkable is Worcester's copy of **368**, which an early eighteenth-century reader had

rebound as two volumes so that he could add extensive notes in several languages.

José Nunes Carreira, *Filologia e crítica de Isaías no comentário de Francisco Foreiro;* Luís de Matos, *Portugais à Paris,* p. 83.

367 Ad sacrum Concilium Tridentinum. . . . sermo quem habuit, Brixiae, apud Ludouicum Sabiensem, 1564. 4°

CUL Acton d.6.8 Lord Acton's library was presented in 1902 (Adams F745).

368 Iesaiae prophetae, vetus & noua ex Hebraico uersio, cum commentario, Venetiis, ex officina Iordani Zileti, 1563. Fol.

BOD E 5.11 Th. Chain mark In the 1605 catalogue **CCCO** Z.50.3 Bequeathed by John Rosewell or Rosewall, who had studied at Corpus from 1655–67, in 1684 **QUO** 77.C.5(2). Oxford binding, with Ker centrepiece ii, in use 1580–97 (Pearson, p. 75). Chain mark **WAD** I37.11 Given by Philip Bisse, 1613 **WOR** D.8.8–9. Rebound as two vols, with many interleaved pages and legible and detailed notes in English, Latin, Greek and Hebrew. Dated Wormstall 1733.

CUL (2 copies) F*.4.23 (C) Acquired before 1715; C.9.29 In the Royal Library, deposited in 1715, and in its MS. catalogue **EMM** 310.4.54, formerly H.1.35, and listed under that shelf-mark in the 18th-century catalogue. Like many books at Emmanuel, it is second-hand and once belonged to the Jesuit college at Padua **TRC** D.16.84 MS. notes. In the catalogue compiled between 1667 and 1675 with the number F 20 (Adams B1580).

369 Iesaiae prophetae vetus & noua ex Hebraico versio, cum commentario . . . Antuerpiae, apud Philippum Nutium [in colophon: excudebat Christophorus Plantinus], 1565–67. 8°

CCCO LC.11.a.3 Extensive and legible annotation in two hands, dated August 1605. Oxford binding with Ker centrepiece xv or xvi, both in use c. 1580–c. 1620 (Pearson, p. 78). **CHC** Allestree L.5.15 With a page of notes, perhaps by Allestree, on the endpaper. From the Allestree bequest of 1681. **CUL** F*.6.7 (F) Acquired before 1715 **G&C** F.12.2 Bequeathed by William Branthwaite, Master, in 1619. He was one of the revisers of the Bible **SJCC** Uu.11.5 From the Crashawe collection, deposited in 1626 (Adams B1583–4).

370 Missale Romanum, ex decreto sacrosancti Concilii Tridentini restitutum, Antuerpiae, ex officina Christophori Plantini, architypographi regii, 1577. 8°

QUO UU.e.70. 16th-century binding; evidence of chaining.

Freitas, Serafim de (?1570–1633) (Freitas, Seraphinus de)

A canonist of Coimbra, whose career took him to Valladolid, where he published **371**. None of his other works, whether published in Spain or Portugal, are in Oxford or Cambridge. In **371** he defends Portuguese claims to rights of navigation on the high seas against the views of Hugo Grotius. There are only two copies, both in Oxford.

Dicionário de História de Portugal, II, 303.

371 De iusto imperio Lusitanorum asiatico, Vallisoleti, ex officina Hieronymi Morillo, 1625. 4°

BOD 4° A 86 Th. BS. Acquired after 1668. **HER** www.02.02 From Magdalen Hall (extinguished 1874–75). With the signature on the title page of Fernão Dias Pinheiro, 1643. This is unlikely to be an early acquisition. For the collection at Magdalen Hall, see Chapter Three, p. lix.

Fróis, Luís (1532–97) (Ludovicus Froes)

Jesuit and missionary, who lived for many years in Japan. The books listed as **372–7** are wholly by Fróis. There are in addition many letters by him in the compendia included in 'Jesuits: Letters from Missions'.

The publications resulting from the Jesuit mission to Japan seldom, if ever, state the nationality of their authors. In addition, none of the books by Fróis in Oxford and Cambridge are in the languages (Portuguese; perhaps also Spanish) in which he originally wrote them. They were translated and retranslated into Italian and Latin, thus obscuring the origin of their author. Fróis was a popular writer in early modern England and all but one of the twelve copies of books by him in the libraries arrived before the mid-eighteenth century, and some much earlier than that.
Biblos: Enciclopédia Verbo das Literaturas de Língua Portuguesa, II, cols 713–15.

372 De rebus Iaponicis historica relatio, *tr. from Italian by Jan Buys,* Moguntiae, ex officina typographica Ioannis Albini, 1599. 8°
    BOD 8° F 58(1) Art. In the 1674 catalogue. Bequeathed by Robert Burton, in 1640 (Kiessling (1988) 619). Bound with **375, 486 BLL** 0905 e 03 (05) With the signature of Thomas Snawfell. The book is bound with medical works of which the latest was printed in 1673, probably from the collection of Nicholas Crouch, fellow, who died in 1690. It is in the 1709 catalogue **WAD** J 13.14 Given by Philip Bisse, 1613.
    CUL N*.6.35 (F) Acquired before 1715 **TRC** W.22.40[2] Probably acquired after 1800 (Adams F1062).

373 Lettera del Giapone degli anni 1591 et 1592, *tr. from Spanish by* Ubaldino Bartolini, Venetia, appresso Gio. Battista Ciotti, 1595. 8°
    BOD 8° L 13 Art. This copy may replace one printed in Milan in 1599 which was listed in the 1605 catalogue.

374 [Lettera del Giapone degli anni 1591 et 1592] Literae annuae Iaponenses anni 1591 et 1592, *tr. from Italian,* Coloniae Agrippinae, apud Henricum Falkenburg, 1596. 8°
    BOD 8° C 583(4) Linc. From the Barlow bequest of 1691. Bound with other religious works of which the latest is 1678.

375 Noua relatio historica de statu rei Christianae in Iaponia, *tr. from Italian,* Moguntiae, ex officina typographica Ioannis Albini, 1598. 8°
    BOD (2 copies) 8° F 58(2) Art. In the 1674 catalogue. Bequeathed by Robert Burton in 1640 and bound with **372, 486** (Kiessling (1988) 620); 8° I 24(1) Art.BS. Acquired from the bookseller Thomas Osborne (bap. ?1704–67).
    CUL N*.6.35 (F) Acquired before 1715. With a motto 'Jesus Deus Meus et Omnia' and initials on the title-page (Adams F1063).

376 Relatione della gloriosa morte di xxvi. posti in croce per comandamento del re di Giappone, *tr. by* Gasparo Spitilli di Campli, Milano, nella stampa del quondam Pacifico Pontio, 1599. 8°
BOD 8° F 14(1) Art. In the 1605 catalogue. Bound with **377**.

377 Trattato d'alcuni prodigii occorsi l'anno M.D.XCVI. nel Giappone, *tr. by* Francesco Mercati Romano, Milano, nella stamparia del quondam Pacifico Pontio, 1599. 8°
BOD 8° F 14(2) Art Bound with **376**.
For letters by him see too the entries for Jesuits: Letters from Missions and Willes, Richard

Galhegos, Pedro de (1597–1665)
Poet and critic. The only copy of **378**, which is in Cambridge, was acquired by a modern collector.
Biblos: Enciclopédia Verbo das Literaturas de Língua Portuguesa, II, cols 745–7.

378 Templo da memoria: poema epithalamico, Lisboa, Lourenço Craesbeeck, 1635.
STCC JPg.5.1008 Bequeathed by H. J. Chaytor, Master 1933–46.

Galvão, António (–1557) (Galvano)
Soldier and governor of Ternate, one of the Spice Islands. His history of the discoveries from the Flood onwards was first published in Portuguese in Lisbon (1563), but Oxford and Cambridge only have the translation printed by Hakluyt (**379**). The translation 'was first done into our language by some honest and well affected marchant of our nation, whose name by no meanes I could attaine unto, and that as it seemeth many yeeres ago', as Hakluyt explains in the dedication to Sir Robert Cecil. Hakluyt compared some of the statements made by Galvão with the chronicles of Barros and Castanheda, probably using the Italian translations, since many proper names quoted are given an Italian form. For further information, and bibliography, see Chapter One, pp. xli–iii.
Biblos: Enciclopédia Verbo das Literaturas de Língua Portuguesa, II, cols 748–9 (article by Evelina Verdelho).

379 [Tratado que compos o nobre e notavel capitão Antonio Galvão] The discoveries of the world from their first originall vnto the yeere of our Lord 1555 . . . published in English by Richard Hakluyt, Londoni, impensis G. Bishop, 1601. 4°
BOD 4° C 107(4) Art. Bequeathed by Robert Burton, 1640. Underlinings (STC 11543; Kiessling (1988) 641) RSL RR. w. 108.
KCC M.18.32 (STC 11543).

Galvão, Francisco Fernandes (1554–1610)

Author of sermons, who spent five years in Rome (1585–90) and was well-known as a preacher in Madrid. According to Barbosa Machado he published only in Portuguese. Writers of devotional literature in that language were not of interest to the early modern universities.
Barbosa Machado, II, pp. 144–5.

380 Sermões das festas de Christo nosso senhor, Lisboa, Pedro Craesbeeck, 1616. 4°
BOD Vet. G2 e.15 Acquired in 1981.

Gama, António da (1520–95) (Gamma)

A jurist, who spent some time in the late 1540s in the Spanish College in Bologna before becoming a judge in Lisbon. It may have been through contacts made in Italy that his book on the cases of the Portuguese supreme court was so widely published abroad, in Madrid, Antwerp and Frankfurt as well as in the Italian centres listed in the short-title catalogue (Venice and Cremona). The preface by Caldas Pereira de Castro, who by the end of the sixteenth century was well known internationally, would also have helped its cause. Deslandes says that King Sebastião commissioned the book and also gave it a twenty-five-year privilege.

Perhaps because Gama had studied in the Spanish College the Frankfurt publisher Palthenius repeatedly refers to him as 'Hispanus', despite abundant evidence in the preliminary matter to the book he was printing that the author was 'Lusitanus'. Five of the six copies of the book in Oxford and Cambridge are certainly of old provenance.
Barbosa Machado, I, pp. 286–7; Deslandes, p. 124.

381 Decisiones supremi senatus inuictissimi Lusitaniae regis, Vlyssippone, excudebat Emanuel Ioannes, 1578. Fol.
BOD H 1.12 Art. Seld. From the Selden bequest of 1659. In the 1674 catalogue SJCO X.4.14 Given by Sir William Paddy, 1633 (Anselmo 724).

382 Decisionum supremi senatus Lusitaniae . . . centuriae quatuor, Cremonae, apud Ioannem Baptistam Pellizzarium, 1598. Fol.
JSO F.2.12 Gall.

383 Decisionum supremi senatus regni Lusitaniae . . . centuriae quatuor, Francofurti, cura et studio Colegii Musarum Novenarum Paltheniani, 1599. Fol.
BOD G 5.1(1) Jur. In the 1605 catalogue and in the 1620 catalogue with the current shelf-mark. Binding stamped Honi soit qui mal y pense. Chain mark.
TRH P*.5.9, formerly K.4.9, K.4.6 and with 4 on the leading edge, which is an indication that it may have been acquired in the seventeenth century. With the college bookplate of 1700. At the end of the volume there is a signature which may be that of Thomas Eden, Master 1626–45, who gave a number of legal works to the college (Adams G202).

384 Decisionum supremi senatus regni Lusitaniae . . . centuriae quatuor, Venetiis, apud haeredes Nicolaum Morettum, 1610. Fol.
BOD L 3.2(2) Jur. Chain mark.

Gândavo, Pero de Magalhães de (16th century)

Writer about Brazil and grammarian. Because his work was published in Portuguese in Lisbon it made no impact abroad for centuries. The first translation into French was published in 1837 and into English in 1922.
Dicionário de história de Portugal, II, pp. 326–7 (article by Luís de Matos).

385 Historia da provincia sancta Cruz, a que vulgarmente chamamos Brasil, *with liminary poems by Camões,* Lisboa, Antonio Gonçalves, 1576. 4°
BOD 233 f.95 Acquired after 1864. Marginalia in Portuguese and French (Anselmo 709).

Gil, Bento (–1623) (Beneditus Aegidius)

A jurist, who studied in Coimbra and practised in Lisbon. It is yet another indication of the relative weakness of Portuguese publishing that there should be four copies of **388**, which was published in Cologne, in Oxford and Cambridge, and only one of **386** and **387**, published in Lisbon. Title-pages state that he was Portuguese.
Barbosa Machado, I, pp. 503–4.

386 Commentaria ad leg. prim. C. de sacrosanct. Eccles., Ulissipone, apud Petrum Crasbeeck, 1609. Fol.
SJCO X.4.19(1) Given by Sir William Paddy in 1633. Chain mark.

387 Tractatus de iure, et privilegiis honestatis, Vlyssipone, typis Petri Craesbeeck, 1618. 4°
BOD 4° A 11 Jur. In the 1635 appendix to the 1620 catalogue.

388 Tractatus de iure, et privilegiis honestatis, Coloniae Agrippinae, apud Petrum Henningium, 1620. 8°
BOD 8° A 10 Jur. Seld. From the Selden bequest of 1659. In the 1674 catalogue JSO E 3.2(1) Gall. Bequeathed by Sir Leoline Jenkins, lawyer and diplomat, in 1685.
CUL O*.15.28(F) Acquired before 1715 SJCC 1.10.28 (1).

Girão, João Rodrigues (1558–1633) (Giram)

Jesuit missionary in Japan. He is frequently confused with another Jesuit, the great Japanese linguist João Rodrigues (see below), even by Backer-Sommervogel. The title-page of **390** ascribes the *Historia Iaponensis* to Ioannis Froes Giram, probably a misreading for Roiz or Rodrigues. Rodrigues Girão's authorship is confirmed by his signature, and the date, which follows the last letter in the volume on p. 80. There is no author's name in **391**, but again the final page (p. 149) is signed Ioannes Roiz Giram, Macau, 1625. It is the only signature. The book is dedicated to

Mutius Vitelleschi, who was the general of the order. The author of **392** is stated on the title-page to be Ioanne Rodriguez. This is not enough to distinguish the two Rodrigues and there is no other signature. The ascription of the book to Rodrigues Girão is, therefore, provisional, but is made by Simoni without supporting evidence.

Anna E. C. Simoni, *Catalogue of Books from the Low Countries 1601–1621*, p. 532, item R89.

389 Histoire de ce que s'est passé au royaume du Iapon, l'année 1624, *tr. from Italian*, Paris, Sebastien Chappelet, 1628. 8°
  CUL F162.d.4.1 Acquired in 1952.

390 Historia iaponensis anni MDCXXIV, continens Christianiae fidei progressum, et varia Iaponensium Christianorum pro fide certamina, *tr. from Italian*, Moguntiae, sumptibus Hermanni Mylii Birckmanni, 1628. 4°
  CUL (3 copies) Mm.15.53 Repaired binding; T.5.16. With the bookplate of the Royal Library, deposited in 1715, and in its MS. catalogue; Syn.7.62.9 Transferred from the British Museum in 1889.

391 Litterae annuae Iaponiae anni M.DC.XXIV, *tr. from Italian into Latin* Dilingae, impensis Caspari Sutoris, 1628. 8°
  TRC V.7.195 Probably acquired in the 19th century.

392 Litterae iaponicae anni MDCVI . . ., Antuerpiae, ex officina Plantiniana, 1611. 12°
  BOD 8° B 1 Med. BS.
  For letters by him see also the entry for Jesuits: Letters from Missions.

Godinho, Nicolau (1559/61–1616) (Godignus)

Jesuit and writer about Africa, who probably did not visit the continent but used his skill as a Latinist to celebrate and defend the missionary work of his order there. Barbosa Machado says that he spent the last ten years of his life in Rome, the head-quarters of the Society of Jesus. Like a number of other Jesuit writers, Godinho does not reveal his nationality on the title-page of his books, though in the dedication of **394** to Claudio Aquaviva, the general of the order, he says clearly that he was Portuguese. Strictly speaking the book is anonymous, but Aquaviva's licence names the author.

Godinho is not a well-known writer, but **393** is present in seven Oxford libraries and four Cambridge ones, probably because of the fascination of the early modern university with Ethiopia, supposedly the home of the first Christian convert (Acts: 8.26–39).

Barbosa Machado, III, pp. 493–4.

393 De Abassinorum rebus . . . libri tres, Lugduni, sumptibus Horatii Cardon, 1615. 8°
  BOD 8° G 22 Art. Seld. From the Selden bequest of 1659 **ASC** SR.106.b.20 **CHC** (2 copies) O.T.6.5, from the Orrery bequest of 1732; Allestree Q.5.20, from the Allestree

bequest of 1681 **JSO** P.1.22 **MER** 67.G.6 17th-century binding **SJCO** HB4/2.d.2.8 Bequeathed by Nathaniel Crynes in 1745 **WOR** XB.7.66 Bequeathed by H. A. Pottinger in 1911.
CUL N*.6.13 (F) Acquired before 1715 **EMM** S.12.4.37 Bequeathed by Archbishop William Sancroft in 1693 **JSC** K.11.32 With the bookplate of Joseph Stillington, 1700, and two pages of MS. notes on the endpapers keyed to the text. Stillington was a fellow from 1694 until his death in 1707 **TRC** W.22.38 In the library's copy of the interleaved Bodleian catalogue of the 18th century.

394 Vita patris Gonzali Sylveriae, Societatis Iesu sacerdotis, in urbe Monomotapa martyrium passi, Lugduni, sumptibus Horatii Cardon, 1612. 8°
BOD Wood 152 (2) Bequeathed by Anthony Wood, antiquarian, in 1695. With legible annotation in Latin, apparently not by Wood (Kiessling (2002) 3239).
CUL Z.14.7 In the Royal Library, deposited in 1715, and in its MS. catalogue.

395 Vita patris Gonzali Sylveriae, Societatis Iesu sacerdotis, in urbe Monomotapa martyrium passi, Coloniae Agrippinae, sumptibus Ioannis Kinckii, 1616. 8°
CUL F.2.92 With the bookplate of the Royal Library, deposited in 1715 **SID** N.7.58 In the catalogue of 1674 **TRC** V.7.55 (2) Bequeathed by John Laughton in 1712. He was college, and later University librarian.

Góis, Damião de (1502–74) (Damianus a Goes)
Historian. Góis spent more than twenty years (1523–45) mostly outside Portugal, in the Low Countries, Germany and Italy. He was the only writer included in the catalogue to have known Erasmus personally, and through that contact there is an indirect link with the world of Sir Thomas More and English humanism (see below). While abroad he wrote the books in Latin, especially his two books about Ethiopia, which brought him great international fame. There are about forty-three copies of his *Fides, religio, moresque Aethiopum* with its companion *Deploratio Lappianae Gentis* in Oxford and Cambridge libraries. Some were printed separately (**404–5**), but most were included in composite volumes organized by Góis himself, or his publisher Rescius (**396**) or by others (**401–2, 406–10** and **826**, where the compiler was Andreas Schottus). The book has been attractive to collectors in modern times, but there are many copies with old provenance. There are five copies too of the earlier *Legatio* which is also about the religion and customs of Ethiopia (**413–5**). John More's very rare English translation (**415**) is held at Emmanuel. John More was the son of Sir Thomas More, but there is no evidence that Góis met any member of the family. Góis was very patriotic and a statement of his nationality appears on the title-page of nearly all his Latin works. Even when it does not (**413**) the title-page makes plain the Portuguese nature of the subject-matter of the book.

On returning to Portugal Góis became the official chronicler of his country, but since **397–9** are all in Portuguese they were of no interest to the early modern English universities and copies were acquired in the nineteenth century or later. All Souls has a copy of two extremely rare translations made by Góis into Portuguese (**403** and **416**), printed in Italy, probably for reasons of secrecy. They may have been bought for the college in the nineteenth century by Peter Frye Hony. For further information about him and about his college see Chapter Three, pp. lix–lx.

Damião de Góis, *O livro de Eclesiastes,* ed. by T. F. Earle; T. F. Earle, 'Damião de Góis, *Deploratio Lappianae Gentis.* Text and Translation'; Elisabeth Feist Hirsch, *Damião de Góis: The Life and Thought of a Portuguese Humanist*; Jeremy Lawrance, 'The Middle Indies: Damião de Góis on Prester John and the Ethiopians'.

396 Aliquot opuscula *with, by Góis,* Fides, religio moresque Aethiopum, Epistolae . . . Preciosi Ioannis, Deploratio Lappianae gentis, Lappiae descriptio, Bellum Cambaicum, De rebus & imperio Lusitanorum . . ., Hispaniae ubertas et potentia, Pro Hispania adversus Musterum . . ., Lovanii, ex officina Rutgeri Rescii, 1544. 4°

BOD 4° D 15 Art. Seld. From the Selden bequest of 1659. It may replace a copy recorded in the 1605 catalogue, with a list of contents **ASC** SR 36.c.16 Perhaps bought at the Stuart sale in 1821 **QUO** Sel.c.28 Bought with money left by Robert Mason, 1841.

CUL O.4.30 From the Royal Library, deposited in 1715, and in its MS. catalogue **CCCC** SP. 369 Bequeathed by Archbishop Matthew Parker in 1575 (Adams G817; Faria (1977), 10).

397 Chronica do felicissimo rei dom Emanuel, Lisboa, em casa de Françisco Correa, 1566. Fol.

BOD Antiq. d.P.1566.1 Acquired between 1883 and 1936. The book came from the collection of Richard Heber, which was sold at auction in London in 1834–7. **ASC** SR 89.d.6 Bound with **399**.

CUL T.9.59 With the bookplate of the Royal Library, deposited in 1715 (Adams G818; Anselmo 491; Faria (1977), 22–6).

398 Chronica do felicissimo rey dom Emanvel, Lisboa, por Antonio Aluarez, impressor, & mercador de liuros, 1619. Fol.

TAY 270.H.39 From the Martin collection, acquired in 1895. (Faria (1977), 52).

399 Chronica do principe Dom Ioam, Lisboa, Francisco Correa, 1567. Fol.

ASC SR 89.d.6 Bound with 397 (Anselmo 492; Faria (1977), 27).

400 Commentarii rerum gestarum in India, Louanii, ex officina Rutgeri Rescii, 1539. 4°

CUL F.153.d.6.1 Acquired in 1957, using money left by Tobias Rustat (1606–93/4) (Adams G819; Faria (1977), 4).

401 De rebus Aethiopicis, Indicis, Lusitanicis & Hispanicis, opuscula qu[a]eda[m] historica doctissima, *with, by Góis,* Fides . . ., Deploratio . . .,

Lappiae Descriptio, Diensis . . . oppugnatio, De rebus . . . Lusitanorum, De bello cambaico, Hispania, *included in* Peter Martyr, De rebus oceanicis . . . decades tres, Coloniae, apud Geruinum Calenium & haeredes Quentelios, 1574. 8°

BOD Crynes 580 From the Crynes bequest of 1745 **HEB** Muller Mont 58Ca25(2) **JSO** P.1.11 Given by Thomas Wilkes **MER** 67.E.1 Oxford binding with Ker centrepiece xvi, in use c.1580-c.1620 (Pearson, p. 78). Given by Thomas Savile, fellow, who died in 1593.

CUL T.11.67 With the bookplate of the Royal Library, deposited in 1715, and in its catalogue, but also with the signature of Sir Thomas Knyvett of Ashwellthorpe, Norfolk, and the date, 25.12.1603. Bishop Moore, the founder of the Royal Library, also acquired Knyvett's library (McKitterick 649) **TRC** (2 copies) W.22.7 Some underlining; Grylls.23.11. Bequeathed by William Grylls in 1863 (Adams M755; Faria (1977), 28).

402 De rebus Hispanicis, Lusitanicis, Aragonicis, Indicis & Aethiopicis . . ., *with, by Góis*: Hispaniae descriptio, Olisiponensis urbis descriptio, Fides . . .; Deploratio . . ., Lappiae Descriptio, Diensis . . . oppugnatio, De bello cambaico secundo commentarii tres, Coloniae Agrippinae, in officina Birckmannica, sumptibus Arnoldi Mylij, 1602. 8°

BOD 8° S 245 Art. Perhaps acquired from the Plately sale, Dec 1810 **CHC** f.9.11 Bequeathed by Robert Burton, 1640 (Kiessling (1988) 689) **SJCO** K.scam.1.upper shelf. 19(1) With the signature of Antony Scattirgood, 1640. He was originally from Trinity, Cambridge, and did not incorporate at Oxford until 1669.

CUL L*.6.28 (F) Acquired before 1715 **CLA** B1.3.40 With the 1701 college bookplate and the shelf-mark P 87 on the fore-edge. In the catalogue of 1677–78 with the same shelf-mark **PET** K.7.4 Probably a 19th-century acquisition **SJCC** E.13.8 From the Crashawe collection, deposited in 1626 (Faria (1977), 45).

See **853** for a work by Teive contained in the same volume.

403 Ecclesiastes de Salamam, con alguas annotações neçessarias, Veneza, per Steuão Sabio, 1538. 8°

ASC SR.70.b.24(1) Bound with **416**.

404 Fides, religio, moresqve Aethiopvm, *with* Deploratio Lappianae gentis, Lovanii, ex officina Rutgeri Rescii, 1540. 4°

CHC Allestree R. 2.2. From the Allestree bequest of 1681, with marginal notes.

TRC Grylls 7.23 Bequeathed by William Grylls in 1863 (Adams G819; Faria (1977), 7).

405 Fides, religio, moresqve Aethiopvm, *with* Deploratio . . . Parisiis, apud Christianum Wechelum, 1541. 8°

BOD Byw. N 5.20 Bequeathed in 1914 by Ingram Bywater. Marginal notes, dated 18 February 1633 **TAY** Arch.12°.P.1541 Acquired in 1936.

CCCC SP.56 (2) Bequeathed by Archbishop Matthew Parker in 1575 (Adams G820; Faria (1977), 8).

406 Fides, religio, et mores Aethiopum, *with* Deploratio . . ., De Lappiae situ, *in* Joannes Boemus, Mores, leges et ritus omnium gentium, Lugduni, apud Ioannem Tornaesium, 1582. 8°

BOD 8° B 90(1) Linc. From the Barlow bequest of 1691 (Faria (1977), 41).

407 Fides, religio, et mores Aethiopum, *with* Deploratio . . ., De Lappiae situ, *in* Joannes Boemus, Mores, leges et ritus omnium gentium, [Geneva], apud Ioannem Tornaesium, 1591. 16°

HER xxx.02.17 From Magdalen Hall (extinguished 1874–75).
CUL N*.13.17 (G) Acquired before 1715 PET I.8.31 (Adams B2271; Faria (1977), 44).

408 Fides, religio, et mores Aethiopum, *with* Deploratio . . ., De Lappiae situ, *in* Joannes Boemus, Mores, leges et ritus omnium gentium, Geneva, I. Tornaesium, 1604.

BOD 8° B 69 Art. Seld. From the Selden bequest of 1659.
CUL Acton e.23.115 Lord Acton's library was presented in 1902 (Faria (1977), 48).

409 Fides, religio, et mores Aethiopum, *with* Deploratio . . ., De Lappiae situ, *in* Joannes Boemus, Mores, leges et ritus omnium gentium, [Geneva], apud Ioannem Tornaesium, 1620. 12°

BOD (2 copies) Crynes 42 Part of the Crynes bequest of 1745; Douce A 33 Part of the Douce bequest of 1834.
EMM S.12.5.82 Bequeathed by Archbishop William Sancroft in 1693 (Faria (1977), 53).

410 [Fides, religio, et mores Aethiopum, *with* Deploratio . . ., De Lappiae situ] The faith, religion and manners of the Aethiopians . . ., *tr. by* Ed. Aston, *in* The Manners, Lawes and Customes of all Nations . . . London, printed by George Eld, 1611. 4°

BOD (3 copies) Wood B 28.1 Bequeathed by Anthony Wood, antiquarian, in 1695 (Kiessling (2002) 1026); 4° Rawl. 535 Bishop Richard Rawlinson's bequest was made in 1755; Douce B. subt. 103. From the Douce bequest of 1834 (STC 3198; Faria (1977), 50).

411 Hispania, Lovanii, excudebat Rutgerus Rescius, 1542. 4°

BOD D 20.12(4) Linc. From the Barlow bequest of 1691, but in the 1674 catalogue, so probably a replacement SJCO Psi.i.4.28(2) Given by William Paddy, 1602 (Faria (1977), 9).

412 Hispania, *in* Robert Beale (Belus), Rerum Hispanicarum Scriptorum Tomus II, Francofurti, apud Andream Wechelem, 1579. Fol.

BOD (2 copies) F 2.3 Art. Seld. From the Selden bequest of 1659; Douce H 249. From the Douce bequest of 1834 BLL 0025 sc 11 NEW BT1.92.11–12 In the catalogue of 1686.
CUL I*.7.15 (B) Acquired before 1715; T.8.32 With the bookplate of the Royal Library, deposited in 1715, and in its MS. catalogue CHR H.13.19. Binding with gilt centrepiece with college arms and motto 'Souvent me souvient'. Number on the fore-edge, which is an indication that the book was acquired in the 17th century G&C L.17.43 (Adams B568; Faria (1977), 30).
See also **396, 401–2** for other editions of this work.

413 Legatio magni Indorum imperatoris presbyteri Ioannis, [Antwerp], Ioannes Graphaeus, [1532]. 8°

BOD 246 g.18 Acquired after 1864 (Faria (1977), 1).

414 Legatio magni Indorum Imperatoris Presbyteri Ioannis, Dordraci, excudebat Iohannes Leonardi Berewout, 1618. 8°

BOD (2 copies) 8° N 66(2) Linc. (Barlow bequest of 1691); Diss. U 90 Bound with other 17th-century travel books JSO Fellows C.16.25(2) (Faria (1977), 51).

415 [Legatio magni Indorum imperatoris presbyteri Ioannis] The Legacye or embassate of the great emperour of Inde prester John, *tr. by John More*, London, W. Rastell, 1533. 4°
EMM S.15.4.56 Bequeathed by Archbishop William Sancroft in 1693 (STC 11966; Faria (1977), 2).

416 Livro de Marco Tullio Ciçeram chamado Catam maior, ou da velhiçe, Veneza, per Steuano Sabio, 1538. 8°
ASC SR.70.b.24(2) Bound with **403** (Faria (1977), 3).

417 Lovaniensis obsidio, *in* Simon Schardius, Historicum opus, Tomus II, Basileae, ex officina Henricpetrina, 1574. Fol. (The work by Góis is on pp. 1869–83.)
BOD D 8.11 CCCO I.22.2 MGO M.11.15.
CUL (2 copies) O.3.62-; L*.3.16- Acquired before 1715 CCCC EP.X.10–12 Bequeathed by Archbishop Matthew Parker in 1575 CHR H.13.28 PET M.3.8 Bequeathed by Andrew Perne, Master, in 1589 QUC D.10.24 Bequeathed by John Smith, fellow, the Cambridge Platonist, in 1652 (See the Benefactors' Register, p. 33) TRC W.11.53 (Adams S623; Faria (1977), 29).

418 Urbis Olisiponis Descriptio, Eborae, apud Andream Burgensem, 1554. 4°
CUL Dd*.4.19 (14) The shelf-mark is one of those associated with the Royal Library, deposited in 1715. One of 21 pamphlets, the latest published in 1658 (Adams G821; Anselmo 384; Faria (1977), 18).

All the Latin works by Góis listed here were republished by Andreas Schottus (**826**). For a summary in French of his Commentarii rerum gestarum in India (**400**) and of De bello cambaico see **659, 660**.

Gomes, Manuel (16th–17th cents)

A doctor, described as 'Lusitani' on the title-page of **419**, but born in Antwerp of Portuguese parents, according to Barbosa Machado. Many Jewish doctors proclaimed their attachment to Portugal despite living abroad. The only copy of his book, in Oxford, is of old provenance.
Barbosa Machado, III, p. 277.

419 De pestilentiae curatione methodica tractatio, Antuerpiae, ex officina Ioach. Trognaesii, 1603. 4°
BOD 4° G 6(1) Med. In the 1620 catalogue, with the current shelf-mark.

Gouveia, António de (?1513–66) (Antonius Goveanus)

Humanist and jurist. Gouveia received a royal bursary enabling him to study in Paris, where he arrived in 1527. Unlike most of his fellow students he never returned to Portugal. Luís de Matos (p. 11) suggests that the reason was circumstantial, his marriage in Cahors in 1549. However, most unusually for a writer of his kind, he never mentions his

nationality on the title-pages of his books. (There is one exception, the first edition of his epigrams, Lyon, 1539; no copy in Oxford or Cambridge). This suggests an antipathy on his part towards Portugal, perhaps because he was suspected there of Lutheranism (Matos, p. 8).
Luís de Matos, *Sobre António de Gouveia e a sua obra.*

420 Alphabetum Græcum, Lugduni, apud Sebastianium Gryphium, 1540. 8°
BOD Byw. N 5.25 (2) Bequeathed in 1914 by Ingram Bywater.

421 De iure accrescendi liber, Tolosae, ex officina Guidonis Boudeuillaei, 1554. 4°
KCC M.28.41 (3) (Adams G912).

422 De iurisdictione libri II, adversus Eguinarium Baronem iureconsultum, Tolosae, apud Ioannem de Fleurs, 1552. 4°
KCC M.36.32 Heavy underlining and annotation. Pp. 43–6 are missing (Adams G913).

423 Epigrammata. *With* epistolæ . . . quatuor, Lugduni, apud Sebastianum Gryphium, 1540. 8°
BOD (2 copies) 300 g.32 Acquired after 1864; Byw. N 5.25(1) Bequeathed in 1914 by Ingram Bywater.
TRC III.8.29 Bequeathed by John Laughton in 1712. He was college, and later University librarian (Adams G914).

424 Epistola ad Guillelmum Bellaium . . . de castigatione harum comoediarum, *by Terence,* eiusdem de versibus Terentianis, necnon de ludis Megalensibus, *included in* P. Terentii Afri poetae lepidissimi Comoediae omnes, Venetiis, apud Bartholomaeum Caesanum, 1553. Fol.
ASC b.4.12.
CUL X.1.19 From the Royal Library, deposited in 1715 **SJCC** Ii.1.61 Given in 1895.

425 Epistola ad Guillelmum Bellaium . . . de castigatione harum comoediarum, *by Terence,* eiusdem de versibus Terentianis, necnon de ludis Megalensibus, *included in* P. Terentii Afri poetae lepidissimi Comoediae omnes, Venetiis, apud Hieronymum Scotum, 1569. Fol.
NEW BT1.92.4 In the catalogue of 1686.

426 Epistola ad Guillelmum Bellaium De castigatione harum comoediarum, *by Terence*; eiusdem de versibus Terentianis, necnon De ludis Megalensibus, atq[ue] etiam annotationes, *included in* P. Terentius Afer cum commentariis, Venetiis, apud Ioannem Gryphium, 1580. Fol.
CHC Oc.2.14 Probably from the Orrery bequest, 1732. Some underlining.

427 Epistola ad Guillelmum Bellaium De castigatione harum comoediarum, *by Terence*; eiusdem de versibus Terentianis, necnon De ludis

Megalensibus, atq[ue] etiam annotationes, *included in* P. Terentius Afer cum commentariis, Venetiis, apud Ioannem Gryphium, 1586. Fol.

TRC Z.16.55 Bequeathed by John Paris who was Fellow in 1707 and Senior Proctor 1725–26 . It also belonged to Henry Molle (?1597–1658), of King's (Adams T371).

428 Ex libro lectionum iuris variarum, Tolosae, apud Ioannem de Fleurs, 1552.

KCC M.28.41 (2) (Adams G916).

429 Lectionum variarum iuris civilis Lib. I, Tolosae, ex officina Guidonis Boudeuillaei, impensis Ioannis Perrioni, 1554. 4°

KCC M.28.41 (1) (Adams G916).

430 M. T. Ciceronis ad C. Trebatium iurisconsultum Topica. In eadem . . . commentarius, Parisiis, apud Thomam Richardum, 1549. 4°

CHC AB.6.9 (3) Marginal notes. Bound with **288**.

431 M. T. Ciceronis ad C. Trebatium iurisconsultum Topica. In eadem . . . commentarius, Parisiis, apud Thomam Richardum, 1550. 4°

CHC Od.3.6 From the Orrery bequest of 1732.

432 M. T. Ciceronis ad C. Trebatium iurisconsultum Topica. In eadem . . . commentarius, Parisiis, apud Thomam Richardum, 1557. 4°

BOD Vet. E1 d.61 Acquired after 1937.

433 Opera iuris ciuilis, Lugduni, apud Antonium Vincentium [in colophon excudebat Symphorianus Barbier], 1564. Fol.

BOD C 1.6(2) Jur. Chain mark. In the 1605 catalogue. Signature of Edmund Marlow, whose name does not appear among the early donors to the library **MER** 64.E.12(3) Oxford binding, Ker rolls xii and xviii, used together between 1575 and 1605 (Pearson, p. 67). Chain mark.

TRH O*.4.13, formerly L.1.13 and with 13 on the fore-edge, indicating early acquisition (Adams G917).

434 Opera quae ciuilis disciplinae claustra continent & reserant, Lugduni, ex officina Vincentii, 1599. 8°

ASC y.infra 2.4.

435 Pro Aristotele responsio adversus Petri Rami calumnias, Parisiis, apud Simonem Colinaeum, 1543. 8°

BOD Byw. N. 5. 26 Bequeathed in 1914 by Ingram Bywater. **MHS** D/ANO.

436 Pub. Terentii Aphri comoediae sex . . ., *edited by Gouveia*, Parisiis, apud Ioannem Lodoicum Tiletanum, 1544 [in colophon 1545]. 4°

BOD Auct. S inf. 2.13 Formerly 4° B 124 Jur. Stated on flyleaf not to be in the Bodleian or the British Museum, so it is likely to be a 19th-century acquisition. The Auct. shelf-mark was used after 1825.

437 Pub. Terentii Aphri comoediae sex . . ., *edited by Gouveia*, Lovanii, Antonius Maria Bergagne, 1552. 4°

CUL X.2.38 From the Royal Library, deposited in 1715 (Adams T342).

438 Pub. Terentii Aphri comoediae sex . . ., *edited by Gouveia*, Parisiis, ex typographia Thomae Ricardi, 1558 (1550). 4°

CUL X.2.34 From the Royal Library, deposited in 1715 (Adams T350).

Gouveia, António de, Bishop of Cyrene (1575–1628)

Augustinian friar, whose life was extremely adventurous even by the standards of his time. He was twice ambassador to Persia, once as a papal legate, and achieved some remarkable diplomatic successes, but ended as a fugitive lucky to escape with his life.

The French translation of **439** was very much an Augustinian enterprise. The translator complains of 'vne langue mal-aisée, obscure, & courte, comme est la langue Portugaise', and was helped by Francisco Muñoz's Spanish version. Gouveia's work was hardly known in the English universities in the sixteenth and seventeenth centuries, and there is only one copy of **439** likely to be of old provenance, at New College. The secret of success was to publish in Latin, as the Jesuits tended to do – though not the next author to be discussed.

Barbosa Machado, I, pp. 294–6.

439 Histoire orientale, des grans progres de l'Eglise cathol. . . . en la reduction des anciens chrestiens, dits de S. Thomas, *tr. from a Spanish version of the Portuguese original by* F. Iean Baptiste de Glen, Bruxelles, par Rutger Velpius [BOD 8° T 151 Art Antwerp par Hierosme Verdussen], 1609. 8°

BOD (2 copies) 8° W 102 Th. Acquired in 1827; 8° T 151 Art. Acquired in 1827. Lacks work by Meneses (**574**) present in the other Bodleian copy KEB 131.02 Bequeathed in 1874 NEW BT3.71.20 Evidence of chaining. Bound with **574**. In the catalogue of 1686, under Meneses.

CUL 6100.d.16 Bound with **574**.

440 Iornada do arcebispo de Goa . . . quando foy as serras do Malauar, Coimbra, na officina de Diogo Gomez Loureyro, 1606. Fol.

BOD Vet. G2 d. 13(1) Acquired after 1937. Bound with **575**.

CUL Hisp.4.60.2 Acquired in 1906.

441 Rellação em que se tratão as guerras e grandes vitorias que alcançou o grande rey da Persia . . ., Lisboa, por Pedro Craesbeeck, 1611. 8°

TAY Finch.G.79 Acquired in 1938, using money left by Robert Finch, of Balliol (1783–1830). The title page has been repaired.

442 Vita, morte, e miracoli del b. Gio. di Dio, *tr. from Spanish by* Bernardo Pandolfo, Madrid, Tomaso Gionta, 1624. 4°

ASC SR.67.b.15.

443 Vita, morte, e miracoli del b. Gio. di Dio, *tr. from Spanish by* Bernardo Pandolfo, Napoli, Lazaro Scoriggio [in colophon et ristampato per Camillo Cauallo 1641], 1631. 4°

BOD Vet. F1 e.185(1) Acquired in 1974.

Guerreiro, Fernão (1550–1614)

Jesuit and publicist, who did not travel to the East but, as he explains in the prologue to the reader of **444**, used letters from missionaries as the basis of a series of narratives intended for the Portuguese and Spanish-speaking publics. The speed with which he and his collaborators worked is evident from the printing history of **445**, which was based on the events of 1600–01, first published in Portuguese in 1603 (no copy in Oxford) and in Spanish translation the following year. It is unlikely that any of the Oxford copies (there are none in Cambridge) are of early provenance.

Francisco Rodrigues, *História da Companhia de Jesus na assistência de Portugal,* III.1, pp. 156–7; Inocêncio, III, p. 184.

444 Relaçam annal das cousas que fezeram os padres da Companhia de Iesus nas partes da India Oriental . . . nos annos de seiscentos & dous & seiscentos & tres, Lisboa, per Iorge Rodrigues, 1605. 4°

ASC (2 copies) SR.63.f.3 Underlining and notes, perhaps in 17th-century hand, some in English, in Livro II, da China; SR. 15. f.7 This copy lacks a title page and all preliminary material.

445 Relacion anual de las cosas que han hecho los padres de la Compañia de Iesus en la India Oriental y Iapon, en los años de 600. y 601., *tr. from Portuguese by* Antonio Colaço, Valladolid, por Luys Sanchez, 1604. 4°

BOD 4° A 49 Jur. BS. Not in any of the early catalogues, up to and including the catalogue of 1738, so acquired after that date ASC SR.63.f.2.

Hakluyt, Richard (?1552–1616)

Geographer, whose compilation of voyages achieved a very wide circulation in early modern Oxford and Cambridge. Some of his information about Portuguese voyages derived from his contacts while in Paris with Dom António, Prior of Crato, the exiled pretender to the Portuguese throne. There is further information about Hakluyt and the extent of his knowledge of Portuguese in Chapter One, pp. xli–iii. For works by Portuguese writers translated in **446** see Pereira, Galeote; Sande, Duarte; Vaz, Lopes.

Oxford Dictionary of National Biography; A.M. and D.B. Quinn, 'Contents and Sources of the Three Major Works', in *The Hakluyt Handbook.*

446 The Principal Navigations, Voyages, Traffiques and Discoveries of the English Nation, London, George Bishop, Ralph Newberie and Robert Barker, 1598–1600. 3 vols. Fol.

BOD (3 copies) H.8.15–16 Art.; Savile X.12 From the bequest of Sir Henry Savile (1549–1622), mathematician and founder of chairs in geometry and astronomy; Douce H.238–9 From the Douce bequest of 1834 **BLL** 575 d 10–11 (3 vols in 2) **CHC** e.2.9 (3 vols in 2) **ENG** YH 43.1 [pri] (3 vols) **EXE** 9M12626 **HER** GGG 5.7 3 vols in 2 **MGO** K.5.11–12 **NEW** BTI.132.1–2 In the catalogue of 1686 **ORI** Pe 1–2 In both the 17th-century catalogues **QUO** Sel.c.175–6 **RSL** RR.x19 (3 vols) **SEH** Fol. R6–7 **SJCO** Sigma 1.33–4 **TRO** B.12.4–5 **WOR** L.5.14–15.

CUL (4 copies) L*.9.34- Deposited before 1715; Peterborough D.11.7 (For Peterborough Cathedral Library, see the Introduction, p. xiv); Syn.1.59.1–2-; RCS. Case.b.104–105 **CHR** Rouse.13.9–10 Presented by William Rouse, a former fellow, in 1940 **EMM** MSS 3.3.21 (-22) 3 vols in 1 **KCC** (2 copies) M.24.19–21; P.3.1–3 **MGC** PL 2111–2 From the collection of the diarist Samuel Pepys (1633–1703), deposited in 1724 **PMC** 2.16.6 Bequeathed in 1626 by Lancelot Andrewes, bishop of Winchester **QUC** D.9.18–19 In the catalogue of the 1680s with the same shelf-mark **SJCC** Aa.4.35–36 **SID** B3.15A–15B **TRC** (2 copies) Capell E.1–2; Grylls 31.148–9 Bequeathed by William Grylls in 1863 (STC 12625–6).

Henriques, Henrique (1520–1600)

A Jesuit and 'the first great European scholar of any Indian language' (Shaw, p. 26). The Tamil catechism is based on a work by Marcos Jorge which Henriques translated into Tamil and then printed in Cochin in South India using specially cast types. Only two other copies are known (and both have disappeared, Shaw p. 27). The Tamil confessionary is the only one known. Though the Bodleian contains other very rare works by Portuguese scholars in or about oriental languages, especially those of João Rodrigues about Japanese, only the works by Henriques have old provenance.

Graham W. Shaw, 'A 'lost' work of Henrique Henriques'.

447 Doctrina christam *with* Confessionairo, Cochin, Colegio da Madre de Deus, 1579–1580. 8°

    BOD Vet. Or. F. Tam. 1 Acquired before 1615 and in the 1620 catalogue.

Homem, Pedro Barbosa (16th–17th centuries)

Canonist and judge, who describes himself as 'Iurisconsulto Portugues' on the title-page of **448**. He excuses himself for writing in Spanish on the grounds that Portuguese is understood by very few foreigners, sig. +7v.

Inocêncio, VI, p. 396.

448 Discursos de la juridica, y verdadera razon de estado, formados sobre la vida, y acciones del Rey don Iuan el II de buena memoria, Rey de Portugal, llamado vulgarmente el Principe Perfecto . . . Coimbra, Nicolao Carvallo, 1629. 4°

    TRC S.15.6 Repaired binding and 3 previous shelf-marks.

Index librorum prohibitorum

Listed here are copies of the Index adapted for use in Portugal. For the use made by Protestant theologians of the Index, see Chapter One, pp. xxxiii–iv.

449 Index librorum prohibitorum, Olysippone, apud Franciscum Corream, 1564. 4°
BOD Broxb. 93.12. From the Broxbourne Library, donated in 1978 (Anselmo 474).

450 Index librorum prohibitorum, *edited by Francisco Foreiro*, Antuerpiae, ex officina Christophori Plantini, 1570. 8°
BOD (3 copies) 8° Z 22(4) Th. Seld. From the Selden bequest of 1659; 8° A 5(2) Jur.BS.; Broxb.93.16. From the Broxbourne Library, donated in 1978.
EMM S7.5.25, also 332.7.4. Bound with two tracts, published in 1614 and 1635. With the Sancroft-Emmanuel bookplate, and part of the bequest of 1693. At the end more than a page of continuous MS. Latin text **JSC** C.6.5(3) With a number on the fore-edge, indicating that it was probably acquired in the 17th century. In the catalogue of 1705 (Adams I96–7).

451 Index librorum prohibitorum, Olysippone, Antonius Riberius, 1581. 12°
BOD 4° C 70(2) Th. In the 1605 catalogue **BLL** LG1 Bequeathed by Paget Toynbee (1855–1932) (Anselmo 947).

452 Index librorum prohibitorum . . ., *ed. by António de Matos de Noronha, Bishop of Elvas,* Olisipone, apud Petrum Craesbeeck, 1597. 8°
BOD 4° M 21 Art.BS. Perhaps acquired in 1734 (Anselmo 515).

453 Index auctorum da[m]natae memoriae, Ulyssipone, ex officina Petri Craesbeck, 1624. Fol.
BOD B 21.20(2) Th. Lacks the title page. Though this book does not have the characteristic Linc. shelf-mark it has the signature of Thomas Barlow, 1629, together with notes in Latin and marginalia in the Latin text. Barlow became bishop of Lincoln in 1675. Chain mark **BLL** 0895 d 05 Probably the copy given by Michael Geddes, after 1691, when he became Chancellor of Salisbury Cathedral. He was chaplain to the English factory in Portugal, 1678–87. In the 1709 catalogue it had the shelf-mark O.6.13 which is still visible in the book today. Evidence of chaining **CHC** Allestree O.2.6 From the Allestree bequest of 1681 **QUO** 8.B.8. 17th-century binding.

Jesuits: Letters from Missions

See also Almeida, Manuel de; Fróis, Luís; Guerreiro, Fernão; Pimenta, Nicolau; Girão, João Rodrigues.

There are one or more letters from Portuguese missionaries, normally Jesuits, in all the collections listed below. For a list of the writers, and brief biographical information about them, see Appendix I.

454 Alcune lettere delle cose del Giappone, paese del mondo novo. Dell'anno 1579 infino al 1581, Brescia, appresso Vincenzo Sabbio, 1584. 8°
BOD Holk. f.98 The Holkham collection was acquired in 1953. It was originally formed by Sir Edward Coke (1552–1634), but the catalogue of Coke's books does not include **454**. Since the volume has no indication of ownership, it is likely that it formed part of the bequest of the 18th-century librarian, Dr Ferrari. See Hassall, *The Books of Sir Christopher Hatton,* p. 6.

455 Alcune lettere delle cose del Giappone. Dell'anno 1579 infino al 1581, Roma, appresso Francesco Zannetti, 1584. 8°
BOD 133 g. 44 The shelf-mark indicates that it was acquired after 1864.

456 Annuae litterae societatis Iesu anni M. D. LXXXV, Romae, in collegio eiusdem societatis, 1587.
BOD 8° L 10 Art. Given by George Trenchard miles.

457 Auuisi della Cina et Giapone, del fine dell'anno 1586, Anuersa, appresso di Christophoro Plantino, 1588. 8°
BOD 8° G 176(2) Art. In the 1605 catalogue with the shelf-mark 8° B 31 Th., now erased but still legible. After 1686 it was bound with another work and given its present shelf-mark.

458 Breuis Japaniae insulae descriptio, *with* insigne quoddam martyrium, Coloniae Agrippinae, in officina Birckmannica, 1582. 8°
BOD 8° H 110(1) Linc. From the Barlow bequest of 1691 CHC WD.8.3(2). From the Wake bequest of 1737.
CUL Dd*.5.37 (G) From the Royal Library, deposited in 1715 EMM 338.4.17 probably acquired after 1800 (Adams F1061 and J94).

459 Cartas que os padres e irmãos da Companhia de Iesus escreuerão dos reynos de Iapão & China, Euora, por Manoel de Lyra, 1598. 2 vols. 4°
BOD 4 C 78 Art. In the 1605 catalogue, where it is dated 1597. Chain mark (Anselmo 774).

460 De nouis Christianae religionis progressibus et certaminibus in Iaponia . . . Monasterii Westphaliae, ex officina typographica Michaelis Dalii, 1627. 4°
BOD Antiq. e.G.1627.1 Bought 1925.
De rebus iaponicis, indicis, et peruanis epistolae . . . See **495**.

461 Diuersi auisi particolari dall'Indie di Portogallo riceuuti, dall'anno 1551 fino al 1558, *tr. from Spanish,* [Venice], Michele Tramezzino, 1558 or 1560. 8°
BOD Vet. F1 f.489 Acquired after 1864.
TRC Grylls 6.107 (2) Bequeathed by William Grylls in 1863 (Adams I108?).
A letter by Melchior Nunes contained in this compilation was translated in **737**, Samuel Purchas, Purchas his Pilgrimes, Vol. III, Book 2, ch. 4.

462 Drey newe Relationes, Augspurg, Chrysostomo Dabersshofer, 1611. 4°
BOD Antiq. e.G. 1611.2 The shelf-mark indicates that it was acquired between 1883 and 1936.

463 Epistolae Iapanicae, Louanii, apud Rutgerum Velpium, 1569 [in some copies 1570]. 8°
BOD Crynes 384 From the Crynes bequest of 1745 ASC SR.63.f.13 Signed L. Van der Burch RSL RR. z. 43 (2) Acquired after 1835, because not in the catalogue of the Radcliffe Library which was printed in that year SJCO K.scam.1.upper shelf. 8 Bound with **465**.

464 Epistolae Indicae, Lovanii, apud Rutgerum Velpium, 1566. 8°

BOD 8° G 66a Th. MS. notes and underlining. It came from the library of an Augustinian monastery in Ingolstadt, which suggests that it was not an early acquisition **CHC** WD.8.5 perhaps from Wake bequest of 1737. With annotations by someone hostile to Jesuits. This copy and the Bodleian one are bound with **47 MER** 74.C.16. 16th or 17th-century binding.

TRC X.7.20 D Signed by John Lumley and in the 1609 catalogue of his collection. It also has the Newton-Puckering bookplate, showing that it was in the library in 1691(Adams A1021 and I110, Lumley 1103).

465 Epistolae Indicae et Iapanicae, 3a. ed., Louanij, apud Rutgerum Velpium, 1570. 8°

BOD (2 copies) 8° E 16 Art. In the 1620 catalogue with the current shelf-mark; 8° N 66 Med. **RSL** RR. z. 43 Acquired after 1835, because not in the catalogue of the Radcliffe Library which was printed in that year **SJCO** K.scam.1.upper shelf. 8 Bound with **463**.

CUL N*.6.48 (G) Acquired before 1715 **G&C** F.35.19 Bequeathed by William Branthwaite, Master, in 1619. He was one of the revisers of the Bible **SJCC** Ee.8.44 Bequeathed by Humfrey Gower, Master, in 1710 **TRC** W.24.37 Bequeathed by James Duport, vice-master, in 1679. Does not include **47**, a text by Andrade (Adams J97 and I111).

466 Epistola patrum Lusitanorum Societatis Iesu ad socios qui Romae versantur. De duodecim eiusdem Societatis pro Catholica fide interfectis, Neapoli, apud Iosephum Cacchium, 1572. 8°

BOD Vet. F1 f.349 The shelf-mark indicates that it was acquired after 1937.

467 Histoire de ce qui s'est passé au royaume d'Ethiopie es années 1624, 1625, & 1626, *tr. from Italian*, Paris, chez Sebastien Cramoisy, 1629. 8°

BOD Antiq. f.F. 1629.1 The shelf-mark indicates that it was acquired between 1883 and 1936.

468 Histoire de ce qui s'est passé en Ethiopie, Malabar, Brasil, et les indes orientales, tirée des lettres escrites és années 1620, iusques à 1624, *tr. from Italian*, Paris, chez Sebastien Cramoisy, 1628. 8°

BOD 8° A 7.8 Jur.

CUL E.13.69 Formerly owned by the monastery of Grunberghen (Brabant) and probably a 19th-century acquisition.

469 Histoire de ce qui s'est passé és royaumes d'Ethiopie, en l'année 1626 . . . et de la Chine, 1629, *tr. from Italian*, Paris, chez Sebastien Cramoisy, 1629. 12°

BOD Vet. E2 f.159 The shelf-mark indicates that it was acquired after 1937.

470 Historica relatio, de potentissimi regis Mogor, *tr. from Italian*, Moguntiae, ex officina typographica Henrici Breem, 1598. 8°

BOD 8° I 24(3) Art.BS Acquired from the bookseller Thomas Osborne (bap. ?1704–67).

471 Historia y anal relacion de las cosas que hizieron los padres de la Compañia de Iesus, por las partes de Oriente, *tr. from Portuguese by*

Christoval Suarez de Figueroa, Madrid, en la Imprenta Real, 1614 [in colophon: 1613], 4°
    BOD (2 copies) 4° S 33 Art. Seld. From the Selden bequest of 1659; 133 f.68 The shelf-mark indicates that it was acquired after 1864. With the printed bookplate of Peter Bardon M.D. ASC SR.63.f.4. 17th-century binding.
    CUL T.10.64 From the Royal Library, deposited in 1715.

472 Iaponica, Sinensia, Mogorana. Hoc est, De rebus apud eas gentes a patribus Societatis Iesu ann. 1598 & 99 gestis, *tr. by* Ioannes Oranus, Leodii, apud Arnoldum de Coerswaremia, 1601. 8°
    BOD 8° I 25 Art. BS. Acquired in 1796 at the sale of the library of Robert Orme (1728–1801), historian of India and East India company servant.

473 Iapponiensis imperii admirabilis commutatio exposita, *tr. from Italian by John Hay,* Antuerpiae, sumptibus viduae & heredum Ioannes Belleri, 1604. 8°
    BOD (2 copies) 8° P 52(6) Art. In the 1605 catalogue with title Relatio Japponiensis and shelf-mark 8° P.51; Wood 893(2) Bequeathed by Anthony Wood, antiquarian, in 1695 (Kiessling (2002) 1424).
    CUL Dd*.5.37 (G) From the Royal Library, deposited in 1715.

474 Lettere annue del Giappone dell'anno MDCXXII e della Cina del 1621 & 1622, Roma, per Francesco Corbelletti, 1627. 8°
    BOD Vet. F2 f.4 Acquired by the Radcliffe Library, which was established using funds left by John Radcliffe (bap. 1650–1714), probably after 1835. It entered the Bodleian after 1937.

475 Lettere annue del Tibet del MDCXXVI e della Cina del MDCXXIV, Roma, appresso Francesco Corbelletti, 1628. 8°
    BOD Vet. F2 f.5 Acquired by the Radcliffe Library, which was established using funds left by John Radcliffe (bap. 1650–1714), probably after 1835. It was transferred to the Bodleian after 1937.
    CUL CRD.62.1.

476 Lettere annue d'Etiopia, Malabar, Brasil, e Goa. Dall anno 1620 fin'al 1624, Roma, per Francesco Corbelletti, 1627. 8°
    BOD 133 g.45 The shelf-mark indicates that it was acquired after 1864.

477 Lettere annue di Ethiopia del 1624, 1625, e 1626, Roma, per l'herede di Bartolomeo Zannetti, 1628. 8°
    BOD (2 copies) Vet. F2 f.1 Acquired by the Radcliffe Library, which was established using funds left by John Radcliffe (bap. 1650–1714), probably after 1835. It entered the Bodleian after 1937; Antiq. f.I. 1628.2 Bought 1927.

478 Lettere del Giapone, et della Cina de gl'anni M.D. LXXXIX & M.D.XC, Venezia, appresso Gio. Battista Ciotti Senese, 1592. 8°
    BOD 8° E 64 Linc. From the Barlow bequest of 1691 ASC SR 63 f 10 A slip included in the book suggests that it was acquired in 1878.

479 Litterae Societatis Iesu, anno MDCII et MDCIII e Sinis, Molucis, Iapone datae, Moguntiaci, e typographeo Balthasari Lippii, 1607. 8°
BOD 8° G 128 Art. Signature of Thomas Parker and Latin marginalia **SJCO** K.scam.2.upper shelf. 12(4) Part of the Crynes bequest of 1745 **WAD** h 31.12 Given by Philip Bisse, 1613.

480 Litterae annuae societatis Iesu anni MDC, Antuerpiae, apud haeredes Martini Nutii & Ioannem Meursium, 1618.
BOD 8° M. 273 Th.

481 Nuoui auisi dell'Indie di Portogallo, *tr. from Spanish,* [in colophon] in Venetia, per Michele Tramezzino, 1559. 8°
BOD Vet. F1 f.438 A cancelled shelf-mark, 133.g.42, indicates that it was acquired after 1864 (see Chapter Three, p. lvii).

482 Nuoui auisi dell'Indie di Portogallo . . . Terza Parte, *tr. from Spanish,* [Venice], Michele Tramezzino, 1562. 8°
BOD 133 g.43 The shelf-mark indicates that it was acquired after 1864 (see Chapter Three, p. lvii).

483 Nuoui auisi dell'Indie di Portogallo, *tr. from Spanish,* Venetia, per Michele Tramezzino [in colofon], 1568. 8°
TRC Grylls.6.107 William Grylls's collection was deposited in 1863 (Adams I109).

484 Relatio historica rerum in Iaponiae regno gestarum anno Domini 1603, 1604, 1605 & parte 1606, *tr. from Italian,* Moguntiae, ex officina Balthasari Lippij, 1610. 8°
BOD 8° B 33 Med. BS. The shelf-mark indicates that it was acquired between 1668 and 1840 **WAD** h 35.25.
CUL Dd*.5.49(G) Repaired binding, but the shelf-mark is one associated with the Royal Library, deposited in 1715.

485 Relatione delle cose piu notabili scritte ne gli anni 1619, 1620 & 1621, dalla Cina, Roma, per l'erede di Bartyolomeo Zannetti, 1624. 8°
BOD Vet. F2 f.6 The shelf-mark indicates that it was acquired after 1937.

486 Relationes de gloriosa morte nouem Christianorum Iaponensium, Moguntiae, ex officina typographica Ioannis Albini, 1612. 8°
BOD (3 copies) 8° F 35(2) Art. In the 1620 catalogue with the current shelf-mark; 8° F 58(3) Art. Bequeathed by Robert Burton, 1640. This copy is bound with **372, 375** (Kiessling (1988) 887); Douce L 543 (2). From the Douce bequest of 1834.
SID S.7.62 (3) With other tracts printed in 1602 and 1612. In the catalogue of 1674, under 'Martyrologium' in Anonymous **SJCC** F.12.8(5) Acquired before 1760.

487 Rerum a Societate Jesu in Oriente gestarum volumen, Coloniae, apud Gervinum Calenium & haeredes Iohannis Quentel, 1574. 8°
BOD (2 copies) 8° I 23 Art.BS. Acquired after 1668; Crynes 531 From the Crynes bequest of 1745 **CHC** W.D.8.3 From the Wake bequest of 1737 **EXE** 9K1574.2.
CUL (2 copies) P.5.36 With the bookplate of the Royal Library, deposited in 1715. Blind-stamped binding with ornaments very similar to Ker 52, which was used 1600–20, (Pearson, p. 89); Ely.e.240 The book, at one time in Ely Cathedral Library, was acquired

by the University Library in 1970 **G&C** F.35.18 Bequeathed by William Branthwaite, Master, in 1619. He was one of the revisers of the Bible (Adams M97).

All copies of this edition include a work by Manuel da Costa of which there is an earlier edition listed as **250**.

488 Rerum memorabilium in regno Iaponiae gestarum litterae an. M. DC. XIX. XX. XXI. XXII. Societatis Iesu. *With* Rerum memorabilium in regno Sinae gestarum litterae annuae Societatis Iesu, Antuerpiae, ex officina Hieronymi Verdusii, 1625. 8°

BOD 8° B 34 Med. BS. The shelf-mark indicates that it was acquired after 1650 **ASC** SR 63.f.9. In this copy the section about China is printed first.

489 Selectarum . . . ex India epistolarum libri iiii, *included in J. P. Maffeius,* Historiarum Indicarum libri xvi, Florentiae, apud Phillipum Iunctam, 1588. Fol.

CULT.8.11 FITZ KCC M.23.8 (Adams M90).

490 Selectarum . . . ex India epistolarum libri iiii, *included in J. P. Maffeius,* Historiarum Indicarum libri xvi, Venetiis, apud Damiamum Zenarium, 1589 [Part 2, 1588], 4°

BOD Vet. F1 e. 223 The shelf-mark indicates that it was acquired after 1937 **MER** 34.H.20 Oxford binding, Ker rolls xii and xviii, used together 1575–1605 (Pearson, p. 67).

CUL Rel.c.58.2 **SJCC** D.10.3 From the Crashawe collection, deposited in 1626 (Adams M91).

491 Selectarum . . . ex India epistolarum libri iiii, *included in J. P. Maffeius,* Historiarum Indicarum libri xvi, Lugduni, ex officina Iunctarum, 1589. 4°

CUL T.10.5 From the Royal Library, deposited in 1715 **STCC** D.9.55 **TRC** X.13.21 Bequeathed by John Laughton in 1712. He was college, and later University librarian. The book had previously belonged to a Fleming, Jacobus Tayardus. With MS. Latin notes to Maffeius's text (Adams M93).

492 Selectarum . . . ex India epistolarum . . . libri iv, *included in J. P. Maffeius,* Historiarum Indicarum libri xvi, Coloniae Agrippinae, in officina Birckmannica, 1589. Fol.

BOD C 2.10(2) Art. Seld., formerly Art C.I.14, so probably not part of the Selden bequest, which entered the library in 1659. A copy is listed in the 1605 catalogue. Chain mark, shelf-mark on leading edge.

CUL (3 copies) N*.6.17(F); O*.5.43(E) Both these entered the library before 1715; Peterborough D.56 (For Peterborough Cathedral Library, see the Introduction, p. xiv). **MGC** PL 2206 From the collection of Samuel Pepys, the diarist (1633–1703), deposited in 1724 **TRC** X.2.34 With 3 previous shelf-marks and the bookplate of John Colbatch, Anglican chaplain in Portugal from 1693–1700, who died in 1748 (Adams M92 and 94).

493 Selectarum . . . ex India epistolarum . . . libri iv, *included in J. P. Maffeius,* Historiarum Indicarum libri xvi, Coloniae Agrippinae, in officina Birckmannica, 1590. 8°

BLL 0695.g.01 **Oriental Institute Library** 512 Maf. S.

MGC G.18.10 17th-century Cambridge binding **TRC** X.13.62 With 3 previous shelf-marks. Signed by John Lumley and in the 1609 catalogue of his collection. It also has the Newton-Puckering bookplate, showing that it was deposited in 1691 (Adams M95, Lumley 1272).

494 Selectarum . . . ex India epistolarum libri iiii, *included in J. P. Maffeius,* Historiarum Indicarum libri xvi, Coloniae, ex officina Birckmannica, 1593. Fol.

BLL 0695.h.08 **MGO** L.9.16 **SJCO** Sigma.2.15.

CUL T.8.39 From the Royal Library, deposited in 1715, and in its catalogue **CLA** F.5.21 The same edition, with reset title-page. With the 1701 college bookplate **JSC** K.2.26b In the catalogue of 1705 **PMC** 8.10.45 Given by Lancelot Andrewes, Bishop of Winchester, in 1589. Binding with blind-stamped centrepiece **QUC** D.2.18 In the catalogue of the 1680s with the same shelf-mark (Adams M96).

495 Selectarum . . . ex India epistolarum libri iv, *with* liber recentiorum epistolarum, *tr. by John Hay. Both included in J. P. Maffeius,* Historiarum Indicarum libri xvi, Antuerpiae, ex officina Martini Nutii, 1605. 2 vols. 8°

BOD 8° M 54 Art. (vol. 1) 8° H 34 Art. (vol. 2). Vol. 1 is in the 1620 catalogue with the shelf-mark M.54. **BNC** Lath. S.2.16. In the catalogue probably compiled in the 17th century with the shelf-mark H.5.2, which is still visible today. Chain mark.

CUL N*.6.16 (F) Acquired before 1715.

496 [Selectarum . . . ex India epistolarum] Una scelta di lettere scritte dell'Indie, *tr. by Francesco Serdonati and included in J. P. Maffeius,* Le istorie delle Indie orientali, Fiorenza, per Filippo Giunti, 1589. 8°

BOD Mortara 986. From a collection acquired in 1852.

497 The Palme of Christian Fortitude, or the glorious combats of Christians in Iaponia, taken out of letters of the Society of Jesus from thence. Anno 1624, *possibly a translation of letters by João Rodrigues Girão,* Douai, widow of C. Boscard, 1630. 8°

CHC WG.8.14 From the Wake bequest of 1737.

CUL Syn.8.63.406 Acquired in 1895 (with no indication of publisher or place) **EMM** 328.7.30 Bequeathed by John Breton, Master, in 1675.

498 Tre lettere annue del Giappone, de gli anni 1603. 1604. 1605. e parte del 1606, Roma, Bartholomeo Zannetti, 1608. 8°

ASC SR. 63.f.14.

499 Tre lettere annue del Giappone, de gli anni 1603. 1604. 1605. e parte del 1606, Bologna [in colophon: printing began in Rome], appresso Gio. Battista Bellagamba, 1609. 8°

BOD 8° A 9.29 Jur. Shelf-mark on leading edge, indicating that it was probably an early acquisition.

500 Tre lettere annue del Giappone, de gli anni 1603. 1604. 1605. e parte del 1606, Milano, P. M. Locarni, 1609. 8°

CUL CRE.60.1.

Jorge, Marcos (−1571)

Jesuit. With the help of Luis de Granada, among others, he compiled a catechism in dialogue form which was first published in Lisbon in 1566 and went through innumerable editions thereafter. It is hardly surprising that the Portuguese version of this work of popular devotion should have found no readers in early modern Oxford or Cambridge. However, the book was much used by Jesuit missionaries, and **501**, a translation into the language of the Congo, was acquired by the linguist Thomas Marshall (died 1685) who had an interest in the languages of Africa. The Jesuit theologian Mateus Cardoso commissioned the translation, but the identity of the translator is not known. The same work was translated into Tamil by Henrique Henriques (**447**).

Francisco Rodrigues, *História da Companhia de Jesus na assistência de Portugal*, II.1, pp. 459–60.

501 Doutrina christaã . . . de novo traduzida na lingoa do Reyno do Congo, Lisboa, por Geraldo da Vinha, 1624. 8°
BOD Mar. 383 Signed Christianus Stenbuckius. Bequeathed by Thomas Marshall, Rector of Lincoln College, in 1685.

502 Doutrina christam . . . representada por imagens, Augusta, 1616. 8°
BOD Douce I 35 Part of the Douce bequest of 1834.

Lacerda, Bernarda Ferreira de (1595−1644/45)

A poet, and the only woman writer represented in the short-title catalogue. She was close to the Carmelite order, but did not profess. Most of the poems in **503** are in Spanish, 'por ser Idioma claro, y casi commun' [because it is a clear language, and almost in general use], as she says in her prologue, but there are poems in Portuguese, fols 112r. and 119r., in Italian, fol. 111v., and a number in Latin. The single copy was probably acquired for All Souls by Peter Frye Hony in the nineteenth century.

Biblos: Enciclopédia Verbo das Literaturas de Língua Portuguesa, 2, cols 1327–8.

503 Soledades de Buçaco, Lisboa, por Mathias Rodrigues, 1634. 8°
ASC nn.17.12.

Lacerda, Manuel de (1569−1634) (Cerda; de la Cerda)

An Augustinian and professor at Coimbra, who proclaims himself to be a Portuguese on the title-page of **504**. There are three copies in Oxford and two in Cambridge, all with old provenance. This is unusual for a book apparently published only in Portugal and not abroad. There may be a connection to **58−9**, by another Augustinian, Egídio da Apresentação, who Lacerda mentions in his prologue to the reader. Those books are also concerned with scholastic theology, were printed by the same Coimbra printer, and are represented in both universities by a number of copies

which may well have arrived together at some point in the seventeenth century.
Barbosa Machado, III, 292.

504 Quaestiones quodlibeticae pro laurea Conimbricensi, Conimbricae, apud Didacum Gomes de Loureyro, 1619. Fol.
BOD L 1.5(2) Th. In the 1674 catalogue **MGO** i.2.6 Chain mark **BNC** Lath E.7.5 With a printed bookplate recording the gift of Henry Mason, prebandary of St Paul's and formerly a student of the college, who died in 1647. Listed under Cerda in the catalogue probably compiled in the 17th century with the shelf-mark T.2.8, which is still visible in the volume today.
CUL I*.4.31 (C) Acquired before 1715 **EMM** S.13.2.42 Bequeathed by Archbishop William Sancroft in 1693.

Lavanha, João Baptista (?1550–1624)
Historian and writer on navigation. Because his work is in the vernacular it is poorly represented in the short-title catalogue. Besides being responsible for **505–8** Lavanha edited volume 4 of Barros's *Décadas* for publication (**113**).
Biblos: Enciclopédia Verbo das Literaturas de Língua Portuguesa, II, cols 1358–60.

505 Nobiliario de D. Pedro Conde de Bracelos, hijo del rey D. Dionis de Portugal, Roma, por Estevan Paolinio, 1640. Fol.
QUO 28.G.1 Chain mark.

506 Regimento nautico, Lisboa, Simão Lopez, 1595. 4°
TRC S.23.29 Probably acquired after 1800 (Adams L294; Anselmo 813).

507 Viage de la catholica real magestad del rei D. Filipe III N.S. al reino de Portugal, Madrid, por Thomas Iunti impressor del Rei N.S., 1622. Fol.
TAY 270 h. 20 Acquired in 1862.

508 Viagem da Catholica Real Magestade del Rey D. Filipe II. N.S. ao Reyno de Portvgal, Madrid, por T. Iunti impressor del Rei N.S., 1622. Fol.
ASC SR.89.d.10.

Leão, Duarte Nunes de (?1530–1608)
A New Christian, chiefly famous today for his work on the linguistics of Portuguese (**511–12**). Early modern Oxford, however, knew only his work in Latin (**509**), which is his reply to José Teixeira's contention that Philip II was not the legitimate ruler of Portugal. The Latin genealogy of the Portuguese kings, also included in **509** but originally published in Spanish in 1569, forms part of the same controversy. The title-page of **509** states that he was 'Lusitanus'.
Biblos: Enciclopédia Verbo das Literaturas de Língua Portuguesa, II, cols. 1380–83.

509 Censurae in libellum de regum Portugaliae origine, *with* De vera regum Portugaliae genealogia liber, Olisipone, ex officina Antonii Riparii, 1585. 4°

BOD (2 copies) 4° N 4 Art. Seld. From the Selden bequest of 1659. Contains De vera . . . genealogia only; Vet. G1 e.11 This copy, acquired in 1950, has both works. There is an entry for both works in the 1605 catalogue (Anselmo 968).

There is another edition of this work, published by Andreas Schottus (**826**).

510 Descrição do reino de Portugal, Lisboa, impresso por Iorge Rodriguez, 1610. 4°

ASC h.11.24.

511 Origem da lingoa portuguesa, Lisboa, impresso por Pedro Crasbeeck, 1606. 8°

TAY Arch.8°.P.1606 Acquired in 1952.

512 Orthographia da lingoa portuguesa, Lisboa, per Ioão de Barreira, 1576. 8°

TAY Arch.8°.P.1576 Acquired in 1952 (Anselmo 225).

513 Primeira parte das chronicas dos reis de Portugal, Lisboa, Pedro Crasbeeck, 1600. Fol.

BOD Fol. DELTA 218 The shelf-mark indicates that it entered the library between 1824 and 1861.

CUL Acton b.38.209 Lord Acton's library was presented in 1902 (Adams N369).

Leão Hebreu (c.1460–after 1523) (Leone Ebreo, León Hebreo, Judah Abarbanel/Abravanel)

The eldest son of Isaac Abravanel (see above), he became a doctor. He left Portugal with his father in 1483 and, like him, never returned. After the expulsion of the Jews from Spain he settled in Italy. None of the copies of his famous *Dialoghi di Amore* make any mention of his Portuguese origin. There are thirty-eight copies of the book, in numerous editions and a variety of languages, across the two universities, about half of old provenance.

Andrés Soría Olmedo, *Los* Dialoghi d'Amore *de León Hebreo: aspectos literarios y culturales*.

514 Dialogi d'amore, Roma, Antonio Blado d'Assola, 1535. 4°

SJCC O.8 Bequeathed by Dominico Antonio Ferrari, 1744 (Adams A59).

515 Dialogi di amore, [in colophon] Vinegia, in casa de' figlivoli di Aldo, 1541. 8°

BOD Auct. 2 R inf. 57 The shelf-mark indicates that it was acquired after 1825 ASC kk.10.4.

CUL Sel.6.31 The shelf-mark indicates that it was probably a 19th-century acquisition TRC (2 copies) M.12.139; M.12.186 Both probably acquired after 1800 (Adams A60).

516 Dialogi di amore, [in colophon] in Vinegia, in casa de' figlivoli di Aldo, 1545. 8°
BOD Auct. 2 R inf. 28 The shelf-mark indicates that it was acquired after 1825. Marginalia in Italian.
CUL Sel.6.6 The shelf-mark indicates that it was probably a 19th-century acquisition
TRC Grylls 11.94 Bequeathed by William Grylls in 1863 (Adams A61).

517 Dialogi di amore, Vinegia, in casa de' figlivoli di Aldo, 1549. 8°
BOD Auct. 2 R inf. 148 Purchased 1828.
TRC (2 copies) M.12.183; M.12.187 Both probably acquired after 1800 (Adams A62).

518 Dialogi di amore, Vinegia, Aldi Filii, 1552. 8°
BOD Auct. 2 R inf. 184 Purchased 1832.
KCC C.10.12.

519 Dialoghi di amore, Vinegia, appresso Domenico Giglio, 1558. 8°
EMM S15.4.60, also 325.6.46 With the Sancroft-Emmanuel bookplate and part of the bequest of 1693. 17th-century Cambridge binding (Adams A63).

520 Dialoghi di amore, In Venetia, appresso Nicolò Beuilacqua, 1572. 8°
SJCO M.scam.1.lower shelf. 30(1) From the Crynes bequest of 1745.

521 Dialoghi di amore, Venetia, appresso Giovanni Alberti, 1586. 8°
BOD 8° A 16 Art. Bequeathed by Robert Burton, 1640 (Kiessling (1988) 767).
CUL Peterborough H.2.39 (4) (For Peterborough Cathedral Library, see the Introduction, p. xiv.)

522 Dialoghi di amore, Venetia, Gio. Battista Bonfadino, 1607. 8°
CUL W.12.57 From the royal collection, deposited in 1715 TRC G.12.230.

523 [Dialogi di amore] De l'amour, Lyon, Jean de Tournes, 1551. 4°
CUL U*.7.33 (F) Acquired before 1715 and signed Yonge (Adams A58).

524 [Dialogi di amore], Philosophie d'amour, tr. by Du Parc, Lyon, chez Guil. Rouille & Thibauld Payen, 1551. 8°
FITZ Given in 1933 (Adams A65).

525 [Dialogi di amore], Philosophie d'amour, tr. by Du Parc, Lyon, chez Guil. Rouille & Thibauld Payen, 1559. 16°
CUL Q*.13.35(G) With the arms of Edward Russell, 3rd Earl of Bedford (1572–1627). Acquired before 1715 (Adams A66).

526 [Dialogi di amore], Philosophie d'amour, tr. by Du Parc, Paris, chez Claude Micard, 1577. 16°
EMM S17.8.81 With the Sancroft-Emmanuel bookplate and part of the bequest of 1693 (Adams A67).

527 [Dialogi di amore], Philosophie d'amour, tr. by Du Parc, Paris, chez Claude Micard, 1580. 16°
WOR QQ.r.09.

528 [Dialogi di amore], De amore dialogi tres, *tr. by* Ioanne Carolo Saraceno, Venetiis, apud Franciscum Senensem, 1564. 8°
BOD Crynes 305 From the Crynes bequest of 1745 CHC f.7.65 Bequeathed by Robert Burton in 1640, with annotation (Kiessling (1988) 766).

529 [Dialogi di amore], De amore dialogi tres, *in* Artis cabalisticae . . . tomus 1, Basileae, per Sebastianum Henricpetri, [in colophon] 1587. Fol.
MGO l.11.15 NEW BT1.49.11 Chain mark QUO 67.A.11 From the Mason bequest of 1841 SJCO Psi.2.27 Given by Ralph or Rudolph Hamor or Hamore, a London merchant, in 1608.
CUL P*.3.3 (B) Acquired before 1715 EMM S.14.2.1 Bequeathed by Archbishop William Sancroft in 1693 KCC A.20.13 In the 17th-century catalogue, which was begun in 1612 SJCC N.4.13 left by Peter Gunning, Master, 1684.

530 [Dialogi di amore], De amore dialogi tres, Basileae, per Sebastianum Henricpetri, 1607. Fol.
TRC X.2.34 In the college's copy of the interleaved Bodleian catalogue used in the 18th century.

531 [Dialogi di amore], Los dialogos de amor, *tr. by J. Costa,* Venetia, [no publisher], 1568. 4°
BOD Vet. F1 e.11 The shelf-mark indicates that it was acquired after 1937.

532 [Dialogi di amore] La traduccion del Indio de los tres dialogos de amor, *tr. by the Inca Garcilaso de la Vega,* Madrid, Pedro Madrigal, 1590. 4°
TRC G.28.16 In the college's copy of the interleaved Bodleian catalogue used in the 18th century (Adams A64).

Lemos, Luís de (1534–) (Ludovicus Lemosius)

A doctor, born in Fronteira or Portalegre, but who was a professor at Salamanca before practising medicine in Llerena, in Spain. Benedito de Castro, cited by Friedenwald, says that he was of a Jewish family. (Castro's *Flagellum Calumniantium* [The Scourge of Calumniators] (Amsterdam, 1631) describes the achievements of a large number of Jewish doctors). There is no indication in his works that Lemos was Portuguese though, unlike some others who rejected their Portuguese origin, he must have remained at least outwardly a Christian. All seven of his books now in Oxford were acquired before 1750. He is less well represented in Cambridge.
Friedenwald, II, pp. 732–3.

533 De optima praedicendi ratione libri sex, Salmanticae, ex officina Ildefonsi a Terranoua & Neyla, 1585 [in colophon: 1584]. 8°
SJCO I.scam.1.lower shelf. 7 Given by William Paddy, 1602 (Fidalgo 1148).

534 De optima praedicendi ratione, libri sex, *with* Judicii operum magni Hippocratis, liber vnus, Venetiis, apud Robertum Meietum, 1592. 8°
BOD 8° L 11 (1) Med. In the 1605 catalogue with the current shelf-mark CCCO

N.18.23 Bequeathed by Richard Samways, fellow, in 1669 **MER** 73.A.7 Ker centrepiece xxiv(a), found only on this book (Pearson, p. 82). Gift of Helen Gulston, widow of Theodore Gulston D. Med and fellow, 1635. See also **535 QUO** NN.s.620 Signed by Martin Aylworth whose name appears in a number of medical books at Queen's. He was a fellow of All Souls, died 1657/58. **SJCO** G.scam.2.lower shelf. 9(4) From the Crynes bequest of 1745.

CUL K.6.20 From the Royal Library, deposited in 1715 **SJCC** Ll.15.18 (Adams L430).

535 In libros Galeni de morbis medendis commentarij, Salmanticae, apud haeredes Mathiae Gastij, 1581. Fol.

MER 50.I.4(2) Gift of Helen Gulston, widow of Theodore Gulston, M.D. and fellow. See **534** (Fidalgo 1035).

536 Paradoxorum dialecticorum libri duo, Salmanticae, haeredes Ioannis a Iunta Florentini, 1558. 8°

CUL Ven.8.55.7 Entered the library in 1889 (Adams L429, Fidalgo 509).

Lisboa, Marcos de (see Silva, Marcos da)

Liturgies and prayer books.

537 Ceremoniale ordinario da missa, *tr.* *by* Antonio Nabo, Lisboa, em casa de Francisco Correa, 1568. 4°

CUL B*.5.48(D) Acquired before 1715 (Adams L981; Anselmo 496).

538 Libro de rezar em linguagem portuguez, Coimbra, per Antonio de Mariz, 1586. 24°

JSO H.13.33.

539 Livro de rezar, em lingoagem, tirado de muytos sanctos, & padres illustres, por Mestre Symão Verepeo, Lisboa, Antonio Alvarez, 1596. 12°

BOD 8° P 138 Th. In the 1674 catalogue. Chain mark. This rare book is probably to be identified with Anselmo 817.

540 Officium duplex cum octava recitandum in civitate et dioecesi Olysiponensi in festo s. Engratiae virginis et martyris, Ulyssipone, typis Gerardi a Vinea, 1625. 4°

CHC Allestree J.4.9(2) From the Allestree bequest of 1681. Bound with **541**.

541 Officia propria Ulyssiponensis ecclesiae, Ulyssipone, ex officina Gerardi a Vinea, expensis Georgii Artur, 1625. 4°

(1) CHC Allestree J.4.9(1) From the Allestree bequest of 1681. Bound with **540**. See also **870–3**.

Lobo, Duarte (c.1565–1646)

A composer, who studied at Évora cathedral, and enjoyed the patronage of the Duke of Bragança, later King João IV. This is the only copy of **542** outside the Iberian world (which in this instance includes Latin America), and the only book of music in this short-title catalogue. It was presented to the Bodleian by the London bookseller George Thomason in 1659 and more recently discovered there by Owen Rees. Owen Rees, 'Adventures of Portuguese 'Ancient Music'', pp. 43–5.

542 Liber Missarum, Antwerp, Balthasar Moretus, 1621. Fol.
BOD Mason EE. 87. Given by George Thomason, a London bookseller, in 1659.

Lobo, Francisco Rodrigues (1573/4–1621)

Corte na aldeia is a classic of Portuguese literature. It is a dialogue on court life, but set in a country village, because under the Hapsburg monarchs there was no court in Portugal. It was nevertheless of interest to contemporary Spanish readers, as the translation (**544**) was printed only three years later. Although the book was only available in the vernacular, the aristocratic or regal nature of the subject-matter appealed to at least one seventeenth-century Cambridge reader and another eighteenth-century Oxford one.

543 Corte na aldea, Lisboa, Pedro Craesbeeck, 1619. 4°
CUL U.13.29 From the Royal Library, deposited in 1715.

544 [Corte na aldea, e noites de inverno], Corte en aldea, y noches de imbierno, *tr. by* Iuan Baptista de Morales, Montilla, por el autor, y a su costa, 1622. 8°
BOD 8° C 37 Art. BS. With the bookplate of Honourable Frederic North, perhaps the younger son of Lord North who matriculated 1782, aged 16.

[Lopes, Fernão] (?1380–?1460)

The anonymous biography of a hero of the wars with Castile has often been attributed to the great medieval historian Fernão Lopes. Most modern scholars doubt the attribution. Lopes, like the majority of the other vernacular historians of Portugal, was of no interest to early modern Oxford or Cambridge.
Crónica do Condestável de Portugal D. Nuno Álvares Pereira, edited by António Machado de Faria, pp. xvi–xxxvii.

545 Coronica do co[n]destabre de Portugal Dom Nunalvrez Pereyra . . ., Lisboa, por Antonio Alvarez Impressor, & Mercador de liuros, 1623. Fol.
TAY 106.H.16 Acquired in 1889.

Lopes, Garcia (–1572) (Garcias Lopius)

A Jewish doctor, and a Portuguese, born in Portalegre, according to the title-page of **546**, who practised in the Low Countries. Later he returned to Portugal, and was burnt at the stake at Évora. In the dedication, from Antwerp, to Dom João de Mascarenhas, he speaks with unusual feeling of his sense of exile from his native land, but he clearly misjudged the mood at home. The work of Portuguese doctors was much prized in the English universities and the three copies of **546** were all acquired in the sixteenth or seventeenth centuries.

Friedenwald, II, p. 737.

546 Commentarij de varia rei medicae lectione, Antuerpiae, apud viduam Martini Nutii, 1564. 8°

BOD (2 copies) 8° L 4(1) Med. In the 1605 cat with unchanged shelf-mark; 8° L 2(1) Med Seld. From the Selden bequest of 1659. In the 1674 catalogue.

CUL N*.14.25 (F) From the bequest of Thomas Lorkin, Professor of Physick, in 1591 (Adams L1469).

Luís, António (after 1490–1565) (Antonius Ludovicus)

New Christian doctor and professor of medicine at Coimbra who, however, was 'Olyssipponensis', according to the title-pages of his books. He seems to have owed much to the protection of the king, João III, to whom he dedicated **549**, the first of the three (**547–9**) to have been printed. (See also Silva Dias, p. 238). In Oxford and Cambridge they have always been bound together. They are among the earliest printed works listed in this short-title catalogue, and it is likely that all of them had arrived in Oxford by the end of the sixteenth century. The copies at Cambridge arrived mostly in the following century.

Silva Dias, *A política cultural da época de D. João III* I, pp. 228–239.

547 De occultis proprietatibus, libri quinque, Olyssippone, Ludouicus Rodurici, 1540. (All copies bound with **548** and **549**.) Fol.

BOD G 2.7(3) Med. **MER** 46.F.2(3) Chain mark. Oxford binding, Ker rolls xi and xix, in use between 1590 and 1620, pp. 210–14. Ker states that the rolls are used together, p. 212. The book belonged to Roger Gifford, D. Med., fellow, who died in 1597 **SJCO** Y.3.19(2) Given by William Paddy, 1602.

CUL N*.8.39 (C) Acquired before 1715 **CCCC** EP.Z.4 (2) Bequeathed by Archbishop Matthew Parker in 1575 **EMM** (2 copies) 303.5.65, formerly Ee.1.5, Q.3.43 With 17th-century Cambridge binding and tab numbered 43, which suggests that it was in a Cambridge library, not necessarily Emmanuel, by that century. It is not in the 18th-century catalogue. Extensive MS. Latin notes; 304.1.65, formerly E.3.42, I.3.51. The book is listed in the 18th-century catalogue with the mark E.3.44 (erased). No book printed before 1712 appears in this part of the catalogue, and it is reasonable to assume that the book entered the library before then (Adams L1690; Anselmo 1009).

548 De re medica opera, Olyssipone, [in colophon] apud Lodouicum Rotorigium, 1540. Fol.

BOD G 2.7(1) Med. In the 1605 catalogue **MER** 46.F.2(2) See **547** **SJCO** Y.3.19(3) See **547**.

CUL N*.8.39 (C) See **547** **CCCC** EP.Z.4 (3) See **547** **EMM** (2 copies) 303.5.65; 304.1.65 See **547** (Adams L1691; Anselmo 1010).

549 Problematum libri quinq[ue], Olyssipone, Ludouicus Rodurici, 1539–40. Fol.

BOD G 2.7(2) Med. **MER** 46.F.2(4) See **547 SJCO** Y.3.19(1) See **547**.
CUL N*.8.39 (C) See item 547 **CCCC** EP.Z.4(1) See **547 EMM** (2 copies) 303.5.65; 304.1.65 See **547** (Adams L1692; Anselmo 1008).

Magalhães, Cosme de (1551–1624) (Cosmas Magalianus)

Jesuit philosopher, theologian and author of commentaries on the Bible. Most of his career was spent in Coimbra. He was one of the 'Conimbricenses', the Coimbra commentators on Aristotle, and was responsible for part of the volume on *De Anima*. In the dedication of **550** to Claudio Aquaviva, the general of the order, he confesses that he had hardly ever been abroad, yet all the numerous works of which he was sole author were first by published by Cardon at Lyon or in the nearby town of Tournon. (For further information on the Coimbra commentators on Aristotle see Chapter Two). It is clear, therefore, that by the early seventeenth century a writer like Magalhães could rely on the good offices of his order to publish in France, despite the risks of piracy at sea to which he more than once refers, in the dedications of **552** and **553**. He was under the protection of Dom Miguel de Castro, who was viceroy of Portugal from 1615 to 1617, as well as holding other political positions, and who may have furthered his career abroad. Castro had access to the imperial post, 'veredarius', which Magalhães made use of for the secure dispatch of manuscripts to foreign printers (see the dedication of **552**).

Of the twenty-three copies of his books in the university and college libraries twenty-one are likely to be of old provenance. It was normal to collect commentaries on the Bible, but **554**, about the origin of the priesthood, which entered the Bodleian, Corpus Oxford and Sidney Sussex soon after publication, may have been of particular interest at a time when the English church was trying to re-establish its roots in the Catholic (though not Roman Catholic) tradition. See also Chapter One, pp. xxxi, xxxiv–v. As is the case with a number of Jesuit writers, the title-pages of Magalhães's books state not his nationality, but his place of origin, Braga. In his commentary on Joshua he uses a number of different versions of the Bible besides the Vulgate: the Septuagint, and others vaguely described as 'aliae versiones'.

Francisco Rodrigues, *História da Companhia de Jesus na Assistência de Portugal*, II.2, p. 46.

550 Commentarii in canticum primum Mosis, Lugduni, sumptibus Horatij Cardon, 1609.

BOD HH 7 Th. Formerly M.8.2 In the 1620 catalogue with the old shelf-mark. Bound with **554**, vol. 2.

CUL Peterborough K.2.9. Bound with an anti-catholic work by Meric Casaubon, *Of the Necessity of Reformation* (London: A. Maxwell, 1664). (For Peterborough Cathedral Library, see the Introduction, p. xiv.)

551 In Mosis cantica et benedictiones patriarcharum commentariorum libri IV, Lugduni, sumptibus Horati Cardon, 1619. Fol.

BOD M 7.14 Th. In the 1635 appendix to the 1620 catalogue, with the shelf-mark unchanged. **BNC** Lath K.5.4 In the catalogue probably compiled in the 17th century with the shelf-mark Q.5.4, now partially obscured by a later bookplate. Chain mark. **CHC** G3.2.7 17th-century binding. Chain mark.

TRC D.6.23 With the arms of Sir William Sedley on the cover. He left money for the purchase of books in 1618.

552 In sacram Josue historiam commentariorum tomi duo, Turnoni, sumptibus Horatii Cardon, 1612. 2 vols in 1. Fol.

BOD M 7.13 Th. In the 1620 catalogue with the same shelf-mark **CHC** D.2.8.41 Chain mark. The dedication to D. Miguel de Castro has been removed **MGO** d.11.04 Chain mark **QUO** 77 D.16 Chain mark. Lacks the title page.

QUC L.2.9 17th-century Cambridge binding with fillets. Author's name and abridged title on fore-edge. College bookplate of 1700. Bought with money given by John Davenant, Bishop of Salisbury, in 1626 (See Benefactors' Register, pp. 10–12). In the catalogue of the 1680s with the current shelf-mark **SJCC** Pp.6.17 Bequeathed by Peter Master, 1684 **TRC** D.4.60 Given by Robert Bennet (d. 1618). 17th-century Cambridge binding stamped R B.

553 In sacram Judicum historiam explanationes et annotationes morales, Lugduni, sumptibus Iacobi Cardon et Petri Cavellat, 1626. Fol.

BOD M 11.2 Th. In the 1635 appendix to the 1620 catalogue, with the same shelf-mark. **EMM** S.7.1.14 Bequeathed by Archbishop William Sancroft in 1693.

554 Operis hierarchici, sive, De ecclesiastico principatu, libri iii, Lugduni, sumptibus Horatij Cardon, 1609. 3 vols in 2. 4°

BOD HH 6,7 Th., formerly M 8.1 Th. Chain mark. In the 1620 catalogue with the old shelf-mark. Vol. 2 is bound with **550 CHC** Jb.1.40 Chain mark **CCCO** L.D.7c.14–15 The book entered the library on 12 April 1616. Chain marks **KEB** 040.09a-b Acquired in 1870, when the college was founded.

CUL (2 copies) E*.4.40 Acquired before 1715. Vols 2–3 only; Acton b.46.11 Lord Acton's library was presented in 1902 **EMM** S.7.3.9 Bequeathed by Archbishop William Sancroft in 1693 **SID** R.5.37 In the catalogue of 1674. With the title on the top edge, a practice which continued until the 1640s (Rogers, p. 78), and the college book-plate of 1701. 3 vols in one.

Mariz, Pedro de (before 1569–1615)

Historian, and author of one of the few books in Portuguese to be listed in the Bodley catalogue of 1605. None of Mariz's other books, which are all in Portuguese, entered Oxford or Cambridge in the early modern period.

Biblos: Enciclopédia Verbo das Literaturas de Língua Portuguesa, III, cols. 485–7.

555 Dialogos de varia historia, Coimbra, na officina de Antonio de Mariz, 1597–98 [in colophon: the second impression, 1599]. 4°

BOD 4° M 22 Art. In the 1605 catalogue with the same shelf-mark **ASC** SR 89.d.7.

CUL (2 copies) Lib.7.59.1, previously T.11.52. With the bookplate of the Royal Library, and in its catalogue with the old shelf-mark. The collection was deposited in 1715; F159.d.12.2 With the bookplate of Harryson Caird. Acquired c.1990 (Adams M603; Anselmo 905).

Mártires, Bartolomeu dos (1514–90)

Dominican and Archbishop of Braga, who attended the Council of Trent from 1561–4. Unlike the majority of religious writers in this list he was neither a missionary nor an academic theologian, but famous for his concern for the spiritual well-being of his flock. So **556–7** are characterized by simplicity and accessibility (see the translator's preface to the reader of **556** and the note, also to the reader, by Luis de Granada included in **557**). The archbishop's work was widely published outside Portugal, at least partly because of his contacts with well-known international figures like Luis de Granada, a fellow-Dominican, and Carlo Borromeo. Copies of his books reached Oxford and Cambridge early, but are largly confined to the Bodleian and to Cambridge University Library. Perhaps they were insufficiently academic to interest the college libraries.
Barbosa Machado, I, pp. 464–71.

556 Catechismo de doctrina christiana, y de practicas spirituales, *tr. into Spanish by* Manuel Rodriguez, Salamanca, Diego Cussio, 1602. 4°
BOD 4° V 2(2) Th. In the 1620 catalogue with the same shelf-mark.

557 Compendium spiritualis doctrinae, Romae, apud Carolum Vulliettum, 1603. 8°
BOD 8° M 44(1) Th. In the 1620 catalogue with this shelf-mark.

558 Stimulus pastorum, Romae, haeredes Julii Accolti, 1572. 8°
SJCC Q.10.43(1) The book belonged to Archbishop Toby Matthew (?1544–1628), while he was bishop of Durham, 1595–1606 (Adams M796).

559 Stimulus pastorum, Paris, apud Iacobum Kerner, 1583. 8°
CUL (2 copies) F*.12.50 (F) Acquired before 1715; Ely e.268 The title-page is damaged. The binding is stamped Edward Gwynn, of Christ Church, who matriculated in 1671, aged 18, and took his BA in 1675–76. The book, at one time in Ely Cathedral Library, was acquired by the University Library in 1970.

560 Stimulus pastorum, ex sententiis patrum concinnatus, Parisiis, apud Michaelem Sonnium, 1586. 8°
BOD 8° M 4 Th. In the 1605 catalogue with the same shelf-mark.

Mendonça or Mendoça, Francisco de (1573–1626) (Mendoza)

Jesuit theologian, who taught at Coimbra, Évora and Lisbon. In the year before his death he went to Rome and died in Lyon, where so much of his work had been and would be published, on the return journey. Limited foreign experience did not prevent his books being published abroad, in Germany as well as in France.

Mendonça, whose title-pages always reveal his place of origin, Lisbon, was an author who at first made slow progress in Oxford. The first two volumes of his commentary on Kings (**561** and **564**) were acquired by Griffith Higgs at an auction held in The Hague on 12 April 1633. Other volumes arrived in ones and twos, but after the whole work had been issued in Cologne in 1633–34 (**569**) and later in Lyon (**570**) eleven early modern libraries acquired it. In all, there are twenty-five copies of the various editions of all or part of the commentary over the two universities. Almost all are of old provenance, as are all nine copies of the *Viridarium* [miscellany] (**571–3**).

Francisco Rodrigues, *História da Companhia de Jesus na Assistência de Portugal*, II.2. p. 46; P. S. Morrish, 'Dr Higgs and Merton College Library', p. 151.

561 Commentarii in quatuor libros Regum. Tomus primus in primum librum, Conimbricae, apud Didacum Gomez d' Loureiro, 1621. Fol.

MER 86.I.17 Given by Griffin Higgs (1589–1659), fellow. There is some underlining (Morrish 399).

562 Commentarii in quatuor libros Regum. Tomus primus in primum librum, Parisiis, apud Michaelem Sonnium, 1622. Fol.

BOD L.7.9 Th. In the 1674 catalogue CHC I.1.3.8 Chain mark. 17th-century binding.
SJCC Pp.6.7 (1) Bequeathed by John Carey, Earl of Dover, in 1677. Bound with item 566.

563 Commentarii in quatuor libros Regum. Tomus primus in primum librum, Lugduni, sumptibus Iacobi Cardon et Petri Cauellat, 1622. Fol.

CUL Q*.8.14 (B) Bequeathed by John Hacket, Bishop of Lichfield (1592–1670).

564 Commentarii in quatuor libros Regum. Tomus secundus in primum librum, Ebora, apud Petrum Craesbeeck, 1624.

MER 86.I.18 Given by Griffin Higgs (1589–1659), fellow (Morrish, 399).

565 Commentariorum in IV. libros regum tomus secundus, Lugduni, sumptibus Iacobi Cardon & Petri Cavellat, 1625. Fol.

BOD L 7.10 Th. Formerly M.9.16 Th, chain mark. In the 1635 appendix to the 1620 catalogue with the old shelf-mark.

566 Commentariorum in IV. libros regum tomus secundus, Parisiis, apud Michaelem Sonnium, 1625. Fol.

SJCC Pp.6.7 (2) Bequeathed by John Carey, Earl of Dover, in 1677. Bound with **562**.

567 Commentariorum in quatuor libros Regum tomus primus & secundus, Coloniae Agrippinae, sumptibus Petri Henningij, 1628. 2 vols Fol.

CCCO G.12.7–8 Chain marks (vol 3 from 1632 ed.).
CUL Peterborough M.6.11- (For Peterborough Cathedral Library, see the Introduction, p. xiv.) EMM S.7.1.23–24 Bequeathed by Archbishop William Sancroft in 1693.

568 Commentariorum in quatuor libros Regum tomus I & III, Lugduni, sumptibus Iacobi Cardon, 1629–33. Fol.

BOD A 16.4(2) Th. (Tomus 3 only). Chain mark.
PMC 5.8.21–2. With the college bookplate of 1700.

569 Commentariorum ac discursuum moralium in quatuor Regum libros tomi tres, Coloniae Agrippinae, sumptibus Petri Henningii, 1632–34. 3 vols in 2 Fol.

BOD M 11.1(1) Th. In the 1635 appendix to the 1620 catalogue **CCCO** G.12.9, (vols 1– 2 from 1628 ed) chain mark **EXE** P 145 Bequeathed by Anthony Clifford, fellow, in 1685 **JSO** B.16.1 **NEW** BT3.116.4–5 In the catalogue of 1686 **ORI** B.d12–13 Chain mark. Bequeathed by Henry Eccleston, fellow, in 1646. In both the 17th-century catalogues.

CUL 2.16.23–5 (3 vols) With the bookplate of the Royal Library, deposited in 1715. 17th-century Cambridge binding with fillets **MGC** B.20.16, formerly G.3.21 Tomus tertius only. Signed Richard Maden, probably the Maden who matriculated in 1639. 17th-century Cambridge binding with fillets **TRC** D.5.25–6 Given with money left by Thomas Whalley, vicemaster, in 1637.

570 Commentariorum in IV libros Regum tomus I [-III], Lugduni, sumptibus Gabrielis Boissat, & Sociorum, 1636–37. Fol.

QUO 77.A.10–12 With a printed note stating that it was the gift of Bernard Robinson, fellow. Since Robinson probably died in 1634, it may be that he left money for the purchase of books. Chain mark **UNI** FF.29.9–10. 3 vols in 2, chain mark. With the signature of John Robinson, M.A. 1657.

CUL F*.2.7-(B) Acquired before 1715 **QUC** L.3.2, formerly 9.3.2. 17th-century Cambridge binding with fillets, parchment pastedown. College bookplate of 1700. In the catalogue of the 1680s with the shelf-mark L.4.2.

571 Viridarium sacrae et profanae eruditionis, Lugduni, sumptibus Iacobi Cardon, 1631 [in some copies, 1632]. Fol.

BOD M 11.8 Th. In the 1635 appendix to the 1620 catalogue **JSO** L.16.2 Bequeathed by Edward Herbert, Baron Cherbury (1583–1648), diplomat and writer on religion. **LIN** LOO.21 With college bookplate dated 1703 and chain mark.

CUL F*.2.6 Acquired before 1715 **SJCC** Dd.7.12 Bequeathed by Ambrose Gilbert, probably the elder, who died in 1649. He had been a student of the college **TRC** F.11.28 Given by Thomas Hill, Master and ardent Calvinist, who died in 1653. On the fly-leaf someone hostile to Hill questions whether he paid for the books with his own money. 17th-century Cambridge binding stamped T H.

572 Viridarium sacrae et profanae eruditionis, Coloniae Agrippinae, apud Petrum Henningium, 1633. 8°

CHC f.2.1 Bequeathed by Robert Burton, 1640, with annotation (Kiessling (1988) 1044).

EMM S.5.3.55 left by Archbishop William Sancroft in 1693.

573 Viridarium sacrae et profanae eruditionis, Lugduni, sumptibus Gabrielis Boissat, 1635. 8°

JSC B.7.16 With the college bookplate of 1700. 17th-century Cambridge binding, with fillets. In the catalogue of 1705.

Meneses, Aleixo de (1559–1617) (Alexis de Menezes)
Archbishop of Goa and later of Braga, he was very much a man of action, governor of India (1602–9) and viceroy of Portugal. His campaign to impose Catholic orthodoxy on the Syrian Christians of Malabar is

described in **440**; his own contribution (**574**) is a version of a Syrian Mass purged of 'Nestorian errors and blasphemies', as the title-page puts it. Most of the copies of his books were acquired in modern times.
Barbosa Machado, I, pp. 88–92.

574 La messe des anciens chrestiens dicts de s. Thomas, en l'evesché d'Angamal, Bruxelles 1609, par Rutger Velpius, 1609. 8°
  BOD 8° W 102 Th. Acquired 1827 **NEW** BT3.71.20 Evidence of chaining. Bound with **439**. In the catalogue of 1686.
  CUL 6100.d.16 Formerly 14.16.88, Dd.12.42 Bound with **439**. In the 19th or 20th century it belonged to a reader with an imperfect command of Portuguese (see endpaper note).

575 Synodo diocesano da igreja e bispado de Angamale dos antigos christãos de Sam Thome das serras do Malabar, Coimbra, na officina de Diogo Gomez Loureyro, 1606. Fol.
  BOD Vet. G2 d.13(2) The shelf-mark indicates that it was acquired after 1937. Bound with **440**.

Meneses, Garcia de (–1484) (Garsias Menesius)

Bishop of Évora and military commander. His oration (**577**), delivered in Rome in 1480 and published there the following year, is the only incunable by a Portuguese writer in either Oxford or Cambridge. The Bodleian acquired it in 1835 and, later, the sixteenth-century reprint (**576**).
Dicionário de história de Portugal, III, pp. 25–6.

576 Garsias Menesius . . . apud Xistum iiij. ponti. max . . . huiuscemodi orationem habuit, Conimbricae, apud Ioannem Aluarum, 1561. 4°
  BOD Vet. G1 e. 20 The shelf-mark indicates that it was acquired after 1937 (Anselmo 83).

577 Oratio . . . apud Xystu. iiii pont. maxi. & apud sacrum cardinalium senatum, Romae, [Georgius Herolt], 1481. 4°
  BOD Auct. 2 Q 6.3 (14) Acquired in 1835 (Bod-inc. G-049).

Mimoso, João Sardinha (–1644)

In **578** Mimoso reports on a play in Latin verse by the Portuguese Jesuit António de Sousa which was staged to celebrate Philip III's progress through Portugal in 1619.
Barbosa Machado, II, pp. 748–9.

578 Relacion de la real tragiocomedia con que los padres de la Compania de Iesus en su Colegio de S. Anton de Lisboa recibieron a la Magestad Catolica de Felipe II, Lisboa, por Iorge Rodriguez, 1620. 4°
  ASC nn.10.12

Miranda, Francisco de Sá de (1487–1558)

One of the most important literary figures of the sixteenth century, because he introduced some of the metrical forms (like the sonnet) and the themes of Italian poetry of the Renaissance into Portugal. As was often the case with vernacular poetry, his work was published long after his death. It was many centuries before there was any interest in him in the English universities.

T. F. Earle, *Theme and Image in the Poetry of Sá de Miranda.*

579 As obras, Lisboa, Manuel de Lira, 1595. 8°
BLL 700 d 07 Imperfect copy, lacking fols 69–168. It is in the 1871 catalogue (Anselmo 764).

580 As obras, *with* a Relação de sua calidade, & vida, Lisboa, Vicente Aluarez, 1614. 8°
TAY Arch.8°.P.1614. Acquired in 1980.

Montalto, Felipe Elias (?–1616) (Philotheus Elianus)

A Jewish doctor, who spent a period in Italy, from about 1599 to 1612, before becoming personal physician to Marie de Médicis, the Queen of France. In his Latin works he is described as 'Lusitanus' on the title-page. His work on mental illness, *Archipathologia,* is very frequently cited by Robert Burton in the *Anatomy of Melancholy,* though Burton probably did not own a copy. See also Chapter One, p. xl.

Friedenwald, II, pp. 468–96.

581 Archipathologia, Lutetiae, apud Franciscum Iacquin, sumptibus Caldorianae Societatis, 1614. 4°
BOD BB 3 Med. In the 1620 catalogue **NEW** BT3.230.18 Oxford binding, Ker centrepiece vi or via, with ornament 52, in use between 1605 and 1620 (Pearson, p. 77). In the catalogue of 1686.
CUL N*.9.24 (D) Acquired before 1715 **G&C** K.5.22 **SJCC** Ll.9.8.

582 Lettre d'Espagne presentee a la royne regente, Paris, chez Iean Brunet, 1614. 8°
BOD Vet. E2 f. 26(4) Acquired 1950.
CUL Acton d.26.410 Lord Acton's library was presented in 1902.

583 Optica intra philosophiae & medicinae aream, Florentiae, apud Cosmum Iuntam, 1606. 4°
BOD D 9.11(1) Linc. From the Barlow bequest of 1691, but in the 1620 catalogue, indicating that it is a replacement copy **BNC** Lath I.4.18 Given by Edmund Leigh, fellow 1611–41. Oxford binding, Ker centrepiece vi or vi a, in use between 1605 and 1620 (Pearson, p. 77). In the catalogue probably compiled in the 17th century, but with the shelf-mark L.5.4, which is not to be found in the book. Chain mark. **ORI** Uf4 In both the 17th-century catalogues.

Montemayor, Jorge de (1520/25–61)

Musician, poet and author of the famous pastoral romance, *La Diana*. Montemayor was born in Portugal, but spent most of his life in the service of the Spanish court and of members of the Spanish nobility. Perhaps because of the ambiguity of his position, there is no statement of nationality on the title-pages of his work. Nearly all his romance is in Spanish, with the exception of a few fragments in Portuguese in Book VII. The Bodleian has had a copy (**588**) since its inception and one came into Cambridge University Library before 1715 (**595**). However, in general early modern scholars did not think that there was a place for vernacular literature in institutional libraries and no more copies were acquired before the eighteenth century.

Jorge de Montemayor, *La Diana,* ed. by Juan Montero, pp. xxvii-xxx.

584 Los siete libros de la Diana, Saragoça, Pedro Bernuz, 1560. 8°
WAD B 1.7 Bequeathed by Richard Warner in 1775. He graduated B.A. in 1734.

585 Los siete libros de la Diana, Anvers, en casa de Iuan Stelsio, 1561. 12°
STCC Chaytor JS/5/1013. Bequeathed by H. J. Chaytor, Master 1933–46 (Adams M1708).

586 Los siete libros de la Diana, . . . agora de nueuo añadido el Triumpho de Amor, de Petrarca . . . *2nd edition,* Alcala, en casa de Andres de Angulo, 1564. 12°
CUL F156.e.8.6 The shelf-mark, and absence from the Adams catalogue, indicate that it was probably acquired in the 20th century, after 1967 (Abad 612, printed by Pedro de Robles and Francisco de Cormellas).

587 La Diana, Venecia, [no publ.], 1568. 12°
TAY 270.A.15 Part of the Martin collection, acquired in 1895.

588 Los siete libros de la Diana de George de Montemayor, agora nueuamente añadida, Anuers, en casa de Pedro Bellero, 1580–81. 12°
BOD 8° M 13,14 Art. In the 1605 catalogue with the same shelf-mark **BLL** 0700 a 12.
CUL F158.e.6.2 Bequeathed by Prof. E. M. Wilson (1906–77) **TRH** H*.6.38. With 19th-century? college bookplate. Extensive cropped annotation in English and Latin, much of it linguistic (Adams M1709 and 1711).

589 Los siete libros de la Diana de George de Montemayor, agora nueuamente añadida, in Venetia, appresso Giacomo Vincenci, 1585. 12°
CUL F158.e.2.2 Acquired in 1960 **PMC** 10.26.122 With the college bookplate of 1700 (Adams M1712–13).

590 Primera y segunda parte de la Diana de George de Montemayor, agora nueuamente corregidas y emendadas, Madrid, por Luis Sanchez, 1599. 12°
CUL Hisp. 8.59.4 From the library of Norman MacColl, presented in 1905 (Adams M1714).

591 Parte primera y segunda de la Diana, Barcelona, Sebastian de Cormellas, 1614. 8°
TAY 270.A.16 Part of the Martin collection, received in 1895.

592 Primera y segvnda parte de la Diana, Madrid, por la viuda de Alonso Martin, a costa de Domingo Gonçalez mercader de libros, 1622. 8°
TAY Vet.Span.I.A.21 Acquired in 1889 **WOR** ZZ.b.13 Bequeathed by William Gower, the second Provost of the college, in 1777.

593 La Diana . . . primera, y segunda parte, Lisboa, por Pedro Craesbeeck Impressor de su Magestad, 1624. 8°
TAY Vet.Span.I.A.4 With Taylor Institution stamp, 1939.

594 Diana, *tr. by Bartholomew Yong*, London, printed by Edmund Bollifant impensis G.B. [George Bishop], 1598. Fol.
BOD Douce M 740 Part of the Douce bequest of 1834 (STC 18044).
CUL Hisp.4.59.2 From the library of Norman MacColl, presented in 1905 (STC 18044)
TRC Munby.b.2.

595 Los siete libros de la Diana, *tr. into French by* S.G. Pavillon *and printed in parallel with the Spanish text*, Paris, [Anthoine du Brueil], 1603. 12°
BOD Douce MM 260 From the Douce bequest of 1834.
CUL Q*.13.10 (G) Title-page damaged. Acquired before 1715.

596 Los siete libros de la Diana, *tr. into French by* S.G. Pavillon *and printed in parallel with the Spanish text*, Paris, Thomas Estoc, 1613. 8°
ASC nn.16.1.

597 Los siete libros de la Diana, *tr. into French by* P.S.G.P. [S. G. Pavillon], Paris, Rolet Boutonné, 1613. 8°
WAD B 14.4 Bequeathed by Richard Warner in 1775. He graduated B.A. in 1734.

598 La Diane, *tr. by* [A. Vitray], Paris, chez Robert Fouet, [1623]. 8°
BOD Douce M 284,285 From the Douce bequest of 1834.

Mota, João Vaz da (−1590) (Joannes Motta)
Author of a number of orations published in Rome, in which he is described as 'Olyssiponensis' and 'Lusitanus'. Barbosa Machado associates him with Aquiles Estaço and Marc Antoine Muret (Muretus), who were both professors in Rome. He was under the patronage of the scholarly cardinal Gugliemo Sirleto (see the dedication of **601**). His Latin orations were printed mostly in collections acquired in the early modern period.
Barbosa Machado, II, p. 785.

599 Encomium in Sanctum Ioannem Apostolum, Romae, apud Ioannem Martinellum, 1585. 4°
BOD (2 copies) 4° W 24(4) With scribbles on the title page. It and **601**, which

immediately precedes it, form part of a collection of pamphlets all published between 1585 and 1592; 4° E 16(6) Th. BS. Acquired after 1668.

600 Funebris oratio in illustrissimum et reverendissimum S. R. E. Cardinalem Gulielmum Sirletum . . . Romae, apud Ioannem Osmarinum Giliotum, 1585. 4°

BOD 4° E 16(18) Th. BS. The shelf-mark indicates that it was acquired after 1668.
CUL Acton c.sel.30 Lord Acton's library was presented in 1902 (Adams V305).

601 Oratio habita . . . cum inciperet explicare lib. Topic. M. Tullij, Romae, apud Iouannem Martinellum, 1585. 4°

BOD (2 copies) 4° W 24(3) Jur. See **599**; 4° E 16(4) Th. BS The shelf-mark indicates that it was acquired after 1668 **MGO** I.18.8(26) One of 33 orations published between 1540 and 1591.
CUL Acton c.50.235 Lord Acton's library was presented in 1902 (Adams V307).

602 Oratio habita . . . in Gymnasio Romano initio professionis suae . . ., Romae, apud Ioannem Martinellum, 1584. 4°

BOD 4° E 16(3) Th. BS. The shelf-mark indicates that it was acquired after 1668.
CUL Acton c.sel.57 Lord Acton's library was presented in 1902 (Adams V306).

603 Oratio habita . . . in Gymnasio Romano . . . quum inciperet explicare Lib. Paradoxorum Marci Tullij . . ., Romae, apud Alexandrum Gardanum, & Franciscum Coattinum socios, 1585. 4°

BOD 4° E 16(5) Th. BS. The shelf-mark indicates that it was acquired after 1668.

Moura, Manuel do Vale de (1564–1650)

Theologian and inquisitor in Évora. Like most other books published only in Portugal **604** made little impact in Oxford or Cambridge. The author's nationality is stated on the title-page. Featherstone and Martin had copies for sale in 1628 and 1639 respectively.
Barbosa Machado, III, pp. 398–9.

604 De incantationibus seu ensalmis, Eborae, typis Laurentii Crasbeeck, 1620. Fol.

BOD 1.18 Jur. Seld. From the Selden bequest of 1659, but in the 1635 appendix to the 1620 catalogue, indicating that this is a replacement copy.
EMM S.14.2.4 Bequeathed by Archbishop William Sancroft in 1693.

Nehemias, Abraão (16th cent.)

A doctor, born in Lisbon, who around 1530 was living in Constantinople. Friedenwald says that **605**, published in Italy and in Latin, was originally written in Hebrew. There are only two copies in the libraries. Nehemias is described as 'Lusitanus' on the title-page.
Friedenwald, I, p. 167.

605 Methodi medendi vniuersalis per sanguinis missionem, & purgationem libri duo, *with* De tempore aquae frigidae in febribus ardentibus ad satietatem exhibendae, liber vnus, 2a ed., Venetiis, apud Bernardum Basam, 1592. 4°

SJCO HB4/4.b.5.12(2) Given by William Paddy, 1602.

CUL K.15.42, possibly from the Royal Library, deposited in 1715, but not in its MS. catalogue (Adams N150).

Nunes, Ambrósio (1529–1611)

A doctor, son of the physician to D. João III, whose career was spent in Coimbra, Salamanca and Lisbon. The only work by him is in Oxford and is in Spanish, but in the prologue 'al lector' he refers to 'nuestra lengua portugueza'. Benedito de Castro, cited by Friedenwald, says he was Jewish (Castro's *Flagellum Calumniantium* [The Scourge of Calumniators] (Amsterdam, 1631) describes the achievements of a large number of Jewish doctors). However, he must have been at least outwardly a Christian, and there is a reference to 'Iesu Christo Dios y Señor nuestro' in the prologue just mentioned. Nunes was also a knight of the Order of Christ (Deslandes, p. 151).

Deslandes, Venâncio, *Documentos para a história da tipografia portuguesa nos séculos XVI e XVII*; Friedenwald, II, pp. 746–7.

606 Tractado . . . que declara el mal que significa este nombre peste, Coimbra, Diogo Gomes de Loureiro, 1601. 4°

BOD E 1.16 Linc. Lacks the title page. From the Barlow bequest of 1691.

Nunes, Pedro (1502–78) (Petrus Nonius)

The best-known Portuguese mathematician of the sixteenth century, who studied for some time in Spain, but most of whose career was spent in Coimbra or in Lisbon, as hydrographer to successive kings. Even if we exclude the brief essay contained in many editions of John of Holywood's *Sphaera* (**611–24**), there are twenty-four copies of his books in Oxford and Cambridge, of which at least nineteen are of old provenance. John Dee, the English Magus, admired Nunes's work greatly and, though the two may never have met, he wished Nunes to be his literary executor in the event of his death.

Nunes was conscious of the need to publish abroad, and wrote **625** in Spanish (further discussion in Chapter Five, pp. lxxxi–ii). During Nunes's lifetime his Latin works appeared both in Basle (**607**) and in Coimbra (**609**). The Coimbra edition was distributed abroad more effectively than some other Portuguese imprints. There are five copies in Oxford and three in Cambridge (one presented in 1860), and it was offered for sale in Frankfurt in 1578, five years after publication (the fair catalogue also dates it, but incorrectly, to 1578). Robert Martin still had a copy in 1639.

Nunes was one of those who preferred to identify himself by his place of birth (Alcácer do Sal) than by his nationality.
Dicionário de história de Portugal, III, 171–2; Peter J. French, *John Dee: The World of an Elizabethan Magus*, p. 177.

607 Opera, Basileae, ex officina Henricpetrina, [in colophon, 1566]. Fol.

BOD (2 copies) S 3.8(1) Jur. MS. corrections. In the 1620 catalogue with the shelf-mark S 3.9; Savile P 5 (3) From the bequest of Sir Henry Savile (1549–1622), mathematician and founder of chairs in geometry and astronomy. Oxford binding, Ker no. 1143, rolls xii and xviii, in use together between 1575 and 1605 (Pearson, p. 67) **SJCO** Delta.3.24 Given by William Paddy, 1602 **NEW** BT3.188.5 Marks of chaining. Probably to be identified with the copy given by Arthur Lake in 1617, on leaving to become bishop of Bath and Wells. In the catalogue of 1686.

CHR Y.17.3 Given by Charles Lessingham Smith in 1860 **PMC** 13.1.15 With the college bookplate of 1879. Signed Roger Long (?1680–1770), Lowndean Professor of Astronomy and Master of Pembroke (Adams N370).

608 Opera, Basileae, Sebastianus Henricpetri, [in colofon, 1592] Fol.

BOD C 7.17(2) Art. In the 1620 catalogue **CCCO** LC.7.b.8 (3)This imperfect copy has De erratis Orontii Finaei and De crepusculis only. The title page is missing. With the signatures of two fellows: Robert Hegge (?1597–1629) and Brian Twine, who died in 1644 **JSO** K.6.14 Gall Bequeathed by Edward Herbert, Baron Cherbury (1583–1648), diplomat and writer on religion **MER** 16.D.6 Oxford binding, Ker rolls xii and xviii, in use together between 1575 and 1605 (Pearson, p. 67).

CUL R*.2.15 (C) Acquired before 1715 **TRC** S.6.3 Given, along with about 60 other mathematical books, by Isaac Barrow, fellow (1649–72) and Master (1672–77), in 1670. Binding stamped with the royal arms and Honi soit qui mal y pense (Adams N371–2).

609 De arte atque ratione nauigandi libri duo, *with* In theoricas planetarum Georgij Purbachij annotationes, In problema mechanicum Aristotelis de motu nauigij ex remis annotatio vna, De erratis Orontij Finoei liber vnus, De crepusculis lib. i., Conimbricae, in aedibus Antonii a Mariis, 1573 [part of the vol. is made up from the 2nd. edition of 1571]. Fol.

BOD (3 copies) H 1.21 Art. Seld. From the Selden bequest of 1659. In the 1674 catalogue; Savile Ee 1 From the donation made by Sir Christopher Wren and John Wallis in 1703; Savile N 12 From the bequest of Sir Henry Savile (1549–1622), mathematician and founder of chairs in geometry and astronomy. Oxford binding, Ker, no. 1454, with centrepiece ii, in use 1580–97 (Pearson, p. 75) **ASC** n.6.15 **MER** 16.D.10(2) Chain marks.

CHR Y.19.28 Given by Charles Lessingham Smith in 1860 **EMM** 304.1.59, formerly I.3.33 With a blind-stamped centrepiece of around 1600 and a medieval pastedown. It belonged to J. Jones of Pembroke, perhaps one of the two John Jones who were recorded as fellows in 1598 and 1601–05. It was given to Emmanuel by M. ?Vassall. Listed in the 18th-century catalogue as I.3.44 **SJCC** Kk.3.1 With the signatures of J. Mansell and Thomas Bendish (?1607–?74), ambassador at Constantinople (Adams N374; Anselmo 861).

610 De crepusculis liber unus, Olyssipone, Ludovicus Rodericus, 1542. 4°

BOD (2 copies) 4° N 1 Art. In the 1605 catalogue with an unchanged shelf-mark; Savile

Y 16 From the bequest of Sir Henry Savile (1549–1622), mathematician and founder of chairs in geometry and astronomy.
CHR Y.24.42 Given by Charles Otway (Bookplate), perhaps the fellow of St John's who died in 1722. A former owner was James Otway (Adams N375; Anselmo 1030).

611 Demonstratio[nem] . . . de inaequali climatum latitudine, *tr. by Élie Vinet*, in Sphaera Ioannis de Sacrobosco emendata . . ., Lutetiae, apud Gulielmum Cauellat, 1561. 8°
CUL M.11.62 Repaired binding, with title on bottom edge, but appears otherwise to be a relatively recent acquisition (Adams H729).

612 Demonstratio[nem] . . . de inaequali climatum latitudine, *tr. by Élie Vinet*, in Sphaera Ioannis de Sacrobosco emendata . . ., Venetiis, apud Hieronymum Scotum, 1562. 8°
CUL White.d.322. Presented to the library in 1962.

613 Demonstratio[nem] . . . de inaequali climatum latitudine, *tr. by Élie Vinet*, in Sphaera Ioannis de Sacrobosco emendata . . ., Lutetiae, apud Gulielmum Cauellat, 1564. 8°
SJCC Kk.11.13(1) left by Peter Gunning, Master, in 1684 (Adams H732).

614 Demonstratio[nem] . . . de inaequali climatum latitudine, *tr. by Élie Vinet*, in Sphaera Ioannis de Sacrobosco emendata . . ., Coloniae, apud Maternum Cholinum, 1566. 8°
CUL White.d.323.

615 Demonstratio[nem] . . . de inaequali climatum latitudine, *tr. by Élie Vinet*, in Sphaera Ioannis de Sacrobosco emendata . . ., Antuerpiae, apud haeredes Arnoldi Birckmanni, 1566. 8°
WHI CR 11:25. Given in 1953.

616 Demonstratio[nem] . . . de inaequali climatum latitudine, *tr. by Élie Vinet*, in Sphaera Ioannis de Sacrobosco emendata . . ., Parisiis, apud Hieronymum de Marnet et Gulielmum Cauellat, 1569. 8°
KCC Bury.SAC.Sph 1569.

617 Demonstratio[nem] . . . de inaequali climatum latitudine, *tr. by Élie Vinet*, in Sphaera Ioannis de Sacrobosco emendata . . ., Antuerpiae, apud Ioannem Bellerum, 1573. 8°
EMM S6.4.53 With the Sancroft-Emmanuel bookplate and part of the bequest of 1693. With a gilt blind-stamped centrepiece of around 1600, stamped TH, and medieval music pastedowns. In 1584 it was presented to an unknown recipient by James Garnet (Adams H733).

618 Demonstratio[nem] . . . de inaequali climatum latitudine, *tr. by Élie Vinet*, in Sphaera Ioannis de Sacrobosco emendata . . . Venetiis, apud haeredem Hieronymi Scoti, 1574. 8°
BOD Vet. F1 f.164 Acquired in 1959.

619 Demonstratio[nem] . . . de inaequali climatum latitudine, *tr. by Élie Vinet*, in Sphaera Ioannis de Sacrobosco emendata, Parisiis, apud Hieronymum de Marnef et viduam Gulielmi Cavellat, 1577. 8°

BOD Rigaud f.1 (2) From the library of Stephen Peter Rigaud (1774–1839), Savilian Professor of Astronomy MER 66.B.1 Perhaps a 16th-century acquisition.

TRC T.22.37 With the signature of Henry Puckering, 1656, and the Newton-Puckering bookplate, indicating that it was left to the library in 1691 (Adams H734).

620 Demonstratio[nem] . . . de inaequali climatum latitudine, *tr. by Élie Vinet*, in Sphaera Ioannis de Sacrobosco emendata . . ., Venetiis, apud haeredem Hieronymi Scoti, 1586. 8°

CUL White.d.324.

621 Demonstratio[nem] . . . de inaequali climatum latitudine, *tr. by Élie Vinet*, in Sphaera Ioannis de Sacrobosco emendata, Coloniae, apud Petrum Cholinum, 1590. 8°

TRO K.1.16(1) Chain mark. Belonged to William Purdue.

622 Demonstratio[nem] . . . de inaequali climatum latitudine, *tr. by Élie Vinet*, in Sphaera Ioannis de Sacrobosco emendata . . ., Coloniae, apud Gosuinum Cholinum, 1594. 8°

CLA C.8.10 Belonged to Humphrey Prideaux of Christ Church, Oxford, in 1660. He gave books to Clare in 1722, through his son Edmund (Adams H735).

623 Demonstratio[nem] . . . de inaequali climatum latitudine, *tr. by Élie Vinet*, in Sphaera Ioannis de Sacrobosco emendata . . ., Coloniae, apud Gosuinum Cholinum, 1601. 8°

CUL Peterborough E.2.48. (For Peterborough Cathedral Library, see the Introduction, p. xiv.)

624 Demonstratio[nem] . . . de inaequali climatum latitudine, *tr. by Élie Vinet*, in Sphaera Ioannis de Sacrobosco emendata, Lugduni, apud Hugonem Gazaeum, 1606. 8°

EMM 326.5.48 In the 18th-century catalogue, with the old shelf-mark 17.2.26, indicating that it probably was not part of Archbishop William Sancroft's collection. It may have belonged to Father Francis Irish (Hyberni) of the Irish mission.

625 Libro de algebra en arithmetica y geometria, Anuers, en casa de los herederos d'Arnoldo Birckman, 1567. 8°

BOD (2 copies) 8° N 16 Art. In the 1605 catalogue with the shelf-mark unchanged; Savile Aa 7 From the bequest of Sir Henry Savile (1549–1622), mathematician and founder of chairs in geometry and astronomy.

SJCC Z.44.98 This copy, printed by biuda y herederos de Iuan Stelsio, was given in the 19th century by Henry Walter (Adams N373).

Oliveira, António Gomes de (16th–17th centuries)

Soldier and poet, whose work is almost entirely in Spanish. The sole copy, in All Souls, cannot be dated but probably was acquired in the nineteenth century.

Inocêncio, I, p. 149.

626 Idylios maritimos y rimas varias, Lisboa, na officina de Pedro Crasbeeck, 1617. 8°
ASC nn.17.11 In 1631 the book belonged to a Don Gonçalo.

Orta, Garcia da (1501–68) (Horta)

A New Christian and 'the first major naturalist to study the main medicinal plants and other therapeutic substances used in coastal Asia' (Pearson, p. 103). He was a physician in Goa and there published **627** in 1563. (For discussion of the linguistic issues raised by the text, see Chapter One, p. xxxviii). Orta's Latin translator was Charles de l'Escluse (Carolus Clusius), who came across the *Colóquios* while on a tour of Spain with his pupil, Jacob Fugger (see the dedication of **628**, p. 4). Clusius was distressed that so valuable a book was only available in a language that few could understand, 'Maxime vero me angebat, quod ea lingua conscriptus esset, quae a paucis intelligatur', so he translated and abridged it, added notes and illustrations, and published it through Plantin. In its Latin form the book became one of the most successful of any written by a Portuguese. Most editions state on the title-page that the translation was made from the 'Lusitanica lingua'.

Altogether in Oxford and Cambridge there are thirty-nine copies, including the first edition and translations made from Latin into other languages. Of these twenty-eight arrived before 1750. Three of the eighteenth-century copies in Oxford are from the collection of William Sherard, a member of a family of botanists who died in 1728. He travelled in the eastern Mediterranean, and there probably acquired his copy of the extremely rare first edition (**627**), which has been extensively annotated by someone with a knowledge of oriental languages. Cambridge's great rarity is the University Library's copy of the same edition, signed and dated by Clusius himself. Some copies in Latin have also been annotated, as is often the case with medical books. See **627, 628, 629, 630, 631**.
M. N. Pearson, 'Hindu Medical Practice', pp. 103–7, with bibliography.

627 Coloquios dos simples, e drogas he cousas mediçinais da India, Goa, por Ioannes de Endem, 1563. 4°
OXS PLS Sherard 167. From the collection of William Sherard, deposited in 1726 and 1728. Marginalia, some in Arabic.
CUL Adv.d.3.21 Carolus Clusius's own copy, signed and dated by him from Lisbon '1564 vi Calend. Januarius'. MS. notes by Clusius (Adams O323; Anselmo 535).

628 [Coloquios dos simples, e drogas he cousas mediçinais da India], Aromatum et simplicium aliquot medicamentorum apud Indos nascentium historia, *tr. from Portuguese by* C. Clusio, Antuerpiae, ex officina Christophori Plantini, 1567. 8°

PLS Sherard 42. From the collection of William Sherard, deposited in 1726 and 1728. This copy lacks the title page and all before p. 17. Marginalia and 16pp. of MS. notes at end **CCCO** N.15.3, left by Brian Twine, fellow, in 1644. Chain marks **SJCO** I.scam.1.upper shelf. 26 With the signature of John Merrick (1671–1757), fellow, or of his son, also John, fellow 1721–33.

CUL (2 copies) P*.6.54 (F) Bequeathed by Thomas Lorkin, Professor of Physick, in 1591 and with annotations by him; Hhh.249 Formerly L.24.49 and with the bookplate of the Royal Library, deposited in 1715. Blind-stamped centrepiece binding of around 1600 with English and Latin aphorisms on the fly-leaf **STCC** G.6.100 Gift of John Addenbrooke (1680–1719), fellow and founder of Addenbrooke's hospital **TRC** S.23.32 The binding, perhaps Cambridge 17th century, has been repaired. In the catalogue compiled between 1667 and 1675 with the number 44. Some MS. notes in Latin and English (Adams O319).

629 [Coloquios dos simples, e drogas he cousas mediçinais da India], Aromatum, et simplicium aliquot medicamentorum apud Indos nascentium historia, *tr. from Portuguese by* Carolo Clusio Atrebate, Antuerpiae, ex officina Christophori Plantini, 1574. 8°

BOD 8° I 68(2) Linc. From the Barlow bequest of 1691 **MGO** R.06.14(04) Given by John Goodyear, who was an important donor of medical books, in 1664. Oxford binding, Ker centrepiece xv, in use c. 1580–1619 (Pearson, p. 78) **NEW** BT3.226.19 Signature of Thomas Hopper, medical practioner, who gave books to the college in 1623. In the catalogue of 1686, under Garcias.

CUL (2 copies) L.6.55 With the bookplate of the Royal Library, deposited in 1715, and in its catalogue. The book also has the signature of Sir Thomas Knyvett (?1539–1618), of Ashwellthorpe, Norfolk, whose library Bishop Moore acquired. Binding with blind-stamped ornaments (McKitterick 379); CCD.47.89 Presented by John Mayor in 1874. Underlining (Adams O320).

630 [Coloquios dos simples, e drogas he cousas mediçinais da India], Aromatum et simplicium aliquot medicamentorum apud Indos nascentium historia, *tr. from Portuguese by* Carolo Clusio Atrebate, 3a ed., Antuerpiae, ex officina Christophori Plantini, 1579. 8°

BOD 8° H 3 Med Seld. From the Selden bequest of 1659. In the 1674 catalogue **CHC** O.k.6.11 Probably from the Orrery bequest of 1731–2. With the signatures of Edward Windsor and Nicholas Wyat. Bound with **243**. Underlining **RSL** RR.z.258(1).

EMM 333.3.13 Probably among those left by Archbishop William Sancroft in 1693 **MGC** H.17.16 (1) Bound with **243** (Adams O321).

631 [Coloquios dos simples, e drogas he cousas mediçinais da India], Aromatum et simplicium aliquot medicamentorum apud Indos nascentium historia, *tr. from Portuguese by* C. Clusio Atrebate., 4a ed. (of Orta), Antuerpiae, ex Officina Plantiniana apud viduam, & Ioannem Moretum, 1593. 8°

BOD Douce O 101 Part of the Douce collection left in 1834 **PLS** Sherard 166. From the collection of William Sherard, deposited in 1726 and 1728. With marginalia and MS. notes on the flyleaf and endpages **RSL** RR. w. 453 Acquired after 1835 Bound with **244 SJCO** HB4/4.a.4.21(2) The gift of Dr Reynolds or Reanolds, President of Corpus (1549–1607).

CUL (2 copies) P*.6.53 (F) Given by Henry Lucas, benefactor and founder of the Lucasian professorship of mathematics, in 1663. It was in his library by 1654; CCD.47.88 Given by John Martyn, Prof. of Botany (1699–1768) and with the signature of John

Banister (1540–1610). Bound with **244 JSC** M.12.12 Bequeathed by Lionel Gatford, D.D. and a former student of the college, in 1715 **PMC** 10.12.19 With a college bookplate of 1879 **SJCC** Ll.11.14 In the catalogue compiled c. 1640 (Adams O322).

632 [Coloquios dos simples, e drogas he cousas mediçinais da India], Aromatum, et simplicium aliquot medicamentorum apud Indos nascentium historia, *with* Christophori a Costa . . . Aromatum & medicamentorum in Orientalis India nascentium liber. *Tr. from Portuguese by Carolus Clusius and included by him in his Exoticorum liber septimus,* 5a ed., Antuerpiae, ex Officina Plantiniana Raphelengii, 1605. Fol. (All copies bound with **245**).

    CHC G.2.4 **MGO** R.17.7 Given by John Goodyear, who was an important donor of medical books, in 1664 **RSL** RR. x. 308 (1) Acquired between 1749 and 1835 **SJCO** Y.2.12 From the Crynes bequest of 1745 **UNI** Given by Elias Wrench and now in **MHS** at P/CLUos **WAD** J 26.7 Bequeathed by Richard Warner, who graduated B.A. in 1734. His library, particularly rich in works on natural history and botany, was left to the college in 1775. A copy is listed in the Bodley catalogue of 1620.

    CUL L.2.6 From the Royal Library, deposited in 1715 **CLA** L1.1.19 With the bookplate of 1701. In the catalogue of 1577–78 with the shelf-mark S.8 **EMM** 314.2.19 Probably among those left by Archbishop William Sancroft in 1693.

633 [Coloquios dos simples, e drogas he cousas mediçinais da India], Dell'historia de i semplici aromati, et altre cose che vengono portate dall'Indie Orientali pertinenti all'uso della medicina, *tr. from Latin by* M. Annibale Briganti, Venetia, appresso Zuane Zenaro, 1597. 8°
    BOD Antiq. f.I. 1597.2 Copy acquired in 1926 from All Souls.

634 [Coloquios dos simples, e drogas he cousas mediçinais da India], Histoire des drogues, espisceries, et de certains medicamens simples, qui naissent és Indes, *tr. from Latin by* Antoine Colin, 2e ed., Lyon, aux despens de Iean Pillehotte, 1619. 8° (Bound with **246**).
    BOD Douce CC 41. From the Douce bequest of 1834 **PLS** Sherard 59. From the collection of William Sherard, deposited in 1726 and 1728.

Osório, Jerónimo (1514–80)

Bishop of Silves, in the Algarve, theologian, controversialist and reluctant, though successful historian, Osório was without any doubt the Portuguese author who made the most impact in sixteenth and seventeenth-century Oxford and Cambridge. There are about 160 copies of books by him in the libraries, well over a hundred of old provenance. Unusually, there are more copies of his books in Cambridge than in Oxford, probably because his chief English opponent, Walter Haddon, was a Cambridge man.

Osório was not only read in university or college libraries. Books by him very frequently appear in inventories, for example, the lists of the goods of Oxford men to be found in *Private Libraries in Renaissance England*. Of the sixty-four such inventories of the 1570s and 1580s twenty-four have at least one book by a Portuguese writer, and in twenty cases that book – more usually several books – is by Osório. White Kennett (1660–1728) of Peterborough Cathedral, but who had been a student at St Edmund Hall, had copies of seven books by him. It is especially surprising to see how often *De Gloria* (probably also with its attendant *De Nobilitate Civili et Christiana*) appears in the collections of young men, perhaps as recreational reading. In Cambridge E. S. Leedham-Green found twenty-eight copies of books by Osório in the probate inventories made for the Vice-Chancellor. He continued to be admired by English Latinists into the eighteenth century, for example, by Alexander Pope (Bourdon, p. 301). There are marginalia or other signs of reading in copies of items **636, 637, 647, 649, 653, 654, 655, 661, 663, 674, 675, 676, 679, 682.**

Osório's life was mostly spent in Portugal, but he made two journeys to Italy, both of which were important to his career as a writer (discussion in Chapter Four, pp. lxvii–ix). Very unusually for a Portuguese writer there are English editions of his Latin works (**642–3**) and translations (**652, 672**). It is clear that, in England, he was not only famous for his controversy with Elizabeth I. He is usually described as 'Lusitanus' on title-pages, but sometimes just as 'Silvensis'.

Léon Bourdon, 'Jerónimo Osório et les humanistes anglais'; T. F. Earle, 'Portuguese Scholarship in Oxford in the Early Modern Period . . .'; E. S. Leedham-Green, *Books in Cambridge Inventories*; Osório, *Cartas*, tr. by A. Guimarães Pinto; *Private Libraries in Renaissance England,* ed. by R. J. Fehrenbach and E. S. Leedham-Green.

635 Opera omnia, Romae, Georgius Ferrarius, 1592. Fol. (4 tom. in 2).
BOD M 10.14,15 Th. In the 1605 catalogue **CHC** H.3.2.1 Bought with money given by Otho Nicolson 1613. Nicolson was a benefactor with no obvious connection to the college (Hiscock, pp. 6–7). **WAD** I 35.2–5 Given by Philip Bisse 1613 **WOR** D.3.1–2 Bequeathed by William Gower, the second provost of the college, in 1777.
CUL (3 copies) H*.1.19- (B) Acquired before 1715; C.8.21 From the Royal Library, deposited in 1715; Acton a.51.83- Lord Acton's library was presented in 1902 (Adams O370).

636 De gloria libri V. De nobilitate ciuili libri II. De nobilitate christiana libri III. Florentiae, apud Laurentium Torrentinum, 1552. 4°
BOD 4° P 54 Jur. Part of the Crynes collection, left in 1745. Annotation in a 16th-century hand. **WOR** D.12.8 Bequeathed by H. A. Pottinger, 1911.
CCCC SP.461 (2) Bequeathed by Archbishop Matthew Parker in 1575. Marginal notes (De gloria only). Bound with **668 PET** (2 copies) D.4.10 (De gloria); D.11.43 (De nobilitate) Both left by Andrew Perne, Master, in 1589 **SJCC** (2 copies) Aa.6.20 (1) With MS. letter by Roger Ascham (in his hand) to Cuthbert Tunstall, Bishop of Durham; Aa.6.20* With a MS. letter of 6pp. to Cardinal Pole by Roger Ascham (in his hand) and marginal notes by Thomas Baker, fellow (1656–1740). Neither copy includes De gloria **TRH** E*.6.29, (De nobilitate civili & christiana only). With a number, 31, on the fore-edge, indicating that it was an early acquisition. The binding has a blind-stamped centrepiece of around 1600 and a medieval pastedown (Adams O371 and 378).

637 De gloria libri V. De nobilitate ciuili et christiana, libri V. Basileae, apud Petrum Pernam, 1571. 8°

CHC WR.8.12 Part of the Wake bequest of 1737. It also had a 17th-century English owner, Robert Fryce. Some pencil marks.

638 De gloria libri V. De nobilitate ciuili et christiana, libri V. Basileae, apud Petrum Pernam, 1573. 8°

CUL W.11.56 From the Royal Library, deposited in 1715 **SJCC** U.5.18 (Adams O372).

639 De gloria libri V. De nobilitate ciuili et christiana, libri V. 3a ed. Basileae, apud Petrum Pernam., 1576. 4°

BOD Lawn f.45 Bequeathed by Brian Lawn in 2001 **EXE** 9F 1576.2 Printed signature of N. Crynes, who died in 1745 **JSO** I.5.28.

CUL Peterborough C.9.24. Given to Peterborough Cathedral Library by White Kennett (1660–1728; see the Introduction, p. xiv). Marginal notes.

640 De gloria libri V. De nobilitate ciuili et christiana, libri V. Coloniae, apud Ludovicum Alectorium, 1576. 16°

EMM 329.6.62 In the 18th-century catalogue by 1712. The library had another copy of this work which it had lost by 1597. See Bush, p. 198 **PMC** 3.7.85 (Adams O373).

641 De gloria libri V. De nobilitate ciuili liber II (sic) Eiusdem de nobilitate christiana, liber tertius, Bilbao, excudebat Mathias Mares, 1578. 8°

CUL Te.56.1 Acquired in 1911 (Adams O374).

642 De gloria, libri V. De nobilitate ciuili & christiana, libri V. Londinii, H. Middletonus, impensis I.H. or F.C. 1580. 16°

BOD (2 copies) Antiq. g.E. 1580.1 The shelf-mark indicates that it was acquired between 1883 and 1936; Vet. A1 g.24 The shelf-mark indicates that it was acquired after 1937 (STC 18884.7).

CUL Syn.8.58.164 (impensis W.N.; STC 18884) **SID** M.7.66 In the catalogue of 1674. With the college bookplate of 1701, and the signature of James Montagu, the first master, who died in 1618, and the price. 16th- or 17th-century binding with blind-stamped centrepiece (STC 18884.7) **TRC** C.7.165 In 1705 it belonged to Edward Rudd (1677–1727), M.A. of Trinity and Fellow (STC 18884.3).

643 De gloria libri V . . . De nobilitate ciuili et christiana, libri V. Londini, excudebat Richardus Field, impensis Iohannis Harrisoni, 1589. 16°

CUL Syn.9.58.3 Acquired from Manley in 1897 (STC 18885) **TRC** C.7.167 In 1621 this book belonged to John Franklyn, perhaps the student of that name at Peterhouse (?1600–1648). It also belonged to Francis Smyth. There were a number of students of that name in late 16th-century Cambridge. The binding of around 1600 has a blind-stamped centrepiece.

644 De gloria libri V. De nobilitate ciuile & christiana libri V. Coloniae, apud Petrum Cholinum, 1612. 12°

BOD 8° G 16 Th. BS. It belonged to Edward Pocock (probably the orientalist, 1604–91, Corpus and Christ Church, though there were other Oxford men of the same name in the 17th century).

645 De gloria libri quinque. De nobilitate ciuili et christiana libri totidem, Rothomagi, apud Romanum de Beauvais, 1616. 12°
BOD Buchanan f.154 Donated by Thomas Buchanan in 1941.

646 De gloria libri V. De nobilitate ciuile & christiana libri V . . . Addita nunc primum authoris vita ab Hieronymo Osorio nepote eleganter conscripta, Coloniae, apud Petrum Cholinum, 1627. 12°
WOR XB.4.50 Bequeathed by H. A. Pottinger, 1911.

647 De iustitia libri decem . . . Ex auctoris codice, misso Coloniam ab hinc plus novem annis, ex quo primum edendos ipse iusserat, transcripti, & emendati . . ., Coloniae Agrippinae, apud haeredes Arnoldi Birckmanni, 1572. 8°
BOD Vet. D1 f.221 Bought from St George's Worcester 1974 **WOR** SS.1.38 Oxford binding, Ker no. 1772, using centrepiece xiii, in use c.1560–73 and c.1590–97 (Pearson p. 78). Much underlining; MS. index. It belonged to Hugo Bowrishe, Thomas Cookes, by whose bequest the college was founded in 1714, and Nicholas Chalmore/Chaulmus (Hart Hall, matriculated 1572, aged 20).
CUL (2 copies) G.12.43 from the Royal Library, deposited in 1715; Peterborough C.9.23 (For Peterborough Cathedral Library, see the Introduction, p. xiv.) **G&C** F.32.27 Bequeathed by William Branthwaite, Master, in 1619. He was one of the revisers of the Bible. The binding has a blind-stamped centrepiece of around 1600 **KCC** B.8.19. **TRC** (2 copies) T.19.6 Signed by John Lumley (1533–1609) and probably no. 448 in the catalogue of his collection. Signed also by Newton, probably Henry Puckering, formerly Newton, whose books were given to the college in 1691. Bound with **662**; F.13.112 (Adams O375).

648 De iustitia libri decem, Coloniae Agrippinae, apud haeredes Arnoldi Birckmanni, 1574. 8°
CUL Peterborough F.2.40 (For Peterborough Cathedral Library, see the Introduction p. xiv.)

649 De iustitia libri decem, Coloniae Agrippinae, apud haeredes Arnoldi Birckmanni, 1581. 8°
CUL Kkk.241 Bound with **667**. Presented to the library in 1915 **TRC** F.13.112 16th–17th-century binding, stamped PS, possibly Peter Shaw, who gave books in 1601. Marginal marks in pencil. In the college's copy of the interleaved Bodleian catalogue used in the 18th century (Adams O376).

650 De iustitia caelesti libri decem, in officina Birckmannica, sumptibus Arnoldi Mylii, Colon. 1586. 8°
BOD Crynes 398 Part of the Crynes bequest of 1745.
CUL Acton d.48.242 Lord Acton's library was presented in 1902 (Adams O377).

651 De nobilitate ciuili, libri duo. Eiusdem De nobilitate christiana libri tres. Olyssipone, apud Ludouicum Rodericum typographum, 1542. 4°
BOD 4° R 11(2) Th. Seld. From the Selden bequest of 1659. In the catalogue of 1674. Bound with **153, 758 MGO** p.15.03 In 1769 it belonged to Thomas Hedman of Pembroke, Oxford (Anselmo 1035).

652 [De nobilitate civile et christiana] A discourse of Civill, and Christian Nobilitie . . ., *tr* William Blandie London, Thomas Marsh, 1576. 4°

BOD (2 copies) C 17.27 Linc. From the Barlow bequest of 1691; Crynes 906(3) From the Crynes bequest of 1745 (STC 18886) **BNC** Lath. H 8.10 (9) **TRO** C.2.3 Given by James Ingram in 1850.

CUL (2 copies) Peterborough G.2.39 Given to Peterborough Cathedral Library by White Kennett (1660–1728; see the Introduction, p. xiv); Syn.7.57.52 Acquired from Quaritch in 1906 (STC 18886).

653 De rebus Emmanuelis Regis Lusitaniae . . . gestis libri duodecim, Olysippone, apud Antonium Gondisaluu[m] typographum, 1571. Fol.

BOD Vet. G1 c.8 Acquired in 1955 **ASC** SR.89.e.2 With the college bookplate no. 6, after 1753 (see Henderson Smith, pp. 21–2); some annotation. Perhaps bought at the Stuart sale in 1821 **MGO** Arch.B.III.5.8 Given by Thomas Mason, Fellow and college Librarian, 30 July 1611.

CUL N.14.20 From the Royal Library, deposited in 1715, and listed in its catalogue (Adams O379; Anselmo 694).

654 De rebus Emmanuelis Regis Lusitaniae . . . gestis libri duodecim, Coloniae Agrippinae, apud haeredes Arnoldi Birckmanni, 1574. 8°

BOD (2 copies) 8° N 50 Art.; 8° S 242 Art. **ASC** SR.89.e.3 Ink and pencil annotation **CCCO** I.15.17 Bequeathed by Thomas Turner, President of the college, in 1714 **CHC** ZN.5.6 Underlinings and notes **EXE** 9K 1574.7 With the signature of John Foulkes **NEW** BT3.64.9 No chain marks, repaired title page, underlining. Probably to be identified with the copy given by Arthur Lake, in 1617, on leaving to become bishop of Bath and Wells. In the catalogue of 1686 **QUO** JJ.s.300 Lacks title page. Signature of Eduardus Fletewood. There are a number of students of this name in Foster but not associated with Queen's.

G&C F.23.12 Bequeathed by William Branthwaite, Master, in 1619. He was one of the revisers of the Bible. The binding has a blind-stamped centrepiece of around 1600. Book 3, Fol. 120v MS. note 'insignis fabula' against discovery of a miraculous cross in S. Tomás de Malipur **QUC** F.19.34. With the signature of Henry Johnson on the pastedown. Stamped coat of arms on binding with motto. A copy was left by John Smith, fellow and the Cambridge Platonist, in 1652 (Benefactors' Register, p. 30). In the catalogue of the 1680s with the current shelf-mark **SJCC** D.11.26 From the Crashawe collection, deposited in 1626 **TRC** W.12.67 In the college's copy of the interleaved Bodleian catalogue used in the 18th century **TRH** F*.3.20 Blind-stamped centrepiece binding of around 1600 and a medieval MS. pastedown. It formerly belonged to Richard Some who became a fellow of St John's, Cambridge in 1571. The book, therefore, is likely to have been in Cambridge since the 16th century. It has a number, 40, on the fore-edge indicating that this was an early acquisition, but not necessarily by Trinity Hall (Adams O380).

655 De rebus Emmanuelis, Regis Lusitaniae . . . gestis, libri duodecim, Coloniae Agrippinae, apud haeredes Arnoldi Birckmanni, 1576. 8°

BOD 8° O 3 Art. Seld. From the Selden bequest of 1659. In the 1674 catalogue. Underlining and marginal notes **SJCO** K.scam.1.upper shelf. 24 Part of the Crynes bequest of 1745.

CUL T.11.66 In the Royal Library, deposited in 1715, and listed in its catalogue. It was part of the library of Sir Thomas Knyvett (?1539–1618), which was acquired by Bishop

Moore (McKitterick 653) **EMM** S.12.4.66 left by Archbishop William Sancroft in 1693 (Adams O381).

656 De rebus Emmanuelis, Regis Lusitaniae . . . gestis, libri duodecim . . . Item: Io. Matalii Metelli Sequani I. C. in eandem historiam praefatio, Coloniae Agrippinae, apud haeredes Arnoldi Birckmanni, 1581. 8°
BOD Antiq. f.G. 1581.3. Acquired between 1883 and 1936, from Ernest Mason Satow, British Legation, Yedo (Tokyo).
TRC W.12.19 Probably a 19th-century acquisition (Adams O382).

657 De rebus Emmanuelis, Lusitaniae regis . . . gestis, libri duodecim . . . Item: Io. Matalii Metelli Sequani i.c. in eosdem libros praefatio, Coloniae, in officina Birckmannica, sumptibus Arnoldi Mylij, 1597. 8°
CHC a.3.39 Bought with money given by Otho Nicolson in 1613. Nicolson was a benefactor with no obvious connection to the college (Hiscock, pp. 6–7). **WOR** G.14.7 Bequeathed by H. A. Pottinger, 1911.
CLA E1.2.16 With the college bookplate dated 1701. There is a previous shelf-mark, P82, on the leading edge, which also appears in the catalogue of 1677–78 (Adams O383).

658 [De rebus Emmanuelis . . . gestis] Histoire de Portugal . . . Comprinse en 20 liures, dont les 12 premiers sont traduits du latin de Ierosme Osorius, *also includes a translation of Castanheda, by Simon Goulart.* Avec un discours du fruit qu'on peut recueillir de la lecture de ceste histoire,[Geneva], De l'imprimerie de François Estienne, pour Antoine Chuppin, 1581. Fol.
BOD Antiq. c.F. 1581.1. The shelf-mark indicates that it was acquired between 1883 and 1936.
CUL F.158.a.3.2 Given by Prof. Alfred Newton, who owned the book in 1879 (Adams O384).

659 [De rebus Emmanuelis . . . gestis] Histoire de Portugal . . . Comprinse en 20 liures, dont les 12 premiers sont traduits du latin de Ierosme Osorius, *also includes a translation of Castanheda, by Simon Goulart, and, in Book 19, a summary of Góis's Commentarii of 1539 and De Bello Cambaico.* Avec un discours du fruit qu'on peut recueillir de la lecture de ceste histoire, Paris, Guillaume de la Nouë, 1581. 8°
BOD Antiq. f.F. 1581.1. The shelf-mark indicates that it was acquired between 1883 and 1936.

660 [De rebus Emmanuelis . . . gestis] Histoire de Portugal . . . Comprinse en 20 liures, dont les 12 premiers sont traduits du latin de Ierosme Osorius, *also includes a translation of Castanheda, by Simon Goulart, and, in Book 19, a summary of Góis's Commentarii of 1539 and De Bello Cambaico.* Avec un discours du fruit qu'on peut recueillir de la lecture de ceste histoire, Paris, Michel Sonnius, 1587. 8°
BOD 8° O 20 Art. In the 1620 catalogue with an unchanged shelf-mark.
See also **165–7** for Castanheda's history.

661 De regis institutione et disciplina libri viii, Olysipponae ex officina Ioannis Hispani, excudebat Franciscus Correa [from colophon], 1571 [colophon 1572]. 4°

BOD 4° P 55 Jur. Oxford binding with blind-stamped centrepiece, Ker xv, in use c. 1580–1619 (Pearson, p. 78). It is stamped BT. The shelf-mark appears on the fore-edge, but the book is not listed in the early catalogues. Marginal notes, drawing attention to important points in the argument. See also **663**.

CUL Peterborough G.2.37 (For Peterborough Cathedral Library, see the Introduction, p. xiv.) Extensive and legible MS. notes. Bound with **671 JSC** O.11.38 Bound with **671**. Not in the catalogue of 1705 **SJCC** Aa/G.27.18 Bequeathed in 1816 **TRH** E*.6.36 Formerly D.3.34. With a blind-stamped centrepiece binding of around 1600, a medieval MS. pastedown and the college bookplate of 1700. The fore-edge is numbered 44 (Adams O385–6; Anselmo 503).

662 De regis institutione et disciplina libri viii, *with* Praefatio by Ioannes Metellus Sequanus, Coloniae Agrippinae, Haeredes Arnoldi Birckmanni, 1572. 8°

EXE 9K 1572 With the signature of N. Crynes, 1745 though Exeter College was not included in Crynes's will. MS. note: Este livro he de Fernando Alvares q*ue* mo emprestou pa*ra* ho ler mas eu naõ lho torney **LIN** N.10.43 With the signature of Thomas Trymington and the price.

EMM S.14.4.33 Bequeathed by Archbishop William Sancroft in 1693 **G&C** F.32.26(2) Bequeathed by William Branthwaite, Master, in 1619. He was one of the revisers of the Bible. Bound with **666 SJCC** Aa/G.27.18 Bequeathed by Thomas Gisborne in 1806 **TRC** T.19.6 [2] In the college's copy of the interleaved Bodleian catalogue used in the 18th century. Bound with 647 (Adams O387).

663 De regis institutione et disciplina libri viii, *with* Praefatio by Ioannes Metellus Sequanus, Coloniae Agrippinae, apud haeredes Arnoldi Birck-manni, 1574.

BOD Wood 458 Bequeathed by Anthony Wood, antiquarian, in 1695. Binding similar to **661** but without stamped initials. Ker centrepiece xv, in use c. 1580–1619 (Pearson, p. 78), so it was in Oxford before Wood acquired it. MS. notes, not by Wood (Kiessling (2002) 4834).

CUL (2 copies) Peterborough F.2.41 Given to Peterborough Cathedral Library by White Kennett (1660–1728; see the Introduction, p. xiv). Underlining; Acton 3.48.56 Lord Acton's library was presented in 1902. **SID** M.7.19 In the catalogue of 1674. With the title on the top edge, a practice which continued to the 1640s (Rogers, p. 78) (Adams O388).

664 De regis institutione et disciplina libri viii, *with* Praefatio by Ioannes Metellus Sequanus, Coloniae Agrippinae, 1582. 8°

EMM 326.7.21 Probably acquired after 1800 (Adams O389).

665 De regis institutione et disciplina libri viii, *with* Praefatio by Ioannes Metellus Sequanus, Coloniae, in officina Birckmannica, sumptibus Arnoldi Mylii,1588. 8°

BOD Tanner 118 From the bequest of Bishop Thomas Tanner (1674–1735) **CHC** f.8.34 Bequeathed by Robert Burton in 1640. Marginal annotations (Kiessling (1988) 1152) **QUO** HH.h.20.

CUL O.12.41 From the Royal Library, deposited in 1715, and listed in its catalogue (Adams O390).

666 De vera sapientia libri v, Coloniae Agrippinae, apud haeredes Arnoldi Birckmanni,1579. 8°
BLL 0625 a 06 Latin marginalia. In the 1709 and 1721 catalogues, with the shelf-mark K.8.15 which is still visible on the title page. Repaired binding.
G&C F.32.26(1) Bequeathed by William Branthwaite, Master, in 1619. He was one of the revisers of the Bible. Bound with item 662 (Adams O391).

667 De vera sapientia, libri v, Coloniae Agrippinae, in Officina Birckmannica, 1582. 8°
BOD Crynes 248. Bequeathed by Crynes in 1745 WAD H 32.1 Given by Philip Bisse, 1613.
CUL Kkk.241 Bound with **649**. Presented in 1915 TRC F.13.17 With the bookplate of John Colbatch, Anglican chaplain in Portugal from 1693–1700, who died in 1748 (Adams O392).

668 Epistola ad serenissimam Elisabetam, Angliae Reginam, Venetiis, ex officina Iordani Zileti, 1563. 4°
BOD 226 i.45 The shelf-mark was in use after 1864 BLL 0650 b 14 Bequeathed by George Coningesby in 1768.
CCCC SP.461 (1) Bequeathed by Archbishop Matthew Parker in 1575. Bound with **636 KCC** A.5.58 (Adams O393).

669 Epistola ad serenissimam Elisabetam, Angliae Reginam, Lovanii, ex officina Ioannis Bogardi, 1563. 4°
CCCC MS.435 (2) Bequeathed by Archbishop Matthew Parker in 1575 (Adams O394).

670 Epistola ad Elizabetam reginam Angliae, Parisiis, apud Nicolaum Chesneau, 1563. 8°
BOD Antiq. f.F. 1563.1 Bought 1917.

671 Epistola ad serenissimam Elisabetam Angliae Reginam, Olysippone, excudebat Antonius Riberius, 1575. 4°
CUL Peterborough G.2.37 (2) Bound with **661 JSC** O.11.38(2) Bound with **661**. Not in the 1705 catalogue (Adams O395; Anselmo 927).

672 [Epistola ad Elizabetham] An epistle . . . to the most excellent Princesse Elizabeth. *Tr.* Richard Shacklock, Antwerp, Aegidius Diest and J. Latius, 1565. 8°
BOD (3 copies) Wood 800 (1), bequeathed by Anthony Wood, antiquarian, in 1695 (Kiessling (2002) 4833); Tanner 15 (2) From the bequest of Bishop Thomas Tanner (1674–1735) (both STC 18888); Vet. B1 f. 78 Bought in the 20th century and bound with item 680 (STC 18887).
KCC A.5.58 (STC 18887) SJCC A.3.28(1) TRC C.7.160[6] (STC 18887).

673 [Epistola ad Elizabetham] Remonstrance a madame Elizabeth, royne d'Angleterre, Lyon, prins sur la coppie imprimée à Paris, 1587. 8°
BOD Vet. E1 f. 41 Bought in 1948.

674 In Gualterum Haddonum Magistrum libellorum supplicum . . . libri tres, Olissipone, Franciscus Correa, 1567. 4°

BOD 4o B 101 Th. **BNC** Latham M.3.13, formerly G.2.10. In the catalogue probably compiled in the 17th century with the shelfmark Arch. G.2.9. Rebound.

CUL (3 copies) Adv.c.8.1 With copious notes by Walter Haddon; Peterborough G.2.38 Given by White Kennett (1660–1728; for the Peterborough Cathedral Library see the Introduction, p. xiv). Many of Kennett's books were second-hand; this copy came from the library of the widely travelled Scottish bishop Gilbert Burnet (1643–1715); Ely c.318 Given by Ralph Perkins to Ely Cathedral Library in 1732, and deposited in Cambridge in 1970. Perkins (1658–1751) had been a fellow of Queens' College **PET** D.11.33 Left by Andrew Perne, Master, in 1589 **SID** Q.4.19 in the catalogue of 1674. Given by Master Sheffelde, possibly Thomas Sheffield who took his M.A. in 1643. Underlining **SJCC** A.2.42 Left by Thomas Baker, fellow (1656–1740) (Adams O396).

675 In Gualterum Haddonum, magistrum libellorum supplicum . . . de religione libri tres. *With* epistola. Dilingae, ex officina Sebaldi Mayer, 1569. 8°

BOD (2 copies) Crynes 397 From the Crynes bequest of 1745. Many marginal notes especially to Epistola; Mason DD 383 from the Mason bequest of 1841 **CHC** WI.8.9 Wake bequest 1737. Marginal annotations **SJCO** HB4/1.a.5.2(1) given by William Paddy, 1602.

CUL (3 copies) Peterborough C.9.22 Given by White Kennett (1660–1728; for the Peterborough Cathedral Library see the Introduction, p. xiv); Hhh.118, formerly C.14.88, and perhaps from the Royal Library, deposited in 1715, though not in the catalogue. Repaired binding; Adams 8.56.2 Marginal notes and underlinings **G&C** F.26.18 The catalogue completed in 1646 states that the college owned the edition of Cologne, 1585 **KCC** K.63.55 **TRC** I.13.113 16th–17th-century binding. Signed by William Hawcroft, possibly the William Havercroft who was admitted to Trinity in 1636 (Adams O397).

676 In Gualterum Haddonum, magistrum libellorum supplicum . . . de religione libri tres. *With* epistola. Dilingae, ex officina Sebaldi Mayer, 1574. 8°

CUL Hhh.77 Formerly C.14.28. With the bookplate of the Royal Library, deposited in 1715, and in its catalogue **PCO** 3.15.41.With the college bookplate of 1700. Legible but cropped Latin marginalia. It is bound with an English Marcus Aurelius (London, Thomas East, 1586), and may have been acquired at the same time.

677 In Gualterum Haddonum Anglum de religione libri tres. *With* epistola, Dilingae, Sebaldus Mayer, 1576. 16°

BOD 8o G 297 Th. Bought from Stark, perhaps the bookseller Adam Stark (1784–1867) **EXE** 9K 1576.6 With the signature of Robert Bradford, who matriculated 1631, aged 19. Binding with Ker centrepiece xxx, in use c.1570–80, according to Pearson, p. 83.

CUL Hhh.77 Probably a 19th-century acquisition **SJCC** U.12.29 With signature of Samuel Otes. There were three generations of students of that name at Cambridge, though none at St John's. The first matriculated in 1568; the last died in 1683 **TRC** Grylls.3.217 From the collection of William Grylls, deposited in 1863 (Adams O399).

678 De religione libri iii in Gualterum Haddonum Anglum *With* epistola. Editio quinta, Coloniae, apud Gosuinum Cholinum, 1525 (really 1585). 12°

CHC OF.6.26 With the signature of Peter de Cardonel, 1649, probably the father of the Christ Church undergraduate of the same name who died in 1699.

679 De religione libri iii in Gualterum Haddonum Anglum *With* epistola. Editio sexta, Coloniae, apud Gosuinum Cholinum, 1588–9. 12°
WAD H 32.2 Given by Philip Bisse 1613.
CUL Peterborough F.2.39 Given by White Kennett (1660–1728; for the Peterborough Cathedral Library, see the Introduction, p. xiv). On the flyleaf there is a note in pencil perhaps reading 'Latinitate pollens, sed argumenta si spectes fecit futilis auctor'.

680 [De religione libri iii in Gualterum Haddonum Anglum] A . . . treatie . . . wherein he confuteth . . . Walter Haddon. *Tr* John Fen, Louanii apud Ioannem Foulerum, 1568. 8°
BOD (2 copies) Vet. B1 f. 131 Acquired after 1861. With the signature of William Herbert 1781; Vet. B1 f.78 Bound with item 672 and bought from Rosenthal in the 20th century.
CUL Peterborough F.2.42 Given by White Kennett (1660–1728; for the Peterborough Cathedral Library, see the Introduction, p. xiv).

681 In Parabolas Salamonis commentarius, denuo recognitus, Antuerpiae, apud Martinum Nutium, 1596. 12°
QUO Tunnel UU.g.580 17th-century binding.
SJCC Pp.14.15 Part of the Crashawe collection, deposited in 1626 (Adams O400).

682 Paraphrasis in Isaiam libri v, Coloniae Agrippinae, apud haeredes Arnoldi Birckmanni, [from colofon] excudebat Godefridus Kempensis, 1579, [colofon 1577]. 8°
CHC f.6.28 Left by Robert Burton 1577–1640 (Kiessling 1153) QUO UU.g.670 Ker no. 1577, with centrepiece xxx, used from the mid or late 1560s to 1608 (Pearson, p. 77). Given by John Langworth. Also belonged to Christopher Webbe. Both these migrated from Cambridge in the 1570s. Underlining.
CUL 2.35.40 From the Royal Library, deposited in 1715 G&C F.12.19 Left by William Branthwaite, Master, in 1619. He was one of the revisers of the Bible SJCC Uu.10.7 Left by Peter Gunning, Master, in 1684 TRC D.38.17, formerly D.1.47 and nothing on the fore-edge With the signature of Will Walker and his motto Will and Walke aright. In the copy of the Bodley catalogue of 1738 used by the library in the 18th century to record its holdings. There were 3 generations of William Walkers at Trinity, admitted between 1640 and 1714 (Adams B1586).

Osório, Jerónimo, the younger (1545–1611)

Osório's nephew and biographer. The biography appears in his uncle's *Opera*, which the younger Osório went to Rome to publish (see **635**, vol I, pp. 1–19). His own commentary on Ecclesiastes was also published there. The English universities have the later, Lyon edition (**683**).
Barbosa Machado, II, pp. 516–8.

683 Paraphrasis et commentaria in Ecclesiasten, *with* Paraphrasis in canticum canticorum, & in ipsam recens auctae notationes, Lugduni, sumptibus Horatij Cardon, 1611. 4°

BOD B 23.9(2) Linc. From the Barlow bequest of 1691, but in the 1620 catalogue, so it is a replacement copy. The shelf-mark is unchanged, except for the addition of 'Linc'. **QUO** 72.B.22.

CUL Z.25.30 With the bookplate of the Royal Library, deposited in 1715. The catalogue of the Royal Library lists a copy with the former shelf-mark (still visible) B.10.9. With the signature of Jo. Morse, perhaps John Morse who was admitted to Emmanuel in 1591 and died in 1648.

Pais, Baltesar (1571–1638) (Balthasar Paez)

A Trinitarian friar who, according to the *Enciclopédia*, took part in the Spanish Armada of 1588, was shipwrecked and then resolved on the religious life. He was a professor at Coimbra and became provincial of his order. There is no evidence that he left Portugal again, but the international ramifications of the religious life made it possible for him to publish in France. The Paris edition of his *Opera* (**684**) is an ambitious publication, in which eight printers collaborated (see colophon). The editor was another Trinitarian, Claude Ralle, who dedicated it to the General of the Order, Louis Petit. Pais himself dedicated item **688**, published in Lyon, to Petit. There is a statement of his nationality on all the title-pages of his works published abroad. Of the nineteen copies of books by him in Oxford and Cambridge at least fourteen were acquired before 1750.

Barbosa Machado, I, pp. 455–6; *Enciclopédia portuguesa e brasileira*, XIX, p. 982.

684 Opera Sacrae Scripturae interpretibus, Parisijs, [in colophon, apud Ioannem Petit-Pas and 7 others], 1631. 2 vols Fol.

BOD P 11.9,10 Th. In the 1635 appendix to the 1620 catalogue **CHC** G.2.2.7 Vol. 1 only **MGO** k.20.10–11 With the signatures of A. Warrant and Godfrey Emondson? May 6th 1631. Chain marks **QUO** 66.c.3–4 Vol. 2 lacks the title page.

CUL (2 copies) C.2.1 From the Royal Library, deposited in 1715; Ely a.108 Binding stamped with the coat of arms of Christopher Hatton (1605–70), of Jesus, created Baron Hatton in 1643. The book was deposited in Cambridge in 1970 **SJCC** Pp.1.16–17 Bequeathed by Lord William Howard in 1640. The 3rd son of the 4th Duke of Norfolk, he became a Catholic in 1584 **TRC** D.6.24 Thomas Whalley, Vicemaster, 1637. The binding is stamped TW.

685 Ad canticum Moysis Exodi xv. commentarij cum annotationibus moralibus, Antuerpiae, apud Gulielmum a Tongris, 1619. 4°

BOD II 12 Jur. The shelf-mark indicates that it was acquired after 1710. Same binding as item 689.

686 Ad canticum Moysis Exodi xv. commentarij cum annotationibus moralibus, Lugduni, sumptibus Ludovici Prost haeredis Rouille, 1622.

CUL E*.4.29 (C) Acquired before 1715.

687 Commentarii ad canticum Moysis, Exod. xv, cum annotationibus moralibus, Ulyssipone, ex officina Petri Craesbeeck, 1618. Fol.

WOR O.a.18 Bequeathed by H. A. Pottinger, 1911.

688 Commentarij in canticum Ezechiae, Isaiae 38, Lugduni, sumptibus Ludovici Prost Haeredis Rouille, 1623. 4°
BOD 4° A 13 Th. With shelf-mark on the leading edge, an indication of early provenance.

689 Commentarii in Epistolam B. Iacobi Apostoli, Lugduni, sumptibus Horatii Cardon, 1617. 8°
BOD II 20 Jur. The shelf-mark indicates that it was acquired after 1710. Same binding as **685 CHC** Hyp.P.45 Chain mark. In the 1665 catalogue **SEH** 4° H 17 With H17 on the leading edge, an indication of early provenance. Repaired binding.
EMM S.7.3.13 Bequeathed by Archbishop William Sancroft in 1693.

690 In Epistolam Beati Iacobi Apostoli Commentarii, Antuerpiae, apud Gulielmum a Tongris, 1617. 4°
QUC G.20.25. With the signature Bardsey on the pastedown. Perhaps George Bardsey, fellow, who was ejected in 1644 and died before the Restoration. Author's name and title on the fore-edge. Cambridge 17th-century binding, stamped QC. In the catalogue of the 1680s with the current shelf-mark.

691 In Epistolam Beati Iacobi Apostoli Commentarii, Antuerpiae, apud Gulielmum a Tongris, 1623. 8°
EMM 334.2.53 There is an old shelf-mark, 18.3.53, under which the book is listed in the 18th-century catalogue. There is a modern note in the catalogue indicating that books belonging to class 18 formed part of the bequests either of John Richardson (1626) or John Breton (1675), but there is no indication of provenance in the book itself. **MGC** A.19.21 Cambridge 17th-century binding with fillets.

Parestrelo, Luís de Beja (1539-after 1609) (Ludovicus de Beia)
The dates come from the autobiographical preface 'ad lectorem' of **700**. Parestrelo was an Augustinian friar, born in Portugal but from a family (Pallastrelli) which had originally come from Italy in the fifteenth century. Perhaps for this reason much of his career was spent in Italy, though he ended as an inquisitor in Coimbra. He is always described as 'Lusitanus', on the title-pages of his books, with the exceptions of **700**, printed in Lisbon, and **692**, which derives from it and was issued after his death. As he explains in the preface, for sixteen years he taught the clergy of Bologna how to resolve cases of conscience. Oxford and Cambridge between them have fifteen copies of the resulting compilation of cases, all with old provenance. They are essentially copies of the same book, which evolved over the years. By the time he returned to Portugal several editions had been published and he was a famous author. This may explain the unusually wide distribution of **700**, printed in Lisbon but in three Oxford libraries and one Cambridge one, all with old provenance. One of the reasons for the Lisbon edition was the difficulty of finding copies in Portugal of the Italian editions of his books.
Barbosa Machado, III, pp. 61–2; *Grande Enciclopédia Portuguesa e Brasileira*, XXI, p. 268.

692 Collegium sacrum Bononiense, seu illustrium casuum conscientiae
. . . accurata decisio, Coloniae Agrippinae, sumptibus Constantini
Münich, 1629. 8°
BOD 8° B 251 Th. In the 1674 catalogue **MGO** l.6.27 Chain mark. Signature of John
Fitzwilliam, Demy 1656, died 1699.

693 Responsiones casuum conscientiae, Bergomi, typis Comini Ven-
turae, & Soc., 1588. 18°
WAD h.14.03 Given by Philip Bisse, 1613.

694 Responsiones casuum conscientiae, *with* duo tractatus, alter quidem
de contractibus liuellarijs, alter verum de venditione rerum fructuosarum
ad terminum, Brixiae, apud Thomam Bozzolam, 1590. 8°
BOD Tanner 446(1) From the bequest of Bishop Thomas Tanner (1674–1735).

695 Responsiones casuum conscientiae, Brixiae, apud Societatem Brix-
iniensem, 1596. 8°
SJCC U.1.4 From the Crashawe collection, which was deposited in 1626, and in the
catalogue compiled c. 1640 (Adams B464).

696 Responsionum casuum conscientiae . . . Pars Secunda, Venetiis,
apud Io. Bapt. & Io. Bernardum Sessam, 1597.
WAD H 29.22 Given by Philip Bisse, 1613.

697 Responsionum casuum conscientiae . . . partes duae, *with* duo
tractatus, alter de contractibus liuellariis, alter de venditione rerum
fructuosarum ad terminum, Venetiis, apud haeredes Melchioris Sessae,
1600. 8°
BOD 8° B 25 Th. In the 1605 catalogue with shelf-mark unchanged.
CUL G*.16.33- (F) Acquired before 1715 **JSC** C.6.36 With the college bookplate of
1700. One of the additions to the catalogue of 1705, probably listed before 1730 (Adams
B465).

698 Responsionum casuum conscientiae . . . partes duae, *with* duo
tractatus, alter de contractibus liuellariis, alter de venditione rerum
fructuosarum ad terminum, Venetiis, apud Sessas?, 1606. 8°
CUL G*.16.24 Deposited before 1715. Tab numbered 24 which suggests that it has
been in the library since the 17th century. Cambridge binding with fillets.

699 Responsionum casuum conscientiae . . . Tractatus quadruplici
partione distinctus, *with* duo tractatus, Venetiis, apud Georgium Valenti-
num, 1621.
EMM 326.3.2, formerly C.4.55. With a 17th-century centrepiece stamped with a gilt
crest and a bookplate recording the gift of John Geoffrays, commensalis, who died in 1660.
Evidence of a tab. In the 18th-century catalogue, where it was probably listed before 1712,
as C.4.55.

700 Variae responsiones casuum conscientiae, *with* duo novi tractatus, de contractu liuellario, & venditione ad terminum, Ulyssipone, typis Petri Crasbeeck, 1610. 4°

BOD B 19.7 Linc. From the Barlow bequest of 1691, but in the 1620 catalogue, so a replacement copy **CHC** Allestree R.2.17 From the Allestree bequest of 1681 **SJCO** HB4/ 1.a.3.5 Given by Sir William Paddy 1633.

EMM S.13.3.46 Bequeathed by Archbishop William Sancroft in 1693.

Paz, Domingos de (16th cent.) (Dominicus a Pace)

A Dominican preacher who spent his career in Italy. For all that he is described on the title-page of **701** as 'Lusitanus'. Oxford has only one copy, and there are none in Cambridge.

Barbosa Machado, I, p. 714.

701 Sermonum in quibus vere Christiani hominis specimen exhibetur, tomus primus [secundus], Venetiis, apud Franciscum Zilettum, 1580. 4°

BOD II 49 Th., formerly P.7.9 Th. The modern shelf-mark shows that the book was reshelved after 1710, but it is in the 1605 catalogue, with the shelf-mark P.5.8 Th.

Pereira, António Pinto (16th cent.)

The editor, Frei Miguel da Cruz, explains that this history of the viceroyalty of Dom Luís de Ataíde (1568–72) was postumous and had been more than thirty years in the printing. The dedication, to King Sebastião, who died in 1578, suggests that the manuscript was completed on or before that date. As is normally the case with vernacular histories, the Oxford copy was acquired in the nineteenth century. The Cambridge copy belonged to John Colbatch, probably the first man in either university to be able to read Portuguese easily. He presented a number of books (seven in all) in the language to his college, Trinity.

Inocêncio, I, pp. 237–8.

702 Historia da India no tempo em que a gouernou o visorey dom Luis d'Ataide, Coimbra, Nicolau Carvalho, 1617. Fol.

BOD Vet. G2 d. 27 The old shelf-mark, 24614 d. 7, indicates that the book was acquired after 1864.

TRC X.13.19 Belonged to John Colbatch, Anglican chaplain in Portugal, 1693–1700, who died in 1748.

Pereira, Galeote (–after 1557)

A nobleman who went out to India in 1534 and was captured by the Chinese in 1549. He was released by 1553. The MS. of his account of his experiences was sent from Goa to Rome in 1561, and included in **481–2**. There is also a translation into English.

C. R. Boxer, *South China in the Sixteenth Century*, pp. l–lv.

Alcune cose del paese della China, in Nuovi Auisi delle Indie di Portogallo (481–2) and, *translated by Richard Willes,* in 902, Richard Willes, The History of Travayle, fols 237–51, 446, Richard Hakluyt, The Principal Navigations, vol. II, Part 2, second numeration, pp. 68–, and 737, Samuel Purchas, Purchas his Pilgrimes, Part III, pp. 199–209.

Pimenta, Nicolau (1546–1614) (Niccolò Pimenta)

Jesuit who, after a career at Coimbra, was appointed visitor of the Indian provinces. He died in Goa. After translation, because Latin is unlikely to have been the original language, his dispatches were circulated in Europe as quickly as possible. On the title-page of 704 the printer of the Mainz edition states that the book had already appeared in Rome 'eodem anno [in the same year]'. Oxford readers quickly had access to 703–4 and 706, since the book in which they are all bound is listed in the 1605 catalogue. There are early copies in Cambridge also. There is no statement of nationality on the title-page, an omission which is normal in the writings of Jesuit missionaries.

Grande Enciclopédia Portuguesa e Brasileira, XXI, 659–60.

703 De felici statu et progresso rei Christianiae in India orientali epistola, Recusa (*sic*) Constantiae, apud Nicolaum Kalt, 1603. 8°

BOD 8° P 52(3) Art. In the library since 1605 and bound with 704 and 706.
CUL I*.14.16 (F) Acquired before 1715.

704 Exemplum epistolae . . . de statu rei Christianiae in India orientali, Moguntiae, apud Ioannem Albinum, 1602. 8°

BOD (2 copies) 8° P 52(2) Art. In the library since 1605 and bound with 703 and 706; Wood 835(2) Bequeathed by Anthony Wood, antiquarian, in 1695 (Kiessling (2002) 5256).

705 Lettera . . . al . . . P. Claudio Aquaviva . . .: da Goa, li 25 di Decembre, 1598, Venetia, appresso Giovanni Battista Ciotti, 1602. 8°

CUL O.12.45 Pencil underlining.

706 Nova relatio historica de rebus in India orientali a patribus societatis Iesu . . . gestis, Moguntiae, Ioannis Albini, 1601. 8°

BOD 8° P 52(1) Art. In the 1605 catalogue with shelf-mark 8° P.51. Bound with 703–4 WAD b13.23.
CUL N*.6.35 (F) Acquired before 1715 STCC L.6.126.1 Given by Thomas Neale, who matriculated in 1584.

Pinel, Duarte (16th cent.) (Eduardus Pinellus)

Pinel has often been identified with the person of the same name who worked on Abraão Usque's famous Spanish translation of the Bible (874–5), published in Ferrara in 1553, and even with Usque himself. In the Bible and the grammar the author (if it is the same author) identifies himself as Portuguese. Only four copies of Pinel's Latin grammar (707) are known besides those in Oxford and in Cambridge.

Samuel Usque, *Consolação às Tribulações de Israel*, I, p. 86; António Manuel Lopes Andrade, 'Os senhores do desterro de Portugal . . .', pp. 100–06.

707 Latinae grammatices compendia, *with* Tractatus de calendis, Vlissipone, apud Ludouicum Rhotorigium, 1543. 4°

BOD 4° D 39 Art. Lacks the calendar.

CUL M*.10.35 (D) In the library before 1715. Bound with William Lily's grammar of 1532 (Adams P1248; Anselmo 1041).

Pinheiro, António (?–1581) (Antonius Pinus)

Pinheiro was one of the 'bolseiros de el-rei', young men who were sent by King João III to study in the Collège de Ste. Barbe in Paris under Diogo de Gouveia. Pinheiro was in France from 1533–1541 (Matos, pp. 53, 72) and there wrote and published his commentary on Book III of Quintilian's *Institutio oratoria* (eleven copies divided between the Universities). The commentary, of thirty-four folios printed in double columns, is dedicated to Gouveia. None of his other works reached England. On his return to Portugal he became tutor to the royal princes and subsequently Bishop of Miranda and Leiria. On the title-page he describes himself as 'Portodemae[us]', i.e., from Porto de Mós, a small town near Leiria.

Luís de Matos, *Les Portugais à l'université de Paris*; *Grande Enciclopédia Portuguesa e Brasileira*, XXI, pp. 740–1.

707.01 In tertium M. Fabii Quintiliani librum luculentissimi commentarii, Parisiis, ex officina Michaelis Vascosani, 1538. Fol.

CUL O*.2.21 (B) In the library before 1715.

707.02 Comme[n]tarius Antonii Pini Portodemaei in tertium [librum M. Fabii Quintiliani . . . De institutione oratoria], Parisiis, ex officina Michaelis Vascosani [in some copies apud Audoenum Parvum], 1542. Fol.

BLL 0640 b 01 Imperfect copy, lacking Pinheiro's commentary CHC AB.2.18 18th-century binding JSO L.8.8 (apud Audoenum Parvum). Oxford 17th-century calf binding with fillets.
CUL W.2.33 From the Royal Library, deposited in 1715 FITZ Presented in 1912. Binding with arms of Louis XIV and XV of France TRC Z.5.19 (Adams Q36).

707.03 Comme[n]tarius Antonii Pini Portodemaei in tertium [librum M. Fabii Quintiliani . . . De institutione oratoria], Parisiis, apud Audoenum Parvum [in some copies apud Vascosanum], 1549. Fol.

ASC b.3.1 Calf binding of the 16th–17th century CHC AC.3.4 Given by Henry Aldritch (1647–1710) MER 24.G.21 Bequeathed by Nicholas Marsh, 1612.
CUL (2 copies) W.1.16 From the Royal Library, deposited in 1715; Rel.a.54.3 (Adams Q39).

Pinheiro, Luís (1560–1620) (Pigneyra)

A Jesuit, but not a missionary. He was sent to Madrid to persuade the government there that Jesuits should be the only religious allowed to visit Japan. As part of his propaganda campaign he composed 708. There is no statement of nationality on the title-page, as there seldom is in writings about the Japanese mission. In the French version (709) he is repeatedly referred to as Pigneyra, but it is a translation, not a different work. Most copies of Pinheiro's work are recent acquisitions, as is normal with history in vernacular languages.

Francisco Rodrigues, *História da Companhia de Jesus na Assistência de Portugal*, III.2, pp. 137–8.

708 Relacion del sucesso que tuvo nuestra Santa Fe en los reynos del Iapon, Madrid, Viuda de Alonso Martin de Balboa, 1617. Fol.
    CHC Arch. Inf. B.3.10(2) With a 17th-century binding QUO 17.g.16 Part of the Mason bequest, 1841.
    CUL Hisp.4.61.8 Probably a recent acquisition.

709 [Relacion del sucesso . . .] La nouvelle histoire du Iapon, *translated from Spanish by* I.B., Paris, chez Adrian Taupinart, 1618.
    CUL Hhh.713 probably a 19th-century acquisition. Repaired binding.

Pinhel, Aires (16th cent) (Arius Pinellus)

A jurist, much of whose professional life was spent in Salamanca, where he died. According to Barbosa Machado, both his legal works were first issued in Coimbra in the 1550s (in Oxford and Cambridge there are copies of only one of them, 712). By moving to Salamanca in 1559 Pinhel got onto the international circuit, because his books were reprinted there and in other European cities. He is invariably described as 'Lusitanus' on title-pages. At least eleven of the fifteen copies of his books in Oxford and Cambridge libraries have been there since early times.

Barbosa Machado, I, pp. 79–80.

710 Omnia quae quidem hactenus extant opera, Lugduni, sumptibus Philippi Tinghi Florentini, 1576. Fol.
    BOD B 4.14 Jur. Mascarenhas. In the 1605 catalogue. Part of the Mascarenhas collection, deposited in 1596. Chain marks and tooled binding.

711 Opera omnia, Antverpiae, apud Ioannem Keerbergium, *with notes by Manuel Soares de Ribeira,* 1618. 2 vols in 1, Fol.
    ASC ee.4.3.

712 Ad constitutiones C. de bonis mater. amplissimi commentarii, Conimbrigae, [António de Mariz?], 1557. Fol.
    MER 70.C.7(3) Chain mark. Title on the fore-edge. MS. contents list.
    CUL S*.3.12 (C) Acquired before 1715. SJCC K.7.22 In the catalogue compiled c. 1640

and with much annotation. One previous Portuguese owner in 1564, but probably from the Crashawe collection, deposited in 1626 (Adams P1249; Anselmo 824).

713 Ad constitutiones Codice de bonis maternis, doctissimi amplissimique commentarii, Salmanticae, excudebat Ioannes Baptista a Terranoua, expensis Ioannis Moreni bibliopolae, 1568. Fol.

ASC z.8.9(1) Bound with **717 SJCO** (2 copies) X.4.15(2) Given by Sir William Paddy, 1633; X.4.38(2) Bought in 1600 with money given by Robert Dow, merchant taylor, for the purchase of 'books in the canon & cyvil laws' (Fidalgo 680).

714 Ad constitutiones C. de bonis mater. amplissimi commentarij, Salmanticae, excudebat Mathias Gastius, 1573. Fol.

MER 46.C.5(2) Oxford binding using rolls xii and xviii, which were used together 1575–1605, Pearson, p. 67. Chain mark. Bound with **718** (Fidalgo 829).

715 Ad constitutiones Cod. de bonis maternis . . . commentarii, Francofurti, per Nicolaeum Bassanum et Ioannem Bellerum,1573. 8°

MER 75.A.13 MS. notes. In Wijffels List C as having entered the library around 1600.

716 Ad constitutiones Cod. de bonis maternis, commentarii, Francofurti, ex officina typographica Nicolaei Bassani, 1596. 8°

TRH M.4.25 Numbered 45 and 130 on the fore-edge. Probably one of the legal books left by Thomas Eden, Master from 1626–45 (Adams P1250).

717 Ad rubric. et leg. secundam Codice de rescindenda venditione, commentarii, Salamanticae, excudebat Ioannes Baptista a Terranoua, expensis Ioannis Moreni bibliopolae, 1568. Fol.

ASC z.8.9(2) Bound with **713**.

718 Ad rub. et l. secun. C. De rescind. vend. commentarii, Salmanticae, excudebat Mathias Gastius, 1573 [in colophon, 1572]. Fol.

MER 46.C.5(3) Chain mark, Oxford binding using rolls xii and xviii, which were used together 1575–1605 (Pearson, p. 67). From the Wijffels List C as having entered the library around 1600. Bound with **714** (Fidalgo 830).

719 Ad Rub. et L. II. C. De rescindenda venditione elaboratiss. & absolutissimi commentarij, *with notes by Manuel Soares de Ribeira*, Coloniae Agrippinae, apud Theodorum Baumium, 1573. 8°

JSO G.3.13.Gall.

TRH D*.3.34 Probably one of the legal books left by Thomas Eden, Master from 1626–45 (Adams P1251).

Pinto, Fernão Mendes (?1510–1583)

Perhaps the most famous of all Portuguese travel writers, whose highly imaginative, but not wholly untruthful account of his wanderings in Asia in the 1540s and 1550s was first published after his death. An English translation of some chapters referring to China appears in Samuel Purchas, Purchas his Pilgrimes (*737*), vol. III, pp. 251–81. In the seventeenth century Pinto was widely read internationally, and there are copies in Oxford libraries of Henry Cogan's complete English translation, in the editions of 1653 and 1663. These, however, fall outside the scope of the present survey. John Colbatch of Trinity Cambridge, probably the first man in either university to be able to read Portuguese fluently, had a copy of the first edition (**720**), but the other copies of that edition, and of the early Spanish and French translations (**721–2**) did not reach Oxford before the nineteenth century.

Fernão Mendes Pinto, *Peregrinação*, tr. by Rebecca Catz.

720 Peregrinaçam, Lisboa, Pedro Crasbeeck, 1614. 8°

BOD Vet. G2 d.19 The shelf-mark indicates that it was acquired after 1937 **RSL** RR. x. 25 Acquired after 1835, because not in the printed catalogue of that year.

TRC U.9.109 The book belonged to John Colbatch, Anglican chaplain in Portugal from 1693–1700, who died in 1748.

721 [Peregrinaçam] Historia oriental de las peregrinaciones de Fernan Mendez Pinto, *tr. by* Francisco de Herrera Maldonado, Madrid, por Tomas Iunti, 1620. Fol.

ASC h.14.1 **CHC** Arch. Inf. B.3.10(1) In 1651 it was in the possession of a Spanish speaker, possibly in the United Provinces. This fact, and the marginal notes in French, suggest that it was not acquired early.

722 [Peregrinaçam] Les voyages advantureux de Fernand Mendez Pinto, *tr. by* Bernard Figuier Gentil-homme Portugais, Paris, chez Mathurin Henault, 1628. 4°

BOD Douce P subt. 85 From the Douce bequest of 1834.

Pinto, Heitor (1524/25–1584)(Hector Pintus)

Pinto, a Hieronymite friar, took his commentary on Isaiah (**730**) with him to Rome when he went there in 1559 on his order's affairs. Armed with licences issued both by the Jesuits and by the Dominicans he had the book printed in Lyon, and his books continued to be published there in his lifetime and afterwards. Pinto was the author of an extremely popular vernacular work, the *Imagem da vida cristã,* which was translated into Latin via French (**724–6**). The *Imagem* is therefore one of the very few works of Portuguese literature which was studied, in Latin translation, in early modern Oxford, and there are marginalia in copies of **725–6**. There was also a translation into Spanish, of which there are single copies in Wadham and Emmanuel. There are twelve copies of various editions of Pinto's collected works in Oxford and Cambridge libraries, all with old provenance, which is an indication of considerable prestige, for these are bulky volumes. All Pinto's books, including the Spanish translation, state clearly his nationality on the title-page.

Anne-Marie Quint, 'À propos de la traduction française de l'*Imagem da Vida Cristã*'.

723 Opera omnia Latina, quae ad hunc vsque diem in lucem peruenerunt, tomus primus [-tertius], Lugduni, apud Bartholomaeum Honoratum, 1584. Fol.

ASC SR. 80.g.8 Oxford binding, Ker no. 1209, roll xxii, in use between 1580 and 1620 (Pearson, p. 71). Bought around 1600 and listed in the catalogue of 1665–89 **BLL** 0565 h 08 With legible MS. Latin notes to the commentaries on Isaiah and Ezequiel. In the 1721 catalogue **MGO** b.5.10 Oxford binding, Ker centrepiece i, in use 1565–1620. The book was bought by the college in 1591, Macray, *Register* III p. 28 **TRO** CUL.H.3.1 Bequeathed by William Fleetwood in 1595, perhaps the lawyer and antiquary (1525–94), who left a number of other books to the college (see Ker, *Pastedowns,* nos. 949–51) **WAD** J 7.22 Given by Philip Bisse, 1613.

EMM 302.2.39, formerly G.2.11, G.2.16. Bequeathed by John Breton, Master, in 1675. The book previously belonged to a Franciscan convent. In the 18th-century catalogue (Adams P1262, Faria (1987), 89).

724 Operum omnium Latinorum, quae ad hunc vsque diem in lucem peruenerunt, *vol. 1,* Lugduni, apud Ioannem Veyratum, 1590, *vol. 2,* Lugduni, apud haeredes Bartholomaei Honorati, 1589, *vol. 3,* apud Ioannem Veyratum, 1590, *vol. 4 with Latin version of Imagem da vida cristã,* apud haeredes Bartholomaei Honorati, 1590. Fol.

BOD O 1.5 Th. In the 1605 catalogue. Oxford binding (Ker centrepiece ii, in use 1580–97. See Pearson, p. 75). Chain mark **SJCO** G.1.26 Acquired in 1613 with money left by Henry Price (1562–1600), fellow.

SJCC Pp.6.2 Bequeathed by Arthur Johnson, fellow, in 1611 (Adams P1264, Faria (1987), 93).

725 Operum omnium quae ad hunc vsque diem in lucem peruenerunt, *vol. 1,* Lugduni, apud Ioannem Veyrat, 1601, *vol. 2,* apud haeredes Bartholomaei Honorati, 1589, *vol. 3,* apud Ioannem Veyratum, 1590, *vol. 4, with Latin version of Imagem da vida cristã,* apud haeredes Barthomaei Honorati, 1589. Fol.

CHC Hyp.K.59 (1–4) 4 vols in one. Marks of chaining. Bought with money given by Otho Nicolson, 1613. Nicolson was a benefactor with no obvious connection to the college (Hiscock, pp. 6–7). In the catalogue of 1665.

TRC D.18.23 4 vols in 1. With gilt crest stamped S E, probably Sylvius Elwes, chaplain, who gave books, mostly of divinity, 1626–30. The provenance is made more likely by the fact that a book known to have belonged to Elwes, Bacon's *History of England* (shelved at VI.6.134), has the same crest and letters (Gaskell, p. 129 n.2). With some Latin annotation in the first of the dialogues of the *Imagem,* De vera philosophia (Adams P1263, Faria (1987), 91, 93, 96).

726 Operum omnium Latinorum, quae ad hunc usque diem in lucem pervenerunt tomus primus (-quartus) *with Latin version of Imagem da vida cristã,* Lutetiae Parisiorum, apud Michaelem Sonnium, 1617. Fol.

QUO 57.E.2 Given by James Davenant M.A. He became a fellow of Oriel in 1661 on the death of his brother George, who had migrated to Oriel from Queen's. Marginal notes to one of the dialogues of the *Imagem,* De mortis memoria.

CUL F*.1.21 (A) Acquired before 1715.

727 [Diálogos da imagem cristã] Dialogos de la imagen de la vida christiana. Segunda parte, *tr. from Portuguese by* Gonçalo de Illescas, Salamanca, por Diego Cusio, 1594. 8°

EMM S15.3.63 With the Sancroft-Emmanuel bookplate recording the bequest of 1593 (Adams P1265; Fidalgo 1388).

728 [Diálogos da imagem cristã] Segvnda parte de los dialogos de la imagen de la vida christiana, *tr. from Portuguese by* Gonçalo de Illescas, Alcala de Henares, en casa de Iuan Iñiguez de Lequerica, 1580. 8°

WAD g 18.5 Given by Charles Godolphin in 1720. Part of the collection of Sir William Godolphin (?1634–96) (Abad 897).

729 In Danielem, Lamentationes Hieremiae et Nahum . . . commentarii, Coloniae, in officina Birckmannica, 1582. 8°

NEW BT3.88.8 Given by Robert Russell. In the catalogue of 1686.

730 In Esaiam prophetam commentaria, Lugduni, apud Theobaldum Paganum, 1561. Fol.

EXE 9F 1562(2) With the title on the fore-edge. Given by Sir William Petre, Rector, in 1567.

CUL F*.4.36 (C) Acquired before 1715. Legible annotation. Bound with **64** and **65**

PET I.13.16 Bequeathed by Andrew Perne, Master, in 1589 (Adams P1267).

731 In Ezechielem prophetam commentaria, Salmanticae, apud Ioannem a Canova, 1568. Fol.

CUL F*.4.41 (C) Acquired before 1715. Formerly owned by a Dr Torres (Adams B1598, Fidalgo 682).

732 In Ezechielem prophetam commentaria, Antuerpiae, in aedibus viduae et haeredum Ioannis Stelsii, 1570. 4°

CUL Ggg.130 Acquired in 1922 **MGC** F.3.20 German? binding with clasps (Adams B1599).

733 In Ezechielem prophetam commentaria, Antuerpiae, in aedibus Petri Belleri, 1582. 4°

SJCC Qq.9.14 Bequeathed by Peter Gunning, Master, in 1684.

734 Polyantheum opus auctoritatibus scripturarum. Cum distichis interpositis compositum: centum et eo amplius sermones continens, *no place, date or publisher. Perhaps Coimbra, 1536. 4°*

BOD Vet. G1 e. 27 (3) Acquired in 1882. Marginal notes (Anselmo 610, who believes the printer to have been Germão Galharde).

Portel, Lourenço de (1541–1641)

A Franciscan and provincial of Portugal, as the title-pages of both his books proclaim. In **735** he discusses canon law as it relates to mendicant friars. He thus explicitly deals, in a shortened form, with the topics treated by another Franciscan, Manuel Rodrigues, in his *Noua collectio* of 1609 (**774**) which was also published by Cardon (see the preface to the reader).

The success of the first edition (Lisbon, 1618, not in Oxford or Cambridge) led Portel to try his luck abroad, following what was by then a well-trodden path. However, the English universities preferred Rodrigues's original text, not this abridgement, and there are only two copies, both in the Bodleian. An early reader of **736** had it bound with a work by another Portuguese religious, the Benedictine Francisco Sanches (**818**).

Barbosa Machado, III, pp. 36–7.

735 Dubia regularia, siue accurata breuisque discussio difficultatum circa religiosam personam atque familiam, Lugduni, sumptibus Laurentii Durand, 1630. 8°

BOD 8° P 27 Jur. In the 1635 appendix to the 1620 catalogue, with the shelf-mark unchanged.

736 Sermones et exhortationes monasticae, *with* vnus tractatus de scrupulis, & alius de impensis factis in templo Salomonis, Vlyssipone, Petrus Crasbeeck, 1617. 4°

BOD BB 12(2) Th. In the 1674 catalogue. Bound with **818**.

Prayer books. See Liturgies.

Purchas, Samuel (bap. 1577–1626)
This compiler of geographical literature, the successor of Hakluyt, was a student of St John's, Cambridge. Like Hakluyt, he travelled very little. There is at least one copy of **737** in nearly every Oxford and Cambridge library. For information about the Portuguese works included in *Purchas his Pilgrimes* see **29, 259, 461, 720, 741** and the entries in the catalogue for Bermudes, Cardim, João de Castro, Galeote Pereira, Queirós and Santos. There is additional discussion in Chapter One, p. xli–iii.

Oxford Dictionary of National Biography; P. A. Neville-Sington, 'The primary bibliography', in *The Purchas Handbook.*

737 Purchas his pilgrimes, London, William Stansby for Henrie Fetherstone, 1625.

BOD (4 copies) K 5.5–6 Art. In the 1635 appendix to the catalogue of 1620;. I 1.3–4 Art. Seld. Part of John Selden's collection, deposited in 1659; Lister E 53–56 Given by Martin Lister (1638?–1712), physician and zoologist; Locke 14.23a-d Formerly owned by John Locke, the philosopher (1632–1704) (STC 20509) **ASC** h.4.8–11 Acquired by the 18th century **BLL** 575 e 1–5 Bequeathed by George Coningesby in 1768 **CHC** Part of the Wake collection, given in 1737 **CCCO** W.g.2.9 **EXE** 9M20509 Given by Edward Glascock, who was in Oxford by 1597 **HER** OH J.46 From Magdalen Hall (extinguished 1874–75) **LIN** K.2.13–18 Acquired by 1703 **MGO** K.18.6–10 Given by John Warner (1581–1666), fellow and major benefactor of the library **HMAN** F1625/3(1) With the signature of Richard Sterne, 1686 **MER** 16.H.15–18 Given by Griffin Higgs (1589–1659) fellow **NEW** BT3.254.7–10 Given by Edward Marowe, Fellow, in 1643. In the catalogue of 1686 **QUO** Sel.c.179–82 Acquired by 1663 **SJCO** Vòls I-III given by Richard Paige, 1654.

He matriculated in 1651; vol. IV acquired in 1656 **TRO** B.14.1–5 Acquired in the 18th century **WAD** K.16.20–3 (5 vols in 4) Given by Mary Dymocke, perhaps in the 18th century **WOR** R.1.12.

CUL (3 copies) Syn.3.62.6-; Young.206- Acquired in 1933; RCS.Case.a.41–4 (STC 20509) **CHR** (2 copies) K.14.19–23 Given by Henry Featherstone, the publisher and a London bookseller, who died in 1647; Rouse 15.10–12 (vols 1,2,4) presented in 1940 by William Rouse, a former fellow **EMM** 307.3.21(-24) Given by Henry Featherstone **FITZ** Presented to the Museum collection in 1809 **G&C KCC** (2 copies) G.28.1–4 Given by Thomas Goad, fellow (1576–1638); M.5.39–42 **MGC** (2 copies) PL 2511; 2512–5 Both copies are from the collection of Samuel Pepys (1633–1703), the diarist, deposited in 1724 **QUC** N.1.29 **SJCC** H.6.24–28 Given by the author, with the encouragement of John Williams, Bishop of Lincoln **SID** Given by John Dixon in 1636, perhaps the John Dixon who took his M.A. in 1609 and died in 1652 **STCC** F.2.39 Presented by Thomas Sherlock in 1761 **TRI** (2 copies) VI.4.30- Given by Isaac Browne, a friend of Dr Johnson (1705–60); Grylls 10.223- Bequeathed by William Grylls in 1863.

Queirós, Pedro Fernandes de (1560–1616) (Ferdinand de Quir)

A navigator who, under the Spanish crown, made a number of voyages between Peru and the islands now known as the New Hebrides, which led him to believe in the existence of a great southern continent. He is one of the very few practical men whose writings appear in the short-title catalogue. His brief memorandum about his achievements and hopes for the future, originally written in Spanish, arrived in Oxford and Cambridge in the early modern period in Latin and English versions. They do not state his nationality, and his English translator believed him to have been a Spaniard (see **740**).

Albino Lapa, *Pedro Fernandes de Queirós: o último navegador português*; *The Voyages of Pedro Fernandez de Quiros, 1595–1606*, 2 vols, tr. by Sir Clements Markham.

738 Discursus ad serenissimum Hispaniae regem, super detecta nuper quinta orbis parte, terra nempe Australi incognita, *in* Gotthard Arthus, Indiae orientalis pars X, Francofurti, in typis viduae Matthiae Beckeri, 1613. Fol. (pp. 13–19).

HER oh.j.50 (10).

CUL (2 copies) F159.a.1.25 Formerly Sel.2.61, L.7.33, Ll.11.21, L.9.17, O.13.3 Binding with armorial stamp Honi Soit Qui Mal Y Pense and Sibi ipsi probitas securitas. Some of the older shelf-marks are typical of those of the Royal Library deposited in 1715, but the book is not listed in the catalogue; F159.a.1.34 Acquired c. 1950.

739 Narratio . . . super tractu, in quinta orbis terrarum parte, cui Australiae incognitae nomen est, Amstelodami, ex officina Hesselii Gerardi, 1612. 4°

BOD Arch. G e. 41 Formerly Art 4° C 106 and in the 1674 catalogue with the old shelf-mark. Oxford binding, Ker no. 1536, with centrepiece vi, in use 1605–20 (Pearson, p. 77). Bound with other items, the latest dated 1613, some with Burton's signature (Kiessling (1988) 848) **JSO** P.1.4(1).

740 [Narratio], Terra Australis incognita, or A new southerne discoverie containing a fifth part of the world, *tr. by W. B.*, London, for John Hodgetts, 1617. 4°
BOD 4° L 78(6) Art. QUO Sel.c.91 (6) 17th-century binding. Chain mark (both listed in STC 10822).
CUL Dd*.3.39 (E) From the Royal Library, deposited in 1715 MGC PL 1431(20) From the collection of Samuel Pepys, the diarist (1633–1703), deposited in 1724 (both listed in STC 10822).

741 Relatio memorialis . . . super detectione quartae orbis terrarum parte, cui nomen Australis incognita, Coloniae Allobrogum, apud Petrum de la Rouiere, 1612. 8°
CHC a.3.311, formerly O.2.5.15. Perhaps from the Orrery bequest of 1732.
See also Samuel Purchas, Purchase his Pilgrimes (**737**), pp. 1422–32.

Ramires, Jerónimo Nunes (16th–17th cents) (Hieronymus Nunius Ramirez)
A doctor who, rather unusually, practised and published in Portugal. He came from Lisbon, as the title-page of **742** states. He dedicated it to Pedro Castilho, viceroy of Portugal and grand inquisitor. This was no doubt a form of self protection, for Ramires had links to many of the New Christians whose careers are described in these notes. One of his teachers in Coimbra was Tomás Rodrigues da Veiga; Ramires's wife and Montalto's wife were sisters; and Estêvão Rodrigues de Castro provided liminary poems to **742**.
Barbosa Machado, II, pp. 509–10; Friedenwald, II, p. 469.

742 Commentaria in librum Galeni de ratione curandi per sanguinis missionem, *with* Tractatus de ponderibus et mensuris, Olisipone, ex officina Petri Crasbeeck, 1608. 4°
BOD 4° R 6 Med. In the 1620 catalogue with the shelf-mark unchanged. The item is bound with medical works printed in Basle in 1609.

Ramusio, Giovanni Baptista (1485–1557)
Italian geographer and publicist whose collections of travel literature include Portuguese material. There are twenty-three copies of his work in the libraries, of which only ten can be said with certainty to be of old provenance. For the items translated see the entries for Francisco Álvares, Duarte Barbosa, João de Barros. There is further discussion in Chapter One, p. xliv.

743 Itinerario di varii rinomati viaggiatori nelle parti dell'Africa, Asia, ed America, Venetia, [in colophon, heredi di Luc'Antonio Giunti], 1550. Fol.
BOD Mason GG 180 Fom the Mason bequest of 1841. The title page is missing.

744 Delle navigationi et viaggi in molti luoghi, 2a ed., Venetia, nella stamperia de Giunti, 1554. Fol.

BOD (2 copies) Mason GG 179 From the Mason bequest of 1841; Vet. F1 c.15 The shelf-mark indicates that it was acquired after 1937 **HER** oh.j.01 **QUO** Sel.c.165 (1).

TRC Grylls 31.137–9 Bequeathed by William Grylls in 1863 (Adams R135).

745 Primo volume . . . delle navigationi et viaggi, 3a ed., Venetia, nella stamperia de' Giunti, 1563. Fol.

BOD (2 copies) HH 86 Art. In the catalogue of 1605; Savile O10 From the bequest of Sir Henry Savile (1549–1622), mathematician and founder of chairs in geometry and astronomy **BLL** 0580 e 01 Vol. 1 Acquired in 1677 from the bequest of Sir Thomas Wendy or Wendie, a former fellow, who died in 1673 **MGO** Q.11.14 Bequeathed by Arthur Throckmorton, who gave many foreign books to the library, in 1626 **TAY** 102.I.2 t.1 Acquired in 1876.

CUL Hanson.b.50 Stamped Cruising Library Association and acquired perhaps in 1961 **MGC** PL 2231 From the collection of Samuel Pepys, the diarist (1633–1703), deposited in 1724 **PMC** LC.2.249 With the college bookplate of 1700 and a note on the flyleaf stating that the marginal annotations are in the handwriting of the poet Thomas Gray (1716–1771), mostly to vols 2–3 which do not contain Portuguese material **ZOO** **(Balfour and Newton Library)** 5 folio 51–53.

746 Primo volume . . . delle navigationi et viaggi, 4a ed., Venetia, nella stamperia de' Giunti, 1588. Fol.

BOD L 1.2 Art. In the 1605 catalogue **BLL** 0580 e 02 Acquired in 1677 from the bequest of Sir Thomas Wendy or Wendie, a former fellow, who died in 1673.

747 Delle nauigationi et viaggi, Venetia, appresso I Giunti, 1606. Fol.

ASC h.5.5 **CHC** Arch. Inf. B.3.4 With the 18th-century college bookplate.

CUL T*.1.27 (c) Acquired before 1715.

748 Primo volume delle navigationi et viaggi, Venetia, appresso i Giunti, 1613. Fol.

BOD Mason GG 176 From the Mason bequest of 1841 **CHC** Arch. Inf. B.3.4.

CUL RCS.Case.a.97 Acquired by the Royal Colonial Institute, London, in 1908.

Rebelo, Fernão (1545–1608) (Fernandus Rebellus/Rebello)

A Jesuit, of a generation that did not need to travel abroad to publish books in Latin with Cardon in Lyon. All five copies of his Latin treatise are of old provenance. The title-page states that he was Portuguese.

Francisco Rodrigues, *História da Companhia de Jesus na Assistência de Portugal*, II.2, p. 131.

749 Opus de obligationibus iustitiae, religionis et caritatis, Lugduni, sumptibus Horatii Cardon, 1608. Fol.

BOD M 1.17 Jur. Seld. From the Selden bequest of 1659, but in the 1620 catalogue, so a replacement copy **SJCO** H.subt.1, given by Ralph or Rudolph Hamor or Hamore, a London merchant, in 1608. Chain mark.

CUL Cc7.22 With the bookplate of John Colbatch, Anglican chaplain in Portugal from 1693–1700, who died in 1748 **SJCC** O.7.14 From the Crashawe collection, deposited in 1626.

750 Opus de obligationibus iustitiae, religionis et caritatis, Venetiis, apud Ioannem Antonium et Iacobum de Franciscis, 1610. Fol.
CUL I*.3.4 (B) Acquired before 1715.

751 Relação das exequias del Rey Dom Filippe, Lisboa, Pedro Crasbeeck, 1600. 8°
TRC W.12.56 [1] Probably acquired after 1800.

Resende, André de (?1500–73) (Andreas Resendius)
A humanist, who studied in Paris and afterwards in Louvain (1529–32) where he came to know members of Erasmus's circle. He never met Erasmus himself, but was one of the few Portuguese writers to make a public statement of his admiration for him. The early modern universities knew Resende's work principally through the compilations published in Germany after his death (**752, 756–7**). Of the twenty-eight copies of books by Resende in Oxford and Cambridge (including in the count the reprint of **753** by Schottus) fifteen are certainly of old provenance, but Resende, like the other humanists and, indeed, Schottus himself, has interested modern collectors also and nine of his books can be shown to have been acquired after 1800.

The publisher, Arnoldus Mylius, dedicated **752** to the wealthy New Christian merchant Simão Rodrigues. Simão, who lived in Antwerp, presumably financed the book, perhaps because his family, like Resende's, came from Évora. (For members of the family who were also authors see André Rodrigues de Évora – often confused with Resende – and the doctor Tomás Rodrigues da Veiga). Resende is normally described as 'Eborensis' on the title-pages of his books, which also make clear that their subject-matter is frequently the history and antiquities of Portugal.

Biblos: *Enciclopédia Verbo das Literaturas de Língua Portuguesa,* IV, cols 710–13 (article by Américo da Costa Ramalho); Odette Sauvage, *L'itinéraire érasmien de André de Resende*; J. Gentil da Silva, *Stratégie des affaires à Lisbonne entre 1595 et 1607,* pp. 3–5.

752 Antiquitatum Lusitaniae, et de municipio Eborensi lib. v. *With* Orationes . . . epistolae historicae & poemata omnia, Coloniae Agrippinae, in officina Birckmannica sumptibus Arnoldi Mylij, 1600. 2 vols in 1. 8°
BOD 8° R 1 Art. In the 1605 catalogue with the same shelf-mark CHC a.3.180 Given by F. Haverfield, 1906.
CUL L*.6.29 (F) Acquired before 1715 (Adams R364).

753 De antiquitatibus Lusitaniae libri quattuor, *completed and with a fifth book by Diogo Mendes de Vasconcelos,* Romae, apud Bernardum Basum, 1597. 8°
BOD Byw. S 2.22 Bequeathed in 1914 by Ingram Bywater.

CUL Mm.19.11 Formerly L.6.31, which is a shelf-mark typical of the Royal Library, deposited in 1715 (Adams R365).
There is another edition of this work published by Andreas Schottus (826).

754 Epitome rerum gestarum in India a Lusitanis anno superiori, Louanii, apud Seruatium Zassenum, 1531. 4°
BOD Vet. B1 e. 6 The shelf-mark indicates that it was acquired after 1937 CCCO LG.5.9 (6).

755 Libri quatuor de antiquitatibus Lusitaniae, Eborae, excudebat Martinus Burgensis, 1593. Fol.
ASC SR.89.d.4 Perhaps bought at the Stuart sale in 1821 (Anselmo 431).

756 Lusitaniae antiquitates, *in* Deliciae Lusitano-Hispanicae, Coloniae Agrippinae, apud Gerhardum Greuenbruch, 1613. 8°
BOD 8° L 61 Art. In the 1635 appendix to the 1620 catalogue, with the same shelf-mark CHC Wf.7.23(1) From the Wake bequest of 1737. Bound with **757**.
CUL (2 copies) L*.6.30 (F) Acquired before 1715. Bound with **757**; Acton d.38.534 Lord Acton's library was presented in 1902 CLA G.8.5 (1). With the college bookplate of 1701, and in the catalogue of 1677–78.

757 Poemata, epistolae historicae, orationes, Coloniae, apud Gerhardum Greuenbruch, 1613. 8°
BOD (2 copies) 8° G 77(2) Art. In the 1635 appendix to the 1620 catalogue with the same shelf-mark; Byw. S 2.23 Bequeathed in 1914 by Ingram Bywater ASC c.3.19 CHC Wf.7.23(2) From the Wake bequest of 1737. Bound with **756**.
CUL L*.6.30 (F) Acquired before 1715. Bound with **756**.

758 Vincentius leuita et martyr, Olisipone, apud Lodovicum Rhotorigium, 1545. 4°
BOD 4° R 11(1) Th. Seld. From the Selden bequest of 1659. In the 1674 catalogue. Bound with **153, 651** (Anselmo 1046).

Resende, Garcia de (?1470–1536)

A courtier, a cousin of André de Resende, and a multi-faceted writer in Portuguese. His life of King João II went through five editions between 1545 and 1622, of which Oxford has only the third (**759**) and Cambridge the fifth (**760**). It is one of the few books in Portuguese to have been in the Bodleian since before 1620. One of Bodley's letters to Dr Thomas James, the first librarian, could be read as meaning that Bodley thought that James could not understand the title-page.
Garcia de Resende, *Livro das obras de Garcia de Resende*, ed. Evelina Verdelho; *Letters of Sir Thomas Bodley to Thomas James,* pp. 127–8.

759 Choronica que tracta . . . do christianissimo dom Ioão ho segundo deste nome, Lisboa, Simão Lopez, 1596. Fol.
BOD DD 64(2) Art. With an earlier shelf-mark Art G.4.13. In the 1620 catalogue, with shelf-mark G.4.3. Chain mark (Anselmo 816).

760 Chronica dos valerosos e insignes feitos del rey Dom Ioão II . . . com outras obras . . . e vay acrescentada a sua Miscellania, Lisboa, por Antonio Alvarez, 1622. 4°
CUL F162.b.12.2 Acquired in 1971.

Ribeira, Manuel Soares da (16th cent.)
A lawyer, who studied under Aires Pinhel in Salamanca, before embarking on a career which took him first to Lyon, which he had to leave because of the outbreak of religious strife there in 1562 (see the dedication to his brother Diogo da Ribeira in **764**), and then to Italy. There are four different editions of his compendium of legal opinions in Oxford libraries, three certainly of old provenance, but only one in Cambridge. The title-pages contain no statement of Ribeira's nationality, and that fact, together with his career in Venice and Padua, suggests that he may have been a New Christian. Barbosa Machado says that he professed 'o Estado Ecclesiastico', but there are no Christian references in the preliminaries to his book.
Barbosa Machado, III, p. 379.

761 Thesaurus receptarum sententiarum, Venetiis, apud Georgium de Caballis, 1568. 8°
ASC z.10.18.

762 Thesaurus receptarum sententiarum, Coloniae Agrippinae, apud Gualtherum Fabricium & Ioannem Gymnicum, 1569. 8°
JSO C.3.23 (2) Bequeathed by Principal Griffith Powell, 1561–1620. In the 1649 catalogue.
TRH B*.6.37 (Adams S1340).

763 Thesaurus receptarum sententiarum, Lugduni, apud heredes Iacobi Iunctae, 1571. Fol.
SJCO X.2.22 Entered the library in 1660. Chain marks. Ker roll ix, used 1600–17 (Pearson, p. 66).

764 Thesaurus receptarum sententiarum, Coloniae Agrippinae, apud Ioannem Gymnicum, 1593. 8°
BOD 8° S 39(2) Th. Seld. From the Selden bequest of 1659, but in the 1605 catalogue, so likely to be a replacement.

Rodrigues, João (1561/62–1633)
Jesuit, man of action, and the 'Father of Japanese Language Studies' (Boxer, p. 363), who first went to Asia when he was fifteen and never returned to Europe. His books about the Japanese language are pioneering works, and he was also largely responsible for the great dictionary (**269**). Like many Jesuits, he tended to work anonymously, and only **765** is signed, 'Ioão Rodriguez Portugues'. The Bodleian has a remarkable

collection of his books, all of them extremely rare, but none arrived there before the 1820s. He is often confused with another Jesuit writer, João Rodrigues Girão (see above).

C. R. Boxer, 'Padre João Rodriguez Tçuzu S.J. and his Japanese Grammars of 1604 and 1620'; Michael Cooper, *Rodrigues the Interpreter*.

765 Arte da lingoa de Iapam, Nangasaqui, no Collegio de Iapão da Companhia de Iesu, 1604 [in colophon, 1608]. 4°

BOD Arch. B d. 14 Purchased in 1827.

766 Vocabulario da lingoa de Iapom, *with* Supplemento deste vocabulario, Nangasaqui, no Collegio de Iapam da Companhia de Iesus, 1603 [supplemento 1604].

BOD Arch. B d. 13. Purchased in 1829.

767 [Vocabulario da lingoa de Iapom] Vocabulario de Iapon, *Spanish tr.*, Manila, Tomas Pinpin y Jacinto Magaurlua, 1630. 4°

BOD 4° L 67 Jur. Acquired in 1826.

For the trilingual dictionary (Japanese, Latin, Portuguese), anonymous but by Rodrigues, see **269**.

Rodrigues, Manuel (1545–1613) (Emanuel Rodericus)

There are not many Franciscan writers in the short-title catalogue; of them, Rodrigues and Felipe Diez are by far the most important. Like Diez, Rodrigues spent most of his career in Spain, and his books were first printed there (see the preliminary matter in **774** and **779**, in which the earliest licence is dated Salamanca, 1597–8). The *Nova collectio* and the *Quaestiones regulares* only reached Oxford and Cambridge in editions published later, by the indefatigable Cardon, of Lyon, but despite being two countries removed from home, Rodrigues is invariably described as 'Lusitanus' on title-pages. There is a Portuguese licence in **773** dated January 1593. Of the thirty-one copies of his books in Oxford and Cambridge all but three are of old provenance. Thomas Barlow studied **774** very closely, probably with the intention of extracting from this compilation of the privileges of monastic orders information damaging to the Catholic cause. For this, see also Chapter One, p. xxxii. Rodrigues's books about the resolution of cases of conscience were also widely acquired, especially in Oxford. His work was given extra publicity through abridgements: **768** is one, done by a group of French friars, and **735** is another, by Lourenço de Portel.

Barbosa Machado, III, pp. 354–5.

768 Compendium quaestionum regularium, Coloniae Agrippinae, apud Ioannem Kinchium, 1618. 4°

BOD 4° C 4 Th. Seld. From the Selden bequest of 1659.

769 Esplicatione della bolla de'morti, e di compositione, *tr from Spanish*, Palermo, per Decio Cirillo, 1621. 4°
TRC C.27.9 [2] With repaired binding. In the college's copy of the interleaved Bodleian catalogue used in the 18th century.

770 Explicacion de la bulla de la sancta cruzada *of Pope Gregory XIII, with* Dos tratados, Alcala, en casa de Iuan Iñiguez de Lequerica, 1590. 4°
BOD 4° R 17 Th. Seld. From the Selden bequest of 1659. With the signature of John Clerke who had it 'apud Calos' 1596 (Abad 1065).

771 Explicacion de la bulla de la sancta cruzada *of Pope Gregory XIII . . ., with* dos tratados, [Lisbon], Alexandre de Siqueyra, 1592. 8°
BOD Vet. G1 f. 12 Acquired 1919. In the 1605 catalogue (Anselmo 1060).

772 Explicacion de la bulla de la sancta cruzada *of Pope Gregory XIII . . ., with* dos tratados, Salamanca, en casa de Juan Fernandez, 1592. 8°
BOD 4° R 5 Th. (Fidalgo 1356).

773 Explicacion de la bulla de la sancta cruzada *of Pope Gregory XIII . . ., with* dos tratados, Salamanca, en casa de Juan Fernandez, 1594. 8°
BLA Binding with gilt blind-stamped ornaments. Number on fore-edge, but acquired by Blackfriars in the 20th century (Fidalgo 1390).

774 Noua collectio et compilatio priuilegiorum apostolicorum regularium mendicantium, et non mendicantium, Turnoni [in some copies Lugduni], sumptibus Horatii Cardon, 1609. Fol.
BOD (2 copies) N 1.13 Jur. Seld. From the Selden bequest of 1659. In the 1674 catalogue; A 21.3 Th. Chain mark CHC OH.2.15. Chain mark QUO 10.D.1 With the signature of Thomas Barlow, July 16th 1633, five pages of notes bound with the book and marginal notes.
JSC K.2.5(2) Bequeathed by Lionel Gatford, D.D. and a former student of the college, in 1715.

775 Noua collectio et compilatio priuilegiorum apostolicorum regularium mendicantium, et non mendicantium, Lugduni, sumptibus Horatij Cardon, 1613. Fol.
EMM 303.3.64 With an old shelf-mark, C.1.18, under which it is listed in the 18th century catalogue. No book printed before 1712 appears in this part of the catalogue, and it is reasonable to assume that the book entered the library before then. The binding has a medieval MS. pastedown and a gilt blind-stamped centrepiece binding of around 1600. There is a tab, typical of Cambridge libraries in the 17th century. There are indications in the volume that it once belonged to a Franciscan monastery.

776 Noua collectio et compilatio privilegiorum apostolicorum regularium mendicantium et non mendicantium, Antuerpiae, apud Petrum & Ioannem Belleros, 1616. Fol.
TRC N.q.5 In the college's copy of the interleaved Bodleian catalogue used in the 18th century.

777 Noua collectio et compilatio privilegiorum apostolicorum regularium mendicantium et non mendicantium, Antuerpiae, apud Petrum & Ioannem Belleros, 1623. Fol.

BOD R 7.10 Jur. In the 1635 appendix to the 1620 catalogue, with the same shelf-mark. Chain mark.

CUL K*.7.25 (A) Acquired before 1715. With an English printed document dated 1620 slipped in, suggesting that it may have arrived in England at that time.

778 Obras morales . . . Contienen la summa de casos de consciencia, y explicacion de la bulla de la cruzada, y addiciones, Madrid, por Luys Sanchez [vol. 2 Miguel Serrano de Vargas], 1601–02. Fol.

QUO 54.D.11 Part of the Mason bequest of 1841. The title page has the author's signature.

779 Quaestiones regulares, et canonicae, Turnoni, sumptibus Horatii Cardon, 1609. Fol.

BOD S 6.5 Jur. Formerly R.5.9 Jur. In the 1674 catalogue, chain mark.

780 Quaestiones regulares, et canonicae, Lugduni, sumptibus Horatii Cardon, 1613. Fol.

EMM 315.4.41 (3 vols in 1). Repaired binding, which may conceal evidence of provenance. Like a number of Emmanuel books, this came from a monastery (details hidden by bookplate). It is listed in the 18th-century catalogue.

781 Quaestiones regulares, et canonicae, Antuerpiae, apud Petrum & Ioannem Belleros, 1616. 3 vols in 2, Fol.

BOD N 1.14,15 Jur. Seld. From the Selden bequest of 1659. In the 1674 catalogue.

CUL Acton a.2.128 Lord Acton's library was presented in 1902 CHR F.2.16–17, formerly D.5.7 (so shelved close to **104**, which is another work of Portuguese theology). Given by Joseph Mede or Meade (1586–1638), fellow. Number on fore-edge.

782 Quaestionum regularium et canonicarum . . . tomi tres, Venice, apud Baretium Baretium, 1616. Fol.

CUL Acton a.2.126- Lord Acton's library was presented in 1902. SJCC K.7.7–8 Given by Thomas Morton in 1628, while he was bishop of Lichfield.

783 Quaestiones regulares, et canonicae, Antuerpiae, apud Petrum & Ioannem Belleros, 1628. Fol.

SJCO U.2.11(1) Bought with money left by William Thomas, 1639.

EMM S.14.1.1 Bequeathed by Archbishop William Sancroft in 1693.

784 Summa de casos de consciencia, Salamanca 1595, por Iuan Fernandez, 1595. 2 vols. 4°

BOD 4° R 19 Th. In the 1620 catalogue with the same shelf-mark (Fidalgo 1412).

785 Summa de casos de consciencia, Lisboa, por Antonio Aluarez, 1595. 2 vols. 4°

ASC s.4.3 The bibliographical information is from the title page of vol. 2. Bequeathed in 1643 by Dudley Digges, fellow, and in the catalogue of his books. Probably to be identified with Anselmo 42.

786 [Summa de casos de consciencia] Summa casuum conscientiae, *tr. from Spanish by* Balthazar de Canizal, Duaci, ex typographia Baltazaris Belleri, 1614. 4°
CHC Hyp.G.111, chain mark. In the 1665 catalogue.
EMM 333.4.52 Bequeathed by John Breton, Master, in 1675. The book belonged at one time to Fr John Geffry, perhaps of a convent in Cavan.

787 [Summa de casos de consciencia] Summa casuum conscientiae, *tr. from Spanish by* Balthasar de Canizal, Venetijs, apud Variscos, 1628. 4°
BOD II 33(1) Jur. In the 1635 appendix to the 1620 catalogue SJCO R.4.11 Bought with money left by William Thomas, 1639.
See also Fr. Bartolomeu dos Mártires.

Rodrigues, Pedro (1542–1628)

A Jesuit, most of whose career was spent in Brazil. His vernacular life of the famous Canarian Jesuit José de Anchieta (1534–85) remains in MS. The Latin version (**788**), a much revised and extended version of the original Portuguese text, was part of the evidence used in the failed process of canonization. Hagiographical writing of this kind was not likely to be of interest to Protestant Oxford and Cambridge, and there is only one copy, in All Souls.
José A. Sánches Marín and María Nieves Muñoz Martín, 'La estructura literaria de la biografía de Anchieta escrita por Sebastiano Berettari', pp. 721–4.

788 Iosephi Anchietae Societatis Iesu sacerdotis in Brasilia . . . vita, *edited by* Sebastiano Beretari, Lvgdvni, sumptibus Horatij Cardon, 1617. 8°
ASC SR.63.g.5.

Sá, Diogo (16th century)

A distinguished soldier in India who, on returning to Europe, spent some years in Paris, not as a student, but because it was a suitable place in which to pursue his intellectual interests and publish the results. In **789**, a treatise on navigation, Sá engages in controversy with Pedro Nunes. His nationality is stated on the title-page. Two years later Sá published another book in Paris, on primogeniture (**790**). This had considerable success in both universities because it was included in a multi-volume collection of legal treatises which was acquired by a number of libraries (see also Pedro de Santarém).
Luís de Matos, *Les Portugais à la université de Paris*, p. 103.

789 De nauigatione libri tres, Parisiis, ex officina Reginaldi Calderii, & Claudii eius filii, 1549. 8°
CHC O.N.6.12 With signature of W. Bradshaw, who matriculated in 1692, aged 19 and died in 1732 as dean of Christ Church.
CUL R*.5.27 (F) Acquired before 1715, and with the signature of John Worth (Joannes Decus), 1552. Notes in Latin and English TRC S.22.27 With 6 previous shelf-marks, but

with a 19th-century college bookplate and perhaps acquired in 1952. Parchment binding stamped Honi soit qui mal y pense (Adams S7).

790 De primogenitura tractatus, Parisiis, apud Martinum Iuuenem, 1551. 8°

CUL J.6.32 From the Royal Library, deposited in 1715 **EMM** S15.4.42(3) With the Sancroft-Emmanuel bookplate, forming part of the bequest of 1693. Bound with two works by the Scottish bishop John Leslie which are concerned with the Scottish succession under Queen Mary. Some underlining (Adams S8).

791 De primogenitura *in* Tractatus illustrium in utraque tum pontificii, tum caesarei iuris facultate iurisconsultorum, De feudis, . . . vol. X.i, Societas aquilae se renovantis, Venetiis, 1584. Fol. (fols 324v-336v).

CHC B.1.2.4 **MER** 64.A.13 **QUO** 35.C.13 **SJCO** U.1.13.

PET A.1.13 Given by Thomas Richardson, Master 1699–1733 **QUC** O.2.14 **TRH** N*.6.13 with the college bookplate of 1700 (Adams T892).

Sá, Manuel (1528–90/1530–96)

One of the most widely read Jesuit theologians in early modern Oxford and Cambridge. There are fifty-seven copies of books by him in the libraries, of which at least forty-eight are of old provenance. Six Oxford colleges and five Cambridge ones, as well as the Bodleian and the University Library, have copies of his aphorisms for confessors, and altogether fifteen colleges have his notes on the complete Bible (*Notationes*), or on the Gospels (*Scholia*), or both. The concision of his writing – the aphorisms in particular form a tiny book – must have made his work attractive to priests whatever their confessional inclination. Sá's book of aphorisms was heavily censored, and the Roman edition of 1608 (no copy in either university) produced many changes. The aphorisms remained, therefore, an authoritive statement of Catholic doctrine and were regarded as such by Thomas Barlow (see his notes in **793**, which he took care to check against **453**, the Lisbon *Index* of 1624).

Sá's very considerable international reputation must have owed much to the fact that nearly his whole career was spent abroad. He taught at Gandía and Alcalá and was close to the Spanish Jesuit general Francisco Borja (see his letter in **813**). He also taught in Rome, was visitor of the Jesuit colleges of Tuscany and the Marche and died in Arona (Piedmont). Early copies of his work have no statement of his nationality on the title-page, but editions of the *Aphorismi* after the Roman one of 1608 all refer to him as 'Lusitanus'.

Francisco Rodrigues, *História da Companhia de Jesus na assistência de Portugal*, I.1, pp. 453–5 and II.2, pp. 122–23.

792 Aphorismi confessariorum, Antuerpiae, ex officina Ioachimi Trognaesii, 1599. 12°

CCCO LD 1c.7 Bequeathed by John Rosewell, who had studied at Corpus from 1655–67, in 1684 **WAD** H 14.4 Given by Philip Bisse, 1613.
SJCC U.11.10 In the catalogue compiled c. 1640. Possibly from the Crashawe collection, which was deposited in 1626 (Adams S1).

793 Aphorismi confessariorum, Coloniae, sumptibus Petri Amorfortij [in colophon, typis Ioannis a Mertzenich], 1599. 12°
QUO UU.b.3125 Signed by Thomas Barlow, 1648. Legible MS. notes.
EMM 324.7.93. Bequeathed by John Breton, Master, in 1675. Pencil marks. Repaired binding (Adams S2).

794 Aphorismi confessariorum, Parisiis, apud Petrum Chevalier, 1600. 32°
BOD 8° S 135 Th. In the 1674 catalogue.
CUL H.16.64 With the bookplate of the Royal Library, deposited in 1715. **EMM** 324.7.93 With an old shelf-mark, 18.6.78, which is typical of Emmanuel, but this book is not listed in the 18th-century catalogue with that mark **SID** Z.7.17 In the catalogue of 1674. With the title on the top edge, a practice which continued until around 1640 (Rogers, p. 78) (Adams S3–4).

795 Aphorismi confessariorum, Parisiis, apud Iacobum Reze, 1601. 32°
BOD Vet. E1 g.31 (1) Acquired in 1960.

796 Aphorismi confessariorum, Madriti, ex officina P. Madrigal, expensis Michaëlis Martinez, 1601. 16°
BOD 1 g.92 Acquired after 1861.

797 Aphorismi confessariorum . . ., Venetiis, apud Gio. Bapt. Ciottum, 1602. 16°
CUL G*.13.43 (G) Deposited before 1715 **G&C** F.31.15 Bequeathed by William Branthwaite, Master, in 1619. He was one of the revisers of the Bible.

798 Aphorismi confessariorum, *corrected by reference to the Roman ed.,* Coloniae, apud Ioannem Crithium, 1608–9. 12°
BOD 8° S 99 Th. In the 1620 catalogue with the same shelf-mark.
EMM S.17.8.20 Bequeathed by Archbishop William Sancroft in 1693.

799 Aphorismi confessariorum, *expurgated and with additions,* Coloniae, apud Ioannem Crithium, 1610. 12°
ORI 3Bg1 This book is not in either of the normally reliable 17th-century catalogues, and is likely to have been acquired later.
CUL F*.13.55 (G) Bequeathed by John Hacket, Bishop of Lichfield (1592–1670).

800 Aphorismi confessariorum, *corrected by reference to the Roman ed.,* Lugduni, apud Ioannem Pillehotte, 1610. 32°
BOD Douce S 310 From the Douce bequest of 1834.

801 Aphorismi confessariorum, *with additions,* Coloniae, apud Ioannem Crithium, 1615. 12°
TRC D.32.20 Bequeathed by James Duport, vice-master, in 1679.

802 Aphorismi confessariorum, *with additions*, Duaci, ex officina Baltazari Belleri, 1618. 16°

CUL Cc.14.33 With the bookplate of John Colbatch, Anglican chaplain in Portugal from 1693–1700, who died 1748.

803 Aphorismi confessariorum, *with additions*, Lugduni, sumptibus Ant. Pillehotte, 1622. 16°

MGO k.1.19 With the signature of John Fitzwilliam, Demy 1656, who died 1699.

804 Aphorismi confessioniorum, *corrected by reference to the Roman ed.*, Lugduni, sumptibus Peter Rigaud, 1624. 16°

JSO I.2.21.

805 Aphorismi confessariorum, Lugduni, sumptibus Iacobi Cardon, 1631. 12°

CCCO LI.1.20 Bequeathed by Richard Samways, fellow, in 1669.

806 Aphorismi confessariorum, Duaci, ex officina Balthazaris Belleri, 1632. 64°

CUL G*.13.44 (G) Acquired before 1715 and in the catalogue of the 'Old Library' with the same shelf-mark.

807 Biblia Sacra vulgatae editionis, Sixti V. Pont. Max. iussu recognita atque edita, cum . . . notationibus Emanuelis Sa . . ., Antuerpiae, ex officina Plantiniana, 1624. 2 vols Fol.

BOD C.4. 12,13 Th., formerly Th. B. 25 1. S. In the 1674 catalogue with the old shelf-mark. Chain mark.

CUL I.22.6- Probably to be identified with the book listed in the catalogue of the Royal Library (deposited in 1715) with the shelf-mark Z.13–14 TRC A.16.21–2. With 17th-century Cambridge binding and gilt crest stamped S E, perhaps the chaplain Sylvius Elwes, who gave books, chiefly of divinity, 1626–30. Two sets of small numbers on the fore-edge, indicating that the volumes entered the library between 1605 and 1660.

808 Notationes in totam Scripturam Sacram, Antuerpiae, ex officina Plantiniana, apud Ioannem Moretum, 1598. 4°

BOD (3 copies) LL 18(1) Th. The 1605 catalogue lists this, the first copy to have entered the library, and states that it is bound with Sá's Scholia, which is indeed the case (see **812**). With chain mark; 4° Z 5 Th. Seld. From the Selden bequest of 1659; EE 22 Th. This copy has the price and date 11/4/1663 on the title page CHC OB.4.7, formerly OB.4.21 With the signature of H. Wotton. From the Orrery bequest of 1732 SJCO F.4.3 Given by the recusant Thomas Tresham in 1599 WAD I 23.3 Given by Philip Bisse, 1613.

CUL (2 copies) E*.4.23 (C) Acquired before 1715 and in the catalogue of the 'Old Library' with the same shelf-mark; 2.25.31, probably to be identified with the book listed in the catalogue of the Royal Library with the shelf-mark B.10.7 SID S.5.48 In the catalogue of 1674. Given by Francis Quarles, perhaps in June 1639 shortly after he was admitted to the college. The binding is stamped with a gilt coat of arms of the Tresham family and the words Credo 1598. Title on the fore-edge and remains of a tab SJCC Qq.5.10 Part of the Crashawe collection, deposited in 1626 (Adams S5).

809 Notationes in totam Scripturam sacram, Lugduni, apud Horatium Cardon, 1601. 4°

BOD D 11.3 Linc. Formerly 4° Z 5 Th. Seld. (the shelf-mark of **808**) and B.4.9. The Lincoln/Barlow books were bequeathed in 1691, and the Selden books in 1659. The presence of a third shelf-mark suggests that the library acquired the book before either bequest was made.

CCCC SP.52 Bought in 1605 **EMM** 333.2.10 With an old shelf-mark, 18.1.66, under which it is listed in the 18th-century catalogue as a missing book. Books belonging to class 18 normally form part of the bequest either of John Richardson (1626) or of John Breton (1675), but there is no indication of this in the volume itself **MGC** B.5.7 With the author's name and the title of the book on the top-edge and fore-edge, indicating acquisition in the 17th century.

810 Notationes in totam Scripturam Sacram, Lugduni, sumptibus Horatii Cardon, 1609. 4°
    ASC Bought around 1600 **MGO** d.05.20 With the signature of John Fitzwilliam, Demy 1656, who died in 1699.
    TRC D.1.15 Numbered with a large 7 on the fore-edge and with a faint sign of a paper tab, indicating that it was acquired in the 1660s (Gaskell, p. 103).

811 Notationes in totam Scripturam Sacram, Moguntiae, sumptibus Ioannis Kinckii, 1610. 4°
    CUL 2.23.51 Probably to be identified with the book listed in the catalogue of the Royal Library (deposited in 1715) with the shelf-mark B.10.6.

812 Scholia in quatuor evangelia, Antverpiae, ex officina Plantiniana, apud viduam & Ioannem Moretum, 1596. 4°
    BOD LL 18(2) Th. Bound with **808**, a fact noted in the 1605 catalogue **CCCO** G.4.3 Bequeathed by Richard Cobbe Bachelor of Theology and fellow, who died in 1597. Binding with Ker centrepiece xiv, used most extensively 1590–1610 (Pearson, p. 78). Chain mark **HMAN** X1596/6 With the bookplate of Exeter Library, i.e. of Exeter Academy, extinguished in the late 18th century. It may have belonged earlier to an academy in Taunton (1670–1759). Harris Manchester College came to Oxford in 1889. Ker centrepiece no. xxii with ornament 62, of around 1600, but Pearson notes that it is not easy to tell if the binding was produced in Oxford or London, p. 82. There is a number on the fore-edge. With the signature of Richard Boles? **WOR** FF.3.5 Oxford binding, Ker centrepiece xxxii, associated with books given by William Paddy, mostly to St John's (Ker, p. 218) **WAD** I 23.2 Given by Philip Bisse, 1613.
    G&C F.14.1 Bequeathed by William Branthwaite, Master, in 1619. He was one of the revisers of the Bible. **QUC** G.20.2, formerly 7.14.2 In the catalogue of the 1680s with the same shelf-marks **SJCC** Qq.5.9 Part of the Crashawe collection, deposited in 1626 (Adams S6).

813 Scholia in quatuor Euangelia, Lugduni, apud Horatium Cardon, 1602. 4°
    CHC Jb.1.41 Oxford 17th-century binding. Chain mark .
    CUL E*.4.33 (C) Acquired before 1715. In the catalogue of the 'Old Library' with the same shelf-mark.

814 Scholia in quatuor Euangelia, Lugduni, apud Horatium Cardon, 1610. 4°
    EMM S.7.3.11 Bequeathed by Archbishop William Sancroft in 1693 **WEST** C H.3.17. Westminster College moved to Cambridge from London in 1899.

Sanches, Francisco (1551–1623) (Franciscus Sanchez)

Sanches's 'rebellion against Aristotle in the *Quod nihil scitur* . . .was to result in a radical form of scepticism that makes him a unique figure in French Renaissance thought' (Sanches, ed. Limbrick, p. 24). This original thinker showed little interest in his Portuguese background (Carvalho, pp. x-xi). He was born possibly in Tuy, in Spain but in the diocese of Braga, where he lived until the age of 11, when he left Portugal with his parents, never to return. There is no statement of his nationality on the title-pages of his books.

Sanches studied in France and then in Rome. The last forty-eight years of his life were spent in Toulouse, where he held chairs in both medicine and philosophy. Like most doctors, Sanches was probably a New Christian and his family may have left Portugal because of fear of persecution. In Toulouse, however, he lived as a Catholic and two of his sons became priests (Limbrick, pp. 6–7). There are fifteen copies of *Quod nihil scitur* in Oxford and Cambridge, of which eight can be shown to be of old provenance, though there are others whose arrival in the libraries cannot be dated. This means that his impact as a thinker was very much less than that of orthodox Aristotelian philosophers like the Coimbra commentators. For further discussion of him see Chapter Five, p. lxxviii.

Francisco Sanches, *Opera Philosophica,* ed. Joaquim de Carvalho; *That Nothing is Known (Quod Nihil Scitur),* edited and translated by Elaine Limbrick and Douglas F. S. Thompson.

815 Qvod nihil scitvr, Lvgduni, apud Ant. Gryphivm, 1581. 4°

ASC k.7.13.

EMM S2.3.24(3) With the Sancroft-Emmanuel bookplate, from Archbishop William Sancroft's bequest of 1693. Cambridge 17th-century binding. With two other medical treatises of the 16th century (Adams S247).

816 De multum nobili et prima universali scientia quod nihil scitur, Francofurti, sumptibus Ioannis Berneri bibliopolae, 1618. 8°

BOD (2 copies) 8° S117(1) Art. A copy is listed in the 1635 appendix to the Bodley 1620 catalogue. It reappears in the 1674 catalogue with the shelf-mark in use today; Crynes 848 (4) Part of the Crynes bequest of 1745 ASC i.11.8 (2) Bound with four other works of which the latest was published in 1674 BNC Lath S.2.2, formerly A.1.10, among other marks. In the catalogue probably compiled in the 17th century with shelf-mark Arch.A.1.9 PMO 10.a.16 With the signature of John Leslie. Bequeathed by H. W. Chandler, 1889 QUO UU.b.1436 (5).

CUL P*.14.2 (F) Acquired before 1715. In the catalogue of the 'Old Library' with the same shelf-mark EMM 324.7.21, previously 17.3.17, probably not part of Sancroft's collection. Repaired binding. Not in the 18th-century catalogue TRC III.8.16. With what may be a 17th-century Cambridge binding. In the college's copy of the interleaved Bodleian catalogue used in the 18th century.

817 Opera medica. His iuncti sunt tractatus quidam philosophici non insubtiles, *including* Quod nihil scitur, Tolosae Tectosagum, apud Petrum Bosc, 1636. 4°

BOD 4° Q8 Med Formerly Med. W. 15 Chain mark. In the 1674 catalogue with the old shelf-mark **QUO** NN.s.1420 Given by Theophilus Metcalfe, M.D., who died in 1757.

G&C K.3.14 **TRC** S.7.27 In the college's copy of the interleaved Bodleian catalogue used in the 18th century. Binding repaired.

Sanches, Francisco, monk of Montserrat (–1604)

A Benedictine, born in Lisbon, according to the title-page of **818**, but who lived in the monastery of Montserrat, near Barcelona, from 1577 to his death. There are only two books published in Barcelona in the short-title catalogue. Salamanca, followed by Madrid, were much more important centres for the trade in learned books with Oxford and Cambridge.

Grande Enciclopédia Portuguesa e Brasileira, XXVI, p. 909.

818 In Ecclesiasten commentarium, Barcinone, Sebastianus Matheuat 1619. 4°

BOD BB 12(1) Th. In the 1635 appendix to the 1620 catalogue. Bound with **736**, which is a Lisbon imprint.

CUL E*.5.18 (D) Acquired before 1715. In the catalogue of the 'Old Library' with the same shelf-mark **EMM** 333.4.66 The old shelf-mark, 18.4.59, is typical of Emmanuel, but the book is not listed with that mark in the 18th-century catalogue.

Sande, Duarte (1547–1600)

Jesuit missionary to China, whose work was only known to early modern Oxford and Cambridge through Hakluyt's translation (**446**).

Grande Enciclopédia Portuguesa e Brasileira, XXVII, p. 42.

[De missione legatorum Iaponensium] An excellent description of the kingdom of China, *translated by Richard Hakluyt,* in Principal Navigations, vol. II, Part 2, second numeration, pp. 379–99.

Santarém, Pedro de (16th–17th centuries)

Jurist and diplomat, who was in the royal service in Italy. However, the title-pages of the various editions of his treatise on insurance state that he was Portuguese. It is most frequently to be found in **821**, a very large compilation of legal works printed in Venice in 1584 (see also Diogo de Sá).

Dicionário de história de Portugal, III, pp. 770–2.

819 Tractatus de Assecurationibus & Sponsionibus mercatorum nunc primum in lucem datus, cum repertorio & summariis, Venetiis, apud Baltassarem Constantinum, 1552. 8°

BOD 8° Rawl. 908. Bishop Richard Rawlinson's collection was left to the Bodleian in 1755.

820 Tractatus de Assecurationibus & Sponsionibus mercatorum nunc primum in lucem datus, cum repertorio & summariis, *in* Selecti tractatus iuris varii . . ., Coloniae, apud Gervinum Calenium & haeredes Iohannis Quentelii, 1569. Fol.
ASC cc.1.10 (2).

821 Tractatus de Assecurationibus & Sponsionibus mercatorum nunc primum in lucem datus, cum repertorio & summariis, *in* Tractatus illustrium in utraque tum pontificii, tum caesarei iuris facultate iurisconsultorum, De contractibus licitis, . . . vol.VI.i, Venetiis, Societas aquilae se renovantis, 1584. Fol. (fols 348r–357r).
CHC A.2.2.11 **MER** 64.A.7 **QUO** 35.C.7 **SJCO** U.1.8.
PET A.1.7 Given by Thomas Richardson, Master 1699–1733 **QUC** O.2.10 **TRH** N*.6.7 College bookplate of 1700. With Latin marginalia to Santarém's text **TRC** N.16.6 With 17th-century Cambridge binding, stamped with gilt crest and ES, indicating that it formed part of Sir Edward Stanhope's large donation of law books of 1608 (Gaskell, p. 88). Stanhope had been a fellow from 1564 to 1572 (Adams T892).

822 Tractatus perutilis & quotidianus de Assecurationibus & Sponsionibus Mercatorum . . . cum repertorio & summariis, Antuerpiae, apud Ioannem Bellerum, 1554. 8°
BOD 8° S 16 Jur. Seld. This copy belonged to Sir Robert Bruce Cotton (1571–1631), a graduate of Jesus College, Cambridge (1585/86) and a politician and antiquary. Many of his books were acquired by Selden.

Santo António, Bernardino de (–1642)
A Trinitarian, who spent his career in Portugal. He published **823**, an account of the redemptionist activities of the order, in Lisbon, which was the city of his birth, according to the title-page. Although there is no record that the book was ever issued in Paris, material by French writers is included in the preliminaries: a licence issued in Paris by the General, identified only as Brother Ludovicus, but probably Louis Petit, and a liminary ode by Claude Ralle. Here is an indication of the international support offered by religious orders to their members. For a Trinitarian who benefited rather more from the encouragement of Ralle and Petit, see Baltasar Pais.
Barbosa Machado, I, pp. 515–6.

823 Epitome generalium redemptionum captiuorum, quae a fratribus Ordinis Sanctissimae Trinitatis sunt factae, Vlyssipone, ex officina Petri Crasbeec, 1623. 4°
BOD FF 34 Th. Marks of chaining.

Santos, João dos (−1622)
Dominican and missionary. His *Etiópia Oriental,* first published in Portuguese (Évora, 1609), was only known to early modern Oxford and Cambridge through Purchas's translation (**737**).
Grande Enciclopédia Portuguesa e Brasileira, XXVII, p. 359.
[Ethiopia oriental, e varia historia de cousas notaveis do Oriente], *translated from Portuguese* in Samuel Purchas, Purchas his Pilgrimes, vol. II, Book 9, Chapter 11.

São Francisco, Luís de (16th. cent.) (Ludovicus a Sancto Francisco/ Ludovicus S. Francisci frater)
Scholar of Hebrew, who left an interesting autobiographical sketch, and an account of the development of his subject in Portugal, in the Praefatio to **824**. He began as a civil and canon lawyer, teaching in Coimbra and Salamanca. He then became a Franciscan. Only at the age of nearly 50 did he begin to study Hebrew, encouraged by Osório (Praefatio, p. 10). His later life was spent in Rome, where his Hebrew grammar, which contains a chapter on Hebrew poetry (Chap. 9), was published. There are nine copies of his works in Oxford and Cambridge, of which seven can be shown to be of old provenance. His nationality is stated on the title-pages.
Barbosa Machado, III, p. 95.

824 Globus canonum, et arcanorum linguae sanctae, ac diuinae Scripturae . . ., Romae, impensis Bartholomaej de Grassis [in colophon, excudebant Alexander Gardanus, & Franciscus Coattinus socij], 1586. 4°
BOD (2 copies) 4° T 73 Th. With the shelf-mark on leading edge, an indication of old provenance; BB 28 Art. Formerly M.3.17 Art. In the 1620 catalogue with the old shelf-mark. The book is listed in the 1605 catalogue with a different shelf-mark, L.2.6. Chain mark JSO N.4.2 MER 46.E.2 Chain mark. Binding of around 1600.
CUL K*.6.1(D) In the library before 1715. Cambridge binding of the 17th century with fillets. Evidence of a paper tab EMM 334.2.35 Old shelf-marks 18.2.1 and 18.6.5, under which it is listed in the 18th-century catalogue. Books in class 18 normally form part of the bequest either of John Richardson (1626) or of John Breton (1675), but there is no indication of provenance in the volume itself PET N.4.18 Bequeathed by Andrew Perne, Master, in 1589 SJCC L.8.17 Bequeathed by Abdias Ashton, fellow, in 1633 (Adams S254).

825 Oratio funebris . . . in obitu . . . F. Marci Valladaris Hispani, Romae, ex typographia Vincentii Accolti, 1587. 4°
BOD 4° W 24(8) Jur. With other orations published between 1585 and 1592.

Schottus, Andreas (1552−1629)
Flemish Jesuit, editor and publicist, who was born in Antwerp. In vol. 2 of **826** he reprinted a number of major works by Góis, Nunes de Leão, André de Resende, and Diogo de Teive.

826 Hispaniae illustratae seu Rerum urbiumque Hispaniae, Lusitaniae, Aethiopiae et Indiae scriptores varii, Francofurti, apud C. Marnium, & haeredes Iohannis Aubrii, 1603–08. 4 vols Fol.

BOD F 6.5–8 Art. Vols 1 and 2 are in the 1605 catalogue, and the rest in the 1620 catalogue CCCO M.24.3–6 Chain mark CHC (2 copies) OV.1.1; Allestree d.2.1–4 From the Allestree bequest of 1681 HER III.5.6.1–4 From Magdalen Hall (extinguished 1874–75) TAY (2 copies) 113.I.9–11, 3 vols in 4. Acquired 1876; Butler.Clarke.Y.1–4 Given to St John's College in 1905 and loaned to the Taylor Institution.

CUL (2 copies) Acton a.38.3- Lord Acton's library was presented in 1902; Syn.2.60.1-Formerly G.7.13. With the bookplate of the Royal Library and in its MS. catalogue with the old shelf-mark. The collection was deposited in 1715. Fine binding with armorial crest SID L.2.28–9 In the catalogue of 1674 SJCC E.4.16–18 In the catalogue compiled c. 1640 TRC W.11.10 probably acquired after 1800.

Sebastião, King of Portugal (1554–1578)

In 1562 King Sebastião was only eight when a speech (827) was made in his name at the opening of the last session of the Council of Trent. The ambassador was Fernão Martins de Mascarenhas.

827 Oratio habita . . . in Concilio Tridentino, Ripae, ad instantiam Petri Antonii Alciatis [in some copies, Baptistae Bozolae], 1562. 4°

BOD (4 copies) 4° A 28(34) Th.; 4° A 84(12) Th. BS; Antiq. e.I.8 Acquired between 1883 and 1936; Vet. F1 e.215(7) The shelf-mark indicates that it was acquired after 1937 CCCO LE.14.32 Chain mark.

CUL Acton D.6.8 (41) Lord Acton's library was presented in 1902 (Adams S1953).

Sena, António de (–1584) (Antonius Senensis)

Sometimes known as António da Conceição, he was a Dominican and a historian of his order. He was also an editor of Aquinas. He studied in Louvain, arriving there in 1564 (see 829, Epistola ad lectorem), and in 1575 went to Rome. After Philip II became king of Portugal in 1580, Sena remained faithful to Dom António, the pretender to the Portuguese throne, and in the summer of 1581 spent some time in exile with him in England. He died, still in exile, in France. Despite his many years abroad Sena is always described as Lusitanus on the title-pages of his books. The three copies of them in the Bodleian are all of old provenance. Jorge Peixoto, *Relações de Plantin com Portugal*, pp. 31–43; *Grande Enciclopédia Portuguesa e Brasileira*, XXVIII, p. 253.

828 Bibliotheca ordinis fratrum ordinis praedicatorum, Parisiis, apud Nicolaum Nivellium, 1585. 8°

BOD 8° A 1 Th. (2) In the 1605 catalogue with the same shelf-mark. Bound with 829.

829 Chronicon fratrum ordinis praedicatorum, Parisiis, apud Nicolaum Nivellium, 1585. 8°

BOD 8° A 1 Th. Bound with 828.

830 Postilla seu expositio aurea sancti Thomae Aquinatis . . . in librum Geneseos, Lugduni, apud Petrum Landry, 1573. 8°
BOD 8° Seld. A 7 Th. From the Selden bequest of 1659.

831 S. Thomae Aquinatatis summa totius theologicae . . ., Antuerpiae, ex officina Christophori Plantini, 1585. Fol.
QUO 54.G.13.

[Silva, Jorge da] (–1578)
A nobleman, who perished in the battle of Alcácer-Quibir. Barbosa Machado claims that **832**, which is anonymous, is by Silva. It is a vernacular devotional work and a recent acquisition.
Barbosa Machado, II, pp. 817–18; Inocêncio, IV, pp. 175–6.

832 Tractado em que se contem a paixam de Christo, Euora, Martim de Burgos, 1589 [in colophon, 1590]. 8°
BOD Vet. G1 f.5 Acquired in 1950 (Anselmo 428).

Silva, Marcos da (1511–91) (Marcos de Lisboa)
A Franciscan and bishop of Oporto, usually known in Portugal as Frei Marcos de Lisboa, or de Bethania. His history of the Franciscan Order, first published in Portuguese in 1557, arrived in Oxford in Italian (**833**) and in Cambridge in Spanish (**835**). Marulo (**834**) is the Croatian philosopher and poet Marko Marulic (1450–1524) whose lives of the saints were translated, via Latin, into many European languages. The English Jesuits printed **836** at St Omer. The volume contains writings by the English Sister Magdalen of St Augustine and a life of St Clare which may have been retranslated from Silva's Portuguese version. It is possible that **834** and **836** have been in the Bodleian since early times.
Inocêncio, VI, pp. 129–32; A. F. Allison, *English Translations from the Spanish and Portuguese,* pp. 166–7.

833 Croniche de gli ordini instituti dal p. s. Francesco, *tr. by* Horatio Diola *from a Spanish version by* Diego Navarro, Venetia, appresso Pietro Miloco, 1617. 4°
BOD Antiq. e.I. 1617.4 Acquired in 1929.

834 Liuro insigne das flores e perfeicoens das vidas dos gloriosos sanctos, *composed by* Marcos Marulo Spalatense de Dalmacia, *and tr. by Silva,* Lisboa, em casa de Francisco Correa, 1579. Fol.
BOD M 9.2 Th. Chain mark (Anselmo 513).

835 Tercera parte de las chronicas de los frayles menores . . ., Salamanca, Alexandro de Canova, 1570. Fol.
CUL Acton.b.3.38 Lord Acton's library was presented in 1902 (Fidalgo 757).

836 The life of the glorious virgin S. Clare, [St. Omer], [no publisher], 1622. 16°
BOD 8° V 70 Th. With the shelf-mark on the leading edge and on the parchment binding.
EMM 328.7.132 (both listed in STC 5350; Allison S.16).

Silva, Semuel da

A Jewish doctor, born in Portugal, who lived in Amsterdam at the beginning of the seventeenth century. His book, which is in Portuguese, on the immortality of the soul is an attack on Uriel da Costa's beliefs. There is only one copy, in Oxford.
Friedenwald, II, p. 761.

837 Tratado da immortalidade da alma, Amsterdam, impresso em casa de Paulo de Ravesteyn, 5383 [i.e. 1623]. 8°
ASC Gallery s.7.11 Perhaps from the bequest made in 1643 by Dudley Digges, fellow, and in the shelf-list of 1756.

Soares, João (1507–72)(Johannes Suarez)

An Augustinian and bishop of Coimbra, controversial both for his dissolute personal life and for the rigour with which he persecuted the New Christians of his diocese. He attended the Council of Trent from 1561–3 and, like several other Portuguese theologians, used the opportunity to publish with Ziletti in Venice. There are copies of **841** in Oxford and Cambridge. Unusually, however, three books by him printed in Coimbra also arrived in Oxford in the early modern period. Special circumstances explain the presence of two of them in the Bodleian. One (**840**) belonged to Bishop Mascarenhas (see Introduction, p. xvi), while the library's copy of **839** is bound with a book printed in Salamanca and may have come from there. Salamanca was closer to the centres of European publishing than any of the Portuguese towns. All the title-pages of his books state that he was bishop of Coimbra.
Grande Enciclopédia Portuguesa e Brasileira, XXIX, pp. 326–8.

838 Commentaria in Marcum et Lucam, Parisiis, apud Sebastianum Nivellium, 1578. 8°
SJCC Uu.11.10 From the Crashawe collection, deposited in 1626 (Adams S2011).

839 Commentarium in . . . Euangelium beati Lucae, Conimbricae, Antonius a Maris, 1574. Fol.
BOD S 8.10(1) Th. Formerly S.4.1 Th, chain marks. In the 1605 catalogue. Bound with a commentary on Hosea printed in Salamanca.
CUL F157.b.12.2 Given by Stephen Gaselee in 1926 (Adams S2012; Anselmo 866).

840 Commentarium in . . . Euangelium beati Marci, Conimbricae, apud Ioannem Barrerium, 1566. Fol.
BOD S 8.11 Th. Part of the Mascarenhas collection, deposited in 1596. In the 1605

catalogue. **SJCO** H.3.25 Given by Ralph or Rudolph Hamor or Hamore, a London merchant, in 1608 (Anselmo 192).

841 Commentarium in . . . Euangelium secundum Matthaeum, Venetiis, ex officina Iordani Ziletti, 1565. 4°
    BOD D 17.8 Linc. Part of the Barlow bequest of 1691, but in the 1620 catalogue also, so a replacement copy. Chain mark.
    CUL F*.5.4 (D) Acquired before 1715. In the catalogue of the 'Old Library' with the same shelf-mark **SJCC** Qq.11.8 From the Crashawe collection, deposited in 1626 (Adams S2010).

Sotomaior, Luís de (1526–1610) (Ludovicus or Luiz Sotomayor)
The title-pages do not record the nationality of this Dominican friar but describe him as a professor of theology at Coimbra. However, there is no doubt that he was Portuguese, born in Lisbon. The twenty-five years that he spent abroad almost certainly include a period in England, during the reign of Mary, as one of the Dominican theologians who, under the direction of Bartolomé Carranza, attempted to restore the universities to the old faith. Barbosa Machado, writing in the early eighteenth century, says that he taught in both Oxford and Cambridge. The *História de S. Domingos* (first edition 1623) says only that he taught Latin in London. Barbosa Machado, however, may well be right, since Tellechea Idígoras prints a letter from Carranza, then at Westminster, dated 15 May 1557, to Juan de Villagarcía, one of the Dominicans resident in Oxford, in which he asks to be remembered to 'Padre fray Luis'.

    Sotomaior was an author of high prestige, and of the fifteen copies of his books now in Oxford and Cambridge eight can be shown to have arrived within ten years of publication. The rest followed not long afterwards. The first edition of his commentary on the Song of Songs (**843,** printed in Lisbon) was dignified by the inclusion of a papal bull by Clement VIII recommending publication. Philip II also urged that it should appear. It was an expensive book, which never recovered the costs of the first edition, though those printed abroad sold well. The royal *alvará* records that Sotomaior had to import printing materials, probably for the elaborately engraved title-page.
Luís Cacegas, *Primeira parte da História de S. Domingos,* I, p. 435; J. Ignacio Tellechea Idigoras, *Fray Bartolomé Carranza y el Cardenal Pole,* p. 260. Barbosa Machado, III, pp. 141–4; Manuel Augusto Rodrigues, *A Cátedra de Sagrada Escritura na Universidade de Coimbra,* pp. 213–27.

842 Ad Canticum canticorum notae posteriores, et breviores, Parisiis, apud Michaelem Sonnium, 1612. 4°
    BOD 4° S 31(1) Th. In the 1620 catalogue with the same shelf-mark **JSO** B.2.8 Given by Thomas Myddleton, 1586–1666, and in the 1649 catalogue.
    KCC A.23.10 Listed in the 17th-century catalogue, which was started in 1612.

843 Cantici canticorum Salomonis interpretatio, Vlysippone, apud Petrum Crasbeeck, 1599 [in colophon, 1601]. Fol.

BOD V 1.9 Th. Chain mark. The old shelf-mark, S.11.3 Th., is the one used in the 1605 catalogue (Anselmo 525).

844 Cantici canticorum Salomonis interpretatio, Parisiis, Michael Sonnius, 1605. Fol.

CCCO LC.17.a.8 Bequeathed by John Rainolds, President of the college, who died in May 1607, chain marks **QUO** 75.B.2 The title page is missing. Oxford 17th-century binding and chain mark **WAD** I 40.9 Given by Philip Bisse, 1613.

CUL F*.2.26 (B) Acquired before 1715 **SJCC** Pp.5.11 From the Crashawe collection, deposited in 1626.

845 Commentarius in priorem ac posteriorem Pauli apostoli Epistolam ad Timothaeum, et item in Epistolam ad Titum, Parisiis, apud Michaelem Sonnium, 1610. Fol.

BOD O 3.10 Th. In the 1620 catalogue **CHC** Hyp.Q.12 In the 1665 catalogue **MGO** c.07.05 Bequeathed by Henry Perier, fellow, who died in 1619. Oxford binding, Ker roll xxv with initials of John Westall, dated by Ker to 1613, p. 219, but Pearson thinks it was in use over a longer period, pp. 71–2 **QUO** 73.B.18. Oxford 17th-century binding and chain mark **WAD** I 40.10 Given by Philip Bisse, 1613.

CUL F*.2.27 (B) Acquired before 1715. In the catalogue of the 'Old Library' with the same shelf-mark.

Sousa, António de (–1632)

A Dominican and an Inquisitor. The books by him in Oxford and Cambridge are concerned with heresy and its extirpation, a subject of keen interest to Protestants. In **847** Sousa includes some material in Portuguese which is specific to Portuguese practice. Of the three copies now in Oxford two arrived in the early period, and **848** may also have done so. Cambridge has one copy with early provenance of **846**. Inocêncio, I, p. 275.

846 Aphorismi Inquisitorum in quatuor libros distributi, Turnoni, sumptibus Laurentii Durand, 1633. 8°

BOD 80 S 27 Jur. In the MS. additions to the 1620 catalogue, and in the 1674 catalogue.

CUL (2 copies) Q*.12.20 (E) Acquired before 1715; Acton.d.1.346 Lord Acton's library was presented in 1902.

847 Relectio de censuris bullae coenae, Vlyssipone, typis Petri Crasbeeck, 1615. 4°

BOD 4° S 15 Jur. Seld. From the Selden bequest of 1659. In the 1674 catalogue.

CUL Acton.d.2.33 Lord Acton's library was presented in 1902.

848 Relectio de censuris bullae coenae, Duaci, ex typographia Baltazaris Belleri, 1632. 8°

BOD 8° C 253 Th.

Sousa, Francisco de (17th cent.)

A lawyer, who studied in Coimbra and practised abroad, in Florence and in Flanders, where **849** was published. The title-page describes him as Portuguese. There is only one copy, in Oxford.
Grande Enciclopédia Portuguesa e Brasileira, XXIX, p. 788.

849 Variae repetitiones ad L. foeminae, ff. de regulis iur., et ad [sect.] actionum Instit. de actionibus; commentariiq. ad Tit. Digest. de pactis Antuerpiae, apud Hieronymum Verdussium, 1618. Fol.
ASC dd.infra 1.5.

Sousa, José Vaz Pinto de (16th-17th cents)

Commentator of Virgil. The book, the only one in the short-title catalogue to have been printed in Braga, was perhaps acquired as a curiosity.
Barbosa Machado, II, p. 909.

850 Thesaurus Musae Virgilianae . . . Pars secunda . . ., Bracharae Augustae, ex thypographia Fructuosi Laurentii de Basto, 1629. 4°
TRC Z.13.76 Bequeathed by John Laughton in 1712. He was college, and later University librarian.

Sousa, Manuel de Faria e (1590–1649)

Literary scholar and historian, much of whose professional life was spent in Spain, as secretary to a succession of noble households. His famous commentary on Camões's *Lusíadas* (**852**) did not reach Oxford or, probably, Cambridge until the nineteenth century. (The copy in Cambridge University Library has a shelfmark used usually, though not invariably, for recent acquisitions). His history of Portugal, though, (**851**) was of more interest to seventeenth-century readers, perhaps especially because it was written in Spanish, and there are three copies with old provenance. The title-pages of both the books in the short-title catalogue make it clear that the subject-matter is Portuguese, though they do not state the nationality of the author.
Edward Glaser, *The "Fortuna" of Manuel de Faria e Sousa* pp. 38–77.

851 Epitome de las historias portuguesas, Madrid, por Francisco Martinez, a costa de Pedro Coello, mercador de libros, 1628. 2 vols in one. 4°
BOD 4° A 46 Jur. BS. Entered the library after 1668 **TAY** Vet.Port.I.B.7 With library stamp 1936 **WAD** G 23.4 Given by Charles Godolphin in 1720. Part of the collection of Sir William Godolphin (?1634–96).
KCC G.16.6 Listed in the catalogue of 1738.

852 Lusiadas de Luis de Camoens . . . comentadas, *with* Informacion en favor de Manuel de Faria i Sousa, Madrid, por Juan Sanchez, 1639. 4 vols in 2. Fol.

TAY 269.G.15,16 Entered the library in 1891.
CUL F163.a.8.1- CHR H.1.6–7 Given by Timothy Hutton in 1862.

Teive, Diogo de (1513/14–after 1569)(Tevius)

In Portugal a well-known humanist and composer of Latin verse and of a tragedy, also in Latin, but represented in Oxford and Cambridge only by a short historical commentary on the siege of Diu (1546), included in a compilation, *De rebus Hispanicis, Lusitanicis, Aragonicis, Indicis & Aethiopicis* (853). There are a number of works by Góis in the same publication (see 402). Teive's commentary was also reprinted by Schottus (826). Teive is identified on the title-page as 'Lusitanus'.

Diogo de Teive, *Tragédia do Príncipe João*, ed. by Nair de Nazaré Castro Soares; Luís de Matos, 'O humanista Diogo de Teive'; Luís de Sousa Rebelo, 'Diogo de Teive, historiador humanista'.

853 Commentarii de rebus a Lusitanis in India apud Dium gestis, Coloniae Agrippinae, in officina Birckmannica, sumptibus Arnoldi Mylii, 1602. 8°

BOD 8° S 245 Art. Perhaps acquired from the Plately sale, Dec 1810, but a copy is listed in the 1605 catalogue CHC f.9.11 Bequeathed by Robert Burton, 1640 (Kiessling (1988) 689) SJCO K.scam.1.upper shelf. 19(1) With the signature of Antony Scattirgood, 1640. He was originally from Trinity, Cambridge, and did not incorporate at Oxford until 1669.

CUL L*.6.28 (F) Acquired before 1715 CLA B1.3.40 With the 1701 college bookplate and the shelf-mark P 87 on the fore-edge. In the catalogue of 1677–78 with the old shelf-mark. PET K.7.4 Probably a 19th-century acquisition SJCC E.13.8. From the Crashawe collection, deposited in 1626 (Faria (1977), 45).

Teixeira, José (1543–1604) (Joseph Teixera)

A Dominican, who remained passionately loyal to António, Prior of Crato, the pretender to the Portuguese throne ousted by Philip II in 1580. He engaged in a polemic with Duarte Nunes de Leão (q.v.) on this issue, which was naturally of interest to contemporary English readers. Part of the polemic is to be found in **856**. He joined Dom António in exile and was in England in 1585 and 1588. The preface to the reader of **865**, published in London, refers to him as 'brother Ioseph Texere a Portuguese, one knowne to the greatest and meanest in Europe, as also here very well'. However, Albuquerque claims that his defence of Salic law in **857** brought him into disfavour with Elizabeth I. In France he became counsellor and confessor to Henri III and his mother, Catherine de Medici. Of the thirty-seven copies of books ascribed to Teixeira across the two universities around twenty-five are of old provenance.

There are doubts about the authorship of some of Teixeira's books. As a political refugee, he may not always have wished to take responsibility for his writings. There is no statement of authorship on the title-page of **854**, but in the unsigned Epistle to the Reader, p. 3, the book is attributed to Teixeira. The author of **855** is said to be 'a Pilgrim Spaniard', though library catalogues normally list it as being by Teixeira. It is substantially the same book as **864**, which has the title 'The Spanish Pilgrime'. Both books show considerable knowledge of Portuguese history and may very well be by the Portuguese Teixeira, whose European fame is proclaimed in **864**, pp. 73–4. The two translations (**859–60**) were also published anonymously. They are attributed to Teixeira in the British Library catalogue. There is no indication of the name of the author or the translator in **859**, but in his long dedication to Ioannes Martin Oltinger the translator of **860** includes some notes about Portugal and recognizes that the original language of the book was Portuguese. The entirely English **865** contains a 'Copie of a Discourse concerning the sucesse of Dom Sebastian' and a number of letters by Teixeira, and two other Portuguese writers, Estêvão de Sampaio and Pantaleão Pessoa de Neiva. The title-pages of all the books stated to be by Teixeira, except **863**, record his nationality as 'Lusitanus' or 'Portugallensis'.

Martim de Albuquerque, 'Acerca de Fr. José de Teixeira e da teoria da origem popular do poder', pp. 571–4; Maria Antonieta Soares de Azevedo, *O Prior do Crato*; Joaquim Veríssimo Serrão, *O reinado de D. António Prior do Crato*.

854 A continuation of the lamentable and admirable adventures of Dom Sebastian King of Portugale . . ., *tr. from French*, London, Iames Shaw, 1603. 4°

    CUL Syn.7.60.157 Acquired in 1906 **TRC** VI.7.46 (3) Bound with **855, 865** (Both copies listed in STC 23866).

855 A Treatise Paraenetical . . . wherein it is shewed by good and euident reasons, infallible arguments, most true and certaine histories, and notable examples; the right way & true meanes to resist the violence of the Castilian king . . . *tr. by W.P. from a French version, by I. Dralymont, of the Spanish original,* London, William Ponsonby, 1598. 4°

    BOD Tanner 325(1) From the bequest of Bishop Thomas Tanner (1674–1735) (STC 19838).

    CUL (3 copies) Dd*.4.3 (E) From the Royal Library, deposited in 1715; Peterborough H.4.12 Given to Peterborough Cathedral Library by White Kennett (1660–1728; see the Introduction, p. xiv); LE.6.89 Acquired in 1886. (One copy recorded in STC 19838) **EMM** 327.5.45, formerly 31.4.56. Bound with three other English pamphlets, the latest printed in 1610. With a 17th-century Cambridge binding, and tab numbered 57 **TRC** VI.7.46 (1) Pencil underlining. Bound with seven other pamphlets, the latest of 1648. Repaired binding, with 78 on upper fore-edge. As there is only one such number this may not be an early Trinity book. Bound with **854, 865**.

856 De Portugalliae ortu, regni initijs, Parisiis, apud Ioannem Mettayer, 1582. 4°

    BOD 4° T 20 Art. Seld. From the Selden bequest of 1659. In the 1674 catalogue.

    CUL (2 copies) I*.10.32 (D) Acquired before 1715. In the catalogue of the 'Old Library' with the same shelf-mark; T.10.3 From the Royal Library, deposited in 1715 (Adams T428).

857 Exegesis genealogica, sive Explicatio arboris gentilitiae . . . Galliarum regis Henrici, ejus nominis iiii, Lugduni Batavorum, ex officina Plantiniana, apud Franciscum Raphelengium, 1592. 4°
BOD 4° T 1 Art. In the 1605 catalogue, with the same shelf-mark **WOR** XT.2.11 Bequeathed by H. A. Pottinger in 1911.
CUL I*.10.8 (D) Acquired before 1715. In the catalogue of the 'Old Library' with the same shelf-mark **EMM** S12.3.30 With the Sancroft-Emmanuel bookplate, so forming part of the benefaction of 1693 (Adams T429).

858 Explicatio genealogiae serenissimi Henrici ii. Condaei, Franciae principis, *with poem* 'In illustrissimam Principum Trimuliorum prosapiae arborem', Parisiis, ex officina Plantiniana, 1596. 8°
BOD (2 copies) 8° T 19(2) Art. Formerly Arts 8 J 18. In the 1620 catalogue with the old shelf-mark; Vet. E1 a. 1(1). The shelf-mark indicates that it was acquired after 1937.

859 Histoire veritable des dernieres guerres aduenues en Barbarie: & du succéz pitoyable du roy de Portugal dernier, don Sebastien, *anonymous tr. from Spanish,* Paris, chez Nicolas Chesneau, 1579. 8°
BOD Godw. subt. 326 (1) From the bequest of Charles Godwyn, who died in 1770 and was a fellow of Balliol.

860 Historia de bello Africano: in quo Sebastianus, serenissimus Portugalliae rex, periit, *tr. from Portuguese into French, and from French into Latin by* Ioannes Thomas Freigius, Noriberga, [in colophon, in officina Catharinae Gerlachin, & Haeredum Iohannis Montani], 1580. 8°
BOD Antiq. f. X.26 (9) Acquired in 1929.
CUL N*.6.60 Acquired before 1715. In the catalogue of the 'Old Library' with the same shelf-mark.

861 Rerum ab Henrici Borbonii Franciae protoprincipis maioribus gestarum epitome, Parisiis, apud Leodegarium Delaz, 1598. 12°
WAD e.30.24 Bequeathed by Alexander Thistlethwaite (1718–71), a student of the college.

862 Speculum tyrannidis Philippi regis Castellae in usurpanda Portugallia, Parisiis, [no printer], 1595. 8°
BOD 8° P 59 Art.
CUL S*.5.43 (F) Acquired before 1715. In the catalogue of the 'Old Library' with the same shelf-mark (Adams T430).

863 Stemmata Franciae, item Navarrae regum, Lugduni Batavorum, apud Ioannem Maire, 1619. 4°
BOD 4° T 19 Art. Seld. From the Selden bequest of 1659. In the 1674 catalogue.
CUL S.3.31 From the Royal Library, deposited in 1715.

864 The Spanish Pilgrime, London, Thomas Archer, 1625. 4°
BOD (4 copies) 4° M 14(3) Th. BS; Pamph. C23 (2); Wood 511 (13). Bequeathed by Anthony Wood, antiquarian, in 1695 (Kiessling (2002) 5973); 243 g.15. (One copy recorded in STC 19838.5) **SJCO** P.scam.1.lower shelf. 7 Part of the Crynes bequest of 1745.

CUL (2 copies) Syn.7.58.24; Acton d.25.80 Lord Acton's library was presented in 1902 MGC Lect.80 (3) Formerly B.6.12. Bound with two other 17th-century pamphlets SJCC Hh.3.25(6) TRC (2 copies) C.11.123 Numbered 59 on the fore-edge. Bound with other English pamphlets of the 1620s, one of which is signed Tho. Scott. There were a number of students of this name in early seventeenth-century Cambridge; VI.10.31. With the Newton-Puckering bookplate, and so forms part of the collection deposited in 1691. Printed with other pamphlets, the latest of 1642.

865 The strangest adventure that ever happened . . . containing a discourse concerning the successe of the King of Portugall Dom Sebastian, *tr. from French [by Anthony Munday]*, London, for Francis Henson, 1601. 4°

BOD Wood 511 (7) Bequeathed by Anthony Wood, antiquarian, in 1695 (STC 23864; Kiessling (2002) 6165).

CUL Syn.7.60.3 Acquired in 1903 (STC 23864) PMC 10.21.27 (2) Given by Mark Frank, fellow, in 1662. TRC VI.7.46 (2) Bound with **854–5**.

Teixeira, Pedro (?1570-after 1610)

Linguist and traveller, whose abridged translation of the Persian chronicler Mir Khvand (1433–98) is the first into a European language. Very little is known about him except that he was probably Jewish. In his preface to the reader Teixeira explains that he had been persuaded by friends to write in Spanish, rather than Portuguese, his native language, in order to be more 'comunicable'. Seven of the ten copies now in Oxford and Cambridge are of old provenance. His work was translated into English in the early eighteenth century by Capt. John Stevens (London, 1711 and 1715).

Eduardo Barajas Sala, *Relaciones de Pedro Teixeira*, pp. xvi, xxxii; Luís Graça, *A visão do oriente*, pp. 25–9.

866 Relaciones . . . d'el origen descendencia y succession delos reyes de Persia, y de Harmuz, y de vn viage hecho por el mismo autor dende la India Oriental hasta Italia por tierra, Amberes, en casa de Hieronymo Verdussen, 1610. 8°

BOD (2 copies) 8° T 12 Art. Seld. From the Selden bequest of 1659, but in the 1620 catalogue, so a replacement copy; 8° Rawl. 920 Bishop Richard Rawlinson died in 1755, but the donation might have been made earlier ASC SR 102. b. 14 Pencil marks. Perhaps bought at the Stuart sale in 1821 WOR (2 copies) MM.2.16 Bequeathed by George Clarke, a benefactor of Worcester and of other colleges, in 1736 and with his bookplate; ZZ.7.13 Bequeathed by William Gower, the second provost of the college, in 1777. This copy also belonged to T. Kelsey.

CUL (2 copies) T*.5.23 (F) Acquired before 1715. In the catalogue of the 'Old Library' with the same shelf-mark; T.12.5 From the Royal Library, deposited in 1715. It was part of the library of Sir Thomas Knyvett (?1539–1618), which was acquired by Bishop Moore. Knyvett bought the book on 17 February 1611/12 (McKitterick 760) CCCC H.10.48 Bequeathed by Henry Gostling (1646/7–1675), fellow PMC (2 copies) 8.13.53 with the college bookplate of 1700; 2.18.63 with the college bookplate of 1879.

Tenreiro, António (15th–16th cents)

Tenreiro, who was born in Coimbra, made two overland journeys from India to Europe, in 1523 and 1528–29. His text indicates that he was a devout Christian. He and his work were of great interest to King John III, who probably saw in the overland route a quicker means of communicating with India than by sea. He wrote in Portuguese, and the only copy of **867**, which is in Oxford, was probably acquired in the nineteenth century.

António Baião, *Itinerários da Índia a Portugal*, pp. xi-xiv; *Dicionário de História de Portugal*, IV, p. 147; Luís Graça, *A visão do oriente*, pp. 14–16.

867 Itinerario de Antonio Tenrreyro, que da India veyo per terra a este Reyno de Portugal, Coimbra, por Ioao de Barreyra, 1565. 8°
ASC Gallery c.2.7 (Anselmo 189).

Toscano, Francisco Soares (16th–17th cents)

Historian, whose highly patriotic series of comparisons between the heroes of Portugal and their Biblical and classical counterparts was written and published during the period of Spanish rule. However, history written in Portuguese was of little interest to the early modern universities. Toscano, despite his surname, was born in Évora and was proud to call himself Portuguese (see the title-page of **868** and the dedication to the reader).

Inocêncio, III, p. 64.

868 Parallelos de principes, e varões illustres antigos, a que muitos da nossa naçam portuguesa se assemelhàrão . . . com a origem das armas de algũas familias deste reino, Evora, por Manoel Carvalho, 1623. 8°
ASC SR 89 d.12 With MS. notes in the dedication which may be the author's proof corrections TAY Vet. Port.I.B.18 Acquired in 1980.

Toscano, Sebastião (–1580) (Sebastianus Tuscanus)

An Augustinian friar, who studied in Salamanca and taught in Naples. In 1558 – during the reign of Queen Mary – he was sent by the General of his Order to England, to restore the suppressed convents. He died in Lisbon. Of his many works, in Portuguese, Spanish and Latin, Oxford and Cambridge possess only one, a commentary on Jonah. Both universities received their copy within fifty years of publication. He is described as 'Lusitanus' on the title-page, which is dedicated to King Sebastião and dated Coimbra 20 October 1571. Two years later the book was published in Venice, and it was this edition that reached the English universities.

Barbosa Machado, III, pp. 702–3.

869 Commentarii pii, docti et catholici in Ionam prophetam, Venetiis, apud Io. Bapt. Somascum, 1573. 8°
BOD 8° S 42(2) Th. In 1605 catalogue with the same shelf-mark.
G&C M.4.22 (3) Bequeathed by William Branthwaite, Master, in 1619. He was one of the revisers of the Bible (Adams T1209).

Trinitarians

870 Institutio siue fundatio, Ordinis sanctissimae ac indiuiduae Trinitatis, & redemptionis captiuorum, *with* Constitutiones . . . prouinciae Portugalliae, Caeremoniale, Vlyssippone, excudebat Emmanuel de Lyra, 1591. 8°
BOD Antiq. f.P. 1591.1 The shelf-mark indicates that it was acquired between 1883 and 1936 (Anselmo 755–6).

871 Officia propria recitanda a fratribus Ordinis sanctissimae Trinitatis, Vlyssipone, ex officina Gerardi de Vinea, 1621. 4°
CHC Allestree J.4.8.(1) From the Allestree bequest of 1681. Bound with **872–3**.

872 Officium de Sanctissimo nomine B. Virginis Mariae. Recitandum a Fratribus Ordinis Sanctissimae Trinitatis, Ulyssipone, ex officina Petri Craesbeeck Typographi, 1627. 4°
CHC Allestree J.4.8.(2) From the Allestree bequest of 1681. Bound with **870, 872**.

873 Officium sanctissimi nominis Iesu cum missa eiusdem recitandum a Fratribus Sanctissimae Trinitatis, [Lisboa], ex officina Antonii Alvarez, 1638. 4°
CHC Allestree J.4.8. (3) From the Allestree bequest of 1681. Bound with **870–1**.
See also Liturgies and prayer books.

Usque, Abraão See Duarte Pinel.

874 Biblia en lengua española, [*in colofon* con yndustria y deligencia de Duarte Pinel Portugues, . . . Ferrara, Jeronimo de Vargas, 1553]. 8°
BOD O.T. Span. c.1. Previous shelf-mark Auctar. M.infra., which indicates acquisition at the end of the 18th century or later. Chain mark.
PMC LC.II.94 Given by Lancelot Andrewes, Bishop of Winchester, in 1589. Detailed and legible marginalia in Spanish (Adams B1254).

875 Biblia en lengua española, con yndustria y deligencia de Abrahã Usque Portugues, Ferrara, Tob Atias, 1553. Fol.
BOD C3.13 Th. Seld. From the Selden bequest of 1659. Lacks the colophon. Signed Bartholomeus Haggatt, Aleppo, 1613. Chain mark.
CUL (2 copies) BSS.212.B53.2; Young. 61 (Adams B1255).

Usque, Salomão (1510–)

Usque, who used the pseudonym Salusque (i.e., Sal.Usque) Lusitanus, is probably to be identified with Duarte Gomes, a New Christian doctor who was educated in Lisbon and Salamanca and taught at the University of Lisbon before leaving for Italy in the late 1530s. His translation into Spanish of Petrarch, though regarded as an important work today, was of no interest to the early modern universities. Lopes Andrade believes that Salomão Usque also worked on the translation of the Bible published by Abraão Usque/Duarte Pinel.

António Manuel Lopes Andrade, 'A figura de Salomão Usque', pp. 19–24.

876 De los sonetos, canciones, mandriales y sextinas del gran poeta . . . Francisco Petrarca, . . . parte primera . . ., en Venecia, en casa de Nicolao Beuilaqua, 1567. 4°

BOD Toynbee 1859. Acquired from Paget Toynbee (1855–1932) in 1929.

Usque, Samuel (after 1497?–)

His famous account of the sufferings of the Portuguese Jewish community (**877**) was first published in Ferrara in 1553 and then many years later in a second, clandestine edition intended perhaps for the crypto-Jews of Antwerp. Neither of the copies in Oxford, which are both of the second edition, is likely to be of old provenance.

Very little is known of Usque's life except that he was born in Portugal and emigrated to Italy. He is unlikely to have been a close relative of Abraão Usque.

Samuel Usque, *Consolação às Tribulações de Israel*, I, pp. 50 and 103–5; António Manuel Lopes Andrade, 'Os senhores do desterro de Portugal . . .', p. 79.

877 Consolacam as tribulacoens de Ysrael, en Ferrare, en casa de Abraham aben Usque, 5313 (1553) (really Amsterdam or Dordrecht, 1599/1600). 8°

BOD Opp.adds.8°1.349 ASC SR. 68.d.16.

Vasconcelos, Agostinho Manuel de (1584–1641) (Vasconcellos)

A historian, all of whose work is in Spanish. The first of his books to reach Oxford, in 1735, is **878**, which is a discussion of the legitimacy of Spanish rule in Portugal after 1580 (see also José Teixeira and Duarte Nunes de Leão). After Portugal had regained its independence Vasconcelos was executed for his adherence to the Castilian cause. Yet **879–80** show him also to have been a patriotic historian of Portugal. Vasconcelos's work was of little interest to early modern Oxford and Cambridge, and six of the nine copies of his books now in the libraries arrived after 1800.

Grande Enciclopédia Portuguesa e Brasileira, XXXIV, p. 271.

878 Sucession del señor rey Don Felipe segundo en la corona de Portugal, Madrid, por Pedro Tazo, [in colophon: por la viuda de Alonso Martin]1639. 8°

BOD Tanner 566. From the bequest of Bishop Thomas Tanner (1674–1735). In 1697 it belonged to Constantin Douffet, a canon of Liège. Much annotation in Spanish.

879 Vida de Don Duarte de Meneses, tercero conde de Viana, y sucessos notables de Portugal en su tiempo . . ., Lisboa, por Pedro Craesbeeck, 1627. 4°

BOD 210 m.394 Acquired after 1864 TAY Finch.H.153.A Acquired in 1941, using money left by Robert Finch, of Balliol (1783–1830) WOR ZZ.8.10 Bequeathed by H. A. Pottinger in 1911.

880 Vida y acciones del rey don Iuan el Segundo . . ., Madrid, en la imprenta de Maria de Quiñones, 1639. 4°

BOD 4° F 36 Med. Purchased in 1825. Some marginal marks and underlinings ASC SR 89 E 1 Perhaps bought at the Stuart sale in 1821 TAY 269.E.6 (Martin) Part of the Martin collection, left in 1895. Marginalia in Portuguese and Spanish WAD G 22.24 With marginalia in Spanish.

CUL T.10.56 From the Royal Library, deposited in 1715.

Vasconcelos, António de (1554–1622)

A Jesuit historian. There are Lisbon licences in **881**, issued in 1618, but Barbosa Machado only records the Antwerp edition. This ambitious publication, which contains engravings of all the kings of Portugal, could perhaps only be printed abroad. The costs were met by Manuel Soeiro, a Portuguese nobleman who was lord of Voorde or Varden in Flanders. The Portuguese subject-matter and authorship of this book are stated on the title-page. One copy at least has been in Oxford since the seventeenth century (none in Cambridge).

Barbosa Machado, I, p. 411; *Grande Enciclopédia Portuguesa e Brasileira*, XXIX, p. 508.

881 Anacephalaeoses, id est, summa capita actorum regum Lusitaniae, *with* epigrammata in singulos reges ab insigni poeta Emmanuele Pimenta eiusdem societatis. Et illorum effigies ad viuum expressae, Antuerpiae, apud Petrum & Ioannem Belleros, 1621. 4°

BOD BB 42(2) Art. Chain mark. The shelf-mark indicates that the book, which may have come from another library, was acquired after 1710, but a copy is listed in the 1635 appendix to the 1620 catalogue ASC ff.infra 10 In the 17th century this book belonged to Valentine Carey (died 1626), Vice-Chancellor of Cambridge and Bishop of Exeter, William Bourchier, Earl of Bath (died 1623) and the arms painter Sylvanus Morgan (1620–93). None of these were connected to All Souls.

Vasconcelos, Pedro Afonso (16th cent.)

A canonist, who was sent by his employer, Dom Teotónio de Bragança, Archbishop of Évora, to Madrid, where he published **882**, the second edition of his treatise on canon law. That was the edition to reach Oxford. As often happened, the first edition, published in Coimbra in 1588 did not succeed abroad. There are no copies in Cambridge.

Barbosa Machado, III, p. 547.

882 De harmonia rubricarum iuris canonici prima, et secunda pars, Madriti, 1590. 4°

BOD II 38 Jur. In the catalogue of 1620. The book was reshelved and given a new shelf-mark after 1710.

Vaz, Álvaro (1526–93) (Alvarus Valascus or Valasco)

A lawyer, whose career was divided between university posts in Coimbra and the royal service in Lisbon, where he was a judge. Most of his work was published postumously, sometimes through the agency of his son, Francisco Vaz de Gouveia (1580–1659), who contributed prefaces to **884** and **887**. However, there are exceptions in **888** and the first volume of the *Decisiones* Lisbon, 1588 (no copy in Oxford or Cambridge). The family were New Christians, and Vaz's son was the subject of a failed Inquisitorial process. He may have had access to international New Christian commercial networks, because his father's work was published widely outside Portugal. All eight copies of books by Vaz in Oxford and Cambridge have early provenance and all of them make reference to Portugal on the title-page.

António Baião, *Episódios dramáticos da inquisição portuguesa*, I, pp. 167–200.

883 Decisiones consultationum ac rerum iudicatarum in regno Lusitaniae, Spirae Nemetum, apud Bernardum Albinum, 1597. 4°

BOD 4° V 5 Jur. Seld. From the Selden bequest of 1659. In the 1674 catalogue **JSO** C.8.5 Gall From the bequest of Sir Leoline Jenkins, lawyer and diplomat, 1685.

TRH B*.7.15 Numbered 9 on the fore-edge, which is an indication that the book was probably acquired in the 17th century. College bookplate of 1700 (Adams V19).

884 Decisiones consultationum ac rerum iudicatarum in regno Lusitaniae, libri duo, Francofurti, e collegio Musarum Paltheniano, [from title page of Liber ii, 1608]. Fol.

BOD V 6.4(1) Jur. In the 1620 catalogue, with the same shelf-mark. Chain mark. Bound with **887**.

885 Decisionum consultationumque ac rerum iudicatarum in regno Lusitaniae, tomi duo, *with* Praxis partitionum et Collationum inter haeredes, Antverpiae, [name of printer illegible], 1621. Fol.

NEW BT1.8.1. 17th-century Oxford binding. Chain marks. In the catalogue of 1686.

886 Praxis partitionum et collationum inter haeredes, Conimbricae, ex officina Didaci Gomez Loureyro, 1605. 4°

BOD AA 11 Med Seld. From the Selden bequest of 1659. In the 1674 catalogue, chain mark.

887 Praxis partitionum et collationum inter haeredes, Francofurti, e collegio Musarum Partheniano, 1608. Fol.

BOD V 6.4(2) Jur. Bound with **884**.

888 Quaestionum iuris emphyteutici liber primus seu prima pars, 2a ed., Olyssippone, excudebat Balthesar Riberius, 1591. Fol.
BOD KK 18(1) Jur. Formerly V.2.4.Jur. In the 1605 catalogue with the shelf-mark V.3.4.Jur. It acquired its present shelf-mark after 1710 (Anselmo 993).

Vaz, Lopes
A historian, of the Spanish empire in America, known to early modern Oxford and Cambridge only through Hakluyt's translation. See also Chapter One, pp. xli–iii.

A discourse of the West Indies and the South sea, written by Lopez Vaz a Portugall, *translated from an MS. in Portuguese by Richard Hakluyt*, Principal Navigations, Vol. III, pp. 778–825 (See **446**).

Vaz, Tomé (1551-after 1620) (Thomas Vallascus)
A lawyer, and a New Christian, who confessed to having reverted to Judaism at his trial, 1618–20, but not related to Álvaro Vaz. His book, which is in the 1674 Bodley catalogue, is one of the very few included in the short-title catalogue to have been published in Oporto. The title-page states that he was Portuguese.
António Baião, *Episódios dramáticos da inquisição portuguesa*, I, pp. 131–8.

889 Allegationum super varias materias primus tomus, in ciuitate Portugalensi, ex officina Fructuosi Laurentii de Basto, 1612. Fol.
BOD AA 9 Med Seld. From the Selden bequest of 1659. In the 1674 catalogue, chain mark. Underlinings.

Veiga, Manuel (1527–1647)
A Jesuit, compiler of a work in Portuguese about Ethiopia and Tibet which came to the Bodleian in 1828.
Inocêncio, VI, pp. 121–2.

890 Relaçam geral do estado da christandade de Ethiopia, Lisboa, por Mattheus Pinheiro, 1628. 4°
BOD 4° L 21 Art.BS. Purchased in 1828.

Veiga, Tomás Rodrigues da (1513–1579/93) (Thomas Rodericus a Veiga)
This New Christian doctor was born in Évora and was a professor in Coimbra. He – or possibly one of his descendants – was the recipient of a bull of Sixtus V, dated 1585, instructing the king of Portugal and his successors to receive members of his family as noblemen and to relieve them from paying any taxes as 'cristãos novos'. All Veiga's children, except one, entered the religious life.

Like his brother André Rodrigues de Évora and the humanist André de Resende, Veiga was pround of his native city, and on the title-page of his books he is described as 'Eborensis'. Évora, the seat of a Jesuit university and a favourite residence of the Portuguese royal family, was a more important centre in the early modern period than it is today, and contemporary foreign readers may not have needed to be reminded what country it was in. However, the next author to be discussed, Brás Viegas, was not so sanguine, and invariably added 'Lusitano' to 'Eborensi'. Rodrigues da Veiga's career was spent in Portugal, but only one copy of one book that he published there reached Oxford, and none reached Cambridge. At least nine of the eleven copies of works by him in the short-title catalogue were acquired in the early modern period. Friedenwald, I, pp. 290–2.

891 Opera omnia in Galeni libros edita . . ., Lugduni, apud Petrum Landry, 1593 [in some copies, 1594]. Fol.
CHC On.2.9. With a binding of around 1600. Chain mark **MGO** r.13.13.
SJCC Mm.3.22 Bequeathed by John Collins, fellow and Professor of Physick, in 1634 (Adams V350).

892 Commentarii in libros Claud. Galeni duos, de febrium differentiis, Conimbricae, apud Ioannem Barrerium, 1578. 4°
SJCO HB4/4.b.5.11 Given by William Paddy, 1602 (Anselmo 226).

893 Tomus primus commentariorum in Claudii Galeni opera, Antuerpiae, ex officina Christophori Plantini, 1564–1566. 2 vols Fol.
BOD V 1.12 Med. In the 1620 catalogue **MER** (2 copies) 46.A.11, 2 vols in 1. Oxford binding using rolls xii and xviii, used together 1575–1605 (Pearson, p. 67). Bequeathed by Robert Barnes, fellow, in 1604, aparently for the exclusive use of his son-in-law, John Euelegus, but also stated to be the gift of Helen Gulston, widow of Theodore Gulston, M.D. and fellow, who died in 1635; 46.F.9(2) Oxford binding similar to that just described. Chain marks **JSO** I.9.4. Gall **PMO** U8d Oxford binding, Ker roll no. HM.d(1), which was in use 1535–75 (Pearson, p. 72). Evidence of chaining **SJCO** Y.2.14 Given by William Paddy, 1602, with underlinings.
CLA L1.2.37 2 vols in 1. With the 1701 college bookplate. In the catalogue of 1677–78 with the shelf-mark U.9 (Adams V349).

Velésio, António
See Manuel Álvares

Viegas, Brás (1553–1599) (Blasio)
A Jesuit, a Portuguese, and a professor at the university of Évora, as every title-page proudly proclaims, except the mysterious **900** which has almost no bibliographical information of any kind. Viegas ensured that his commentary on the Apocalypse would be known internationally by dedicating it to an Italian cardinal, Odoardo Farnese, the son of Alexander Farnese and the Portuguese Maria of Bragança, and it

obtained the enthusiastic backing of Claudio Aquaviva, the General of the Order (see the dedication included in **894, 895** and **897**). Of the seventeen copies of books by him in Oxford and Cambridge fifteen can be shown to be of old provenance. Most copies of the editions of the commentary printed outside Portugal arrived shortly after publication, and in the case of the copy of **895** now in St John's Oxford, in the year of publication.

Francisco Rodrigues *História da Companhia de Jesus na Assistência de Portugal*, II.2., p. 125.

894 Commentarii exegetici in Apocalypsim Ioannis apostoli, Eborae, apud Emmanuelem de Lyra, 1601. Fol.

BOD C 17.8 Th. The statement on the first page of the index, 'Do Collegio de S. Jeronymo', indicates that it was probably not an early acquisition **QUO** 70.B.13. Oxford 17th-century binding. Chain mark.

895 Commentarii exegetici in Apocalypsim Ioannis apostoli, Lugduni, sumptibus Horatii Cardon, 1602. 4°

BOD B 23.1 Linc. Part of the Barlow bequest of 1691, but in the 1605 catalogue also, so a replacement copy. Chain mark **SJCO** G.4.25 Given by the recusant Thomas Tresham in 1602 **WAD** I 23.1 Given by Philip Bisse in 1613.

SID R.5.1 In the catalogue of 1674. With the title on the top edge, a practice which continued until the 1640s, and on the fore-edge (Rogers, p. 78) **SJCC** Qq.9.11 Part of the Crashawe collection, deposited in 1626.

896 In Apocalypsim Ioannis apostoli commentarii exegetici, Coloniae Agrippinae, apud Ioannem Honthemium, 1603. 4°

CHC Jb.1.37. Oxford 17th-century binding. Chain mark.

CUL E*.5.34 (D) Acquired before 1715. In the catalogue of the 'Old Library' with the same shelf-mark.

897 Commentarii exegetici in Apocalypsim Ioannis apostoli, Parisiis, apud viduam Petri Bertault, 1606.4°

CCCO Z.50.4 Bequeathed by John Spenser, president of the college, who died 3 Apr 1614. Chain mark.

CLA N.6.6. The gift of William Bridon, a former student, who took his M.A. in 1582. With the college bookplate of 1701 and the shelf-mark Aa.32 on the fore-edge. In the catalogue of 1677–78 with the same shelf-mark **G&C** L.23.24 (Printed by Dionysius Binet). With the signature of Walter Parker, Sept. 1639.

898 Commentarii exegetici in Apocalypsim Ioannis apostoli, Venetiis, apud Societatem Venetam,1608. 4°

CUL U*.5.66 (D) Acquired before 1715.

899 Commentarii exegetici in Apocalypsim Ioannis apostoli, Parisiis, apud viduam Petri Bertault, 1615. 4°

UNI K.4.8. Oxford 17th-century binding. Chain mark.

TRC D.8.112 Numbered 84 and 26 on the fore-edge. Stamped armorial centrepiece with S E., perhaps the chaplain Sylvius Elwes, who gave books, chiefly of divinity, 1626–30.

900 Vaticinium de Babylonis et meretricis Romanae excidio, [no place or publisher, but this edition is based on **896**], 1632. 4°
   JSO R.6.19 (6) Gall.
   CUL Dd*.3.14 (E) From the Royal Library, deposited in 1715.

Visitação, Cristóstomo de (−1604) (Chrysostomus a Visitatione/ Chrysostome de la Visitation)
A Cistercian, much of whose career was spent in Rome and Venice, where he wrote his work in two volumes about the Virgin Mary (see the dedication of **901**). However, his Portuguese origin is proclaimed on the title-page, and reinforced in the dedication of vol. 2 to Duke Ramusio Farnese, whose mother was the Portuguese Maria de Bragança. Both Oxford and Cambridge have a copy acquired shortly after publication.
Barbosa Machado, I, pp. 565–6.

901 De verbis Dominae. Hoc est, De verbis quae Maria Deipara ad angelum, & ad Elisabeth cognatam locuta est, Venetiis, apud Iacobum Vincentium, & Ricciardum Amadinum, socios, 1600. 2 vols. 4°
   BOD 4° C 13 Th. In the 1605 catalogue with the same shelf-mark.
   SJCC P.9.24 From the Crashawe collection, deposited in 1626 (Adams V887).

Willes, Richard (1546–79?)
A compiler of geographical information and the predecessor of Hakluyt and Purchas. He translated two short texts (neither of them in Portuguese) by Luís Fróis and Galeote Pereira. See Chapter One, p. xli.

902 The History of Travayle in the West and East Indies, imprinted at London by Richard Jugge, 1577. 4°
   BOD (2 copies) D.11.12. Linc. From the Barlow bequest of 1691; Douce E 258 From the Douce bequest of 1834 CHC Arch.Inf.B.5.19.
   FITZ Acquired in 1818 (STC 649).

Zacutus Lusitanus (1575–1642)
Zacutus lived and practised in Portugal until the age of 50, when for religious reasons he moved to Amsterdam. All his printed works appeared after that date, and in all of them he is described as 'Lusitanus'. Of the nineteen copies of his books in Oxford and Cambridge, fifteen were acquired before 1750.
Encyclopaedia Judaica, XVI, cols. 909–10.

903 De medicorum principum historia libri sex, Coloniae Agrippinae, ex officina Iohannis Frederici Stam,1629. 8°
   JSO I.6.12 Gall Bequeathed by Griffith Davies, M.D. and fellow, in 1724.

904 De medicorum principum historia, liber primus [-sextus], Amstelodami, sumptibus Henrici Laurentii, 1636–39 [some sets are made up from the 1st and 2nd eds]. 4 vols. 8°

BOD 8° L 27–31 Med. In the MS. additions to the 1620 catalogue **JSO** I.6.13–16 (2) Gall. Bequeathed by Griffith Davies, M.D. and fellow, in 1724 **SJCO** Hb4/4.b.6.5–6 With the signature of John Merrick (1671–1757), fellow, or of his son, also John, fellow 1721–1733.

CUL Hh.17.16 Vol. 1 only. Given by John Worthington (1663–1738), who had been a fellow of Peterhouse **SJCC** Ll.7.4–8 Signed Wrench, 1639, perhaps Richard Wrench who was a fellow, 1636–46.

905 De praxi medica admiranda, libri tres, *with* ad philiatros candidissimos exhortatio, Amstelodami, typis Cornelii Breugeli, sumptibus Henrici Laurentii, 1634. 8°

BOD 8° L 26 Med. **CHC** f.2.9 From the bequest of Robert Burton, 1640. Chain mark (Kiessling (1988) 1730) **JSO** I.6.17 Gall. Bequeathed by Edward Herbert, Baron Cherbury (1583–1648), diplomat and writer on religion **SJCO** HB4/4.b.6.2 MS. notes, probably of the 17th century.

CUL K.17.40 From the Royal Library, deposited in 1715 **PMC** 10.12.33 Given by William Quarles (?1607–?74), fellow and medical practitioner, in 1640. **SJCC** Ll.7.3 **TRC** S.10.169. Belonged to Timothy? Ashenhurst. In the catalogue compiled between 1667–75 with the number 7.

906 Praxis medica admiranda, Lugduni, apud Ioannem-Antonium Huguetan, 1637. 8°

BOD Vet. E2 e. 9 Acquired in 1938 from the Radcliffe Library, which was established using funds left by John Radcliffe (bap. 1650–1714).

CUL K.17.4 From the Royal Library, deposited in 1715 **EMM** 324.8.50, formerly E.5.63, under which it is listed in the 18th-century catalogue. No book printed before 1712 appears in this part of the catalogue, and it is reasonable to assume that the book entered the library before then. The book has a 17th-century Cambridge binding, no tab, and the title inscribed on the fore-edge (unusual at Emmanuel), perhaps indicating that it came from another library **G&C** K.21.28 Cambridge 17th-century binding with fillets **SJCC** Mm.12.43.

BIBLIOGRAPHY

The Bibliography is divided into six sections, as follows:

1. Library Catalogues and Benefactors' Registers (where these consist mostly of donations to libraries) pp. 183–7.
2. Works on the history and content of libraries pp. 188–91.
3. Works on printers and printing-houses pp. 191–2.
4. Other bibliographical works pp. 192–3.
5. Early modern sources consulted (other than those listed in previous sections) pp. 193–6.
6. Works written after 1750 consulted (other than those listed in previous sections) pp. 196–206.

1. Library Catalogues and Benefactors' Registers (where these consist mostly of donations to libraries):

Libraries in Oxford:

Bodleian Library (and dependent libraries)

Bibliotheca Radcliviana, 1749–1949: Catalogue of an Exhibition (Oxford: Bodleian Library, 1949).

Coates, Alan, et al. (eds), *A Catalogue of Books Printed in the Fifteenth Century now in the Bodleian Library*, 6 vols (Oxford: Oxford University Press, 2005).

[Hyde, Thomas, et al.], *Catalogus impressorum librorum Bibliothecae Bodleianae* (Oxford: Sheldonian Theatre, 1674).

[James, Thomas], *The First Printed Catalogue of the Bodleian Library, 1605: a facsimile* (Oxford: Clarendon Press, 1986).

James, Thomas, *Catalogus universalis librorum in bibliotheca Bodleiana* (Oxford: John Lichfield and James Short, 1620). The copy shelved at BOD 4o Rawl. 597 has MS additions on interleaved pages.

[James, Thomas], *Appendix ad catalogum librorum in bibliotheca Bodleiana qui prodiit anno domini 1620* . . . (Oxford: John Lichfield, 1635).

[Kidd, John] *Catalogue of the Works in Medicine and Natural History Contained in the Radcliffe Library* (Oxford: Collingwood, 1835).

College Libraries

Morgan, Paul, *Inter-Collegiate Catalogue of Pre-1640 Foreign Books in Oxford Libraries outside the Bodleian,* 16 vols (Oxford: 1979). This work, described as a 'provisional printout', is shelved at BOD R.Bibl.121/1–16.

All Souls College

L.R.4.d.2 MS. 418: 'Catalogus librorum in Bibliotheca Chichleiana juxta seriem alphabeticam'. In use between 1665–1689.

L.R.4.d.3 MS 416: A shelf-list, by author, dated June 12 1756.

L.R.5 1.10: 'Catalogus librorum ad Bibliothecam Collegii Animarum omnium Fidelium defunctorum de Oxon[ia] spectantium et donatorum eorundem'.

MS 421c, fols 68v-85: Transcription of 'Catalogue of Dudley Digs books bequeathed by him unto our colledg and placed in ye study of ye Wardens lodging untill room be made for some of them in our Colledg library and the rest be disposed of for ye Colledg use', made by Edmund Craster 16 Nov 1949.

MZ.7.ST: *A Catalogue of a Choice and Valuable Collection of Books in all Classes of Spanish Literature . . . to be sold by John Bohn* (no place, date, or name of publisher, but after 1826).

Balliol College

MS Balliol College: 'Catalogus librorum et benefactorum bibliothecae collegii de Baliolo, Oxon'. This incomplete catalogue of the library contains only authors A-M. It was compiled around 1673.

MS 865 a 4: A catalogue without a title but dated 1721.

MS 895.f.7: 'Catalogus impressorum librorum in bibliotheca Balliolensi', dated at end 1709.

[Rathbone, John] *Catalogue of Printed Books in Balliol College Library* (Oxford: Combe, 1871).

Brasenose College

MS Brasenose 88: A catalogue probably of the seventeenth century.

MS S/Folio 2.6: A catalogue which may have been compiled in 1717.

Christ Church

'Catalogus librorum omnium in Bibliotheca Aedis Christi', dated 1665.

[Hyde, Thomas, et al.], *Catalogus impressorum librorum Bibliothecae Bodleianae* (Oxford: Sheldonian Theatre, 1674). The college used its copy of the Bodley catalogue to record the additions to its holdings made as a result of the Wake bequest of 1737.

'A Catalogue of the Library of Charles late Earl of Orrery and which was sent down to Christ College in Oxford' (1732).

Corpus Christi College

Sigma. 12. 1: 'Catalogus Librorum Collegii Corporis Christi'.

Hertford College

Hertford College now incorporates the much older Magdalen Hall which was extinguished in the late nineteenth century. The old catalogues all relate to books belonging to the former hall.

'Catalogus Benefactorum Aulae Magd. Bibliotheculae quae extructa fuit in istam formam per H. Wilkinson S. Theo. Doctor et aulae Magdalae principalem anno MDCLVI' (1656).

'Catalogus Librorum in Aul. Mag. Bib. Oxon'. Perhaps compiled in the seventeenth century.

Wilkinson, Henry, *Catalogus librorum in bibliotheca Aulae Magdalenae* (Oxford: H. Hall, 1661).

Jesus College

C.1: 'A perfect and intire catalogue of all the Books belonging unto Jesus College in Oxford. A catalogue of Books belonging of old unto the Library of the said College.' The catalogue lists the books given by Dr Mansell in 1649.

LI.3: This catalogue includes 'Dr Mansell's books which are not allready in Jesus College Library'.

Magdalen College

MS 777: 'Catalogus Benefactorum Bibliothecae'. The first entry is dated 1637.

New College

BT1.4.6, New Coll. Archive 3582: 'Hunc catalogum memoriae omnium illorum qui hanc bibliothecam libris instruxerunt libentissime dicavit Arthurus Lake providentia divina Bathon: & Wellensis Episcopus huius collegii custos, prid. Kal. Iulii AD MDCXVII' (1617).

BT1.10.6: Untitled MS catalogue with the date of 1686 on the flyleaf.

BT1.12.12: A much shorter MS catalogue, perhaps of the mid 17th-century.

Oriel College

Case D.c.V.22. Catalogue of Oriel Library, of around 1684. It is dated 1625, but the date refers to the *Decretum* regulating library use, not to the catalogue.

Case D.c.V.21. Untitled MS catalogue. It seems to be a fair copy of D.c.V.22 and is in a similar hand.

Pembroke College

Catalogue of the Aristotelian and Philosophical Portions of the Library of the late Henry William Chandler . . . Preserved in the Library of Pembroke College, Oxford (Oxford: Clarendon Press, 1891).

St Edmund Hall

KK 167 'St Edmund Hall Library Catalogue', 2 vols., of the late eighteenth or early nineteenth century.

KK 169 is a second catalogue, dated 1792.

Trinity College

'Catalogus librorum in bibliotheca exteriori Collegii S. Trinitatis'. The so-called 'chained catalogue', probably of the early eighteenth century.

'Nomina et cognomina eorum spectabilium virorum quorum munificentia locupletat bibliothecam collegii hujus Stae. et Individuae Trinitatis'. The

first part of the book was compiled probably in the late 1620s when one of the
fellows was appointed librarian.

Libraries in Cambridge:

Adams, H. M., *Catalogue of Books Printed on the Continent of Europe, 1501–1600, in
Cambridge Libraries*, 2 vols (Cambridge: Cambridge University Press, 1967).

Cambridge University Library

UA.ULIB 7/3/2: An author catalogue of the 'Old Library', before the arrival of
the royal library in 1715.
UA.ULIB 7/3/3: A note on the flyleaf states that this catalogue 'represents the
arrangement and contents of the UL before 1715, when George I added
Bishop Moore's collection to the library'. It completes the information in UA.
ULIB 7/3/2.
UA.ULIB 7/3/36: A four-volume catalogue of the royal library (RL), the usual
name for the library of John Moore (1646–1714), Bishop of Ely, which was
bought by George I and presented in 1715.

Clare College

G1.3.28: 'Catalogus librorum omnium in Bibliotheca Aulae Clarensis'.
According to an MS note in the library's copy of Mansfield Forbes, *Clare
College,* (see Section 6 below) it was compiled in 1677–78.
Early Printed Books to the Year 1500 in the Library of Clare College, Cambridge
(Cambridge: Cambridge University Press, 1919).

Emmanuel College

Lib.1.2: The eighteenth-century class catalogue. An untitled catalogue, of
Archbishop Sancroft's library (1693) and other material, mostly listed before
1712.

Gonville and Caius College

MS 644/784: This MS catalogue, arranged by shelf, was mostly made between
1632 and 1642, but contains additions up to 1646.
Collett, W. R. *A List of the Early Printed Books in the Library of Gonville and Caius
College, Cambridge* (Cambridge: Deighton, 1850).

Jesus College

B.13.16: 'Catalogus librorum in Bibliotheca Coll. Jesu A.D. 1705'. This was
added to in a different hand, and contains some items given by Lionel Gatford
in 1715 (see for an example item 774).
B.13.8: An author catalogue, compiled in 1730.

King's College

Lib MS 1: 'Index Bibliothecae Regalis Collegii, in quo continentur dispositio
columnarum nomina benefactorum'. It was begun in 1612.
Lib MS 4: 'Catalogus Librorum', dated 1738.

Lib MS 5, 40.B.1: 'Catalogue of the library of King's College by [John] Woodyere Bookseller 1778 for the use of the Provost'.

Magdalene College

Smith, N. A. (ed.), *Catalogue of the Pepys Library at Magdalene College Cambridge*, 7 vols (Cambridge: Brewer, 1978–91).

Queens' College

MS F.IV.22: 'Nomina eorum, qui bibliothecam hanc suis donariis locupletarunt, hoc libro signantur'. This register begins in 1562 and continues to the eighteenth century.

'Collegium Reginale': This MS, which has no shelf-mark, is an alphabetized author and title combined catalogue. The bulk of it seems to have been completed in the 1680s.

Horne, Thomas Hartwell, *Catalogue of the Library of the College of St Margaret and St Bernard, commonly called Queen's College, in the University of Cambridge*, 3 vols (London: The Society of Queen's College, 1827).

St Catharine's College

Catalogus librorum in bibliotheca Aulae Divae Catharinae, Cantabrigiae (Cambridge: Archdeacon, 1771)

St John's College

MSS U.1: An author catalogue, compiled around 1640.

MSS U.3: 'Catalogus librorum Bibliothecae Johannensis, quo libri quotquot ibi extant disponuntur ordine prout singulis forulis cuiusque classes reponuntur'.

Sidney Sussex College

'Catalogus librorum in Bibliotheca collegii Sidney Sussex'. This is the first catalogue of the library, compiled in 1674.

'Catalogus Librorum in Bibliotheca Collegii Dominae Franciscae Sidney Sussex', of 1814.

Trinity College

Add MS a 101a: A catalogue compiled by Thomas Griffith, Librarian, 1667–75, with shelf marks.

Add MS a 104: 'Catalogue of the New Library', which is a fuller catalogue, with shelf marks, compiled 1675–95 (see Gaskell, *Trinity College Library: the First 150 Years*, p. 214).

Add. MS. A. 135: [Hyde, Thomas, et al.] *Catalogus impressorum librorum Bibliothecae Bodleianae*, 4 vols (Oxford: Sheldonian Theatre, 1738). In the eighteenth century the library used this interleaved copy of the catalogue to record its own holdings.

Add MS a 150: 'A Catalogue of Books given to Trinity College'.

2. Works on the history and content of libraries:

Beddard, R. A., 'The Official Inauguration of the Bodleian Library on 8 November 1602', *The Library*, 7th series, 3 (2002), 255–83.

Bloomfield, B. C. (ed.), *A Directory of Rare Book and Special Collections in the United Kingdom and the Republic of Ireland* (London: Library Association, 1997).

Bodley, Sir Thomas, *Letters of Sir Thomas Bodley to Thomas James*, edited by G. W. Wheeler (Oxford: Clarendon Press, 1926).

Briggs, G. M., 'The General Removal 1723', *Bodleian Library Record*, 3 (1951), 213–22.

Bruni, Roberto L. and D. Wyn Evans, *Italian Seventeenth-Century Books in Cambridge Libraries: a Short-Title Catalogue* (Florence: Olschki, 1997).

Bullard, M. R. A., 'Talking Heads: the Bodleian Frieze, its Inspiration, Sources, Designer and Significance', *Bodleian Library Record*, 14 (1994), 461–500.

Bush, Sargent and Carl J. Rasmussen, *The Library of Emmanuel College Cambridge* (Cambridge: Cambridge University Press, 1986).

Carron, Helen, 'William Sancroft (1617–93): A Seventeenth-Century Collector and his Library', *The Library*, 7th series, 1 (2000), 290–307.

Chambers, D. D. C., 'A catalogue of the library of Bishop Lancelot Andrewes', *Transactions of the Cambridge Bibliographical Society*, 5 (1970), 99–121.

Coates, Alan, 'The Bodleian Library and its Incunabula', *Bodleian Library Record*, 18 (2005), 608–43.

——, 'The Lawn Collection', *Bodleian Library Record*, 18 (2003), 197–9.

—— and Richard Gameson, *The Old Library Trinity College, Oxford* (Oxford: Trinity College, 1988).

——, 'The Old Library of Trinity College, Oxford', *Bodleian Library Record*, 13 (1991), 466–78.

Costin, W. C., 'The Inventory of John English, BCL, Fellow of St John's College', *Oxoniensia*, 11–12 (1946–7), 102–31.

Craster, Sir Edmund, *History of the Bodleian Library, 1845–1945* (Oxford: Bodleian Library, 1981).

——, 'John Rous, Bodley's librarian, 1620–52', *Bodleian Library Record*, 5 (1954–6), 130–46.

——, *The History of All Souls College Library*, edited by E. F. Jacob (London: Faber, 1971).

Davidson, Alan, 'Catholics and Bodley' *Bodleian Library Record*, 8 (1967–72), 252–57.

Earle, T. F., 'Portuguese Scholarship in Oxford in the Early Modern Period: The Case of Jerónimo Osório (Hieronymus Osorius)', *Bulletin of Spanish Studies*, 81 (2004), 1039–49.

——, 'Three Portuguese Best-Sellers in Early Modern Oxford and Cambridge, with a finding list', in Teresa Pinto Coelho (ed.), *The Treaty of Windsor (1386) and 620 Years of Anglo-Portuguese Relations*, 2006, 12 pp. http://www.clpic.ox.ac.uk/home.shtml

Fordyce, C. J. and T. M. Knox, 'The Library of Jesus College, Oxford', *Oxford Bibliographical Society Proceedings & Papers*, 5 (1937), 53–115.

Gaskell, Philip and Robert Robson, *The Library of Trinity College, Cambridge: A short history* (Cambridge: Trinity College, 1971).

Gaskell, Philip, *Trinity College Library: the First 150 Years* (Cambridge: Cambridge University Press, 1980).

Grierson, Philip, 'John Caius' Library', in John Venn et al. (eds), *Biographical History of Gonville and Caius College*, VII (1978), pp. 509–25.

J. J. Hall (ed.), *Peterborough Cathedral Library: A Catalogue of Books Printed before 1800 and now in Cambridge University Library* (Cambridge: Cambridge University Library, 1986).

Hampshire, Gwen, *The Bodleian Account Book, 1613–1646* (Oxford: Oxford Bibliographical Society, 1983).

Hanna, Ralph. *A Descriptive Catalogue of the Western Medieval Manuscripts of St John's College Oxford* (Oxford: Oxford University Press, 2002).

——, 'An Oxford Library Interlude: The Manuscripts of John Foxe the Martyrologist', *Bodleian Library Record*, 17 (2002), 314–26.

Hassall, W. O., *A Catalogue of the Library of Sir Edward Coke* (London: Yale University Press, 1950).

——, *The Books of Sir Christopher Hatton at Holkham* (London: The Bibliographical Society, 1950).

Hearne, Thomas, *Reliquiae Bodleianae: or Some Genuine Remains of Sir Thomas Bodley* (London: John Hartley, 1703).

Hinton, Lavinia, *Trinity Hall: The Story of the Library* (Cambridge: Trinity Hall, 2000).

Hiscock, W. G., *A Christ Church Miscellany* (Oxford: privately printed, 1946).

Jayne, S., *Library Catalogues of the English Renaissance* (Godalming, 1983).

Jayne, Sears and Francis R. Johnson, *The Lumley Library: The Catalogue of 1609* (London: British Museum, 1956).

Ker, Neil R., 'Oxford College Libraries in the Sixteenth Century', *Bodleian Library Record* , 6 (1957), 459–515.

——, *Records of All Souls College Library, 1437–1600* (Oxford: Oxford Bibliographical Society, 1971).

——, 'The Library of John Jewel', *Bodleian Library Record*, 9 (1973–78), 256–65.

Kiessling, Nicolas K., *The Library of Anthony Wood* (Oxford: Oxford Bibliographical Society, 2002).

——, *The Library of Robert Burton* (Oxford: Oxford Bibliographical Society, 1988).

Liddell, J. R., 'The Library of Corpus Christi College, Oxford, in the Sixteenth Century', *The Library* 18 (1938), 385–416.

Macray, William Dunn, *Annals of the Bodleian Library Oxford* 2nd edn. (Oxford: Clarendon Press, 1890; reprinted Bodleian Library, 1984). This book was first published in 1868.

Madan, Falconer and H. H. E. Craster, *Summary Catalogue of Western MSS in the Bodleian Library* (Oxford, Clarendon Press, 1922).

Mandelbrote, Scott, *Donors of Books to Peterhouse: An Exhibition to mark the opening of the Gunn Gallery 1 October 2005* (Cambridge: Rampant Lions Press, 2005).

McKitterick, David, *Cambridge University Library, A History: The Eighteenth and Nineteenth Centuries* (Cambridge: Cambridge University Press, 1986).

McKitterick, David, *The Library of Sir Thomas Knyvett of Ashwellthorpe c. 1539–1618* (Cambridge: Cambridge University Library, 1978).

McLachlan, H. John, 'Manchester College Library: Its History and Contents', undated typescript in Harris Manchester College library.

Morgan, Paul, 'Manchester College and its books', in Barbara Smith (ed.), *Truth, Liberty, Religion: Essays celebrating Two Hundred Years of Manchester College* (Oxford: Manchester College, 1986), pp. 111- 26.

——, *Oxford Libraries Outside the Bodleian: A Guide* (Oxford: Bodleian Library, 1980).

——, 'The Vicar's Library, St Mary's, Marlborough, Wiltshire', *Bodleian Library Record*, 12 (1985), 76–7.

Morrish, P. S., *Bibliotheca Higgsiana: A Catalogue of the Books of Dr Griffin Higgs (1589–1659)* (Oxford: Oxford Bibliographical Society, 1990).

Mortlock, D. P., *Holkham Library: A History and Description* (for presentation to members of the Roxburghe Club, 2006).

Ovenell, R. F., *Brian Twyne's Library* (Oxford: Oxford Bibliographical Society, 1952).

Page, R. I., 'Audits and replacements in the Parker Library: 1590–1650', *Transactions of the Cambridge Bibliographical Society*, 10 (1991), 17–39.

Philip, Ian, *The Bodleian Library in the Seventeenth and Eighteenth Centuries* (Oxford: Clarendon Press, 1983).

[Pogson] K. M. P., 'A Grand Inquisitor and his library', *Bodleian Quarterly Record*, 3 (1922), 239–44.

Pointer, Oliver, 'The Library', in C. S. L. Davies and Jane Garnett (eds), *Wadham College* (Oxford: Wadham College, 1994), pp. 92–9.

Private Libraries in Renaissance England, edited by R. J. Fehrenbach and E. S. Leedham-Green, 6 vols (Binghampton: Medieval and Renaissance Texts and Studies; Marlborough: Adam Matthew Publications, 1992–2004).

Rogers, Nicholas, 'The Early History of Sidney Sussex College Library' in D. E. D. Beales and H. B. Nisbet (eds), *Sidney Sussex College Cambridge* (Woodbridge: Boydell & Brewer, 1996), pp. 75–88.

Rothesay, Charles Stuart de, *Catalogue des livres de la bibliothèque du chevalier Stuart* (Paris: imprimé à l'hôtel de Sa Majesté Britannique, 1821).

——, *Catalogue of the valuable library of the late right honourable Lord Stuart de Rothesay . . . which will be sold at auction, by Messrs. S. Leigh Sotheby & John Wilkinson . . . 31st day of May 1855.*

Sargent, Clare, 'Two Sixteenth-Century Book Lists from the Library of Queens' College, Cambridge', *Transactions of the Cambridge Bibliographical Society*, 12 (2001), 161–78.

Silveira, Luís (ed.), *Livros do século XVI impressos em Évora: núcleo da Biblioteca Pública e Arquivo Distrital de Évora* (Évora: Imprensa Moderna, 1941).

Simoni, Anna E. C., *Catalogue of Books from the Low Countries 1601–1621 in the British Library* (London: The British Library, 1990).

Smith, J. Henderson, 'The Book-Plates of All Souls' College, Oxford', *Journal of the Ex-Libris Society* 9 (1899), 19–23.

Streeter, B. H., *The Chained Library: a Survey of Four Centuries in the Evolution of the English Library* (London: Macmillan, 1931).

Stubbings, Frank, *A Brief History of Emmanuel College Library* (Cambridge: Emmanuel College, 1996).

Ungerer, Gustav, 'The Earl of Southampton's Donation to the Bodleian in 1605 and its Spanish Books', *Bodleian Library Record*, 16 (1997–9), 17–41.

Gregory Walker, Mary Clapinson and Lesley Forbes (eds), *The Bodleian Library: A Subject Guide to the Collections* (Oxford: Bodleian Library, 2004)

Wallis, P. J., 'The Library of William Crashawe', *Transactions of the Cambridge Bibliographical Society*, 2 (1956), 213–28.

Warner, Lyndan, 'Fellows, Students, and their Gifts to Jesus College Library', *Transactions of the Cambridge Bibliographical Society*, 11 (1996–99), 1–48.

Wheeler, G. W., 'Bodleian Press-Marks in Relation to Classification', *Bodleian Quarterly Record* , 1 (1916), 280–92 and 311–22.

——, *The Earliest Catalogues of the Bodleian Library* (Oxford: Oxford University Press, 1928).

Wijffels, Alain, *Late Sixteenth-Century Lists of Law Books at Merton College* (Cambridge: LP, 1992).

——, 'Law Books in Cambridge Libraries, 1500–1640', *Transactions of the Cambridge Bibliographical Society*, 10 (1993), 359–412.

Wilkinson, C. H.,'Worcester College Library', in *Transactions of the Oxford Bibliographical Society*, 1 (1927), 263–326.

3. Works on printers and printing-houses:

Abad, Julián Martín, *La imprenta en Alcalá de Henares*, 3 vols (Madrid: Arco, 1991).

Almeida, M. Lopes de, *Livros, livreiros, impressores em documentos da Universidade, 1600–1649* (Coimbra: Arquivo de Bibliografia Portuguesa, 1964).

——, *Livros, livreiros, impressores em documentos da Universidade, 1587–1835* (Coimbra: Arquivo de Bibliografia Portuguesa, 1966).

Baudrier, Président, *Bibliographie lyonnaise: recherches sur les imprimeurs, libraires, relieurs et fondeurs de lettres de Lyon au XVIe siècle*, 13 vols (Paris: F. de Nobele, 1964).

Deslandes, Venâncio, *Documentos para a história da tipografia portuguesa nos séculos XVI e XVII* (Lisbon: Imprensa Nacional, 1888; facsimile Lisbon: Imprensa Nacional, 1988).

Dias, João José Alves, *Craesbeeck: uma dinastia de impressores em Portugal* (Lisbon: Associação Portuguesa de Livreiros Alfarrabistas, 1996).

Evans, R. J. W., *The Wechel Presses: Humanism and Calvinism in Central Europe, 1572–1627* (Oxford: Past & Present, 1975).

Fidalgo, Lorenzo Ruiz, *La imprenta en Salamanca*, 3 vols (Madrid: Arco, 1994–5).

Fletcher, H. George, 'The final disposal of the Henric-Petri shop: a 1659 Leipzig witness', *Gutenberg-Jahrbuch*, 70 (1995), 184–5.

Griffin, Clive, *Journeymen-Printers, Heresy, and the Inquisition in Sixteenth-Century Spain* (Oxford: Oxford University Press, 2005).

Gutenberg comes to Japan: The Jesuit Mission Press, 1590–1620, catalogue of an exhibition held at the Bodleian Library, 16 January to 11 March 2006.

Gutiérrez, Luisa Cuesta, *La imprenta en Salamanca: avance al estudio de la tipografía salmantina (1480–1944)* (Salamanca: Excma. Diputación Provincial de Salamanca, 1960).

Hellinga, Lotte, 'Printing History as Cultural History', *Gutenberg-Jahrbuch*, 76 (2001), 20–6.

Loureiro, José Pinto, *Livreiros e livrarias de Coimbra* (Coimbra: Biblioteca Municipal, 1954).

Maclean, Ian, 'André Wechel at Frankfurt, 1572–1581', *Gutenberg-Jahrbuch*, 63 (1988), 146–76.

Norton, F. J., *Italian Printers 1501–1520* (London: Bowes & Bowes, 1958).

Peixoto, Jorge, *Relações de Plantin com Portugal: notas para o estudo da tipografia no século XVI* (Coimbra: Faculdade de Letras da Universidade de Coimbra, 1962).

Voet, Leon, *The Golden Compasses: A History of the Printing and Publishing Activities of the Officina Plantiniana at Antwerp*, 2 vols (Amsterdam: Vangendt, 1972).

4. Other bibliographical works:

Allison, A. F., *English Translations from the Spanish and Portuguese to the Year 1700* (London: Dawsons, 1974)

—— and D. M. Rogers, *The Contemporary Printed Literature of the English Counter-Reformation between 1558 and 1640*, 2 vols (Aldershot: Scolar, 1989–94)

Anselmo, António Joaquim, *Bibliografia das obras impressas em Portugal no século XVI* (Lisbon: Biblioteca Nacional, 1977). This a reprint of a work first published in 1926.

Barbosa Machado, Diogo, *Bibliotheca Lusitana*, 4 vols (Coimbra: Atlântida, 1965–67; 1st edition Lisbon: Antonio Isidoro da Fonseca, 1741–59).

Barlow, Thomas, *De Studio Theologiae or Directions for the Choice of Books in the Study of Divinity* (Oxford: Lichfield, 1700).

De Backer, Augustin, Auguste Carayon Aloys, and Carlos Sommervogel, *Bibliothèque de la Compagnie de Jésus*, 9 vols (Brussels: Schepens and Paris: Picard, 1890–1900).

Delerue, Paul Esmeriz, 'Pedro Nunes: contributo para uma síntese referenciada da sua bibliografia', *Revista da Biblioteca Nacional*, 7 (1992), 129–148.

Draudius [Draut], Georgius, *Bibliotheca Classica, siue Catalogus Officinalis, in quo singuli singularum facultatum ac professionum libri, qui in quavis fere lingua extant, quique intra hominum propemodum memoriam in publicum prodierunt . . .* (Frankfurt: Balthasar Ostern, 1625).

Fabian, Bernhard (ed.), *Die Messkataloge des sechzehnten Jahrhunderts*, 5 vols (Hildesheim and New York: Georg Olms, 1972–2001).

Faria, Francisco Leite de, 'As muitas edições de obras de Dom Jerónimo Osório', *Revista da Biblioteca Nacional*, 1 (1981), 116–35.

——, *Estudos bibliográficos sobre Damião de Góis e a sua época* (Lisbon: Secretaria de Estado da Cultura, 1977).

——, 'O maior sucesso editorial do século XVI: a *Imagem da Vida Cristã* de Frei Heitor Pinto', *Revista da Biblioteca Nacional*, Second Series, 2 (1987), 83–110.

Featherstone, Henry, *Catalogus librorum in diuersis locis Italiae emptorum, anno 1628* (London: John Legate, 1628).

Glendinning, Nigel, 'Spanish books in England: 1800–1850', *Transactions of the Cambridge Bibliographical Society*, 3 (1959–63), 70–92.

Heller, Martin J., *The Sixteenth-Century Hebrew Book: an Abridged Thesaurus*, 2 vols (Leiden: Brill, 2004).

Inocêncio [Innocencio Francisco da Silva], *Diccionario bibliographico portuguez*, 22 vols (Lisbon: Imprensa Nacional 1858–1923).

Jackson, K. David, *Camões and the First Edition of* The Lusiads, *1572* (Portuguese Literary and Cultural Studies: Dartmouth, 2003) [On CD-ROM].

Ker, Neil R., *Fragments of Medieval Manuscipts used as Pastedowns in Oxford Bindings* (Oxford: Oxford Bibliographical Society, 1954; reprinted, with corrections and additions [edited by David Rundle and Scott Mandelbrote], 2004).

Lee, Brian North, *Early Printed Book Labels: a Catalogue of Dated Personal Labels and Gift Labels Printed in Britain to the Year 1760* (Pinner: Private Libraries Association, 1976).

Leedham-Green, E. S., *Books in Cambridge Inventories: Book-Lists from Vice-Chancellor's Court Probate Inventories in the Tudor and Stuart Periods*, 2 vols (Cambridge: Cambridge University Press, 1986).

Martin, Robert, *Catalogus librorum, ex praecipiis Italiae emporiis selectorum . . .* (London: Thomas Harper, 1639)

Neville-Sington, P. A., 'The Primary Bibliography', in L. E. Pennington (ed.), *The Purchas Handbook*, 2 vols (London: The Hakluyt Society, 1997), II, pp. 465–573.

Palau y Dulcet, Antonio, *Manual del librero hispano-americano*, 28 vols (Barcelona: Palau, 1948–77).

Pearson, David, *Oxford Bookbinding, 1500–1640* (Oxford: Oxford Bibliographical Society, 2000).

Pfister, Louis, *Notices biographiques et bibliographiques sur les Jésuites de l'ancienne mission de la Chine (1552–1775)* (San Francisco: Chinese Materials Center, 1976).

Pollard, A. W. and G. R. Redgrave, *A Short-Title Catalogue of Books Printed in England, Scotland, & Ireland, and of English Books Printed Abroad (1475–1640)*, 2nd edition, revised by W. A. Jackson and F. S. Ferguson, completed by Katharine F. Pantzer, 3 vols (London: The Bibliographical Society, 1976–91).

Sá, Artur Moreira de, *Índices dos livros proibidos em Portugal no século XVI* (Lisbon: Instituto Nacional de Investigação Científica, 1983).

Streit, Robert, *Bibliotheca Missionum*, IV–V (Aachen: Verlag der Aschendorffschen Buchhandlung, 1928–9).

Verzeichnis deutscher Drucke des 17. Jahrhunderts <www.vd17.de>

5. Early modern sources consulted (other than those listed in previous sections):

Ascham, Roger, *Letters,* translated by Maurice Hatch and Alvin Vos (New York: Peter Lang, 1989).

Barbosa, Duarte, *O Livro de Duarte Barbosa*, edited by Maria Augusta da Veiga e Sousa, 2 vols (Lisbon: Ministério da Ciência e da Tecnologia, 1996)

Barlow, Thomas, *Exercitationes aliquot metaphysicae de Deo* (Oxford: A. Lichfield, 1658).

Barreiros, Gaspar, *Chorographia* (Coimbra: João Álvares, 1561; reprinted Coimbra: Por ordem da Universidade, 1968).

Boxer, C. R., *South China in the Sixteenth Century: being the narratives of Galeote Pereira, Fr. Gaspar da Cruz, O.P., Fr. Martín de Rada, O.E.S.A. (1550–1575)* (London: Hakluyt Society, 1953).

Burton, Robert, *The Anatomy of Melancholy*, edited by Thomas C. Faulkner and others, 6 vols (Oxford: Clarendon Press, 1992–2000). The Introduction to vol. 1, and the Commentary, which occupies vols 4–6, are by J. B. Bamborough.

Cacegas, Luís, *Primeira parte da História de S. Domingos*, edited by Luís de Sousa, 2 vols (Lisbon: Panorama, 1866).

Cardim, Fernão, *Tratados da Terra e Gente do Brasil*, edited by Ana Maria de Azevedo (Lisbon: Comissão Nacional para as Comemorações dos Descobrimentos Portugueses, 1997).

Castro, Estêvão Rodrigues de, *Obras poéticas em português, castelhano, latim, italiano*, edited by Giacinto Manuppella (Coimbra: Acta universitatis conimbricensis, 1967).

Costa, Cristóvão da, *Tratado das drogas e medicinas das Índias orientais*, translated and edited by Jaime Walter (Lisbon: Junta de Investigações do Ultramar, 1964).

Crashaw, William, *Romish Forgeries and Falsifications* (London: Matthew Lownes, 1606).

——, *The Bespotted Jesuite* (London: Batholomew Alsop, 1641).

Crónica do Condestável de Portugal D. Nuno Álvares Pereira, edited by António Machado de Faria (Lisbon: Academia Portuguesa da História, 1972).

Delgado, João Pinto, *Poema de la reina Ester, Lamentaciones del profeta Jeremías, Historia de Rut y varias poesías*, edited by I. S. Révah (Lisbon: Institut français au Portugal, 1954).

Dictionarium Latino Lusitanicum, ac Iaponicum (facsimile edition of item 269, Tokyo: Tokyo Bunyo, 1953).

Earle, T. F., 'Damião de Góis, *Deploratio Lappianae Gentis*. Text and Translation', *Humanitas*, 58 (2006), 347–67.

Évora, André Rodrigues de, *Sentenças para a ensinança e doutrina do Príncipe D. Sebastião*, edited by Luís de Matos (Lisbon: Banco Pinto & Sotto Mayor, n.d.).

Ferreira, Francisco Leite, *Noticias chronologicas da Universidade de Coimbra*, edited by Joaquim de Carvalho, I–II (Coimbra: Por ordem da Universidade, 1937–38).

Foxe, John, *Against Ierome Osorius Byshopp of Silvane in Portingall and against his slanderous Inuectiues. An Aunswere Apologeticall: For the necessary defence of the Evangelicall doctrine and veritie. First taken in hand by M. Walter Haddon, then undertaken and continued by M. Iohn Foxe, and now Englished by James Bell . . .* (London: John Daye, 1581).

——, *Contra Hieron. Osorium, eiusque odiosas insectationes pro Evangelicae veritatis necessaria Defensione, Responsio Apologetica. Per clariss. Virum Gualt. Haddonum inchoata: Deinde sucepta & continuata per Ioan. Foxum* . . . (London: John Daye, 1577).

——, *De Christo gratis iustificante contra Osorianam Iustitiam* (London, Thomas Pursue, 1583).

Geddes, Michael, *Several Tracts against Popery* (London: Lintott, 1715).

——, *The Church-History of Ethiopia* (London: Chiswell, 1696).

——, *The History of the Church of Malabar* . . . *Together with the Synod of Diamper* . . . *Done out of Portugueze into English* (London: Sam. Smith, 1694).

Góis, Damião de, *O livro de Eclesiastes,* edited by T. F. Earle (Lisbon: Fundação Calouste Gulbenkian, 2002).

Gunning, Peter, *The Paschal or Lent-Fast Apostolical & Perpetual* (London: R. Norton, 1662).

Haddon, Walter, *A Sight of the Portugall Pearle*, translated by Abraham Hartwell (London: William Seres, 1565).

Hakluyt, Richard (translator), *The Discovery and Conquest of Terra Florida, by Don Ferdinando de Soto and six hundred Spaniards his Followers, written by a Gentleman of Elvas* . . . *and translated out of Portuguese*, edited by William B. Rye (London: Hakluyt Society, 1851).

Hooker, Richard, *Works,* edited by W. Speed Hill, 7 vols (Cambridge, Mass: Harvard University Press, 1977–93).

Laud, William, *A Relation of the Conference between William Lawd* . . . *and Mr Fisher the Jesuite* (London: Richard Badger, 1639).

Leo the Moor, *A Geographical Historie of Africa*, translated by John Pory (London: George Bishop, 1600).

Lobo, Francisco Rodrigues, *Corte na Aldeia,* edited by José Adriano de Carvalho (Lisbon: Presença, 1991).

Montemayor, Jorge de, *La Diana,* edited by Juan Montero (Barcelona: Crítica, 1996).

Osório, D. Jerónimo, *Cartas,* translated and edited by A. Guimarães Pinto (Silves: Câmara Municipal de Silves, 1995).

——, *Tratado da Glória,* translated and edited by A. Guimarães Pinto (Lisbon: Imprensa Nacional-Casa da Moeda, 2005).

——, *Tratado da Justiça,* translated and edited by A. Guimarães Pinto (Lisbon: Imprensa Nacional-Casa da Moeda, 1999).

——, *Tratado da Verdadeira Sabedoria,* translated and edited by A. Guimarães Pinto (Lisbon: Imprensa Nacional-Casa da Moeda, 2002).

——, *Tratados da Nobreza Civil e Cristã,* translated and edited by A. Guimarães Pinto (Lisbon: Imprensa Nacional-Casa da Moeda, 2006).

Pinto, Fernão Mendes, *Peregrinação,* translated by Rebecca Catz (Chicago: University of Chicago, 1989).

Pinto, Fray Héctor, *Imagen de la vida cristiana,* edited by Edward Glaser (Barcelona: Juan Flors, 1967).

Purchas, Samuel, *Purchas his Pilgrimes*, 4 vols (London: William Stansby for Henrie Fetherstone, 1625).

Quiros, Pedro Fernandez de, *The Voyages of Pedro Fernandez de Quiros, 1595–1606*, 2 vols, translated by Sir Clements Markham (London: Hakluyt Society, 1904).

Resende, Garcia de, *Livro das obras de Garcia de Resende*, edited by Evelina Verdelho (Lisbon: Fundação Calouste Gulbenkian, 1994).

Sanches, Francisco (Franciscus Sanchez), *Opera Philosophica*, edited by Joaquim de Carvalho (Coimbra: Revista da Universidade de Coimbra, 1955).

——, *That Nothing is Known (Quod Nihil Scitur)*, edited and translated by Elaine Limbrick and Douglas F. S. Thompson (Cambridge: Cambridge University Press, 1988).

Statutes of the University of Oxford Codified in the Year 1636 Under the Authority of Archbishop Laud, edited by John Griffiths (Oxford: Clarendon Press, 1888).

Syllabus aliquot synodorum et colloquiorum, quae auctoritate et mandato Caesarum et regum, super negotio religionis, ad controversias conciliandas, indicta sunt: doctorum item aliquot ac piorum virorum utriusque religionis, tam Catholicae Romanae, quam Protestantium, libri & epistolae, vel ex iis excerpta; ex quibus videri potest, quam non difficilis controversiarum in religione conciliatio, si pugnandi vincendique animus absit, veritatis vero studium cum pacis studio conjungatur. (Orléans: no publisher, 1628.)

Taylor, Jeremy, *Ductor Dubitantium, or the Rule of Conscience in all her General Measures*, 2nd edition (London: Norton, 1671). The first edition was published in 1660.

Teive, Diogo de, *Tragédia do Príncipe João*, edited by Nair de Nazaré Castro Soares (Lisbon: Fundação Calouste Gulbenkian and Fundação para a Ciência e a Tecnologia, 1999).

Teixeira, Pedro, *Relaciones de Pedro Teixeira del origen, descendencia y succession de los Reyes de Persia, y de Harmuz, y de un viage hecho por el mismo autor dende la India Oriental hasta Italia por tierra*, edited by Eduardo Barajas Sala (Madrid: Miraguano & Polifemo, 1994).

Usque, Samuel, *Consolação às Tribulações de Israel*, edited by Yosef Hayim Yerushalami and José V. de Pina Martins, 2 vols (Lisbon: Fundação Calouste Gulbenkian, 1989).

Warren's Book, edited by Alfred William Winterslow Dale (Cambridge: Cambridge University Press, 1911).

Willes, Richard, *The History of Travayle in the West and East Indies* (London: Richard Jugg, 1577).

Willet, Andrew, *Synopsis papismi or a general view of the Papacy, with confutations of Romish errors from the Scriptures, Fathers, Councils, et. Etc*, edited by John Cumming, 10 vols (London: British Society for Promoting the Religious Principles of the Reformation, 1852).

6. Works written after 1750 consulted (other than those listed in previous sections):

Albuquerque, Martim de, 'Acerca de Fr. José de Teixeira e da teoria da origem popular do poder', *Arquivos do Centro Cultural Português*, 5 (1972), 571–86.

Almeida, Fortunato de, *História da Igreja em Portugal*, edited by Damião Peres, 4 vols (Oporto: Portucalense, 1967–1971).

Alves, Hélio J. S., *Camões, Corte-Real e o sistema da epopeia quinhentista* (Coimbra: Universidade de Coimbra, 2001).

Anderson, Benedict, *Imagined Communities* (London: Verso, 2006). First published in 1983.

Andrade, António Manuel Lopes, 'A figura de Salomão Usque: a face oculta do humanismo judaico-português', in *Gramática e humanismo: actas do colóquio de homenagem a Amadeu Torres,* 2 vols (Braga: Aletheia, 2005) II, pp. 15–25.

——, 'Os senhores do desterro de Portugal: judeus portugueses em Veneza e Ferrara em meados do século XVI', *Veredas* 6 (2006), 65–108.

Ashton, T. H. (ed.) *The History of the University of Oxford,* 8 vols (Oxford: Clarendon Press, 1984–2000).

Azevedo, Maria Antonieta Soares de, *O Prior do Crato* (Coimbra: Universidade de Coimbra, 1974).

Baião, António, *Episódios dramáticos da inquisição portuguesa,* 3 vols (Lisbon: Seara Nova, 1936–8).

——, *Itinerários da Índia a Portugal por terra* (Coimbra: Imprensa da Universidade, 1923).

Bedouelle, Guy and Bernard Roussel (eds), *Le temps des Réformes et la Bible* (Paris: Beauchesne, 1989)

Bethencourt, Francisco, *L'Inquisition à l'époque moderne* (Paris: Fayard, 1995).

Biblos: Enciclopédia Verbo das Literaturas de Língua Portuguesa, edited by José Augusto Cardoso Bernardes et al., 5 vols (Lisbon: Verbo, 1995–2005).

Binns, J. W., *Intellectual Culture in Elizabethan and Jacobean England: The Latin Writings of the Age* (Leeds: Cairns, 1990).

Boase, Charles William, *Register of the Rectors, Fellows and Other Members on the Foundation of Exeter College, Oxford with a History of the College and Illustrative Documents* 2 vols (Oxford: Oxford Historical Society and Baxter's, 1894).

Borges, Armindo, *Duarte Lobo (156?-1646): Studien zum Leben und Schaffen des portugiesischen Komponisten* (Regensburg: G. Bosse, 1986).

Bossy, John, *The English Catholic Community, 1570–1850* (London: Darton, Longmann, Todd, 1975).

Bourdon, Léon, 'Jerónimo Osório et les humanistes anglais', in *L'Humanisme portugais et l'Europe* (Paris: Fondation Calouste Gulbenkian, 1984), pp. 263–333.

——, 'Jerónimo Osório et Stanislas Hosius (1565–1578)', *Boletim da Biblioteca da Universidade de Coimbra,* 23 (1958) 1–105.

——, *La Compagnie de Jésus et le Japon, 1547–1570* (Paris: Fondation Calouste Gulbenkian, 1993).

——, 'Novas investigações sobre a viagem de Jerónimo Osório à Itália (1576–1577)', offprint from *Ocidente,* 171 (1952).

Bouza Álvarez, Fernando J., *Del escritorio a la biblioteca: la civilización escrita europea en la alta edad moderna (siglos XV–XVII)* (Madrid: Síntesis, 1992).

Boxer, C. R., 'Padre João Rodriguez Tçuzu S.J. and his Japanese Grammars of 1604 and 1620', *Boletim de filologia,* 11 (1950), 338–63.

——, *The Christian Century in Japan* (Berkeley: University of California Press, 1967).

——, *The Portuguese Seaborne Empire, 1415–1825* (Manchester: Carcanet, 1991).

——, *The Tragic History of the Sea, 1589–1622* (Cambridge: Hakluyt Society, 1959).

Brasenose College Register, 1505–1909, 2 vols (Oxford: Blackwell, 1909).

Brooke, Christopher, 'Learning and Doctrine', in Victor Morgan and Christopher Brooke, *A History of the University of Cambridge, 1546–1750* (Cambridge: Cambridge University Press, 2004), pp. 437–63.

——, 'The Syllabus, Religion and Politics 1660–1750', in Morgan and Brooke, pp. 511–41.

Buchan, John, *Brasenose College* (London: Robinson, 1898).

Burke, Peter, *Languages and Communities in Early Modern Europe* (Cambridge: Cambridge University Press, 2004).

Bylebyl, Jerome J., 'The School of Padua: Humanistic Medicine in the Sixteenth Century', in Charles Webster (ed.), *Health, Medicine and Mortality in the Sixteenth Century* (Cambridge: Cambridge University Press, 1979), pp. 335–70.

Carreira, José Nunes, *Filologia e crítica de Isaías no comentário de Francisco Foreiro (1522?–1581),* (Coimbra: privately printed, 1974).

Castle, Robert Sidney, *Pembroke College Cambridge, 1347–1947* (pamphlet probably printed in Cambridge in 1947).

Castro, José de, *Portugal no Concílio de Trento,* 6 vols (Lisbon: União Gráfica, 1944–1946).

Castro, Manuel de, *Escritores de la Provincia Franciscana de Santiago: siglos XIII–XIX* (Santiago de Compostela: no publisher, 1996).

Chartier, Roger, 'Crossing Borders in Early Modern Europe: Sociology of Texts and Literature', *Book History,* 8 (2005), 37–50.

——, *The Culture of Print: Power and the Uses of Print in Early Modern Europe,* translated by Lydia G. Cochrane (Cambridge: Polity, 1989).

Chouraqui, André, *Between East and West: A History of the Jews of North Africa,* translated by Michael M. Bernet (Philadelphia: Jewish Publication Society of America, 1968).

Collinson, Patrick, *Archbishop Grindal* (London: Cape, 1980).

Cooper, Michael, *Rodrigues the Interpreter* (New York: Weatherhill, 1974).

Coquillette, Daniel R., *The Civilian Writers of Doctors' Commons, London* (Berlin: Duncker & Humblot, 1988).

Costa, Mário Júlio de Almeida, 'O direito (cânones e leis)', *História da Universidade em Portugal, I.2 (1537–1771)* (Coimbra: Universidade de Coimbra, 1997), pp. 823–34.

Costello, W. T., *The Scholastic Curriculum at Early Seventeenth-Century Cambridge* (Cambridge, Mass.: Harvard University Press, 1968).

Costin, W. C., *The History of St John's College Oxford, 1598–1860* (Oxford: Clarendon Press, 1958).

Couto, Aires Pereira do, 'O poema *Fontelum* de António de Cabedo', *Humanitas,* 46 (1994), 333–49.

Coxito, Amândio A., 'O curso conimbricense', *História do Pensamento Filosófico Português,* II, edited by Pedro Calafate (Lisbon: Caminho, 2001), pp. 503–43.

Curtis, Mark H., *Oxford and Cambridge in Transition 1558–1642* (Oxford: Clarendon Press, 1959).

Curto, Diogo Ramada, *O discurso político em Portugal (1600–1650)* (Lisbon: Universidade Aberta, 1988).

Daniel, Charles Henry and Wilberforce Ross Barker, *Worcester College* (London: Routledge, 1998; reprint of the edition of 1900).

Davis, C. S. L. and Jane Garnett (eds), *Wadham College* (Oxford: Wadham College, 1994).

Davis, H. W. Carless, *A History of Balliol College,* revised by R. H. C. Davis and Richard Hunt (Oxford: Blackwell, 1963).

Dent, C. M., *Protestant Reformers in Elizabethan Oxford* (Oxford: Oxford University Press, 1983).

Dias, José Sebastião da Silva, *A política cultural da época de D. João III,* 2 vols (Coimbra: Universidade de Coimbra, 1969).

——, *Camões no Portugal de Quinhentos* (Lisbon: Biblioteca Breve, 1981).

——, 'O cânone filosófico conimbricense (1562–1606)', *Cultura-História e Filosofia,* 4 (1985), 257–370.

——, *Os descobrimentos e a problemática cultural do século XVI* (Coimbra: Universidade de Coimbra, 1973).

Dicionário de História de Portugal, edited by Joel Serrão, 4 vols (Lisbon: Iniciativas Editoriais, 1963–71).

T. F. Earle, *Theme and Image in the Poetry of Sá de Miranda* (Oxford: Oxford University Press, 1980).

Emden, A. B., *A Biographical Register of the University of Oxford A.D. 1501 to 1540* (Oxford: Clarendon Press, 1974).

Encyclopaedia Judaica, 16 vols (Jerusalem: Keter, 1972).

Farrell, Allan P., *The Jesuit Code of Liberal Education: Development and Scope of the Ratio Studiorum* (Milwaukee: Bruce, 1938).

Feingold, Mordechai, 'The Humanities' and 'The Mathematical Sciences and New Philosophies', in Nicholas Tyacke (ed.), *The History of the University of Oxford: the Seventeenth Century* (Oxford: Clarendon Press, 1997), pp. 211–357 and 359–448.

Fincham, Kenneth, 'Early Stuart Polity', in Nicholas Tyacke (ed.), *The History of the University of Oxford: the Seventeenth Century* (Oxford: Clarendon Press, 1997), pp. 179–210.

Firth, C. H., *Modern Languages at Oxford* (Oxford: Oxford University Press, 1929).

Fletcher, J. M., 'The Faculty of Arts', in James McConica (ed.), *The History of the University of Oxford: the Collegiate University* (Oxford: Clarendon Press, 1986), pp. 157–99.

Forbes, Mansfield D., *Clare College, 1326–1926,* 2 vols (Cambridge: Clare College, 1928–30).

Foster, Joseph, *Alumni Oxonienses: the members of the University of Oxford, 1500–1714,* 4 vols (Oxford: Parker, 1891–92).

Frank, Robert G., 'Medicine', in Nicholas Tyacke (ed.), *The History of the University of Oxford: the Seventeenth Century* (Oxford: Clarendon Press, 1997), pp. 505–58.

French, Peter J., *John Dee: The World of an Elizabethan Magus* (London: Routledge, 1972).

Friedenwald, Harry, *The Jews and Medicine,* 2 vols (Baltimore: Johns Hopkins, 1944).

Galvão, António, *Tratado dos Descobrimentos*, edited by Luís de Albuquerque (Lisbon: Alfa, 1989).

Gams, Pius Bonifacius, *Series episcoporum ecclesiae catholicae* (Graz: Akademische Druck-U. Verlagsanstalt, 1957).

Gardiner, Robert Barlow, *The Registers of Wadham College, Oxford*, 2 vols (London, Bell, 1889–95).

Gascoigne, John, 'Isaac Barlow's Academic Milieu: Interregnum and Restoration Cambridge', reprinted in Gascoigne, *Science, Politics and Universities in Europe, 1600–1800* (Aldershot: Ashgate, 1998), pp. 249–90.

——, 'The Universities and the Scientific Revolution: The Case of Newton and Restoration Cambridge', reprinted in Gascoine, *Science, Politics and Universities*, pp. 391–434.

Gomes, Pinharanda, *Os Conimbricenses* (Lisbon: Biblioteca Breve, 1992).

González de la Calle, Pedro Urbano, 'Contribución a la biografía de Manuel da Costa "Doctor Subtilis" ', *Revista da Universidade de Coimbra*, 11 (1933), 310–73.

Graça, Luís, *A visão do oriente na literatura portuguesa de viagens: os viajantes portugueses e os itinerários terrestres (1560–1670)* (Lisbon: Imprensa Nacional-Casa da Moeda, 1983).

Grafton, Anthony, 'Traditions of invention and inventions of tradition in Renaissance Italy: Annius of Viterbo', reprinted in Anthony Grafton, *Defenders of the Text: the Traditions of Scholarship in an Age of Science, 1450–1800* (Cambridge Mass.: Harvard University Press, 1991), pp. 76–103.

Grafton, Anthony and Lisa Jardine, *From Humanism to the Humanities: Education and the Liberal Arts in Fifteenth- and Sixteenth-Century Europe* (London: Duckworth, 1986).

Grande Enciclopédia Portuguesa e Brasileira, 40 vols (Lisbon: Enciclopédia, n.d.).

Griffin, Nigel, 'Italy, Portugal, and the Early Years of the Society of Jesus', in T. F. Earle and Nigel Griffin (eds), *Portuguese, Brazilian and African Studies: Studies Presented to Clive Willis on his Retirement* (Warminster: Aris & Phillips, 1995), pp. 133–49.

Haigh, Christopher, *English Reformations: Religion, Politics and Society under the Tudors* (Oxford: Clarendon Press, 1993).

Hall, Basil, 'Biblical Scholarship: Editions and Commentaries', in S. L. Greenslade (ed.), *The Cambridge History of the Bible, Volume III: the West from the Reformation to the Present Day* (Cambridge: Cambridge University Press, 1963), pp. 38–93.

Hardy, Ernest George, *Jesus College* (London: Routledge, 1998).

Hastings, Adrian, *The Construction of Nationhood: Ethnicity, Religion and Nationalism* (Cambridge: Cambridge University Press, 1997).

Helmholtz, R. H., *The Canon Law and Ecclesiastical Jurisdiction from 597 to the 1640s, The Oxford History of the Laws of England*, I (Oxford: Oxford University Press, 2004).

Hirsch, Elisabeth Feist, *Damião de Góis: The Life and Thought of a Portuguese Humanist* (The Hague: Nijhoff, 1967).

Hopkins, Clare, *Trinity: 450 Years of an Oxford College Community* (Oxford: Oxford University Press, 2005).

Howell, W. S., *Logic and Rhetoric in England, 1500–1700* (New York: 1961).

Ijsewijn, Jozef, 'Achilles Statius, a Portuguese Latin Poet in Late 16th-Century Rome', in *Humanismo português na época dos descobrimentos* (Coimbra: Instituto de Estudos Clássicos, 1993), pp. 109–23.

Israel, Jonathan I., *European Jewry in the Age of Mercantilism, 1550–1750* (Oxford: Clarendon Press, 1989).

——, *Radical Enlightenment: Philosophy and the Making of Modernity 1650–1750* (Oxford: Oxford University Press, 2001).

Jardine, Lisa, *Erasmus, Man of Letters: The Construction of Charisma in Print* (Princeton: Princeton University Press, 1993).

——, 'Humanism and the sixteenth-century Cambridge arts course', *History of Education*, 4 (1975), 16–31.

——, 'The place of dialectic teaching in sixteenth-century Cambridge', *Studies in the Renaissance*, 21 (1974), 31–62.

Kaplan, Yosef, *Judíos nuevos en Amsterdam: estudio sobre la historia social e intelectual del judaísmo sefardí en el siglo XVII* (Barcelona: Gedisa, 1996).

Kearney, Hugh, *Scholars and Gentlemen: Universities and Society in Pre-Industrial Britain* (London: Faber, 1970)

Lake, Peter, *Anglicans and Puritans? Presbyterianism and English Conformist Thought from Whitgift to Hooker* (London: Unwin Hyman, 1988).

Lapa, Albino, *Pedro Fernandes de Queirós: o último navegador português* (Lisbon: Agência Geral do Ultramar, 1951).

Lawrance, Jeremy, 'The Middle Indies: Damião de Góis on Prester John and the Ethiopians', *Renaissance Studies*, 6 (1992), 306–24.

Levack, Brian P., *The Civil Lawyers in England, 1603–1641: A Political Study* (Oxford: Clarendon Press, 1973).

Lewis, Gillian, 'The Faculty of Medicine', in James McConica (ed.), *The History of the University of Oxford: the Collegiate University* (Oxford: Clarendon Press, 1986), pp. 213–56.

Frei Marcos de Lisboa: cronista franciscano e bispo do Porto (1511–1591) (Oporto: Centro Interuniversitário de História de Espiritualidade, 2002).

Lohr, Charles H., 'Renaissance Latin Aristotle Commentaries', *Renaissance Quarterly*, 28 (1975), 689–741.

MacCulloch, Diarmaid, *Reformation: Europe's House Divided, 1490–1700* (London: Allen Lane, 2003).

——, *The Later Reformation in England, 1547–1603* (Basingstoke: Palgrave, 2001).

Maclean, Ian, 'Mediations of Zabarella in Northern Germany, 1586–1623' in Gregorio Piaia (ed.), *La presenza dell'aristotelismo padovano nella filosofia della prima modernità* (Rome-Padua: Antenore, 2002), pp. 173–98.

——, 'The market for scholarly books and conception of genre in Northern Europe, 1570–1630', in Georg Kauffmann (ed.), *Die Renaissance im Blick der Nationen Europas* (Wiesbaden: Harrassowitz, 1991), pp. 17–31.

Macray, William Dunn, *A Register of the Members of St. Mary Magdalen College, Oxford* 8 vols (London: Frowde, 1894–1915).

Marques, A. H. de Oliveira, *História de Portugal*, 3 vols (Lisbon: Presença, 1997–1998).

Marques, Maria Alegria F., *Estudos sobre a ordem de Cister em Portugal* (Lisbon: Colibri, 1998).

Marshall, P. J., 'The Portuguese in Asia in British Historiography', *Portuguese Studies*, 20 (2004).

Martin, G. H. and J. R. L. Highfield, *A History of Merton College, Oxford* (Oxford: Oxford University Press, 1997).

Martin, Henri-Jean, 'Renouvellements et concurrences', in Henri-Jean Martin and Roger Chartier (eds), *Histoire de l'édition française*, I (Paris: Promodis, 1982), pp. 379–403.

Matos, Luís de, *Les Portugais à l'université de Paris entre 1500 et 1550* (Coimbra: Por ordem da universidade, 1950).

——, *Les Portugais en France au XVIe. siècle: études et documents* (Coimbra: Por ordem da universidade, 1952).

——, 'O humanista Diogo de Teive', *Revista da Universidade de Coimbra*, 13 (1937), 215–270.

——, *Sobre António de Gouveia e a sua obra* (Lisbon: Fundação Calouste Gulbenkian, 1966).

McConica, James, 'Humanism and Aristotle in Tudor Oxford', *The English Historical Review*, 94 (1979), 291–317.

McKenzie, D. F., *Bibliography and the Sociology of Texts*, revised edition (Cambridge: Cambridge University Press, 1999).

Mendes, António Rosa, 'A vida cultural', in *História de Portugal*, edited by José Mattoso, III (Lisbon: Estampa, 1993), pp. 375–421.

Milne, J. G., *The Early History of Corpus Christi College, Oxford* (Oxford, Blackwell: 1946).

Milton, Anthony, *Catholic and Reformed: The Roman and Protestant Churches in English Protestant Thought, 1600–1640* (Cambridge: Cambridge University Press, 1995).

Morgan, John, *Godly Learning: Puritan Attitudes towards Reason, Learning and Education, 1560–1640* (Cambridge: Cambridge University Press, 1986).

Moss, Ann, *Printed Commonplace-Books and the Structuring of Renaissance Thought* (Oxford: Clarendon Press, 1996).

Muller, Richard A., *Post-Reformation Reformed Dogmatics I* (Grand Rapids: Baker Book House, 1987).

Nascimento, Aires A., *'Laudes studiorum*: o humanismo jesuítico dos primórdios (no cenário de Anchieta e da *Ratio studiorum)'*, in *Actas do congresso internacional Anchieta em Coimbra – Colégio das Artes da Universidade (1548–1998)* (Oporto: Fundação Eng. António de Almeida, 2000), pp. 39–63.

Netanyahu, Benzion, *Don Isaac Abravanel, Statesman and Philosopher* (Ithaca, NY: Cornell University Press,1998).

New Catholic Encyclopaedia, 15 vols (Detroit: Thomson/Gale, 2003).

Nutton, V., 'Humanist Surgery', in Andrew Wear (ed.), *The Medical Renaissance of the Sixteenth Century* (Cambridge: Cambridge University Press, 1985), pp. 75–99.

Olmedo, Andrés Soría, *Los* Dialoghi d'Amore *de León Hebreo: aspectos literarios y culturales* (Granada: Universidad de Granada, 1984).

O'Malley, John W., *The First Jesuits* (Cambridge, Mass.: Harvard University Press, 1993).

O'Reilly, Terence, 'The scriptural scholarship of the early Spanish Jesuits – a survey', *Journal of the Institute of Romance Studies*, 4 (1996), 135–43.

Oxford Dictionary of National Biography <http://www.oxforddnb.com/>

Parker, John, 'Contents and Sources of *Purchas his Pilgrimes*', in L. E. Pennington (ed.), *The Purchas Handbook*, 2 vols (London: The Hakluyt Society, 1997), II, pp. 383–464.

Patterson, W. B., *King James VI and I and the Reunion of Christendom* (Cambridge: Cambridge University Press, 1997).

Pearson, M. N., 'Hindu Medical Practice in Sixteenth-Century Western India: Evidence from Portuguese Sources', *Portuguese Studies*, 17 (2001), 100–13.

Pinto, António Guimarães, 'Damião de Góis e D. Jerónimo Osório: a *Crónica de D. Manuel* e *De rebus Emmanuelis gestis*', in *Actas do Congresso Internacional: Damião de Góis na Europa do Renascimento* (Braga: Faculdade de Filosofia, 2003), pp. 307–48.

——, *Humanismo e controvérsia religiosa: lusitanos e anglicanos*, 3 vols (Lisbon: Imprensa Nacional-Casa da Moeda, 2006), and see, in Section 5, Osório, D. Jerónimo de.

Quinn, A. M. and D. B., 'Contents and Sources of the Three Major Works', in D. B. Quinn (ed.), *The Hakluyt Handbook*, 2 vols (London: The Hakluyt Society, 1974), II, pp. 333–460.

Quint, Anne-Marie, 'À propos de la traduction française de l'*Imagem da Vida Cristã* de Frei Heitor Pinto', *Bulletin des Études Portugaises et Brésiliennes*, 35–6 (1975–76), 65–92.

——, *L'Imagem da Vida Cristã de Frei Heitor Pinto*, (Paris: Centre Culturel Calouste Gulbenkian, 1995).

Racine, Matthew, '*A Pearle for a Prynce:* Jerónimo Osório and Early Elizabethan Catholics', *The Catholic Historical Review*, 87 (2001), 401–27.

Ramalho, Américo da Costa, 'Um humanista em viagem: Gaspar Barreiros (1546)', in Américo da Costa Ramalho, *Para a História do Humanismo em Portugal IV* (Lisbon: Imprensa Nacional-Casa da Moeda, 2000), pp. 81–93.

Rebelo, Luís de Sousa, 'Diogo de Teive, historiador humanista', in *A Tradição Clássica na Literatura Portuguesa* (Lisbon: Horizonte, 1982), pp. 255–79.

Rees, Owen, 'Adventures of Portuguese "Ancient Music" in Oxford, London, and Paris: Duarte Lobo's "Liber Missarum" and Musical Antiquarianism, 1650–1850', *Music & Letters*, 86 (2005), 42–73.

Reynolds, David (ed.), *Christ's : a Cambridge College over Five Centuries* (London: Macmillan, 2005).

Richards, George Chatterton and Charles Lancelot Shadwell, *The Provosts and Fellows of Oriel College* (Oxford: Blackwell, 1922).

Roberts, Julian, 'Importing Books for Oxford, 1500–1640', in James P. Carley and Colin G. C. Tite (eds), *Books and Collectors, 1200–1700: Essays presented to Andrew Watson* (London: The British Library, 1997), pp. 317–33.

——, 'The Latin Trade', in *The Cambridge History of the Book in Britain, Volume*

Four: (1557–1695), ed. John Barnard and D. F. McKenzie (Cambridge: Cambridge University Press, 2002) pp. 141–73.

Rodrigues, João, *João Rodrigues's Account of Sixteenth-Century Japan*, translated and edited by Michael Cooper (London: Hakluyt Society, 2001).

Rodrigues, Francisco, *História da Companhia de Jesus na Assistência de Portugal*, 3 vols (Oporto: Apostolado da Imprensa, 1931–44).

Rodrigues, Manuel Augusto, *A Cátedra de Sagrada Escritura na Universidade de Coimbra*, (Coimbra: Faculdade de Letras, 1974).

——, 'Algumas notas sobre a vida e a obra de Diogo de Paiva de Andrade', *Revista Portuguesa de História*, 15 (1975), 301–27.

——, 'Alguns aspectos da obra exegética de Fr. Jerónimo de Azambuja (Oleastro), O.P.', *Revista Portuguesa de História*, 17 (1977), 25–36.

Rowse, A. L., *Ralegh and the Throckmortons* (London: Macmillan, 1962).

Ruderman, David B., *Jewish Thought and Scientific Discovery in Early Modern Europe* (New Haven: Yale University Press, 1995).

Russell, P. E., 'A Stuart Hispanist: James Mabbe', *Bulletin of Hispanic Studies*, 30 (1953), 75–84.

——, 'English Seventeeth-Century Interpretations of Spanish Literature', *Atlante*, 1 (1950), 65–77.

Sánches Marín, José A. and María Nieves Muñoz Martín, 'La estructura literaria de la biografía de Anchieta escrita por Sebastiano Berettari', in *Anchieta em Coimbra*, edited by Sebastião Tavares de Pinho, 3 vols (Oporto: Fundação Eng. António de Almeida, 2000), II, pp. 721–37.

Sauvage, Odette, *L'itinéraire érasmien de André de Resende* (Paris: Fundação Calouste Gulbenkian, 1971).

Schmitt, Charles B., 'Aristotle among the Physicians', in Andrew Wear (ed.), *The Medical Renaissance of the Sixteenth Century* (Cambridge: Cambridge University Press, 1985), pp. 1–15.

——, *Aristotle and the Renaissance* (Cambridge, Mass.: Harvard University Press, 1983).

——, 'Philosophy and Science in Sixteenth-Century Universities: Some Preliminary Comments', reprinted in Charles B. Schmitt, *Studies in Renaisance Philosophy and Science* (London: Variorum, 1981), pp. 485–530.

——, 'Thomas Linacre and Italy', in Francis Maddison, Margaret Pelling and Charles Webster (eds), *Essays on the Life and Work of Thomas Linacre, c.1460–1524* (Oxford: Clarendon Press, 1977), pp. 36–75.

Scott-Warren, Jason, 'News, Sociability and Bookbuying in Early Modern England: the Letters of Sir Thomas Cornwallis', *The Library*, 7th series, 1 (2000), 381–402.

Serrão, Joaquim Veríssimo, *O reinado de D. António Prior do Crato* (Coimbra: Universidade de Coimbra, 1956).

——, *Portugueses no Estudo de Toulouse* (Coimbra: Por Ordem da Universidade, 1954).

Seton-Watson, Hugh, *Nations and States: An Enquiry into the Origins of Nations and the Politics of Nationalism* (London: Methuen, 1977).

Shadwell, Charles Lancelot, *Registrum Orielense: an Account of the Members of Oriel College, Oxford*, 2 vols (London: Henry Frowde, 1893–1902).

Shaw, Graham W., 'A "lost" Work of Henrique Henriques: the Tamil Confessionary of 1580', *Bodleian Library Review*, 11 (1982–85), 26–34.

Sillery, Valentine, *St John's College Biographical Register, 1660–1775* (Oxford: privately printed, 1990).

Silva, J. Gentil da, *Stratégie des Affaires à Lisbonne entre 1595 et 1607: Lettres marchandes des Rodrigues d'Évora et Veiga* (Paris: S.E.V.P.E.N., 1956).

Smith, Anthony J., *Nationalism* (Cambridge: Polity, 2001).

Soares, Nair de Nazaré Castro, *O príncipe ideal no século XVI e a obra de D. Jerónimo Osório* (Coimbra: Instituto Nacional de Investigação Científica, 1994).

Standaert, Nicolas, 'The Transmission of Renaissance Culture in Seventeenth-Century China', in Daniel Carey (ed.), *Asian Travel in the Renaissance* (Oxford: Blackwell, 2004), pp. 42–66.

Stevenson, W. H. and H. E. Salter, *The Early History of St John's College, Oxford* (Oxford: Oxford Historical Society, 1939).

Tellechea Idígoras, J. Ignacio, *Fray Bartolomé Carranza y el Cardenal Pole* (Pamplona: Diputación foral de Navarra, 1977).

Thorndyke, Lynn, *The Sphere of Sacrobosco and its Commentators* (Chicago: University of Chicago, 1949).

Trevor-Roper, H. R., *Archbishop Laud, 1573–1645* (London: Macmillan, 1940).

Trim, D. J. B., 'Sir Thomas Bodley and the International Protestant Cause', *Bodleian Library Record* 16 (1998), 314–340.

Trueman, Carl R. and R. S. Clark (eds), *Protestant Scholasticism: Essays in Reassessment* (Carlisle: Paternoster, 1999).

Truman, R. W., 'Dr Bartolomeu Filipe of Coimbra: Reader of Machiavelli and Furió Ceriol', in Aires A. Nascimento and others (eds), *Humanismo para o nosso tempo: homenagem a Luís de Sousa Rebelo* (Lisbon: Fundação Calouste Gulbenkian, 2004), pp. 303–10.

——, 'Jean Matal (Johannes Matalius Metellus), ami fidèle de Jerónimo Osório et son *De rebus Emmanuelis* à Cologne', in *Humanismo português na época dos descobrimentos* (Coimbra: Instituto de Estudos Clássicos, 1993), pp. 333–342.

——, 'Jean Matal and his relations with Antonio Agustín, Jerónimo Osório da Fonseca and Pedro Ximenes', in M. H. Crawford (ed.), *Antonio Agustín Between Renaissance and Counter-Reform* (London: Warburg Institute, 1993), pp. 247–63.

Twigg, John, *A History of Queens' College Cambridge, 1448–1986* (Woodbridge: Boydell, 1987).

Tyacke, Nicholas, *Aspects of English Protestantism, c.1530–1700* (Manchester: Manchester University Press, 2001).

Üçerler, M. Antoni J., 'Alessandro Valignano: Man, Missionary and Writer', in Daniel Carey (ed.), *Asian Travel in the Renaissance* (Oxford: Blackwell, 2004).

Venn, John and J. A., *Alumni Cantabrigienses: A Biographical List of All Known Students, Graduates and Holders of Office at the University of Cambridge, from the Earliest Times to 1900*, 4 vols (Cambridge: Cambridge University Press, 1922–27).

Venn, John et al. (eds), *Biographical History of Gonville and Caius College*, 7 vols (Cambridge: Cambridge University Press, 1897–1978).

Wells, Joseph, *Wadham College* (London: Routledge, 1898).

Whiteway, R. S. (ed.), *The Portuguese Expedition to Abyssinia in 1541–1543 . . . with . . . the short account of Bermudez* (London: Hakluyt Society, 1902).

Willis, Clive (ed.), *China and Macau* (Aldershot: Ashgate, 2002).

Wilson, Edward M., 'Spanish and English Religious Poetry of the Seventeenth Century', in Edward M. Wilson, *Spanish and English Literature of the 16th and 17th Centuries*, edited by D. W. Cruickshank (Cambridge: Cambridge University Press, 1980), pp. 234–49.

Winius, George Davison, *The Black Legend of Portuguese India: Diogo do Couto, His Contemporaries, and the* Soldado Prático (New Delhi: Concept, 1985).

APPENDIX 1

Letters from Jesuits

There is no space here except for the briefest biographical notes about the ninety Jesuit missionaries whose dispatches are included in items 454–500. Some are known by one letter only; others, like Luís Fróis, by several, and in addition whole works by Jesuit missionaries are listed elsewhere in the short-title catalogue, under authors' names.

The university and college libraries have a very large collection of the letters. The writers of them who are known to be Portuguese are listed below. Variant forms of names are given, since translation and retranslation caused some of the authors almost to lose their identity. Whenever possible their dates of birth and death are recorded, and the geographical area where their activity was principally concentrated. The number or numbers following each entry are of the item or items in the short-title catalogue where letters by the writer concerned are to be found. Normally biographical information comes from de Backer & Sommervogel; in a few cases from Barbosa Machado and Francisco Rodrigues (*História da Companhia de Jesus na assistência de Portugal*) or from examination of the letters themselves.

Abreu, João de (Giovan d' Abra). In Molucca around 1549 **461**
Alcaceva, Pedro de (Petrus Alcaceva, Pietro d'Aliacena, Petrus Dalcena). Japan, died 1579 **459, 461, 463, 465, 487, 495**
Almeida, António de (Antonius Dalmeida). China; died 1591 **457, 478, 495**
Almeida, Luís de (Aloisius or Ludovicus Dalmeida). Japan; died 1583, aged about 60 **459, 463, 465, 487, 490, 492, 495**
Almeida, Manuel. Ethiopia, 1578–1646 **469**
Almeida, Pedro de (Pietro Dalmeida). Goa; died 1579 **482**
Andrade, António de. Tibet **1580–1634 468, 475, 476**
Anonymous
     Rector of the College of the Company in Goa, written 12/12/57 **456, 480**
Antunes, Diogo (Iacobus Antonius). China; born 1552 **479**
Araújo, Miguel de (Michele Daraijo). In Brazil around 1621 **476**
Azevedo, Luís de. Ethiopia, 1561–1634 **468, 476**
Barreto, Sebastião. Goa, 1567–1625 **468, 476**
Barros, Tomás de. India and Ethiopia, 1591–1658 **468, 476**
Blasquez, António. In Brazil 1557–61 **482**
Brandão, Aires (Ariae Blandonii, Arius Brandonius or Bandonius. One of the first missionaries in the East; born 1529 **459, 464, 465, 487, 495**
Cabral, Francisco (Franciscus Capralis). Japan, China and India, 1528–1609 **454–5, 458, 459, 490, 492, 495**

1520–1600 **461, 464, 465, 481, 482.** For works in Tamil by him see under Henriques in the short-title catalogue.

Lameira, Manuel. India and Ethiopia, 1571–c.1633 **468, 476**

Lopes, António. Japan, 1548–99 **459**

Lopes, Baltasar. Japan, 1542–1609 **459**

Luís, Gaspar (Gaspar Ludovicus, Gaspard Louys). Japan, 1586-after 1639 **468, 476, 488**

Martins, Pedro (Petrus Martinus). India and Japan, 1542–98 **495**

Mascarenhas, Pedro de (Petrus Mascarenas). Moluccas, died 1583 **463, 465, 487, 495**

Matos, Gabriel de. Japan, 1572–1633 **479**

Mendes, Fernando. Perhaps the famous traveller Fernão Mendes Pinto, c.1510–83 **461**

Mesquita, João (Giovanni di or Iohannes Meschita). South India, born 1529 **465, 482**

Mexia, Lourenço. Japan and China, 1540–99 **454–5, 459**

Moura, Belchior de. Japan, born 1545 **459**

Nóbrega, Manuel de. Brazil, 1519–70 **461, 463, 465, 482**

Nunes, Baltasar (Baldassar Nugnez). South India, born 1544 **461, 495**

Nunes, Melchior. (Belchior Nunes Barreto, Nuno Barreto, Melchior Nunezius, Melchior Nugnez, Melchior Nunnez). India and Japan, 1520–71 **461, 463, 464, 465, 481, 482, 487, 490, 492, 495**

Nunes, Nicolau (Nicolaus Nunnis). Moluccas, died 1576 **461, 487, 495**

Pais, Gaspar. Ethiopia,1593–1635 **467, 477**

Pereira, Jacinto (Iacinthe Pereria). Malabar, 1598–1657 **468, 476**

Perez, Francisco (Francesco). Malacca, 1515–83 **459, 461, 478**

Pimenta, Nicolaus. India, 1546–1614 **495.** See also under Pimenta for works wholly written by him.

Pinheiro, Manuel (Emmanuelis or Emmanuele, Pigneiro or Pinnero). India, 1556–1618 **472, 470, 495**

Pires, Ambrósio (Ambrosio Pera). In Brazil in 1555 **461**

Quadros, António de. India, 1528–72 **461, 463, 464, 465, 482**

Rebelo, Gonçalo. Japan, 1544–1610 **459**

Ribeiro, Cristóvão (Christoforo Ribero). São Tomé, died after 1553 **461**

Rodrigues, António. Brazil, 1516–68 **482**

Rodrigues, Francisco. Goa, 1515–73 **461**

Rodrigues, Gonçalo. Ethiopia and Goa, 1527–64 **461, 482**

Rodrigues, Jerónimo (Hieronymus Ruizius). Macau, **487, 495**

Sá, Simão. India, 1560–1614 **495**

Sanches, Aires (Arias Sanctius). Japan, 1527/30–1590 **459, 487, 490, 492, 495**

Semedo, Álvaro. China, 1585–1658 **460, 474**

Silva, Duarte da (Duartis a Sylva, Duarte di Selva, Eduardus Sylvius). Japan, 1536–1564 **459, 461, 463, 465, 487, 490, 492, 495**

Silva, João da. Goa, 1597–1624 **468, 476**

Silva, Martim (Martinus Sylva). India, 1535-? **487, 495**

APPENDIX 2

Index of Current Locations

All Souls College, Oxford 18, 27, 29, 39, 50, 73, 76, 96, 104, 107, 134–8, 146, 156, 177–8, 184, 195, 203, 212, 220, 222, 228, 259, 262, 268, 290–1, 317, 335, 340–1, 393, 396–7, 399, 403, 416, 424, 434, 442, 444–5, 463, 471, 478, 488, 498, 503, 508, 510, 515, 555, 578, 596, 609, 626, 653–4, 707, 711, 713, 717, 721, 723, 737, 747, 755, 757, 761, 785, 788, 810, 815–6, 820, 837, 849, 866–8, 877, 880–1.

Balliol College, Oxford 107, 172–3, 187, 214, 229, 241, 279, 296, 306, 354, 372, 412, 446, 451, 453, 493–4, 579, 588, 666, 668, 707.02, 723, 737, 745–6.

Blackfriars, Oxford 194, 222, 773.

Bodleian Library, Oxford 2, 6, 11, 15, 17–24, 27, 31, 33, 35–7, 40, 42–9, 51–4, 56, 58–9, 61, 63, 67–9, 71–5, 77, 79–83, 86, 88–90, 92, 94, 96, 103–16, 119, 123, 125, 132, 135, 139–41, 143–5, 150–1, 153, 155–6, 160–3, 166–9, 172–3, 175–9, 181–2, 185, 189–93, 196, 198, 200, 202, 204, 207, 209, 211, 213, 217–9, 221–3, 226–8, 232, 234–235. 05, 235.07–8, 235.10–240, 242, 244, 246, 248, 250, 252, 256–7, 259, 261–4, 269–70, 272, 276, 281, 284, 287, 291–5, 297–303, 306, 309–11, 315–8, 320–7, 332, 336–7, 339–42, 346, 350–1, 353–5, 357–60, 363–6, 368, 371–7, 379–81, 383–5, 387–8, 392–4, 396–7, 401–2, 405–6, 408–14, 417, 419–20, 423, 432–3, 435–6, 439–40, 443, 445–7, 449–82, 484–8, 490, 492, 495–6, 499, 501–2, 504, 509, 513, 515–8, 521, 528, 531, 534, 539, 542, 544, 546–57, 560, 562, 565, 568–9, 571, 574–7, 581–3, 588, 594–5, 598–604, 606–10, 618–9, 625, 629–31, 633–6, 639, 642, 644–5, 647, 650–6, 658–61, 663, 665, 667–8, 670, 672–5, 677, 680, 683–5, 688–9, 692, 694, 697, 700–4, 706–7, 710, 720, 722, 724, 734–7, 739–40, 742–6, 748–9, 752–4, 756–9, 764–8, 770–2, 774, 777, 779, 781, 784, 787, 794–6, 798, 800, 807–9, 812, 816–9, 822–30, 832–4, 836, 839–43, 845–8, 851, 853, 855–60, 862–6, 869–70, 874–84, 886–90, 893–5, 901–2, 904–6.

Brasenose College, Oxford 18, 35, 68, 127, 223, 495, 504, 551, 583, 652, 674, 816.

Cambridge University Library 1, 3–10, 12–4, 16–8, 21, 24, 27, 34–5, 38, 43, 45–7, 48–50, 54–5, 58–60, 64–8, 77, 80, 85–6, 91, 96, 99, 104, 106, 109–10, 115, 117–9, 122–5, 127–30, 132–3, 139–40, 142, 158–62, 164–5, 167, 171, 173, 188, 198, 207, 216, 225, 228–9, 234238, 244–5, 247–8, 255, 258, 264–7, 271, 273, 279, 283, 285, 289, 290, 292, 298, 300–1, 308, 325, 327, 331, 334, 344, 347, 349, 354, 356, 358–9, 367–9, 372, 375, 388–90, 393–7, 400–2, 407–8, 412, 417–8, 424, 437–40, 446, 458, 465, 468, 471, 473, 475, 484, 487, 489–91, 494–5, 497, 500, 504, 513, 515–6, 521–3, 525, 529, 534, 536–7, 546–50, 554–5, 559, 563, 567, 569–71, 574, 581–2, 586, 588–90,

594–5, 600–2, 605, 608, 611–4, 620, 623, 627–9, 631–2, 635, 638–9, 641–
3, 647–50, 652–3, 655, 658, 661, 663, 665, 667,671, 674–7, 679–80, 682–
4, 686, 697–8, 703, 705–9, 712, 726, 730–2, 737–8, 740, 745, 747–50,
752–3, 756–7, 760, 777, 781–2, 789–90, 794, 797, 799, 802, 806–8, 811,
813, 816, 818, 824, 826–7, 835, 839, 841, 844–7, 852–7, 860, 862–3, 865–
6, 875, 880, 896, 898, 900, 904–6.

Christ Church, Oxford 18, 21, 27, 45, 47–8, 59, 66, 79, 87, 96, 109, 168, 170,
187, 195, 205, 212, 222, 229, 233, 243, 245, 250, 280, 288, 291, 297, 302–
3, 322, 340–1, 353, 362, 369, 393, 402, 404, 426, 430–1, 446, 453, 458,
464, 487, 497, 528, 540–1, 551–2, 554, 562, 572, 630, 632, 635, 637, 654,
657, 665, 675, 678, 682, 684, 689, 700, 707.02–3, 708, 721, 725, 737, 741,
747–8, 752, 756–7, 774, 786, 789, 791, 808, 813, 821, 826, 845, 853, 871–
3, 891, 896, 902, 905.

Christ's College, Cambridge 8, 104, 412, 417, 446, 607, 609–10, 737, 781,
852.

Clare College, Cambridge 7, 17, 28, 35, 98, 165, 185, 245, 292, 300, 316,
328, 402, 494, 622, 632, 657, 756, 853, 893, 897.

Corpus Christi College, Cambridge 18, 87, 396, 405, 417, 547–9, 636, 668–9,
809, 866.

Corpus Christi College, Oxford 21, 35, 43, 45, 66, 96, 98, 139, 162, 198, 206,
215, 223, 277, 296, 354, 356–7, 360, 368–9, 417, 534, 554, 567, 569, 608,
628, 654, 737, 754, 792, 805, 812, 826–7, 844, 897.

Emmanuel College, Cambridge 46, 56, 67, 99, 104, 110, 152, 157, 165, 198,
207, 216, 225, 230, 243, 245, 250, 255, 272, 274, 284, 305, 319–20, 323,
325, 368, 393, 409, 415, 446, 450, 458, 497, 504, 519, 526, 529, 547–9,
553–4, 567, 572, 604, 609, 617, 624, 630, 632, 640, 655, 662, 664, 689,
691, 699–700, 723, 727, 737, 775, 780, 783, 786, 790, 793–4, 798, 809,
814–6, 818, 824, 836, 855, 857, 906.

Exeter College, Oxford 17, 162, 214, 446, 487, 569, 639, 654, 662, 677, 730,
737.

Fitzwilliam Museum, Cambridge 489, 524, 707.02, 737, 902.

Gonville and Caius College, Cambridge 44, 48, 66, 118, 121–2 , 126, 139, 162,
179, 185, 189, 324, 331, 363, 369, 412, 465, 487, 581, 647, 654, 662, 666,
675, 682, 737, 797, 812, 817, 869, 897, 906.

Harris Manchester College, Oxford 101, 120, 737, 812.

Hertford College, Oxford 113–5, 135, 166, 187, 371, 407, 445, 737–8, 744,
826.

History of Art Library, Oxford 313.

Jesus College, Cambridge 96, 104, 185, 393, 450, 494, 573, 631, 661, 671, 697,
774.

Jesus College, Oxford 18, 46, 59, 75, 93, 95, 104, 161, 187, 198, 211, 220, 251,
344, 354, 382, 388, 393, 401, 414, 538, 569, 571, 608, 639, 707.02, 719,
739, 762, 804, 824, 842, 883, 893, 900, 903–5.

Keble College, Oxford 439, 554.

King's College, Cambridge 96, 187, 355, 379, 421–2, 428–9, 446, 489, 518,
529, 616, 647, 668, 672, 675, 737, 842, 851.

Lincoln College, Oxford **17, 100, 571, 662, 737.**
Magdalene College, Cambridge **17, 46, 101, 110, 154, 214, 229, 235, 243, 278, 446, 492–3, 569, 630, 691, 732, 737, 740, 745, 809, 864.**
Magdalen College, Oxford **18, 46, 49, 58, 70–2, 74–6, 81, 87, 98, 132, 162, 187, 195, 204, 212, 221, 230, 245, 310–1, 340–1, 353, 417, 446, 494, 504, 529, 552, 601, 629, 632, 651, 653, 684, 692, 723, 737, 745, 803, 810, 845, 891.**
Merton College, Oxford **57, 96, 109, 123, 130, 139, 170, 174, 198, 201, 210, 225, 229, 253–4, 296, 331, 338, 348, 393, 401, 433, 464, 490, 534–5, 547–9, 561, 564, 608–9, 619, 707, 712, 714–5, 718, 737, 791, 821, 824, 893.**
Museum of the History of Science, Oxford **169, 245, 435, 632.**
New College, Oxford **46, 66, 72, 78, 96, 119–20, 123, 141, 180, 185, 198, 205, 212, 221, 229, 243, 340, 353, 361, 365, 412, 425, 439, 446, 529, 569, 574, 581, 607, 629, 654, 729, 737, 885.**
Oriel College, Oxford **68, 101, 185, 188, 197, 202, 208, 214, 224, 227, 230, 344, 446, 569, 583, 799.**
Oriental Institute Library, Oxford **493.**
Oxford Centre for Hebrew and Jewish Studies Library **401**
Pembroke College, Cambridge **35, 67, 96, 185, 331, 446, 494, 568, 589, 607, 631, 640, 745, 865–6, 874, 905.**
Pembroke College, Oxford **96, 194–5, 199, 202, 207, 211, 216, 219, 225–6, 231, 278, 285, 340–1, 345, 352, 816, 893.**
Peterborough Cathedral Library (now in Cambridge University Library) **49, 110, 167, 273, 325, 446, 492, 521, 550, 567, 623, 634, 639, 647–8, 652, 661, 663, 671, 674–5, 679–80, 855.**
Peterhouse, Cambridge **21, 44, 162, 331, 340–1, 343, 402, 407, 417, 636, 674, 730, 791, 821, 824, 853.**
Philosophy Faculty Library, Oxford **219, 347.**
Queens' College, Cambridge **17–8, 72, 74, 99, 104, 311, 417, 446, 494, 552, 570, 654, 690, 737, 791, 812, 821.**
Queen's College, Oxford **17, 24, 48, 58–9, 67–8, 71, 78, 95, 111, 113–4, 120, 127, 131, 144, 164, 203, 233, 256, 264, 292, 304, 340–1, 354–7, 366, 368, 370, 396, 446, 453, 505, 529, 534, 552, 570, 654, 665, 681–4, 708, 726, 737, 740, 744, 774, 778, 791.**
St Catharine's College, Cambridge **378, 491, 585, 628, 706, 737.**
St Edmund Hall, Oxford **205, 211, 225.**
St John's College, Cambridge **6–7, 11, 17–8, 21, 32, 46, 49, 54, 56, 59, 67–8, 84, 87, 96, 110, 160, 162, 169, 172, 185, 187–8, 198, 207, 216, 225, 234, 244, 286, 311, 323, 331–2, 356–7, 360, 369, 388, 402, 424, 446, 465, 486, 490, 514, 529, 534, 552, 558, 562, 566, 571, 581, 609, 613, 625, 631, 636, 638, 654, 661–2, 672, 674, 677, 681–2, 684, 695, 712, 724, 733, 737, 749, 782, 792, 808, 812, 824, 826, 838, 841, 844, 853, 864, 891, 895, 901, 904–6.**
St John's College, Oxford **18, 56, 76–7, 90, 96–7, 110, 117, 120, 128, 132, 141, 194, 205, 211, 222, 229, 243–5, 249, 258, 284, 296, 305, 310, 312, 316, 322, 331, 340–1, 343, 354, 381, 386, 393, 402, 411, 446, 463, 465,**

INDEX

This is an index to the people and places mentioned in the Introduction, in the notes to the Short-Title Catalogue, and in the Catalogue itself. It includes authors, readers and donors of books, printers and publishers, and places of publication. Names of languages are also referenced. Roman numerals refer to pages of the Introduction, and Arabic numerals to pages of the notes. Arabic numerals in **bold** refer to items included in the Catalogue. The two Appendixes contain additional indexes, to authors of letters written by Jesuit missionaries, and to the current location of items in the Catalogue.